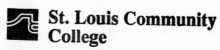

OFFSIDE

....

PRINCETON STUDIES
IN CULTURAL SOCIOLOGY

──────── EDITORS ────────

Paul J. DiMaggio
Michèle Lamont
Robert J. Wuthnow
Viviana A. Zelizer

*Origins of Democratic Culture: Printing, Petitions,
and the Public Sphere in Early-Modern England*
by David Zaret

*Bearing Witness: Readers, Writers,
and the Novel in Nigeria*
by Wendy Griswold

*Gifted Tongues: High School Debate
and Adolescent Culture*
by Gary Alan Fine

Offside: Soccer and American Exceptionalism
by Andrei S. Markovits and Steven L. Hellerman

OFFSIDE

SOCCER AND AMERICAN EXCEPTIONALISM

....

Andrei S. Markovits and
Steven L. Hellerman

PRINCETON UNIVERSITY PRESS   PRINCETON AND OXFORD

Library of Congress Cataloging-in-Publication Data

Markovits, Andrei S.
Offside : soccer and American exceptionalism / Andrei S. Markovits
and Steven L. Hellerman.
p. cm.
Includes bibliographical references and index.
ISBN 0-691-07446-1 (alk. paper)
ISBN 0-691-07447-X (pbk. : alk. paper)
1. Sports—United States—Sociological aspects. 2. Soccer—Social
aspects—United States. I. Hellerman, Steven L., 1958– II. Title
GV706.5.M363 2001
796.334′0973—dc21   00-061115

This book has been composed in Centaur and Sabon

The paper used in this publication meets the minimum
requirements of ANSI/NISO Z39.48-1992 (R1997)
(*Permanence of Paper*)

www.pup.princeton.edu

Printed in the United States of America

10   9   8   7   6   5   4   3   2   1

10   9   8   7   6   5   4   3   2   1
(Pbk.)

Contents ....

Preface ....

THE STORY of this book begins on Saturday afternoon June 21, 1986, when I boarded a plane in Frankfurt on my way home to Boston after completing a lecture tour in a number of European countries. Having been caught up by the World Cup of soccer then being played in Mexico, I bought a number of German newspapers to saturate my interest in the impending—and much anticipated—quarterfinal game between Brazil and France, which I was to miss on account of my transatlantic journey. Needless to say, all papers bristled with detailed pregame analyses and massive previews of the match between two of the best teams playing in that tournament. Upon my arrival in Boston, I proceeded to ask the immigration officer the result of the game that had just ended in Mexico. Whereas the equivalent immigration officer in any European country would have obliged me with delight, this Boston-based officer completely conformed to the expected habitus of the average American male sports fan by looking at me with a mixture of amazement, estrangement, incredulity, and perhaps even some hostility while professing his total ignorance of the event, let alone the outcome, with equanimity bordering on pride. In the corner of his glass booth, however, I detected a small television set broadcasting a Saturday afternoon game between the Boston Red Sox and the Baltimore Orioles then being played at Fenway Park. The officer's demeanor became much more friendly when I asked him the score of this game, and he informed me that the Red Sox were enjoying a comfortable lead in the late innings with their star pitcher Roger Clemens ("The Rocket") well on his way to winning his thirteenth game in a row in what was to become a very impressive personal fourteen-game winning streak (in a superb season culminating in Clemens's garnering the first of his still unprecedented five Cy Young awards). When I arrived at home later that afternoon, I managed to catch the last few minutes of a tape-delayed and abbreviated telecast of the France-Brazil game that NBC had advertised with much fanfare as one of its new (and few) international features in its competition with ABC's *Wide World of Sports* in the summer lull between the NBA playoffs and the beginning of football season that—with all the exhibition games—had gradually encroached on much of August. I was compelled to resort to a number of cross-Atlantic telephone calls that evening to indulge my need to discuss France's victory over Brazil (on penalty kicks)—and the latter's relegation from the tournament—with a bevy of knowledgeable friends in Europe, since the handful of American friends who knew and cared about this match and the tournament as a whole were either in Mexico or in Europe.[1]

As so often in my life, the lecture trip in June 1986 once again highlighted for me perhaps the single most essential and visible hiatus in the public sphere and cultural interest of American and European males who constituted my world on either side of the Atlantic. Part of the trip involved my job as a lecturer to well over one hundred American college alumni and alumnae on a boat that journeyed down the Danube from Vienna to the Black Sea. In addition to delivering daily lectures on the politics, society, and culture of the region we traversed, my "upstairs" and daytime life on the boat consisted of discussing the then ongoing NBA finals between the Boston Celtics and the Houston Rockets, a topic of such great interest among many male passengers of the cruise that we spent the better time of our "day-leave" in Budapest desperately trying to find a copy of the most recent *International Herald Tribune* so as to be better apprised of the latest events in the series. At night my world changed entirely. I was the only passenger to join the ship's crew of Russian, Ukrainian, Bulgarian, and Austrian men in the "downstairs" section of the boat to watch one of the nightly soccer games broadcast from the World Cup in Mexico via Eurovision and commented upon in the language of the country that our boat happened to be traversing at the time. On this trip I found myself deeply involved in two worlds that in some ways were so similar, in that they both followed sports events centered on competitive team sports with their requisite identities, histories, legacies, and iconographies. Above all, both worlds exhibited interests and passions that were visible and tangible, and that had been nurtured for years. For both worlds, the actual events—the NBA finals for the American passengers, the World Cup tournament for the European crew—were merely acute and current manifestations of cultural acquisitions that formed important ingredients of the identities of their respective observers. Thus, for most American followers of the Celtics-Rockets series, the passion of following the series via the sports pages of the *International Herald Tribune* and the hope of catching a glimpse of some highlights on Belgrade television's sports news was part of a much larger package, containing a general interest in basketball and a particular awareness of the importance of the NBA finals in the American sports scene as a whole. "Talking sports"—in this case basketball—was clearly an integral part of male American culture. Same with the Europeans and their passion for the World Cup, underlined by the fact that nightly viewership in the boat's "downstairs" section did not vary according to the identity of the teams in the games being broadcast. To be sure, passions were higher when a team close to the viewers' hearts participated in a game, but viewership hardly diminished when a match between, say, two far-away Latin American contestants was aired by Bulgarian or Romanian television in languages often not understood by many of the viewers, a fact that did not detract anything from the overall interest in the event. Just as "talking basketball" was an integral, indeed important, part of their culture for the American male passengers, so "talking soccer" was to the boat's multinational European crew.

Despite these obvious similarities and affinities, these worlds could not have been more different from each other. Indeed, in terms of the contents of their respective passions, they had nothing to say to each other. As such, I had yet again witnessed something that had baffled me all my life. Having been brought up completely biculturally, I had noticed one major and consistent hiatus between my American and European male friends: the world of sports. Even totally Eurocentric and Europhile American friends and colleagues in my milieu who are deeply steeped in the latest Parisian debates on culture and politics, relish reading Ernst Bloch, Walter Benjamin, and Jürgen Habermas, and much prefer most things European to American, find themselves following American sports (provided, of course, they are sports fans). And the same pertains vice versa: Among my European colleagues who have become academic experts on the United States and the few who happen to love this country—there are only a handful of European intellectuals who fit this bill—very few, if any, have abandoned their passion for and loyalty to soccer and replaced it with an equivalent knowledge of and affect for any of the American team sports. I could never reconcile my own two worlds of, on the one hand, knowing the names of every player on the Hungarian World Cup team of 1954 and every national soccer champion in Romania, Hungary, Austria, Germany, England, and Italy since 1950, and on the other hand, instantly recognizing the historical significance, and according the proper awe, to such American icons as the 1927 Yankees, the Boston Celtics of the 1960s, and the Green Bay Packers. The content of my conversations on either side of the Atlantic was always different, yet their function, form, role, and substance were surprisingly similar, if not indeed identical. The milieus were virtually the same, yet my experiences in them were mutually exclusive. Thus, in deciding to research soccer's relationship to the United States and American culture I embarked on a highly autobiographical venture.

Like many immigrants and naturalized Americans, comparing the United States with one's place of origin—Central Europe in my case—has been a daily occurrence throughout my life. As a historically oriented political science major at Columbia University, I was deeply influenced by a comparative macrosociology that featured the study of this intercontinental comparison with scholarly rigor. In addition to Werner Sombart, Max Weber, and Karl Marx—whose work addressed the similarities and differences between the New and the Old World—I was deeply influenced by the writings of Seymour Martin Lipset, whose prodigious scholarship revolved around a constant comparison of the United States with Europe as well as Canada, the latter as a sort of hybrid and synthesis between the two competing models. Hence, it was a foregone conclusion that my decision to spend the summer of 1986 researching why soccer had failed to become culturally hegemonic in the United States would be framed in the epistemologies that had informed not only much of my scholarly work but also my quotidian existence. And so it was that following my boat experience on the Danube in June, I submerged myself in the stacks of Harvard University's Widener Library to shed some light on the "other" American exceptionalism, the original—of course—being the absence of a European-style socialism or social democracy as a systemically dominant political force in American politics throughout much of the twentieth century.

When by October I had finished a draft of the paper, I gave a copy to my dear friend Peter Hall at the Center for European Studies at Harvard, whose views and criticisms I, along with the multitude of colleagues and students all over the world who have been the beneficiaries of Peter's generosity, erudition, and brilliance over the years, cherish. As expected, Peter returned the paper with two pages of detailed, single-spaced comments; to my complete surprise, however, he also suggested that I offer the paper in a forthcoming meeting of the seminar on "The State and Capitalism since 1800," the Center's first and most prestigious study group, a kind of informal but well-known institution in the world of historically oriented political economy and sociology in the United States, as well as in Europe. A huge crowd appeared for my presentation, which was followed—as has often been the case in this seminar's tradition—by the richest intellectual discussion that I have ever experienced. Charles S. Maier's comments were so witty and insightful that in July 1988 they were published together with my paper "The Other 'American Exceptionalism'—Why Is There No Soccer in the United States?" in *Praxis International*, then under the editorship of Seyla Benhabib. That was the beginning of what subsequently proved to be far and away my most successful academic article, as it appeared in four languages in addition to English—German, French, Italian, Swedish—and generated cross-disciplinary interest beyond any of my expectations. The reason for this international interest in my work on soccer's absence in the United States was evident: In the well-known framework of a scholarly debate that had attained a distinguished profile in comparative historical sociology, I had approached a topic that had much popular appeal and had crossed the minds of many a European academic soccer fan. Thus, my study on soccer's absence in American culture complemented the existing scholarship on other American exceptions, notably—of course—the Sombartian thesis of socialism's manifest absence in the United States. The enthusiastic response to my extensive lecturing on this topic in many European countries, Israel, as well as in the United States, was my own confirmation that a serious engagement of this topic met with the interest of an intellectually minded community well beyond the stricter confines of the most relevant academic disciplines, sports history and sociology in particular.

It was thus no surprise, though an immense honor, that only such an eclectically oriented, interdisciplinary, and profoundly international academic center like the Wissenschaftskolleg zu Berlin—Institute for Advanced Study Berlin—would extend an invitation for me to spend the academic year 1998–99 as a Fellow, with the completion of this book as my project. Anybody who knows the *Kolleg* and its brilliant *Rektor*, Wolf Lepenies, can immediately understand how this institution extended itself on behalf of an author with such an academically unorthodox task. But since Mr. Lepenies is as conversant with the writings of Theodor Fontane as he is with the adventures of Donald Duck, and as insightful and erudite in all topics of the humanities and social sciences as he is with the German Bundesliga and the National Basketball Association, my year in Berlin proved to be far and away the most intellectually rewarding of my academic career. Mr. Lepenies' request for me to write a detailed position paper on the decline of the hook shot in professional basketball was merely one of the highlights of this amazing year. The fact that I completed this manuscript was another. I owe the *Kolleg*, its wonderful *Rektor*, its Fellows, and its able staff much more than I can express on paper.

I also would like to extend my most heartfelt thanks to my coauthor, Steven L. Hellerman. The story of Steve's involvement with this project parallels the book's central argument and its epistemology. I first met Steve in January 1993 when he enrolled in my political sociology seminar featuring the writings of Karl Marx, Max Weber, Emile Durkheim, as well as those of Werner Sombart, Seymour Martin Lipset, Barrington Moore Jr., and a number of other major political sociologists of the nineteenth and twentieth centuries. Steve, an aspiring journalist and struggling sportswriter at the time, had just enrolled as a student at the University of California, Santa Cruz, to complete his undergraduate education, which he had interrupted for a number of years. As we discovered our mutual passion and admiration for the beauty and genius found in the works of Marx, Weber, Durkheim, and Garcia (Jerry, that is) as well as for the Big Three American team sports, we soon established a common cultural interest that formed the basis of our friendship. As the years progressed, Steve became increasingly involved in this project. By the time we had coauthored two articles on this topic—one published in Germany, the other in the United States—Steve had become a full-fledged partner in this endeavor. He remained so throughout the writing of this book. While he shares all of this work's contributions, its shortcomings are my responsibility alone. The fact that Steve never showed any signs of truly embracing soccer in an emotional way beyond the intellectual task at hand—that it never became part of his culture the way baseball, basketball, and football so clearly have been—constitutes my only regret in what otherwise has been an excellent collaborative relationship. Then again, it confirms the book's main thesis: that hegemonic sports cultures are very "sticky" and "path dependent" and cannot be acquired through intellect but only through emotion and identity, which is what ultimately sustains them in a historically lasting way. An understanding of them on an intellectual level is simply not deep enough for this to occur.

I am grateful to the United States Soccer Hall of Fame in Oneonta, New York; to Major League Soccer (MLS) in New York City; and to the Fédération Internationale de Football Association (FIFA) in Zurich for their readiness to supply us with materials and to answer our many questions. While those individuals who have helped us over the years by giving so generously of their time and knowledge are far too numerous to list here, I would like to mention only Seamus Malin, one of the most knowledgeable people on soccer in the world. I hope that this book will, if anything, increase the number of conversations that I have with Seamus; when talking with him, hours pass like minutes chock-full of enjoyable details pertaining to the wonderful game of soccer. Paul DiMaggio's national reputation as a careful commentator, brilliant sociologist, and one of the most conscientious and thoughtful colleagues in the social sciences was yet again corroborated by his eleven-page single-spaced comments on a draft manuscript of this book. I remain unsure as to whether our revisions meet Paul's exacting standards. I am absolutely certain, however, that they much improved the published product. I owe Walter Lippincott's interest in this book to his passion for and expertise in soccer. What could easily have become dry meetings solely devoted to discussions of editorial matters invariably evolved into rich and nuanced conversations about soccer, indeed sports in general. Without Walter's patience and commitment to this project, this book would most likely not have been written; Princeton University Press most certainly would not have published it. Ian Malcolm's editorial guidance deserves utmost praise and much gratitude, as does Marsha A. Kunin's expert copyediting. Tim Sullivan was a wonderful production editor, and Sylvia Coates an excellent indexer.

I owe everything in the world to my wonderful wife, Kiki, who always indulges me with humor, if also a slight incredulity, as I continue to watch thousands of hours of baseball, basketball, football, hockey, and soccer on two continents, all under the guise of research. And as usual, without

Kelly's warmth and companionship—which she has brought to bear in so many other projects—this book would not have been written.

Lastly, I dedicate this book to my late father, Ludwig Markovits, lifelong fan of MTK Budapest and Austria Wien, the two most prominent "Jewish" clubs of Habsburg Europe, who so lovingly took me to dozens of soccer games during my childhood in Timişoara (Temesvár), where I first experienced the emotions of the game in the town's local "derby" between the blues of Stinţa (which became my team) and the reds of CFR (that soon turned into a prominent object of my contempt and fear). It was also my beloved father who in 1960—soon after our very first arrival in the United States—took me to my first baseball game, to Yankee Stadium of all places, where I witnessed yet another "derby," between the hometown Yankees and the visiting Red Sox. Even though my father never learned to understand baseball, let alone love it, he still continued to take me to games, fully appreciating my enthusiasm for this new discovery but also perhaps sensing that "talking baseball" was a helpful, if not necessarily required, ingredient for a young immigrant boy's comfortable acculturation to the United States. The moments that I shared with my father watching sports have remained among the happiest and most serene in my life. I know that he would have loved every page of this book.

Andrei S. Markovits
Ann Arbor, Michigan
October 2000

First and foremost, I would like to extend heartfelt thanks and gratitude to Andrei Markovits for giving me the opportunity, privilege, and honor of participating in this project (in which I learned such a great deal while attaining immense enjoyment); for all the interest, generosity, and patience Andy has exhibited in graciously providing wisdom, guidance, and mentoring to me over several years; for our many conversations covering such a breadth of subjects; and, most of all, for his friendship. I would like to add my gratitude and appreciation to Andy's in thanking all those who generously gave their time to make this a better book.

I would like to thank the faculty and staff, as well as my friends and colleagues at Claremont Graduate University's School of Politics and Economics, for providing an excellent and intellectually stimulating environment in which I have sought to learn the tools of the academic trade. I would also like to thank the friends who over the years have shared many moments and hours with me watching and talking sports, including those at the John Barleycorn in San Francisco and at the Bandbox in North Bellmore, New York.

I dedicate this book to my parents, Leon and Francine Hellerman, for a lifetime's worth of love, encouragement, and support, and also to the memory of my great aunt, Minnie Weissman, and her husband (my uncle), Jack Weissman—a soccer player on two continents, baseball fan on one.

Steven L. Hellerman
Claremont, California
October 2000

OFFSIDE

....

Introduction ....

A DEFINITE trend toward cultural convergence has been one of the main aspects of globalization. In the course of the twentieth century, especially among countries of the advanced industrial world, a set of common icons has developed that have become part of what we call Western culture. While this has been true on all levels, elite as well as mass, this commonality has been particularly pronounced in what has come to be known as popular culture. Whereas this cultural convergence has to a considerable degree coincided with America's rise to political and economic prominence in the twentieth century—thus comprising part of what has been termed "Americanization"—it would be erroneous to see this development as purely a one-way street in which an all-powerful America imposes its cultural icons on the rest of the world. Any visit to the United States, where wine drinking, coffee culture, sushi, and other aspects of the European as well as the Far Eastern culinary worlds have become commonplace from coast to coast, demonstrates that global culture—though featuring American items—is far from identical with American culture. Moreover, important pockets of popular culture exist that have remained completely resistant to any kind of Americanization in the course of the twentieth century. Nowhere is this more pronounced than in the crucial world of mass sports. In this area, Europe and much of the rest of the world took a different path from that of America. Indeed, it is our contention that in the area of sport as culture, the differences between the United States on the one hand and much of the world on the other remain more persistent and noticeable than the similarities.

To wit: whereas both male Americans and Europeans of a certain age (between twenty-five and sixty-five), occupational and employment-related profile (university professor, researcher, social scientist, publicist, student), status (relatively highly educated, urbane, cosmopolitan), class (middle and upper middle), lifestyle, and milieu (urban, "postmaterial-ist"),[1] of a certain habitus and in possession of particular cultural capital[2] (well-read consumers of high-brow media—both domestically and internationally—well traveled and well connected), all follow the same, or very similar, events, watch the same movies, read the same books, follow the same academic debates, listen to the same music, have very similar, if perhaps not identical, consumption habits. In short, though they share a common public persona, lifestyle, and preoccupation in much of their daily lives of work and leisure, there seems to be one major exception to the surprising commonality of this male milieu: that of sports. Americans know details and become passionate about the World Series, the playoff games of the National Football League, batting averages, earned run averages, triple doubles, and March Madness, and they remember and revere—perhaps even idolize—legends such as Mickey Mantle, Willie Mays, Ted Williams, and Henry Aaron in baseball; Jim Brown, Joe Montana, Bart Starr, and Walter "Sweetness" Payton in football; Wilt Chamberlain, Bill Russell, Michael "Air" Jordan, and Earvin "Magic" Johnson in basketball; and Bobby Orr, Maurice "Rocket" Richard, Mario Lemieux, and Wayne Gretzky ("The Great One") in hockey. Europeans have identical relationships of affect and admiration for the likes of Bobby Charlton, Franz "Kaiser" Beckenbauer, Gianni Rivera, Ferenc "Öcsi" Puskas, Johan Cruyff, Pelé, and other greats of the world of soccer. While to Americans, Fenway Park, Yankee Stadium, Lambeau Field, and Madison Square Garden invoke history, memory, and awe, Europeans experience identical sentiments and associations with names such as Old Trafford, Anfield, Wembley, Ibrox Park, San Siro, Estado Bernabeau, Nou Camp, Nép Stadion, Maracana, and the Boekelberg.

The question, of course, is why. Why has the United States remained so aloof from the world's most popular sport? Why in a sports-crazed society like the American one has soccer played such a marginal role?[3] Why has this remained true despite the United States hosting the World Cup with great success in 1994? Why was this still the case four years later when the World Cup played in France was watched and followed by a hitherto unprecedented global audience estimated at 40 billion cumulative television viewers over one month, and after a well-financed professional league had completed three seasons in the United States?[4] Why is this arguably the only global phenomenon wherein the United States counts for little and has continued a marginalized existence throughout all of the twentieth century? Why do many consider the twentieth century the "American century"—with this "nowhere more evident than in the landscape of sports"[5]—yet, concerning soccer, Paul Gardner's words could not be a more accurate characterization: "Not even the most chauvinistic American could claim that the United States has had any influence on the development of soccer."[6] After all, the United States has most certainly mattered in this era's global politics, economics, all aspects of cultural production and consumption (popular as well as elite), science, and education; and, of course, in sports, too, where, for example, the United States has garnered the largest number of Olympic medals among all countries since the inception of the modern games in 1896?[7] Even in the Winter Olympics, where the United States most certainly never attained the prominence it has had throughout the twentieth century in the summer games, Americans proved quite successful over the years in such glamorous events as figure skating and Alpine skiing. Hence, it is simply not true that America has lived in "splendid isolation" throughout the twentieth century, apart from the rest of the world, content to enjoy life on its own continental expanse buffered by two seemingly impenetrable oceans. The twentieth century would not be called the "American Century" had the United States behaved as parochially on the world scene as some have argued. Yet, in the world's most popular sport by any measure, this has been exactly the case.

Whereas it would be quite impossible to write a history of the twentieth century in virtually any field without having the United States present in some prominent (if not necessarily predominant) manner, this is simply not the case in the world of soccer. Crudely put, America did not matter. What are the origins and manifestations of this particular "American exceptionalism"?[8] Answering this question forms the core of this book.

In presenting this introduction, which is the basis for our consideration as to why we believe soccer never became a dominant player in America's sport culture, as it did in that of other advanced industrial societies, permit us this comment: We want the reader to know that we are in equal awe of the accomplishments of athletes in all of the sports we examine in this book. In our research for this project and in our lives as sports fans on both sides of the Atlantic, we have often observed and experienced a great deal of contempt for the other continent's sports on the part of fans, writers, commentators, and analysts. To many Europeans, American sports appear to be not only awkward and strange (perfectly understandable in view of their unfamiliarity) but also inferior and easy (less excusable, one might think). The exact same thing pertains to the ways in which many Americans view the most dominant European sport, soccer. But to us—the authors of this book—hitting a small, hard ball traveling in excess of ninety miles per hour with a thin wooden bat sixty feet away is just as difficult and impressive as threading a beautiful fifty-yard cross from the back of the field into the opposing team's penalty area as an assist to a possible goal. Fade-away jump shots are every bit the equals of headers, and a great run by an American football player remains as aesthetically pleasing, emotionally exciting, and intellectually impressive to us as a great run by a European or Latin American soccer player. These athletes are akin to artists whose creativity, no matter the medium, has earned our utmost respect. Most important, the appreciation of these sports has given us a degree of joy and fulfillment in our lives that only other true sports fans will understand and appreciate.

Chapter 1 presents our argument and its framework. The next two chapters offer a historical overview of the development of team sports in the United States, from their origins in the nineteenth century through the end of World War II. Chapter 2 features a discussion of those team sports that formed what we have termed America's "hegemonic sports culture":

baseball, football, basketball, and (to a lesser extent, but still with a legitimate and palpable presence) ice hockey. These four sports are what we
have come to call the "Big Three and One-Half" of America's "sport
space." Soccer's history of turmoil in the United States during the same
period comprises chapter 3. The second half of the twentieth century is
considered in the book's next section, with the Big Three and One-Half
featured in chapter 4, and soccer in chapter 5. Chapters 6 and 7 provide
respective case study accounts of World Cup 1994 (hosted by the United
States) and World Cup 1998 (hosted by France). A brief conclusion reex-
amines the book's thesis and offers some thoughts regarding soccer's possible and potential future in the United States.

One ....

The Argument: Sports As Culture in Industrial Societies

AMERICAN CONFORMITIES AND EXCEPTIONS

ERIC HOBSBAWM brilliantly argued that throughout the twentieth century in "the field of popular culture the world was American or it was provincial" with one unique exception: that of sport. Hobsbawm credits soccer as the universalizing agent for sport in the twentieth century the way American culture was for much of everything else. Hobsbawm states: "The sport the world made its own was association football, the child of Britain's global presence. . . . This simple and elegant game, unhampered by complex rules and equipment, and which could be practiced on any more or less flat open space of the required size, made its way through the world entirely on its merits."[1] But not in the United States. Our study is to shed light on this matter. In particular, we harness the classics of modern and contemporary political sociology as well as comparative politics and political economy to gain a conceptual understanding of this major difference between the United States (and Canada) on the one hand, and Europe, indeed much of the rest of the world, on the other. As such, this book is a study in the comparative political sociology of advanced industrial societies and their public cultures from the late nineteenth century to the present and beyond. It is also a study of the United States and a major aspect of its popular culture. In particular, we locate and analyze the United States as an advanced industrial democracy that shares many cultural facets with other countries of comparable economic development and political rule but also exhibits features that are clearly sui generis and different from features found in other industrial societies. The literature on American exceptionalism is vast.[2] Still, let us offer a cursory sketch of its major arguments so as to better contextualize our own.

In the conventional parlance of comparative political sociology, American exceptionalism refers to the curious situation in which the United States was the only major industrial country of the twentieth century without the presence of a significant socialist/social democratic and/or communist party in its polity. Erroneously, though conveniently labeled "socialism," this formation based on parties advocating the interests of the male, skilled, industrial working class as an expression of progressive politics remained ephemeral in the United States compared to all European industrial democracies, as well as Australia and New Zealand. Even Canada and Japan featured social democratic and socialist (as well as communist) parties, respectively, that attained much greater importance in the history of these two countries than similar parties had in the course of American politics throughout the twentieth century. The title of Werner Sombart's famous book *Why Is There No Socialism in the United States?* has formed the core concern and the central topic of the "American exceptionalism" debate.[3]

Briefly, here are seven of the main reasons provided by political sociologists for this American exceptionalism:

1. The early political enfranchisement of white American males by virtue of citizenship rendered moot their gathering in oppositional parties whose platforms featured the extension of the franchise to workers, unlike the case with socialist/social democratic parties in Europe. The American worker saw himself as a citizen first instead of as a laborer (or proletarian), unlike his European counterpart (who might indeed have been a "subject," not a citizen).

2. Yet another side of this early "embourgeoisement" of the American male worker hailed from an absence of a feudal order in the United States that never created entrenched reactionary institutions such as the landed aristocracies and the established churches of Europe, which could only be dislodged via revolutions or other forms of radical political commitments on the part of workers and the commercial middle classes.

3. The vast space of the American continent allowed for a geographic mobility unparalleled in Europe, offering an escape from conflicts that otherwise would have lent themselves to the creation of the collective enmities often expressed in class antagonisms in Europe.

4. The abundance of cheap land allowed individuals to seek their fortune apart from inhabited areas, fostering the creation of independent farmers as individuals, rather than indentured peasants as a collective.

5. The myth of the individual's ability, resolve, and resources as the sole mechanisms for professional advancement and personal happiness mitigated against collective action in pursuit of both. The American Dream was predicated on the individual's achievements, not on the collective's entitlements.

6. The multiethnic nature of the American populace (brought about by the immigration of people from many different cultures, countries, and ethnic groups) endowed ethnic identity with a much greater potency in politics than did class. To be sure, identities at the point of production did emerge in the United States to create class as a viable social collective. But identities formed at home and in the neighborhoods—at the point of reproduction—overrode the former and gave rise to the dominant cleavages in American political history throughout the twentieth century and before.[4] Thus, the American worker saw

himself as an American citizen first, a member of his ethnic group second, and only then as a laborer in a particular factory or industry.

7. Perhaps the most important common denominator of all exceptionalisms and the single most pervasive underlying variable for an understanding of American politics and society is the quintessentially bourgeois nature of America's objective development and subjective self-legitimation from its very inception to the present. This "natural," hence all the more comprehensive bourgeoisification of American politics and society created certain structures and an accompanying atmosphere that differentiated the United States from all other countries in the Old World (as opposed to the New World, which, as a concept, remained tellingly reserved almost exclusively for the United States)[5] and from the latter's mere colonial extensions overseas. At the core of this burgeoning "Americanism" was the free individual who was to attain *his* fulfillment by being an independent, autonomous, sovereign, and rational actor in a free market unfettered by any oppressive collectivities, be they the state or social classes, organized religion, or the army. In short, bourgeois America created a new *liberal* identity priding itself on being of European origin, yet also on transcending—and bettering—this origin's old aristocratic framework by a new republican virtue in a new world.[6] Or, to paraphrase Alexis de Tocqueville's brilliant observation regarding this point, America had the luxury of being born bourgeois without having to become so.[7]

Hegemonic Sports Culture

Our study offers yet another dimension to the comparative analysis that sees the United States as an integral, yet at the same time "exceptional," representative of advanced industrial societies. Indeed, we argue that America's sports exceptionalism is deeply rooted in other exceptionalisms that constitute essential features of modern American life. But before we embark on a detailed discussion of these exceptionalisms, of what makes the United States different from the rest of the world, we would first like to present a few overall points differentiating the sports cultures of *all* modern industrial societies, including that of the United States. In this context, it is important to emphasize that what we mean by *sports culture* is what people breathe, read, discuss, analyze, compare, and historicize; what they talk about at length before and after games on sports radio; what they discuss at the office watercooler; and what comprises a significant quantity of barroom (or pub) talk; in short, what people *follow* as opposed to what people *do*. In other words, while activity (doing) and culture (following) overlap to a certain crucial degree (as will become evident in this study), they are separate entities in which we view the "following" as more essential for our conceptualization of a society's

sports culture. To be more precise, we are interested in what we call "hegemonic sports culture," meaning the sports culture that dominates a country's emotional attachments rather than its calisthenic activities. This
domination need not be exclusive or total; indeed, it never is. Rather, it is
hegemonic in the sense that Raymond Williams has used this concept
so fruitfully in his pathbreaking studies on culture: "The reality of any
hegemon, in the extended political and cultural sense, is that, while by
definition it is always dominant, it is never either total or exclusive. At
any time, forms of alternative or directly oppositional politics and culture
exist as significant elements in society."[8] Put differently, this book is less
about the world of athletes than it is about that of couch potatoes. Indica-
tors of what we mean by hegemonic sports culture occur with greater
frequency on sports radio call-in programs than on the sports fields, arenas, and courts themselves.

Thus, to stay with the United States as an example, we are much less
interested in the fact that there are currently 19 million (largely youthful
and upper-middle-class) soccer players in the country than we are with
the fact that the *Boston Globe*—very typical for any comparable daily
paper in a city with major sports teams—ran a minimum of six articles
every day on the New England Patriots during the last three weeks of the
1997 football season, a number that regularly ballooned to ten on the
Monday following an important game, and that such coverage of a local
football, baseball, basketball, and—in some parts of the United States—
hockey team is nothing unusual.[9] Yet another example of sports culture
as opposed to activity would be the immense prominence accorded to the
annual drafts for new players in the National Basketball Association
(NBA) and the National Football League (NFL), which have been televised live and nationally for years and are always subject to passionate
debates among fans all over the country. This book focuses on those
sports that garner as much—in certain cases more—public attention off
the field (court, rink) as in their actual performance. It views the lengthy
pre-game analyses and post-game assessments in the media, especially on
the hundreds of sports radio shows dotting the land, as perhaps more
salient for hegemonic sports culture than the actual contests themselves.
Sport culture need not comprise atheletes themselves (although they are
certainly involved). Instead, it features anyone with a love of sports, regardless of whether they ever participated in them in their own lives.
Again, following is much more central to our argument than doing; culture supersedes activity.

To clarify further: There are 30 million pool and billiards players in the
United States and 45 million engaged in fishing on a regular basis. Even
though both these numbers far exceed the number of basketball, football,
and baseball players, we would not classify billiard playing or fishing as
part of American sports culture. Instead, what we mean by sports culture

is an intense, frequent, perhaps even constant, preoccupation of a large public on at least a national—but also often on an international—scale that reaches well beyond the activities of the (professional) actors and the (amateur) spectators concerning the sports themselves, thereby rendering the "following" much more important than the actual "doing." Of course, all activities entail "culture": Recreational fishermen exist in a culture wherein they swap stories; discuss where, when, and how to fish; and the merits of bait, lures, or flies. Billiard players might meet a few nights a week in the bar or pool hall to play (engaging in both friendly and serious competition) and discuss their game. Indeed, in this sense, stamp collectors have a culture of their own, which also entails interest, passion, and know-how. However, the key to our premise and interpretation is this: These cultures (e.g., of fishing, pool playing, or stamp collecting) are inextricably tied to the activists/practitioners and their immediate entourages, whereas the culture of what we have defined as hegemonic sports is much more diffuse, and elicits passions and interest far beyond those of the participants and their physical space.

Hegemonic sports culture receives ample representation in other outlets of popular culture such as films, television shows, and, of course, literature. For example, Suzanne Wise, a specialist on American literature with sport themes, has compiled a bibliography of 4,500 adult works on baseball, 4,100 on football, 2,800 on basketball, and—tellingly—only 15 on soccer.[10] There have been many films, television shows, musicals, novels, and short stories that feature baseball, football, basketball and hockey, boxing and even golf. Such staples of American culture as *The Boys of Summer, Field of Dreams, Damn Yankees, Brian's Song, Hoosiers, The Natural, Bull Durham, Cobb, White Men Can't Jump, Flubber, Hoop Dreams, North Dallas Forty, The Eighty-Yard Run, End Zone, A Fan's Notes,* and *Tin Cup*—to mention just a few at random—have become part of the American vernacular. Everybody knows them, including people who are not sports fans by any stretch of the imagination. To be sure, here too exists a hierarchy in which baseball—"the national pastime"— receives the greatest and perhaps the best representation in American literature and film. As framed by author George Plimpton: "The smaller the ball, the better the literature."[11] In contrast, we could only find a few American films in which soccer was featured. Sure enough one was set outside the United States, in a German prisoner-of-war camp during World War II: in *Victory,* released in 1981, Allied prisoners led by Michael Caine, Sylvester Stallone, and Pelé manage to escape from their German captors by using their formidable soccer skills. Revealingly, Hollywood had to use Pelé—the only truly recognizable soccer star to a wide American audience—to give the movie any chance for commercial success; moreover, the only American actor, Sylvester Stallone, played goalie (naturally). Another American film on soccer was *Lady Bugs,* a Rodney Dangerfield vehicle aimed toward adolescents wherein the plot—tellingly—revolves around a *girls'* soccer team. Films such as *The Big Green, Manny's Orphans, Hotshot, Soccer Dog,* and *The Boys in Company C* featured soccer in some fashion but have remained obscure to the American public.

These phenomena about the cultural representation of hegemonic sports in the United States have their counterparts in other cultures and countries with the parallel representation of their own hegemonic sports. Be it cricket in the West Indies, India, and Pakistan, or soccer in Argentina, Austria, or Romania, these team sports have attained a cultural representation over the years that renders them social forces in their countries well beyond the actual playing fields on which they occur as a mere physical activity.[12] To use an example from the world of soccer: What we mean by hegemonic sports culture is not so much that Brazil has sent a team to every one of the sixteen World Cups thus far contested, but that the team's departure from the Rio de Janeiro airport has been televised, that its practice sessions are broadcast live back to Brazil, and that over one thousand journalists cover the team's every move on and off the field for a country of 140 million self-professed soccer coaches. Similar situations of sports culture in the guise of "following" pertain to virtually all countries in the world during the quadrennially held World Cup, except the United States, of course, where equivalent passions emerge around baseball's World Series, football's playoffs and Superbowl, and the championship games in basketball.

To be sure: there *is* an overlap between what people do—and have done since childhood—and what they follow. Sport as a topic for our book is a Durkheimian construct of a collective experience subject to formal rules, norms, and agreements but whose main attribute lies in its inherently cohesive and solidaristic nature. Few social phenomena embody Durkheim's "conscience collective" better than modern hegemonic sports.[13] This pertains to team sports to a far greater extent than to individual sports. For example, nobody would argue that cycling was not immensely popular in France throughout the twentieth century and that the Tour de France, particularly, had not attained near iconic dimensions in France's sport space. French Tour de France winners such as Louison Bobet, Jacques Anquetil, and Bernard Hinault became national heroes after repeatedly winning this grueling contest, undoubtedly the world's premier bicycle race. And still, none of them once brought 1 million people out into the streets of Paris in celebration of their amazing feats, let alone three times within five days, as was the case with the two final victories of the French soccer team during the 1998 World Cup.[14] Celebrating crowds of similar quantities welcomed the French team in July 2000 after it had just won the European Championship in Holland, thereby becoming the sole national side ever to hold the two most prestigious crowns in international soccer at the same time: World and European champions.

Lending additional support to our argument that team sports exercise much greater emotional power and collective cohesion than individual sports is that such unprecedented celebrations occurred in a country where soccer had allegedly enjoyed much less public enthusiasm and cultural hegemony than in neighboring Germany, Italy, Spain, and England. The sport may differ, but the phenomenon does not. With their shared belief system, common sentiment, mutually intelligible rules and norms, sports—particularly team sports—create a culture that varies by country and society in its empirical manifestations but appears compellingly similar in its analytic construct (as culture). And here we see some fascinating features common to all industrial societies. It is to a discussion of these that we now turn before embarking on a presentation of the "exceptions" informing the American experience.

Common Features of Industrial Societies

Modern sports as culture are inextricably tied to the development of mass societies. Sport in its organized form of regulated leisure and, subsequently, of commodified culture, has proceeded hand in hand with such major components of "modernization" as urbanization, industrialization, education, and the perpetually expanding participation of a steadily growing number of citizens in the public spheres of politics, production, and consumption. Modern sports everywhere became inextricably linked to the most fundamental aspects of modernization: discipline exacted by regulated industrial life, the strict separation of leisure and work, the necessity of organized and regularized recreation for the masses, cheap and efficient public transport by train, later airplane (intercity) and bus as well as trolley (intracity), prompt and widely available mass communication via the press (introduction of the sport pages in newspapers and the establishment of sport journalism) followed by telegrams (crucial for the development and proliferation of betting), radio and then television, and the development and rapid expansion of modern education. Nobody has written more insightfully than Allen Guttmann about the inextricable link between societal modernization and modern sports the way both came to be understood throughout the twentieth century. In adopting concepts from Max Weber, Emile Durkheim, Ferdinand Toennies, and Talcott Parsons, Guttmann convincingly demonstrates how mechanisms as decisive as secularism, equality of opportunity to compete and the conditions of competition, specialization of roles, rationalization, bureaucratization, quantification, and the quest for records transformed "premodern" games, play, and contests into "modern" sports.[15] The creation and— perhaps more important—dissemination of modern sports as culture are thus part and parcel of a public life defined by the (often conflicting) interaction between modernization's two most important social agents: the bourgeoisie and the working class. Modern sports have also become a major forum as well as a replica of the contradictions of modern life. Concretely, modern sports are totally achievement oriented, hence egalitarian, yet at the same time also inherently unequal, thus elitist. They are liberal and decidedly not collectivist in one essential way: Their equality of opportunity is accompanied by a singularity of results. All can participate and start, but only one emerges as winner. Vince Lombardi's famous dictum that "winning is not everything, but the only thing" comes closer to being a superb characterization of the essential quality of modern sports than he likely cared to realize.

One of the most interesting analyses of culture in political sociology focuses on culture's retarding nature, on its "stickiness," particularly in relation to the perceived innovative impulses of the economy and the allegedly progressive tendencies of technology. Karl Marx and William Ogburn described culture's "lagging" tendencies in perceptive detail, and attributed to this "stickiness" an important impediment to social change.[16] The contemporary literature on globalization picks up this theme of a discrepancy between a rapidly developing "global" technology and a persistence of a "local" culture, often enhanced precisely in reaction to the globalizing tendencies of technology and the economy.[17] It is safe to say that such stickiness pertains to sport cultures in all advanced industrial societies, exhibiting a resilience that has rendered them alive and well for over one hundred years. In contrast, as well as complementary to Marx and Ogburn, Max Weber also discerned the salience of such stickiness as an explanation for history's durability, though not so much in a society's culture as in its institutions. According to Weber, it has been the resilience of such institutions—their adaptability, their resourcefulness, their staying power—that shaped culture and the social world wherein these institutions existed.[18] Joseph Schumpeter also emphasizes the stickiness of institutions in explaining the complexity of social change: "Social structures, types and attitudes are coins that do not readily melt. Once they are formed they persist, possibly for centuries."[19] While institutions in general are sticky, change of, in, and by them is further slowed by the stickiness of cultures laden with tradition, habit, custom, and simple inertia. We argue that even though one can currently detect critical junctures in the existence of many of these sports cultures, their longevity will prevail to safeguard the traditional formation of each country's sport space.

The story is pretty much the same in all advanced industrial societies. Once a nation's "sport space" is filled, there are very few changes in this space.[20] To be sure, the notion of "space" is twofold. It refers first to a sheer logic of quantity. So, as in a popular restaurant where tables are full and there is a waiting list for patrons, who can only be seated once space has become available by departing guests, sport space also describes a finite entity of entrants, a limited capacity to give all participants equal prominence and presence. Thus, the concept of "sport space" is indeed physically determined and quantitatively defined, since the capacities of all such spaces are limited. Above all, timing matters immensely. The sequence as to which sport came first, which managed to modernize most efficiently, and how this modernization process related sequentially to the particular society's overall modernization all represent crucial ingredients in the formation of a society's sport space. [21] But more important, sport space denotes a qualitative dimension of cultural construction and group contestation that reflects power relationships in society at large, and in sport in particular. Sport space is not "filled" simply on a first-come, first-served basis, but rather disputed and contested by social groups and actors with particular sets of interests. Positions within any society's sport space can thus be denied by dominant groups and alliances of interests.[22] This sense of sport space as contested cultural territory, as well as a sphere of established institutional interests, complements—rather than contradicts—the previously mentioned notion of sport space as merely a physical entity, a quantity that once filled, remains so forever.[23]

However, one thing is clear: Whichever sport entered a country's sport space first and managed to do so in the key period between 1870 and 1930, the crucial decades of industrial proliferation and the establishment of modern mass societies, continues to possess a major advantage to this day. Put differently, the contingent trajectory, of sport culture—what social scientists would call its "path dependence"—is very high. Early arrival does not guarantee late survival, but it most certainly helps, because choices are very rapidly narrowed once sport spaces become filled both quantitatively and spatially, and qualitatively in that any newcomer must exert a great deal of power and expend major resources to be given, using the previous example, a seat at the restaurant's increasingly limited tables from which few want to depart. The "liability of newness" becomes increasingly burdensome once the topography of a country's sport space has been established.[24] Tellingly, the window of arranging the sport spaces of virtually all industrial democracies roughly occurs in that crucial period between 1870 and 1930. Once the occupants have settled in, they are virtually impossible to dislodge. The continually reinforcing feedback of escalating success provide them a cultural and institutional presence that render them virtually invincible.[25] Exit options as well as entrance possibilities become severely limited, relative costs increase considerably, and the whole compact is driven by loyalties that are constantly reproduced. Moreover, their reproduction in turn helps enhance the staying power of the existing arrangements.[26] A "mechanism of reproduction" develops that creates a self-reinforcing and positive feedback process that strengthens those that are already present and weakens the entrance options for all newcomers.[27] This led to a situation that permitted substantial shifts *within* many a country's sport spaces over the past century, although few entrants were accorded the status of cultural importance and popular following accorded to that enjoyed by the early arrivals. In other words, once the window of opportunity between 1870 and 1930 was missed, it was virtually impossible to break into a country's sport space successfully for the ensuing seven decades. The "barriers to entry" remain exceedingly high, since the existing occupants enjoy significant cost advantages vis-à-vis all newcomers, have a fine and widely appreciated product differentiation, and benefit from substantial economies of scale.[28] Factor in that newcomers will inevitably suffer from an inadequate demand for their product, and it is clear that a belated entrance into this virtually closed world is almost prohibitive.[29] Newcomers, in effect, remain "crowded out."

While markets differ immensely, it is clear that in situations with few but very powerful players—that is oligopolies, indeed virtual monopolies in cases with only one dominant sport occupying a country's sport space—factors that deter entry also forestall exit, and elements that impede exit restrict entry.[30] This deterrence need not be part of a manifest or conscious strategy on the part of the incumbents to keep out newcomers; the structural power of incumbency is sufficient.[31] One way to alter entrance requirements and exit options is through unexpected exogenous influences or shocks that change the playing field in a major way. Whatever these exogenous factors may be—new technologies, new discoveries, new channels of communication, major social shifts, political upheavals, or a combination of some or all of these—they certainly reorder and reorient the existing structures of incumbency and might indeed threaten it with potential newcomers and even some departures from the old order. As to the sport space of the United States and other advanced industrial societies, it is possible that just such a period of restructuring and realignment is taking place that might perhaps make the current era a potential "critical juncture" somewhat analogous to the situation one century ago—though we doubt it, at least as far as the short run is concerned.[32]

If the path dependence just described pertains to the macrolevel of sport space and the collective dimension of the social, there is an equally significant—and profoundly related—path dependence on the microlevel of the individual that is crucial to the establishment of hegemonic sports cultures. It is mostly when one is a child that the lifelong attachment to a sport takes root. A potent mixture of the roles of spectator, participant, and then of fan creates an allegiance to a sport at a young age that seems almost irrevocable for life. Here we have noticed the pre-dominance of teams, and thus of team sports, as opposed to individual sports, in the

perpetuation of such dominant cultures in all advanced industrial societies. Teams have the modern power of continuity; they are institutions
whose presence continues regardless of the individuals on the team. Teams
are modern complex entities that exhibit "organic solidarity" in the best
Durkheimian sense, meaning that the entity itself is far more important
and lasting than any individual in it (no matter how prominent the individual). Additionally, individual sports do not exact solidarity in the act
of performing, in the process of production. They are thus of a less complex and modern order than team sports. To cite Durkheim once again,
individual sports remain stuck in the world of "mechanical solidarity" in
which the collective is incidental. In team sports, the collective is essential,
the whole always more than the sum of its individual parts.

   This is not to say that success is meaningless and the affective equivalent
to failure, as there are plenty of "fair weather fans" who support a team
only when it is victorious. But it is to say that teams—as continuous institutions with clear identities apart from those of their individual players—
are particularly powerful vehicles for establishing affective relationships
with their fans very early in life. Individual sports are different: When a
boxer, tennis player, figure skater wins a major following and becomes an
icon clearly enjoying mass appeal—be it for achievement of style, as a
"hometown favorite" (i.e., for patriotic reasons), or as a "personality"—
the attraction and loyalty remain ephemeral because they are totally tied
to this particular individual's persona, character, charisma. Once the
boxer, tennis player, figure skater loses his or her charisma through decline, defeat, and/or retirement, fans are left in a void, in need of finding
a new icon. Teams, on the other hand, endure. To be sure, Celtics fans
mourned the departure of Larry "Legend" Bird just like Bayern Munich
fans still invoke the days when Franz "Kaiser" Beckenbauer graced their
team's uniform. And nobody in the world bemoaned the departure of
Michael Jordan more emphatically than Chicago Bulls fans. But even
without Michael Jordan's charisma, the Chicago Bulls continue as an institution. Very few fans of these respective teams—indeed of all other
team sports—desert their team or lose their love for the sport because of
the loss of a spectacular player's charisma. As such, team sports are more
modern and enduring entities than individual sports; they not only capture our imagination at an earlier age, but they do a much better job of
shackling our affect for life. And these affective feelings and deep-seated
partisanships are nontransferable. Once an Arsenal fan, always an Arsenal fan, even when one's fate leads to a move far away from Highbury.

   The same pertains to team sports in America, where it is not only the
fans who have been mobile but—unlike anywhere in Europe—also the
teams. Notice the continued loyalty of many Brooklynites after the
Dodgers moved to Los Angeles in 1958,[33] or of the denizens of Oakland,

whose allegiance to the Raiders was so powerful that it was one of the main reasons for the team's return to Oakland after a fifteen-year "desertion" to Los Angeles. Moreover, team allegiances and affect supersede that which is directed at individual players regardless of the power of the individual's particular charisma. Fans of Borussia Mönchengladbach did not switch their allegiance to Real Madrid when their beloved Günter "*in die Tiefe des Raumes*" Netzer joined that club and faced his old team in the European Champion's Cup. Conversely, the Candlestick faithful celebrated and cheered Darryl Strawberry when he joined the San Francisco Giants, though he hailed from and had last played for much-hated Los Angeles and had been roundly jeered by the very same fans every time he took the field in a Dodgers uniform. Celtics fans were delighted to welcome Larry Bird back to Boston as the head coach of the Indiana Pacers, but while they continued to pay homage to their beloved idol, all of them rooted for their Celtics to defeat Bird's Pacers. This institutionalized, nonnegotiable, and virtually irreplaceable loyalty to teams on the part of their fans gives team sports a cultural continuity and a level of involvement unparalleled in individual sports. As Roman Horak, Austria's leading student of sport culture, argues: Love of, loyalty for, and identification with one's team remains arguably the only emotional constant in one's life. Horak characterizes the relationship between the fan and his soccer club in terms that are perfectly applicable to fans' relations with their teams in American sports: "Moreover, there remains only one single constant in the life of people, particularly of men, and that is the soccer club and all the ties to it associated with being a fan. Marriages fail, relationships end, jobs disappear, anything can happen; only one red thread remains reliably through life: team loyalty."[34]

This continuity is further accentuated by the presence of a certain Kantian relationship on the part of fans vis-à-vis their teams. At its base, this relationship is quite pure in that it is largely interest free. Most fans do not derive any monetary rewards or any other tangible benefits from their team's fortune. They want their team to win for the simple reward of winning in itself; no ulterior motives here, no hidden agendas, just pure interest-free affect. To be sure: Every team has its fair-weather fans, and winning always creates "free riders" who only express interest when the home team is in contention. But affect in team sports is amazingly long lasting and sturdy. How else to explain the great loyalty of long-suffering Boston Red Sox and Chicago Cubs fans in baseball, New York Rangers fans in hockey, New York Jets fans in football, and countless loyal fans of any number of unsuccessful clubs in British and continental soccer? Marketers are fully aware of this early path dependence and the ensuing increasing returns that a lifelong allegiance to a team and its sport entails. In its attempt to woo youngsters from their increasing attraction toward

rival team sports, the National Football League hired a former MTV executive who clearly recognized that "it's all about getting a football . . . into
a kid's hands as soon as you can. Six years old, if possible. You want to
get a football in their hands before someone puts a basketball in their
hands, or a hockey stick."[35]

"Frozen Spaces" and the Dialogue with History

Following the pioneering work of Seymour Martin Lipset and Stein Rokkan in terms of their historical explanation of the contemporary topography of party spaces in advanced industrial democracies, we adapt the
concept of the "freezing" of party spaces to the world of sport.[36] In a
comparative analysis of the party landscape in the advanced industrial
democracies of Europe, Lipset and Rokkan conclude that it was largely
four major cleavages that—by their prominence and acerbity—gave rise
to voter alignments that continue to define the party system that these
countries exhibit to this day. In particular, Lipset and Rokkan argue that
with the last—and most pronounced—of these cleavages (that between
capital and labor, which they label the "owner-worker" cleavage) well
established following the Great War, the cleavage system and its reflection
in a nation's party topography was by and large in place by 1920. Indeed,
it became so ensconced, Lipset and Rokkan aver, that it remained "frozen" well into the 1960s and beyond. While there are clearly flaws in this
scheme (for example, the failure to account for fascism in a number of
the countries critical to Lipset and Rokkan's analysis and the ensuing
major alteration of the party landscape in the countries concerned), we
remain impressed by how accurate the analysis has proven over time and
how the cleavages that defined the party topography of industrial democracies at the early part of the twentieth century remarkably still pertained
at its end. Some edges frayed, as newcomers entered the party space, and
there were a few exits, but on the whole, the landscape that was frozen
after World War I is still intact and quite recognizable.

We believe that such an analogy to the situation in sports is apt and
strong, as it appears that sport spaces in virtually all of the advanced
industrial countries were frozen by the end of World War I and virtually
no significant thawing occurred until, perhaps, the current period. Whatever sport (or sports) managed to become culturally dominant—or hegemonic—by 1930 remained so through the end of the twentieth century.
Of course, changes occurred in sport—its institutions, rules, and venues—
over the years. Just like political parties adapted to—and in turn co-
opted—political change, these "frozen" sports proved to be highly adapt-
able, malleable, and energetic. Hence, it was only their presence in the

existing sport spaces that was "frozen," not the sports themselves. And just as in the world of party politics it has become an all but impossible task to melt away the frozen structures, in the sports world, too, traditional groups have by and large succeeded in demonstrating an immensely impressive resilience and remain ensconced in the core of each country's sport space, leaving only the margins to various newcomers.

Whereas we take seriously Friedrich Nietzsche's dictum that anything with a history defies precise categorization and a useful definition, we argue emphatically that in all manifestations of sport as culture—as opposed to activity—that intangible thing called "history" matters immensely. While to some degree this is a truism, it needs to be addressed, as it is so essential for the continued legitimation of each of the dominant sports and for the reproduction of sports culture. All hegemonic sports reproduce and legitimate themselves through constant acts of loyalty, legends, colors, and icons. Thus, every contemporary game becomes—implicitly, to be sure, but also quite often explicitly—a discourse with history. The culture of continuity and comparability develops over time and space, and this gives the already established sports an attraction that virtually no newcomers can match. Indeed, all established sports prolifically utilize a constant appeal to history to discredit their potential rivals. The Big Three in the United States, just like hockey in Canada, and soccer in the rest of the world invoke their alleged aesthetic, even moral, superiority over any newcomers by appealing to history. What makes this history so potent is that it is relived and reconfirmed in every contest: *Any* game in Yankee Stadium is an often explicit discourse with baseball's past; the same pertains to games in such hallowed places as Fenway Park or Wrigley Field. While it is true that modern stadiums are disdained by the games' purists precisely for lacking this essential historical ingredient, they, too, become part of the game's history quite quickly by being forums where the sport continues to be played. Of course, Lambeau Field invokes a different—definitely more revered, perhaps bordering on the sacred—reaction from most football aficionados (let alone Green Bay Packer fans) than the modern-day run-of-the-mill concrete megaplex situated at some suburban highway exit. But there, too, the game's legitimacy and its attractiveness to millions of fans is quickly reproduced and well established by dint of tradition. Retired numbers of former greats may grace the walls of outdoor stadiums (or the rafters of indoor arenas), but they are mere decoration and largely ephemeral items in the constant reliving of tradition that reaffirms the hegemonic position of the particular sport as mass culture.

The historically significant venues featuring baseball and football have their parallels in all dominant sports cultures. All have their Meccas, their hallowed grounds distinguished by their respective age and the pedigree of their occupants: Hockey boasted its Montreal Forum (replaced by the Molson Centre in the 1990s) and its Maple Leaf Gardens (hailing from the 1920s and rendered obsolete by the Air Canada Centre in 1999); basketball its Boston Garden (also replaced in the 1990s by the Fleet Center, which, however, incorporated in its design the Garden's famed parquet floor precisely for reasons of tradition and continuity, at least until Christmas 1999 when it was removed) and its Madison Square Garden (despite having changed its location three times in the course of the twentieth century); and soccer its Old Trafford, Maine Road, Anfield, White Hart Lane, Highbury, Ibrox Park, Estado Bernabeau, Nou Camp, Betzenberg, Boekelberg, San Siro, Hütteldorf, Wembley, Maracana, and many others of comparable fame, each sporting its own legends, legacies, and myths. All claim to be unique for their special place in their sport's history, yet all serve as coalescing icons in that their specialness is acknowledged, accepted, even revered by all of that sport's fans and participants, regardless whether they be friends or foes of the particular team concerned. And nothing more eloquently conveys the reification of history in sports than the various halls of fame in the United States and Canada, veritable shrines to the legends (both human and material) of the respective games, designed to keep memory alive and history palpable and visible, thereby further enhancing the sports' already considerable legitimacy.

History plays yet another legitimating part in the sense that every contemporary game serves at least as an implicit, but very often as an explicit, comparison with the past. Nowhere is this more the case than in the Big Three and One-Half of American sports where constant statistics and measurability permit at least a pro forma comparison between present achievements and performance with those of past teams and players. When Barry Sanders of the Detroit Lions amassed over two thousand rushing yards in the 1997 season, the major attraction of his amazing feat was not so much the contemporary achievement itself, but rather the comparison—and implicit competition—with other running greats, Eric Dickerson and O. J. Simpson in particular (the only other two runners to have attained two thousand yards in one season), but also with Jim Brown, Earl Campbell, and other comparably prominent NFL running backs. Discoursing with history is as essential for baseball, basketball, and hockey as it is for football. Is Mark McGwire the equal of Henry Aaron, and are they both in Babe Ruth's "league"? How does Kareem Abdul Jabbar compare to Wilt Chamberlain, Bill Russell, or even George Mikan (a player from a truly different era)? Is Wayne Gretzky definitely the best hockey player ever to have played the game, or might it be Bobby Orr (as commonly heard in Boston)? Is Steve Young really "the best quarterback ever," as claimed in an article in the *New York Times Magazine* based on a statistical comparison of Young's achievements with those of other quarterback greats such as Milt Plum, Sammy Baugh, Otto Graham, Johnny Unitas, Bart Starr—each from an era of the game preceding Young's—as well as Dan Marino, Joe Montana, and John Elway, each Young's contemporary?[37] These comparisons need not remain confined to individual players. They clearly involve teams as well. Thus, were the 1998 Yankees really as good, perhaps even better than, their 1927 predecessors? Were the Chicago Bulls with their six NBA championships in the 1990s as good—or better than—the Bill Russel–led Boston Celtics that amassed eleven championships in the 1950s and 1960s? Endless fodder for spirited debates anchored in history.

While statistics facilitate the historicization of sports and furnish one measure of a sport's modernity, they are in no way essential to history's pride of place in the affirmation of every sport culture's continued vibrancy. In the case of soccer, where goals scored were—until very recently at least—the only quantified criteria in the game, longitudinal comparisons have been as commonplace and as integral to the game's culture as they have in the more statistically oriented North American sports.[38] Was Franz Beckenbauer as great a player as Fritz Walter? How did either of them compare to Lothar Matthäus? None of these players' undoubtedly great careers can ever be measured in a quantitatively precise manner the way greatness can be ascertained in all four North American sports. And yet, all soccer fans acknowledge and know about their greatness, though the debate as to which one is greater than the other will never abate and is precisely the meat of what we have here termed "hegemonic sports culture." Indeed, all three players would be ranked higher on soccer's firmament than such prolific goal scorers as Gerd Müller, Jürgen Klinsmann, and Oliver Bierhoff, to stick with our German examples. Were the great Real Madrid teams of the late 1950s and early 1960s as good as the dominant AC Milan teams of the late 1980s and early 1990s, and was either comparable to the Johan Cruyff–led Ajax Amsterdam teams of the 1970s? Was the German national team that won the World Cup in 1990 as good as its precursors that attained the same feat in 1954 and 1974, respectively, or were none of them close to the brilliance that distinguished the side that won the European championship in 1972? To this penchant for diachronic comparison one can add a similar built-in obsession with synchronic comparison (How does Zinedine "Zizou" Zidane's midfield play at Juventus Turin compare to that of his performances for the French national team? Is Michael Owen a more talented striker than Ronaldo?), and it is clear that comparability over time and space serves as an essential mechanism in the constant legitimation and reaffirmation of sports culture. These constant comparisons over time and space—whether quantified, as in all American team sports, or qualitative, as in the world of soccer—form a ubiquitous and necessary ingredient to all hegemonic sports cultures. An acute awareness of, and a keen appreciation for, history is essential for any kind of sport discourse.

Critical Junctures, Agents, and Agency

Critical junctures are crucial in the establishment of every sport. Serendipity and chance have a major role in determining a sport's successful establishment as either mass culture or mere activity for a select group of interested participants, especially in its nascent phases. While critical junctures are unique and random events, somewhat akin to accidents and thus quite unpredictable, the context wherein they occur is much more determined and structurally compelling. Whereas we cannot predict accidents, with reasonable certainty we can predict when, where, and how they might happen if we know the constituent framework and the necessary prerequisites for their occurrence. Marc Bloch's brilliant misstep theory of history pertains to the development of each sport space as well.[39] While we know that the misstep that led to the climber's lethal fall from the mountain was a decisive—though completely unpredictable—random act of misfortune, we must also take into account various other measures that explain the mishap: the visibility on the mountain that day; weather conditions that might have made the path slippery; the physical shape of the climber, his mental preparation, and the quality of his equipment; and a host of other factors. In short, while critical junctures may be acts of serendipity and randomness, the framework wherein they occur is not. Whereas each hegemonic sport can point to a few critical junctures that turned out to be fortuitous events in its development toward cultural dominance, the context wherein each of these serendipitous acts occurred was actually quite predictable and uniform: those of major demographic changes, massive urbanization, the introduction of mass transit, uniformization, large-scale commodification of most aspects of public life, increased competition, growing public participation of an ever-increasing percentage of the population—in short, the process of what has become widely known by the problematic and controversial term of "modernization." Put differently, agency mattered in the successful establishment of every sports culture. As usual, it never overrode structure, but by seizing the right moment it proved indispensable in reinforcing structural predispositions and launching these sports on the path of cultural prominence. On the one hand, one can discern everywhere an interesting combination that defines agency: There exist traits that could best be characterized as "entrepreneurial" or "charismatic." On the other hand, "managerial" or "bureaucratic" attributes are of equal importance in the establishment of hegemonic sports. As with all structures discussed by Schumpeter and Weber, in sports, too, we find the former characteristics more prevalent in the early "premodern" stages of their development. Thus, it is interesting to note that in the establishment of each country's sport space, entrepreneurs and innovators, typically strong-willed individuals with courage and vision—in short persons with charismatic authority—proved instrumental in the introduction and further development of the sport. This pertains as much to the business side of the sport (the ownership of teams, the most important factor) as it does to the establishment of the sport: its institutionalization in some competitive framework, usually in the form of a league, as well as the development of mutually intelligible and accepted rules to guarantee the sport's appeal beyond that of a local game, and its transformation into a competitive contest on the national and international scale.

With the sport's maturation and its establishment as a modern commodified entity, the "managerial" and "bureaucratic" attributes assume unquestioned dominance. Thus, when one hears that sports today are primarily a business, this not only describes a reality that the modernization process exacts of any successful structure but it also connotes in its wistfulness and lamentation a desire on our part to have sports exempted from this modernization process, to maintain the pristineness of a pastoral game while continuing the innocence of a childhood activity. This built-in desire to extol sports of the "good old days," to create myths of its alleged innocent past, untainted by the commodification and bureaucratization of the modern world, adds further immediacy to the historicization of all the dominant sports described herein. Yet again, history matters. And in a curious way, sports do indeed maintain a personalization, an immediacy, a "charismatic" stage unparalleled in other businesses and commodified entities of similar size and importance. This is obvious, of course, on the production side, where all sports—including team sports—thrive on individual achievement and contribution. Michael Jordan's charisma is completely personal and unique; it is nontransferable. The same pertains to Alfredo Di Stefano, Ruud Gullit, Jürgen Klinsmann, Wayne Gretzky, John Elway, and Sammy Sosa. Of course the team's overall success is of paramount importance, but the very fact that individuals on losing teams can still be celebrated personalities and revered stars attests to the appeal of individuals with charisma.[40] Just think of Ernie Banks as a nationally revered star on the perennially poor Chicago Cubs, and parallel cases in the soccer histories of Europe and Latin America. But even regarding ownership, sports continue to be more personalized, more charismatic than businesses of comparable importance and commodification. Thus, for every Walt Disney or Molson Brewery or MSG Corp. ownership, there exists a George Steinbrenner, Ted Turner, Charles Finley, Art Modell, Wayne Huizinga, Jerry Reinsdorf, Jerry Jones, and Peter Angelos. In the world of first-class soccer, too, rich individuals such as Bernard Tapie (former flamboyant owner of Olympique Marseilles), Silvio Berlusconi (owner of AC Milan), the Agnelli Family (Juventus Turin), Sir John Hall (Newcastle United), Jack Walker (Blackburn Rovers), and Alan Sugar (Tottenham Hotspurs) exist side by side with huge conglomerates as owners of prominent soccer teams. Charisma and bureaucracy interact in the organizational landscape of modern sports to a degree rarely seen in other comparable institutions of advanced industrial capitalism. This interaction continues to give agency a major presence in the structure of hegemonic sports cultures.

In each of these advanced industrial societies, all dominant sports have been the exclusive domain of men. Until recently, few realms of modern industrial life have been so gender exclusive as hegemonic sports cultures in all countries. This pertains at *all* levels: to owners, fans, spectators, to the daily consumers of this culture via television, radio, and the sports pages in newspapers and magazines, and, of course, most important, to the activists themselves, the players. While women have participated in these dominant sports, this participation—again until recently—has remained completely marginal. Whereas one of the new structural ingredients we are currently witnessing on an international level—and that might in fact offer a prerequisite for a critical juncture to occur in the next few years—is the increasing participation on the part of women on all levels of hegemonic sports culture (as spectators, fans, viewers, readers, and, most important, as players), the past century's "gender apartheid" is far from over.[41] Underlying the inclusive nature of hegemonic sports for men—and thus their a fortiori exclusive characteristic for women—is that these sports often form a bond and discourse transcendent of class, status, ethnicity, geography, and religion. Of course, allegiances to teams heighten such differences and exacerbate existing ones: Consider the serious religious tensions between Catholics and Protestants at every Celtic-Rangers derby in Glasgow, or the class rivalries in Viennese soccer between the fans of formerly "upper class" and "urbane" Austria on the one hand, and the "proletarian" supporters of Rapid on the other. Yet, when taken to the more abstract, but still very real, level of the sport itself—when severed from the immediate passions of partisanship and team identification—hegemonic sports culture offers men one of the very few true venues of communication devoid of the baggage that otherwise impedes communication. Think of how a well-healed banker or a highly educated professor can strike up a fine sense of bonding with a taxi driver or a construction worker over sports, the only topic and venue of communication—appropriately known as "guy talk"—that would ever afford both such a level of verbal exchange, perhaps even a few moments of mutual respect and affection. Briefly put, few structures in modern life have remained such a male preserve as hegemonic sports cultures. In recent years, the interest of females as spectators and fans, and as players and participants in many recreational sport contexts, has risen considerably in most advanced industrial societies, especially in the United States. In the future, perhaps, a modern major spectator team sport might include girls and young women at its foundation. In the United States, soccer—with its "egalitarian access" and its current popularity as a girls', women's, and coeducational sport—might have that potential. But for the foreseeable future, the success of any spectator sport, particularly when large sums of money are involved, will continue to depend overwhelmingly on the play and interest of males.[42]

To be sure, women entered the sports world in the last two decades of the twentieth century to an unprecedented degree. As activists and participants, they now contest on a regular basis in virtually all the disciplines formerly the exclusive domain of men at international events such as the Olympics and world championships. As discussed in subsequent chapters, professional basketball witnessed the birth of two women's leagues in the United States in the late-1990s, among which the NBA-sponsored WNBA survived on seemingly solid ground into the twenty-first century. If anything, women's soccer has been more important than the men's game in the United States. It has most certainly been more successful, with the American women's team winning the first world championship of women's soccer in 1991, attaining the first gold medal awarded in that sport at the summer Olympics of 1996, and triumphing in the third world championship held in the United States in the summer of 1999, undoubtedly the very first soccer event in the United States with a genuine mass following and popular involvement on the part of the general American public. Indeed, affection for and interest in the U.S. women's soccer team represented the very first time in American sports history that soccer attained the accoutrements of a hegemonic sports culture in the United States—if only for a few weeks—comparable to what was the norm in Europe and Latin American throughout the twentieth century.

In terms of viewership in the 1980s and 1990s, women in the United States and Europe have also shown remarkably increased interest. Thus, for example, it has been estimated by European advertising analysts that a hitherto unprecedented number of women watched the World Cup tournament in the summer of 1998. Nearly 50 percent of France's female population watched the games, especially in the latter stages of the tournament; in Italy, as many women as men watched Italy's matches, while in the Netherlands the numbers were the same for men and women for games screened at 9:00 P.M. local time.[43] But the long-term trend still remains: While it is true that women have become much more involved and interested in special events such as major national and international contests, they still lag considerably behind men when it comes to daily partisanship and a continued identification with a sport and a team. To use the example from the World Cup in the summer of 1998, while it may be true that women became interested in the matches of this event to nearly the same numerical degree as men, it has simply not been the case that this temporary enthusiasm translated into a consistent and long-term interest in and identification with club-level soccer. French women might very well have been swept up by the general enthusiasm for the French team's winning ways, but this did not make them enthusiastic Paris St. Germain, St. Etienne, or Lens fans during the French regular soccer season following the special event of the World Cup. This part of French soccer reverted to its usual pre–World Cup male milieu. Even though women in the advanced industrial societies have made major gains in virtually all aspects of sports (as spectators, participants, managers, coaches, journalists) in the wake of the attainments of the modern women's movement, which has altered public life in these societies since the mid-to-late 1970s, it is safe to say that the organized professional sports that constituted societies' hegemonic sports cultures at the end of the twentieth century remained nearly as much the domain of men as they had at the century's beginning. Participation in sports as activity became much more female during the last two decades of the twentieth century, but following it as culture still remained an overwhelmingly male domain, as it had been since its inception a century before. In short, women now *do* but men still *follow*.[44]

This continued gender divide is further maintained—even reinforced—by issues of class, which play a crucial role in the creation and maintenance of each country's sport space and the dominant sports cultures therein. Everywhere, the maturation of sports cultures exhibits the following trajectory of social transformation with respect to class: A sport in its nascent phases is played by upper-class or upper middle-class gentlemen who revel in its activities, good fun, and gamesmanship. In this atmosphere of proud amateurism, playing the game is far more important than winning the contest. Indeed, the ethos of "value rationality," so prevalent at this stage of the sport's existence, exacts a certain disdain for winning and instead extols participation in the game as well as camaraderie among all contestants (teammates and opponents alike). With the sport's modernization—featuring, among other things, an inclusion of a large number of new participants as fans, players, and followers—the "pure" phase of the sport (i.e., that of merely playing it, of enjoying the process and not the outcome) shifts significantly. Suddenly, the ultimate "means rationality" emerges with a vengeance, as the game itself becomes a mere means to the single end of victory. This process is accompanied by the sport's early professionalization and commodification; as camaraderie gives way to competition, rules of contest emerge that are there to be broken, if need be, to satisfy the sport's new and paramount raison d'être: that of winning. Subsequently, games for fun develop into contests for remuneration. Hence, enter the era of professional players, managers, coaches, owners—the protagonists of the modern sport culture.

Class and Path Dependence

The main social carrier of this transformation of sport from activity and games to culture and contest has been the male, industrial working class. Analogous to Barrington Moore Jr.'s well-known dictum of "no bourgeoisie, no democracy," we would like to assert a parallel construction for the contemporary presence of modern sport cultures: no working class and commercial middle class, no modern sport as mass culture.[45] Be it soccer in England, Austria, Germany, Argentina, Italy, France, Romania, or baseball, football, and basketball in the United States, and hockey in Canada, they all began as amateur games played by gentlemen and were then transformed into mass cultures by the participation and inclusion of the working and middle classes, mainly as professional players (i.e., skilled workers as producers) and as fans (consumers). In every country where soccer developed into the premier occupant of the country's sport space, the game became inextricably identified with a "proletarian" culture. Tellingly, this has not been the case in the United States, particularly during the country's so called "soccer boom" begun in the late 1970s and early 1980s where the sport—other than in some Latino milieus—has been touted as a middle-class, egalitarian, communitarian, suburban game precisely in contrast to the proletarian, rugged, macho football and hockey, even baseball and basketball. Elsewhere in the world, soccer maintains its aura (or stigma, depending on one's point of view) of being an exclusively male, working-class, vulgar, rough, and occasionally even violent sport. Any kind of American-style "yuppiefication" or "sanitation" of its original milieu is disdained by true soccer fans, as well as players. For example, during the World Cup in the summer of 1998, members of the successful French squad—in particular, team captain Didier Deschamps, goalie Fabien Barthez, and defender Frank Leboeuf—bemoaned the fact that the stadiums of the tournament (particularly the Stade de France in Saint-Denis) were populated by men in three-piece suits with ties who, in the players' view, lent these events the air of a funeral or a theatrical play rather than that of a soccer match, while the true soccer fans milled about outside these venues unable to afford the price of tickets and with no access to them at all.[46] Leboeuf suggested putting up a sign outside the Stade de France for the championship final that would read: "No suits allowed." He continued, "It's an offense to soccer, which is a sport of the masses. Put on a T-shirt. Paint your face and start shouting."[47] Added Deschamps: "I get to the field and look up at the tribune and all I see is guys in black. They look more like they are attending a funeral than a World Cup game! . . . We're missing the worker, who thinks red, white and blue from morning till night. There is no sense of communion with the people in the stadium." The colorful Barthez concurred: "It's not a classical music concert with flutes. We should have seen 80,000 people letting go a little. This is the VIP's World Cup."[48]

That a hegemonic sport's image is mainly defined by its milieu and *not* the actual activity on the field is best exemplified by the fact that the much rougher game of rugby continues to enjoy a certain "refined" and upper-class image, whereas soccer—wherever it is culturally hegemonic—is seen as proletarian. Hence, the old saying that rugby is a rough game played by gentlemen whereas soccer is a gentle game played by ruffians aptly mirrors the different class participation in the modernization process of these two related sports. Further corroboration of the point that the respective class involvement in the sport rather than the game itself coined the sport's image as culture in its particular sport space is the telling difference between rugby played by professionals (Rugby League) and by amateurs (Rugby Union): The former is perceived as commercial, thus vulgar and proletarian, whereas the latter has maintained an aura of gentlemanliness as an elite game that extends throughout Britain. Interestingly, it is the only team game in which Ireland retains a united team. Exported to Britain's colonies, with the exception of the West Indies, Union has historically been strictly amateur. Union was played predominantly by grammar and public schools (the only winter sport played at both), although there were a few comprehensives that also took it up. Tellingly, the more popular but proletarian soccer remained in a subordinate position at these "elite" institutions. Played by universities, the annual Oxford-Cambridge Union game has the kind of national interest in Britain that could be compared to the annual Army-Navy game in American football in contemporary America. Characteristic of its amateur standing and gentlemanly ethos, Union had no leagues. Various cup competitions at the club level were only introduced in the 1970s, the period in which Union, too, began a process of overt professionalization.

Rugby League, in contrast, was a regional game, largely confined to Yorkshire and Lancashire, decidedly working class and professional. Union and League remained steadfastly separate entities and cultures strictly based on class lines to the extent that if a player shifted from Union to League and thus received remuneration for playing the game of rugby, he would be barred from Union's amateur ranks for life. This class distinction has also been transferred to Britain's former colonies as well as to a few other countries (especially the southwest region of France, Romania, Italy, Japan) where rugby has attained a respectable, if decidedly subordinate, foothold in their respective sport spaces. The League game has witnessed the emergence of the Australians as the best in the world, whereas global preeminence in the Union game is usually contested among Australia, New Zealand (the "All Black"), and South Africa, where—until recently—rugby was unquestionably the game of the dominant whites, especially Afrikaaners (with the "Springbok" national team being one of the most powerful symbols of apartheid), and soccer decidedly the game of the blacks, thus reinforcing rigid class distinctions with ethnic and racial ones. Despite these changes, Rugby League's strength remains confined to the geographic and social core of its origins.

This class-bound image pertains to the American sport scene as well. The Big Three and One-Half have often been associated with "lower class," "mass," "popular," perhaps even vulgar, (if not so much "proletarian," since the concept of "proletarian" is less common in the United States than in other comparable industrial democracies as a result of American exceptionalism). The rule of thumb in terms of a sport's image is this: If it has attained mass status, meaning that it has become a culture that masses follow rather than an activity that gentlemen perform, it is routinely perceived as commercial, lower class, common, and unrefined. If it failed (or never attempted) to become a mass phenomenon, or—tellingly—if its introduction into a country's sport space occurred only recently, that is, in the age of postindustrialism and not at the height of the creation of mass democracy in the era of industrial development, then the sport maintains an aura of refinement and exclusivity, of being decidedly non-, indeed anti-proletarian. We can thus observe the following mirror images in the contemporary sports world: In the United States, the Big Three and One-Half still maintain a decidedly mass-based image, despite major attempts to transform these sports into "family entertainment"; soccer, on the other hand, continues to be identified as a "yuppie" and 'preppy" sport indulged by a mixture of suburban "soccer moms," along with Hispanic immigrants.

In Europe, soccer maintains a decidedly popular and mass-based—if also occasionally less proletarian—image, whereas imports of the American Big Three have attained an aura of middle-class "cool" and "yuppie" acceptability. The equivalent social strata (middle-class professionals, urban yuppies) that have recently begun to play and follow soccer in the United States have discovered baseball in Italy and Holland, basketball in Germany, France, Italy, Greece, Spain, and football in Germany and the

Scandinavian countries. Everywhere, the gradual weakening of working-class culture and the concomitant lessening of traditional communities centered around the old ball park, the home pitch, the team pub, or the neighborhood bar is associated with a loss of authenticity and a commercialization that any true fan of the respective sport decries. Even though all mass sports had become subject to the logic of capitalism sooner or later in the course of the twentieth century, commodification on a grand scale, which began characterizing sports in both the United States and Europe in the late 1980s and 1990s, was met with much disdain by the true fan on both sides of the Atlantic. Megaplexes, corporate skyboxes, pay-per-view television, the ubiquitous presence of multinational corporations as sponsors, the globalization of markets all seemed to undermine the old working-class roots that characterized the milieus of these sports without eradicating them completely. To be sure: The New York Yankees, the Chicago Bulls, the Montreal Canadiens, the Dallas Cowboys, AC Milan, Bayern Munich, Ajax Amsterdam, Manchester United, and Arsenal London have crucial tie-ins with entities such as Nike, Opel, Umbro, Molson, Sharpe, Continental, and other multinational corporations. Their logos might have attained global identification and might indeed have generated a following far from the respective teams' actual activities. At least until Michael Jordan's retirement, the Chicago Bulls had a coterie of ardent and knowledgeable fans in Europe, just as AC Milan, Bayern Munich, or any of the prominent European soccer clubs have their modest American followings. Yankee caps and Cowboy jerseys are as readily available in Paris and Rome as European soccer shirts are in any larger American city. And still, this globalization is merely another layer that exists in addition to—not instead of—the teams' local roots and parochial milieus. In no way does globalization displace local attachments. Indeed, it does not even come close to the intensity of emotions and enthusiasm garnered by the traditional identities that will continue to receive pride of place for years to come. The Yankees will become better known on a global level in the course of the next decades, but true love for them will not reach much beyond New York (or for those who at least grew up there), thereby rendering the situation not all that different from the one that existed one hundred years ago. The same pertains to Real Madrid and Boca Juniors Buenos Aires. Knowledge of these teams will become global; true affection for them, however, will remain local.

Hegemonic sports have yet another commonality, concerning class: Their players have disproportionately hailed from the lower strata of their respective societies. So, just as a statistically significant number of Brazilian soccer stars have emerged from the favelas of Rio de Janeiro and São Paolo, the inner core of many American cities furnishes a good number of the country's talent in the Big Three, basketball in particular. Stars of all hegemonic sports emanate from the poor and underprivileged segments of their societies, both urban and rural: This is as true of Italian, Austrian, and English soccer players as it is of West Indian cricketers, Canadian hockey players, Caribbean baseball players, and American football players. The reason is obvious: Hegemonic sports have historically offered the poor but talented one of the very few venues of unimpeded upward mobility and genuine societal recognition usually denied them by most other institutions of modern capitalism. Over the years, dominant sports have accorded financial rewards (class mobility) and social recognition (status mobility) to a few highly talented members of otherwise marginalized groups (be they economic, ethnic, religious) to an extent only paralleled by a close cousin: the world of popular entertainment.

To confirm this phenomenon, we looked at the social backgrounds of the 22-man rosters of the Austrian, German, Italian, English, Dutch, and French teams that played in the World Cup tournament of 1998. We picked these six teams because they hailed from countries whose level of economic development was comparable to that of the United States. We are quite certain that the pattern found with these squads pertained to most others in the tournament as well, particularly since many came from countries that enjoyed a lower standard of living than these six affluent European societies. Of the 132 individuals on these six teams, only 12 had at least one parent—though never both—with a university degree and/or an occupation such as doctor, lawyer, university or college teacher, researcher, or middle manager. Virtually all of these players hailed from families where the parents either held typically working-class jobs (both blue collar such as truck driver or industrial worker, and white collar such as office clerk or secretary) or were part of the lower middle class in that their parents had a bakery, owned a local pub, or were engaged in some sort of small business on the most parochial level, be it in the countryside, a small town, or the "wrong side of the tracks" in a big city. Significantly, this was much less the case with the American team, whose players had parents much more solidly middle class. Moreover, in notable contrast to all European players, only 1 of whom (out of 132!) had completed a postsecondary education, a large majority of the Americans had either attained a college degree or attended college for at least two or three years. Compounding the difference between European and American soccer players at this World Cup, none of the American players hailed from a truly underprivileged, proletarian, or "rough" background as had a large number of the Europeans on all six teams considered in our study. The social and class equivalents to the European soccer players in North America regularly populate the ranks of the National Basketball Association, the National Football League, Major League Baseball, and the National Hockey League. However, most of the American players in the Big Three do indeed spend some time in college, thanks to the American exception of college athletics (discussed in this chapter and in chapters 2 and 4).

Hegemonic sports' formative years (as opposed to origins) in working-class culture are best illustrated by the fact that audience noise and vocal participation, often bordering on the raucous and unruly, are part of this world's cultural package. The boisterous support of the home team and the concomitant taunting of opponents bespeaks a discourse in which winning is once again primary. Loyalties and emotions are to be displayed with pride and vigor both in victory and defeat. Contrast this to the demeanor for upper-class sports: Overt partisanship needs to be checked, loud support is openly disdained, the visitor is to be accorded as much respect, if not necessarily affection, as the hometown favorite; and an atmosphere of gentility and quiet pervades the whole ambience. That these atmospheric differences are socially constructed and vary according to time and place is best demonstrated by the following: With cricket exhibiting more of an upper-class sports culture in England than in the West Indies, India, Pakistan, and Sri Lanka, the spectators have on the whole continued to behave with much greater restraint in the former than they have in the latter, where cricket audiences have exhibited behavior much more akin to, say, soccer crowds in England or those attending comparable dominant sports in other countries. There is also the example of the completely differing behavior on the part of Rugby Union and Rugby League supporters. What compels the spectators of the amateur sport to cheer with applause, leads the followers of the professional game to ridicule with jeers. A look at tennis in this context reveals that the commercialization of the game, its overt commodification engendered by the so-called "open era," which abolished the old "elitist" distinction between amateurs and professionals in the early 1970s, caused the previously accepted habitus of gentlemanly behavior on the part of players and spectators alike to disappear. Stars such as Ilie "Nasty" Nastase, Jimmy Connors, and John McEnroe derived much of their charisma by being the "bad boys" of tennis, meaning they spurned the old genteel conventions of the game to assume a demeanor well established in such dominant sport cultures as the Big Three and One-Half in the United States and soccer in the rest of the world. Tennis audiences also shed their former gentility and became much more akin to their counterparts in dominant sports in terms of open partisanship and boisterousness. In short, class in its myriad manifestations has deeply shaped the world of sports and will continue to do so.

Nationalism and National Pride as a Feature in Hegemonic Sports Cultures

Lastly, nationalism is without any doubt among the most decisive and ubiquitous factors influencing sports as a cultural phenomenon. This should come as no surprise since both—organized sports and nationalism—are essential expressions of modernity. Even though international and transnational in their actual exercise, activity, implementation, and—most important for their common intelligibility—rule structure, most modern sports are nationally organized, institutionalized, and represented. The contestants at international events are national actors providing modern sports in such venues an immense attraction and general appeal well beyond the contestants themselves, and often even beyond the circle of the sports' followers and fans. How else can one explain an entire country's excitement—even fanaticism—for "its" contestant at an international event, be it the quadrennial Olympics, the annual Tour de France, one of the four annual Majors (or the biannual Ryder Cup) in golf, one of the four annual Grand Slams (or the annual Davis Cup) in tennis, and any of the annual, biannual, and quadrennial world championships that determine any sport's very best on the globe (with the quadrennial world championship of soccer receiving a special pride of place for being far and away the world's most popular sporting event). Examples abound: The medal count in any Olympics is of paramount importance to every participating country. The dominant countries take account of their total medal tallies and tout their victories—implicitly or explicitly—as evidence of their respective countries' achievements and superiority over others. The countries that win medals more rarely are filled with perhaps even greater joy and pride than the habitués when one of their athletes succeeds in gaining a medal. Americans, Russians, and Germans measure their national pride in large quantities of medals, yet, Israeli or Surinamese national pride was no less palpable when a woman judo fighter (Yael Arad) won a silver medal at the Barcelona Olympics in 1992 for the former and a swimmer (Anthony Nesty) won a gold medal at the Seoul Olympics in 1988 for the latter, furnishing both nations with their first Olympic medals.

The three victories by American rider Greg LeMond at the Tour de France in the late 1980s and 1990 not only made this event much more popular and better known among American sports fans and the population as a whole but, as is often the case—and as a clear testimony to the unequaled power of nationalism in the dissemination of interest in sports—spawned an entire generation of excellent and well-known American riders as evidenced by the popularity, respect, and results of Andy

Hampsten and Bobby Julich at the most difficult races in the world, including the Giro d'Italia (won by Hampsten) and the Tour de France (where Julich placed third in 1998). Lance Armstrong's victory at the road-racing world championship in 1993—a first for an American—still paled to his accomplishment in 1999 as only the second American to win the Tour de France. By having conquered testicular cancer with its terrible side effects before winning one of the most grueling events in any sport, Armstrong became an American hero whose achievements and popularity among the American public will likely further cycling's presence in America's sport space, perhaps even beyond the level of activity into that of culture. Only because French national pride was particularly hurt that an American (of all people) was about to triumph in one of France's most hallowed cultural events did Le Monde, the country's "paper of record," attempt to tarnish Armstrong's amazing feat by falsely attributing it to the rider's alleged use of performance-enhancing and illegal drugs. His repeating this amazing feat in 2000 had certain American sports commentators hail Armstrong in the "legend" category of Michael Jordan and Wayne Gretzky.

But the French are not exceptional in their ardent nationalism, which enhances their interest in and support for one of their countrymen's participation in any sport. For example, Germans had always expressed some interest in the Tour de France, especially when their fellow Germans Rudi Altig and Hennes Junkermann performed solidly, though never spectacularly, in this major event in the 1960s. But the popularity of this event skyrocketed into a completely different—and previously unimaginable—zone among Germans when in 1997 Jan Ullrich became the first German rider to win this prestigious race. This can be observed in other sports as well. Consider the growth of golf's popularity in Germany as a consequence of Bernhard Langer's victories at prestigious international tournaments such as the Masters in Atlanta. The same applies to golf's immense growth in Spain in the wake of the success of Spanish golfers Seve Balesteros and Jose Maria Olazabal. The Grand Prix world champions Jochen Rindt and Nikki Lauda spawned an entire generation of superb Austrian race-car drivers and rendered Grand Prix car racing one of that nation's most popular sports. Michael Schumacher's success made auto racing much more popular in Germany than at any time since a German aristocrat—the late Graf Berghe von Trips—performed superbly on the Grand Prix circuit in the late 1950s and early 1960s, yet, unlike Schumacher, never won a world championship.[49]

The formidable winning ways of Bjorn Borg singlehandedly placed Sweden on the tennis world's map, creating in their wake a bevy of brilliant Swedish tennis players who have made tennis a truly popular sport in Sweden. The same occurred with Boris Becker in Germany, without whom one could not imagine the dominating presence of Steffi Graf on the women's side, nor the presence of excellent German male players such as Michael Stich. Becker's popularity set in motion the transformation of tennis in Germany from a decidedly upper class and elite sport into a mass activity by the 1990s. Corroborating nationalism's immense primacy in driving such popular interest is the fact that since Boris Becker's and Steffi Graf's respective retirements, tennis has taken a nose dive in terms of its presence in Germany's sports culture. Television ratings for the Grand Slams and other major tournaments have declined drastically. The French love their "Open" at Roland Garros every June, but when French players such as Cedric Pioline advance in the tournament, or even such nominally French contestants as Mary Pierce show a feeble sign of success, the partisanship and enthusiasm on the part of the French crowd assume dimensions of a completely different order from the general appreciation shown for the tournament as a whole.[50] Nationalism's frightening power in sports is well exemplified by the fact that even in such traditionally genteel and reserved sports as tennis where the contestants' nationality is allegedly of secondary importance, and where fairness demands that the opponent be treated with the same courtesy and support as the hometown hero, annual Davis Cup contests, where individual players represent their countries, develop into cauldrons of nationalistic frenzy, particularly in the finals—and especially against the United States. It is hard to forget the batteries and nails thrown at American players in Bucharest or Recife as expressions of support for the host team, or the nationalistic excesses in the Swedish, French, Austrian, and German arenas when the United States contested the finals in the Davis Cup against teams from these nations. Even the habitually fair-minded English team's fans mutated into a crowd of partisan nationalists when their team, consisting of the fine Tim Henman and hard-serving Greg Rusedski, had a realistic chance of beating the much-hated Yanks. It was not to be thanks to the heroics of American Davis Cup veteran Jim Courier. Indeed, even such feeble and largely nonexistent a nationalism as "Europeanism" has received a concrete manifestation with all the flag waving, cheering of the home side, and jeering of the opponents in the Ryder Cup, the biannual golf competition between the best players of Europe and America for the elusive team superiority in this most individualistic of sports. Indeed, it has only been at Ryder Cup events that one observes the European flag used as an actual symbol and object of shared passion on the part of regular people, as opposed to its still common existence as an abstract construct of distant bureaucrats. Only in this sport setting has anything resembling a European identity thus far attained a tangible sense of affection and community that has otherwise so commonly—and tragically—been associated with national identities in Europe throughout the nineteenth and twentieth centuries.

If anything, nationalism plays an even greater role in team sports than it does in individual sports. Whereas it could be argued in the case of the former that the contestant represents him or herself as much—if not more—than their countries, in the case of a team's collective entity and very being, the collective in the form of the country, city, or region most definitely supersedes any identification with the individual. Indeed, any placement of individual loyalties and achievements over those of the collective are seen as selfish, wrong, detrimental to the collective good—and often unpatriotic. Because soccer is the world's most widely performed team sport played internationally by more nations than are represented in the United Nations, nationalism has enjoyed a greater presence in this game than in perhaps any other sport. In most cases, this has been benign. In many, however, it has led to ugly riots, furthered nationalist excesses, spawned national hatreds and prejudice, while appealing to hostility and contempt toward opponents. In the case of El Salvador and Honduras in the 1970s, a disputed soccer game exacerbated the already present hostility between these two Central American neighbors, leading to a brief "soccer war" between them.

The case of the World Cup in France played in the summer of 1998 serves as a good example of parallel developments in other countries in which soccer comprises the dominant sports culture. At the outset of the tournament, there was convincing evidence that many French—Parisians and women, in particular—had little, if any, interest in the World Cup.[51] Indeed, there were many derisive voices bemoaning France's hosting of this seemingly extravagant and very expensive month-long event. Yet, with every victory of the French team, millions of formerly skeptical Frenchmen—and French women—jumped on the bandwagon. By the semifinal, France was engulfed in a sea of national pride that brooked no dissent, no doubting. When the French team attained the previously unreachable by winning the World Cup, all of France—from the political class to the millions celebrating the victory for days in the streets of French cities—basked in the glory of a nationalism unleashed by the success of twenty-two young men in shorts kicking a round ball on a large manicured soccer field. The team had become synonymous with France's hopes and aspirations. Indeed, we suspect that the impressive television ratings for French women (noted earlier) had more to do with their being caught up in French nationalism and national pride than in a newly attained love for the game of soccer. To be sure, the uglier sides of nationalism, which have become commonplace in Europe, also appeared during the World Cup: English hooligans singing patriotic songs and hollering racist slogans while preparing to battle North African denizens of Marseilles; German neo-Nazi thugs traveling to France like predatory military units (mobile phones and all) with the expressed desire of hurting, possibly killing,

a French state official, a "feat" they nearly achieved by crippling a policeman for life in the city of Lens; Croatians beating up Bosnian Muslims
every time their team scored a goal; and the Croatian coach explaining
his team's success and the Yugoslav team's early relegation from the tournament by claiming that Croats are Europeans, thus superior to Serbs,
who hail from the Balkans.[52] Not to excuse the Serbs so easily in terms of
their own ugly display of nationalism: one need only remember the deri-
sory whistling, booing, and jeering of the American anthem by Serb supporters before the game between Yugoslavia and the United States, a singularly rude and unsportsmanlike conduct even in the nationalistic annals
of international soccer. There exists no country whose sports establishment happens to be less nationalistic than the country's overall culture.
Indeed, typically, most sports associations are invariably among the most
vociferous exponents of a country's nationalism. Alas, hegemonic sports
cultures remain fertile breeding grounds for both chauvinisms, that of the
nationalistic and of the male variety, which—to be sure—are related.

Yet one more piece of evidence confirms nationalism's crucial role in
the construction and maintenance of sports cultures: Television data con-
clusively demonstrate that in every country the viewership of any international sporting competition drops by at least one-half, often more, whenever representatives of that country no longer participate in that event
due to elimination, disqualification, or any other reason for departure. To
be sure, a hard core of "real" sports fans will remain interested in the
event for sport's sake regardless of the nationalism of the contestants.
However, the less committed observers invariably lose interest once their
country's representatives are no longer present.

The role of nationalism in culturally hegemonic sports also manifests
itself in the constant and ubiquitous "rhapsodization" by intellectuals,
poets, sports writers, and ethicists of various kinds, as illustrated earlier
in this chapter regarding the Big Three and One-Half in the United States.
Just as there are hundreds of books on baseball—but also on football and
basketball—that invoke the allegedly singular beauty of the game and its
innate ability to convey something deep about the American character,
life, happiness, the yearly seasons, work, manhood, collective values, or
just about any topic the respective interpreter of the game deems important, so one finds the exact equivalent regarding soccer's unique
beauty, its expression of national character, the elegance of its simplicity,
and its being a fine allegory of life rather than merely a game and a sport.
Soccer in Germany, Italy, England, Argentina, and Brazil—only the most
prominent among soccer nations—has constantly been used to explain
and interpret many larger issues in politics and society that reach well
beyond the game itself.[53] Hockey has played the identical role in Canada's
fabric where the game has repeatedly served as an allegory for explaining
and understanding everything, from the Canadian soul to the country's

linguistic divide. Tellingly, this rhapsodization of sports on a large scale happens only in the case of what we have termed in our study hegemonic sports, and (as noted earlier) is precisely another marker of the respective sport's cultural dominance in that particular society.

To reiterate the point: No single factor in any sport has exerted stronger attraction and engendered greater enthusiasm for participants, fans, observers, and outsiders than nationalism. But here, too, the United States has been slightly, to more than a bit, different. It is to a discussion of America's exceptions that we now turn.

American Exceptions

Central to our argument is the assessment that America's dominant sports culture—though exhibiting many structural parallels with that of other countries with comparable levels of industrialization and modernization—developed sufficient differences and indigenous peculiarities to create a sport space that can be justifiably labeled singularly American. Thus, in sports, too, the United States is similar yet sufficiently different from comparable modern democracies to warrant the analytical, if not normative, categorization of an exception. America's sports exceptionalism, we submit, remains inextricably linked to the other exceptionalisms that have rendered American politics, American social relations, and American culture so similar yet at the same time so different from other comparable phenomena, particularly in Europe, the United States's most important progenitor.

America's sports exceptionalism is also rooted in America's powerful bourgeois order. As argued previously in this chapter, modern sports everywhere in the industrial world are embedded in the development of mass societies. The creation and—perhaps more important—dissemination of modern sports is thus part of the bourgeois mode of life. While most modern sports were actually "invented" by members of society's "higher stations" (either of aristocratic or, more often, quasi-aristocratic bent), they soon became the purview of the bourgeoisie and the "masses" if they gained any significance beyond that of polo or croquet. It was the bourgeoisie's commodification of sports—especially those that were to comprise each country's dominant sports culture—that led to the complex structure and ubiquity of contemporary sports in all advanced industrial societies. Not surprisingly, it was the two most bourgeoisified societies of the nineteenth century, Great Britain and the United States, that founded organized professional team sports played and enjoyed by the masses in their own countries and—in the case of Britain's "inventions," primarily soccer—everywhere in the world. [54] The dissemination of the respective national sports correlated positively with the two countries' global positions. Great Britain was still the leading imperial power and as such the main opinion leader and cultural "hegemon" of the time. People all over the world emulated British ways, especially those related to recreation, relaxation, and sports.[55] The United States, on the other hand, was still by and large an isolated "new world" that fascinated (both positively and negatively) the European and global public.

Yet, despite America's economic might and prowess by the end of the nineteenth century, its concrete political and cultural presence remained marginal in world affairs at the time. To be sure, this isolation was in part self-imposed by America's self-identification as on the one hand related to Europe, and on the other hand distinctly non-European, perhaps even anti-European. Whereas the British bourgeoisie derived much of its pride and self-legitimation from being part of the center of a global empire, its American counterpart attained much of its identity precisely from having spurned this very empire and—in contrast to its Canadian and Australian cousins—in having established a successful "frontier" republic in the wake of its opposition to this empire. This strong ambivalence toward Great Britain in particular (and Europe more generally)—manifesting itself in a clear affinity fostered by a common language and culture on the one hand, and a disdain for the old colonial master and its ways on the other—greatly influenced the development of public discourse in the United States during the latter half of the nineteenth century. This "special relationship," marked by both admiration and rejection, proved particularly significant for the development of American sports.[56] As such, this American ambivalence toward things British and European and the attempt to create a cultural niche in line with—yet independent of—British and European culture, constitutes an integral part of American exceptionalism. Hence, both football and baseball developed into American sports par excellence within the framework of this ambivalent and largely one-sided dialogue that America conducted with Britain about its ways. Both sports evolved out of largely preindustrial British team games. Both tried to define their respective identities by claiming to be American originals, by underlining their indigenous "Americanness" and by establishing themselves as distinctly non-European. This conscious Americanization—though present in all of the Big Three sports—was especially pronounced in baseball. Through complete bourgeoisification, all three American team sports became adapted to a new, commercialized industrial order in a new world. By the time Britain's own mass sport, soccer, had been successfully exported all over the world, America's sport space was already occupied by former British imports now converted into genuine American sports plus an indigenous American invention that was to prove vastly popular in the cramped quarters and indoor activities of America's newly arrived immigrants and their American-born children.

Why was soccer crowded out in the United States? First, the American bourgeoisie had successfully established its own national game, baseball, while rejecting a sport closely associated with old England and its aristocratic ethic, cricket. Baseball's "downward dissemination" to the American masses (including immigrants, or at least their children) subsequently coincided with soccer's proliferation as a mass sport in England. Second, the young elites at the top American universities were keener on playing—and then altering—what had developed into a British elite sport, rugby, than in expressing their Anglophilia by importing soccer, which by that time had undergone a process of commercialization, professionalization, and "vulgarization" in England similar to that of baseball in the United States. Third, there was the invention, presence, and dissemination of basketball. Important for our argument, America's sport space thus became filled very early and, it seems, to capacity. Indeed, no other modern industrial country has developed a sport space in which three major team sports—and very possibly a fourth if one includes ice hockey (as one must for key areas in the United States such as Detroit, tellingly dubbed "Hockeytown," Chicago, Boston, New York, the Great Lakes region, and New England)—have played crucial roles in defining hegemonic sports culture, as has been the case in America. All modern countries have at least one such sport, usually soccer. Many have two, with the second sport differing from country to country. A few have three, but with a major drop between the first (usually soccer) and the next two, one of which is often not a team sport. Thus, basketball has been a very solid and respectable second in the Mediterranean countries (Spain, Italy, Croatia, Yugoslavia, Greece, Turkey, Israel). Indeed, basketball in Lithuania has enjoyed such popularity over the years that it is soccer's equal, perhaps even superior, in terms of the game's prominence in that small Baltic nation's sports culture. Cycling (though only tangentially a team sport when compared to such games as soccer, hockey, and the American Big Three) has enjoyed major popularity in France, Italy, Belgium, Holland, Spain, and—to a lesser degree—Denmark, Switzerland, and Germany. Downhill skiing has been prominent in Austria's sport space during the winter months when—as a fine measure of sports culture—offices virtually close down to watch the major races of the winter season, particularly the Olympics and world championships. This sport—though very seasonal and clearly not of the team variety—also enjoys popularity in France, Switzerland, Germany, Italy, and, of course, the United States. Cross-country skiing is downhill skiing's exact counterpart in the sport space of the Nordic countries, including Norway, Sweden, and Finland. Cricket and rugby are definitely present in England's sports culture, though with nowhere close to soccer's popularity. The list could go on but the point is clear: Nearly all modern industrial countries feature soccer as the unquestioned hegemon in their respective sport spaces. Many also have a second and sometimes even a third sport—though often not of the team variety—that clearly qualifies as culture: more than a mere activity in that people follow it passionately, are interested in it on the professional level, talk about it at their place of work or while socializing, and bestow stardom on its successful practitioners in the usual manner of adoration while rewarding (or punishing) them with immense publicity and constant attention. Yet, none have three major national team sports (baseball, football, basketball) plus another important one in key regions (hockey) that have shaped the country's sports culture for at least a century, as in the United States.

● Yet another aspect of American exceptionalism germane to our argument of America's different sports culture and sport space lies in the major role assumed by universities and colleges in the creation, dissemination, and continued reproduction of the American sport space and American sport culture. Simply put, in no other country of the advanced industrial world have colleges and universities played such paramount importance as continuous producers, consumers, foci, and loci of sports as in the United States. As we will see in later chapters, this exceptionalism has helped reinforce soccer's marginalization in the American sport space.

There are several reasons for American higher education's prominent role in sports. America's elite institutions on the East Coast—Harvard in particular, but also Yale, Columbia, Princeton, Williams, Amherst, Rutgers—were originators of organized sports and major loci of their implementation in postbellum America. As in the case of their English counterparts, Oxford and Cambridge, these American universities and colleges created an atmosphere of gentlemanly gamesmanship in which the ethos of mens sana in corpore sano fostered organized sports as an equivalent activity to academic pursuits. An educated gentleman—in this view—had to be as well versed in the realm of athletics as in his knowledge of literature and the classics. These universities—Harvard in the case of the United States and Cambridge in the case of England—became the founding institutions of the two versions of football that, respectively, would develop into the preeminent games of the American and the British (indeed global) sport spaces.

Bespeaking America's true bourgeois ethos and mission, the country developed a concept of education that emphasized the inclusion of large numbers on all levels, even that of the postsecondary colleges and universities. In notable contrast to Britain and the Old World, where higher education remained the preserve of a privileged few until the education explosion of the late 1960s and early 1970s, higher education in the United States rapidly developed into a mass structure with the establishment of land-grant colleges and public universities that had the clear mission of educating the country's large middle class. By the eve of World

War I, the United States had a large network of universities and colleges that became an attainable goal to a degree unparalleled anywhere else in the world.[57] Higher education and its institutions developed into an integral part of American middle-class culture well before it did so in Europe and elsewhere. Particularly in the world of public institutions, these universities often evolved into the primary foci of state and local pride, becoming the leading producers of the respective state's professionals, bureaucrats, and other key middle-class representatives. Since these institutions often existed in states with few large cities and thus in areas where the presence of professional sports made no economic sense, universities and their teams soon became the sole purveyors of sport on a meaningful competitive level for large areas of the country. Being a Sooners fan in Oklahoma, a Huskers fan in Nebraska, a Longhorns fan in Texas, a Wildcats fan in Kentucky, or a Wolverines fan in Michigan has been every bit the iconographic, spiritual, and affective equivalent to being an Arsenal supporter in North London, a Rangers fan in Glasgow, a Rapid supporter in the Hütteldorf district of Vienna, and a Barca fan in Barcelona. As in the case of major European soccer clubs with their clear identities, milieus, and networks, the football and basketball teams of American universities became essential representatives of the identity and culture of their respective regions, states, cities and towns. With their involvement in and dedication to sports, they merely underlined one of the key ingredients of America's bourgeois ethos: that of meritocracy.

On the European continent, sports never entered the realm of the universities, since these were seen as research institutions, training grounds for state bureaucrats, or domains of the church. In all three cases, they remained strictly in the realm of the mind and had little, if any, tolerance for pursuits of the body. In England, Oxbridge did in fact engage in organized and competitive sports as part of its students' educational ethos. But this engagement remained confined to amateur, extracurricular, and purely avocational pursuits, never leaving the realm of the gentlemanly. Not so in the United States. By dint of this country's meritocratic ethos and the proliferation of its institutions of higher learning—itself a consequence of this meritocratic ethos—sports became an integral part of university life and thus of public identity. Even though college sports in America continue to maintain the self-legitimating myth of a precapitalist, aristocratic amateurism, those sports that developed into America's dominant sport cultures through their presence in American college life (football and basketball in particular) lost this attribute long before the multi-million-dollar television contracts of the contemporary era. The meritocratic achievement-oriented nature of modern competitive team sports and the meritocratic ethos of the modern American university developed an institutional synthesis that rendered the realm of higher education into one of the major purveyors of modern American sport culture, a situation unparalleled anywhere else in the advanced industrial world.

The National Collegiate Athletic Association (NCAA) was established by 1910 as the authoritative body in charge of all collegiate sports. This major institution has dominated the workings of college athletics in form and content to a degree unparalleled in the higher education of other societies. It has decreed the length of playing seasons, defined rules of participation, legislated eligibility for institutions and players; in short, the NCAA has served as an agent as well as a structure that helped define the topography of the American sport space. As we shall see, the NCAA's strict scheduling rules regarding the timing of each sport's official season of competition constituted yet another factor in soccer's continued structural marginalization in America's dominant sports culture.

There are further American peculiarities that qualify as subsidiary exceptionalisms in that they are secondary to the larger factors of American exceptionalism already described, particularly the hegemony of bourgeois power in politics, culture, and society. While comparatively minor, these exceptionalisms also helped shape the American sport space into a different configuration than its counterparts in other advanced industrial societies.

First and foremost, American professional sport teams have always been businesses best described by that quintessential American term, "franchise." Owners could, did, and continue to move these franchises at will, as long as they do not violate league rules, which, in turn, are decreed by the owners' collective and its representatives, the so called "league commissioners." The point here is that unlike the Vereine (clubs) in Germany and Austria, for example, where professional sports teams are bodies of public law in addition to being commodified institutions in pursuit of profits in a capitalist market place, franchises in the United States are purely market-based entities devoid of public obligations and responsibilities beyond those exacted by their immediate ownership and that of the league in which they operate. In short, team ownership and league formations have always been much more overtly capitalist enterprises in the United States than in Europe, where there have always been more public constraints on the operation of both. American team sports and their leagues have been much more thoroughly commercialized than was the case, until recently, with soccer in Europe.[58] From its very beginning as a professional sport, soccer in Europe developed in the manner of what Rudolf Hilferding so aptly called "organized capitalism," that is, a balanced mixture of state and market.[59] Clubs, though privately owned like American franchises, joined leagues that exhibited characteristics best described by Peter Katzenstein's apt concept of "para-public institutions," meaning that though private in their ownership and their mission to make money for their owners, the clubs' existence and the leagues' governance remained subject to institutions, rules, and regulations clearly beyond the immediate purview of the clubs. [60] Hence, in each country there developed a para-public soccer league with a multiplicity of levels that—once established—attained a position of market monopoly sanctioned by the league as a para-public or quasi-statist entity—no American-style, periodic new-league formations here, nor any league disappearances. Moreover, clubs in Europe could not simply pack up their belongings and depart from one city to another merely at the owner's whim, as has often occurred in the much more laissez-faire atmosphere of America's franchise-style sport structure. While no Major League Baseball club has ceased to exist in the twentieth century, and no National Football League or National Basketball Association franchise has done so since the early 1950s, teams in American sports proliferate and move from one location to another with a facility and regularity completely unknown to the soccer (and club) world in Europe and Latin America. Owners may come and go, but teams stay put in their long-established environs. Moreover, poor-playing European teams face the punishment of relegation from the "majors"—the Premier League, the Serie A, the Bundesliga—into a country's second, third, or even fourth division. Conversely, teams performing exceptionally well in the lower leagues have been rewarded by promotion into the next higher division, with the ultimate reward of elevation to the country's premier level.

All these conventions of soccer have been governed by an international body called Fédération Internationale de Football Association (FIFA), established in 1903. Nothing comparable has ever existed in the structure of American professional sports, which have never been governed by para-public institutions. With the possible major exception of organized baseball, there exist no de jure monopolies in the presence and governance of American sports. Teams, no matter how consistently poor their performance, are never punished with relegation to a lesser league or division while even the best AAA baseball team or the finest team of the Continental Basketball League is never rewarded for its efforts with a spot in its sport's respective premier or major league. In contrast to virtually all soccer leagues in the world, U.S. sports leagues—including the country's myriad soccer leagues—have always been self-contained and "hermetic."[61] Lastly, none of the American professional sports, their leagues and their teams, have ever entered a structure in which their existence is governed by a supranational body, à la FIFA in soccer. In short, all major American professional sports that defined the dominant sports culture in the United States in the course of the twentieth century exhibited a much more unimpeded capitalist style and ethic than their European counterparts, particularly in the world of soccer. Moreover, American sports and their structures remained content, until very recently, to define their world purely in North American terms. Their horizon of legitimation and self-perception did not extend beyond the confines of the American continent—in the beginning, not much beyond the confines of the eastern seaboard, or New York City for that matter. Hence, the American champion in baseball, football, and basketball has blithely usurped the sobriquet "world" champion; in hockey, and recently in baseball and basketball the "world" extends a bit beyond the immediate confines of the United States to include Canada. There has been vague talk that this strictly North American horizon might be extended to include some hockey clubs from European countries contending for the Stanley Cup. Similarly distant plans are in discussion as to the NBA's global reach. But even if such an internationalization of these sports were to be implemented in the future, their epicenter would still remain in the United States.

In their institutional presence and their culture, American sports are like American education and American religion: independent of the state, market driven, and ultimately subject to few, if any, regulating bodies outside those of their own creation. Anybody can start a league or a team, just as anybody can found a religion or a church, or an institution of learning from kindergarten to university. The barriers of entry and the subsequent maintenance of operations are dictated only by money. There exists no sports minister in the United States as there does in many countries. Similarly, there also exists no chief rabbi, priest, minister, mullah, or any other chief religious figure in the United States who would represent his flock and speak for it in an official capacity sanctioned by the state as that religion's sole legitimate interlocutor. To a degree unparalleled in any other modern industrial country, sports, religion, and education are chaotic structures in the United States with no common rules and no clear centers. The history of American sport, as we shall soon see, is littered with new leagues, newly founded teams, as well as those departed and defunct. All of these phenomena simply do not exist in the sports worlds of other countries, which all possess a much more orderly arrangement in which the chaos of the market has been bridled by much stricter rules of conduct than have ever existed in American sports.

The Big Three American sports—and hockey until the 1970s—also exhibit a very different relationship to nationalism than do global team sports, soccer in particular. As essentially North American, the most important competition in these sports occurs domestically (if one excuses the inclusion of Canada into the United States for the purposes of hockey). In other words, rivalries and loyalties are not attached to national entities as in the world of soccer, but almost exclusively to subnational ones. Football is so much an American sport that it basically does not exist anywhere else; there are no meaningful international competitions in American football. The same pertains to baseball, though with the game an Olympic sport as of 1996, there now exists a Team USA in baseball whose fate is completely secondary to most American sports fans, if indeed it registers at all.

While baseball's international reach has always been much larger than that of football, it still remains almost exclusively an American sport at the top level of the game, namely the major leagues. The same pertains to basketball, far and away the most international of the Big Three, indeed, the second most popular team sport in the world after soccer. To most American sports fans, basketball remains an exclusively American affair, so much so that when the United States finally fielded its truly elite best players as Team USA in the form of the first legendary "Dream Team" at the Barcelona Olympics in 1992, many American basketball fans decried this as completely unfair, unnecessary, and overbearing, since—as indeed happened—the rest of the world's top basketball teams were no match at all for the best American players. No analogous development would ever be conceivable—let alone occur—in any other country, where fielding the very best national team in international competition and playing for it is perceived as an obligation, honor, and privilege on the part of that country's very best athletes in the sport, amateur or professional. Thus, Europeans might have envied or held in awe the Dream Team's prowess, but in no way did they decry its supremacy or blame the United States for fielding its very best athletes, as many Americans did. Indeed, Europeans rejoiced that by sending their very best basketball players to the Olympics, Americans were perhaps on their way to taking this unique international competition more seriously in this sport than they had in the past. Whereas in other countries, basketball world championships engender much interest, a great sense of national pride and competition, these events barely register in the United States, where the game remains tied to the National Basketball Association on the professional level and to the colleges on the nominally amateur level. When the NBA players decided to boycott the basketball world championship in Greece in the summer of 1998 in response to management's lockout of its players, the American media all but ignored this tournament, relegating it to obscure sections of the sports pages and canceling existing television broadcasts for lack of interest among the American public. Only when a ragtag group of American players (led by the widely respected coach of the two-time NBA champion Houston Rockets, Rudy Tomjanovich) hailing from various European professional leagues, colleges, and the Continental Basketball Association came away with a surprisingly respectable bronze medal did this event receive short-lived but visible media coverage. A few days after the tournament, the players who had so valiantly represented their country and who would have been heroes for their effort and its results anywhere else sank back into complete oblivion in the American sports world, where such national efforts on the international scene matter little, if at all.

One can see the same thing in hockey, though Team Canada and Team USA attained some homegrown interest in various international competitions, particularly when the Canadians went head-to-head with the Soviet Union's great teams of the 1970s and 1980s. But on the whole, this aspect of the game remains far less interesting to the average North American hockey fan than the intraleague rivalries of the National Hockey League. This has been so much the case that the NHL is in the process of reconsidering its participation in future winter Olympics due to disappointing fan interest in the NHL stars' first Olympic appearance in Nagano in 1998, though the league agreed reluctantly to have its players participate in the 2002 Olympic Games in Salt Lake City. Still, an argument could be made in the case of hockey that—beginning with that memorable series between Canada and the Soviet Union in the fall of 1972—the game has become more internationalized than any of its other North American counterparts.

Further confirmation of this marked isolationism in the world of American sports is that the Davis Cup competition in tennis—far and away the most important tennis event to most countries in the world and every bit the equal to the four Grand Slams in prestige—barely registers on the radar of American sports fans, including tennis fans and tennis players. Whereas it would border on national betrayal if a nation's top player ever recused himself from his country's quest for the Davis Cup, such behavior remains completely standard and accepted fare in the United States, where it is the exception instead of the rule when its best players comprise its national team. And when one of those rare occasions does indeed occur, the players convey unmistakable feelings that they regard their "service" for their national team as little more than a chore, an unwelcome interruption in their relentless pursuit of individual championships and, of course, money. American golfers' attitudes toward the Ryder Cup are not dissimilar. In notable contrast to their European counterparts, a number of Americans let it be known that they view this tournament as an "exhibition," a sort of burdensome nuisance one simply has to perform as a star player in the game, but something that simply never measures up to the important tournaments, particularly the "Majors." Perhaps the memorable comeback by the U.S. team from a virtually hopeless position at the Longwood Club in Brookline, Massachusetts, in September 1999 leading to an emotional victory over the Europeans might lend the Ryder Cup a greater importance to American golfers and the American public than had been previously the case. Still, it is rare to have the best American players represent their country as a matter of course on various Team USAs, be they in basketball, hockey, tennis, or golf. And the American public accepts this, not because it is less nationally minded than the publics in other countries but because the horizon of its sports world remains largely national. It is only for this reason that Americans cannot really appreciate how the fans of other countries express such ardent forms of nationalism when their teams enter international tournaments. Thus, two essential and complementary sides of soccer remain enigmatic to American sports fans: its deeply anchored nationalism, and the equally thorough international presence of the game upon which such nationalism is based. While soccer fosters highly national sentiments and identities, it also offers an international language of communication and an international cultural code that is truly binding and bonding. None of the hegemonic American sports offers either of these sentiments. American sports neither engender a deep sense of nationalism nor provide a genuine forum for internationalism. They remain confined to a world all their own. Here, too, America is different.

America's sports exceptionalism—linked to a certain kind of self-contained nationalism acting apart from the rest of the international arena—also exists in perhaps the most modern of sports, auto racing. Popular in most advanced industrial societies throughout much of the twentieth century, it attained a truly international flavor after World War II with the establishment of the Grand Prix Formula One world championship races, spanning literally every continent and hosted in more than twenty countries on an annual basis. This nearly year-long international circuit represents the very best in auto racing, with the winner declared the uncontested world champion. Moreover, in all the countries where a race occurs in the course of a season, Formula One racing has attained something akin to what we have termed "hegemonic sports culture": Its drivers are popular stars recognized everywhere except, of course, in the United States. While Formula One driving existed in this country, and two American drivers—Phil Hill and Mario Andretti—did indeed win the world championship, it never came close to rivaling the indigenous and completely American events of NASCAR racing, the Indianapolis 500, and other races followed by a large American public. Unlike nations where Formula One has become part of culture by dint of an internationally recognized and respected identification with one traditional circuit that has featured this race for decades (Silverstone in England, Nürburgring and Hockenheim in Germany, Monza in Italy, etc.), the U.S. Grand Prix migrated from an old airport in Watkins Glen in upstate New York to downtown Detroit; Long Beach, California; and Las Vegas, only to disappear for years with few American racing fans truly missing it. Formula One returned to the United States in the fall of 2000 when over two hundred thousand spectators watched its debut at the famous Indianapolis

Speedway. Bespeaking American exceptionalism is the fact that the only Formula One race in North America that has become traditional and enjoys genuine popularity is the Canadian Grand Prix, held annually in Montreal. That the French Canadian driver Gilles Villeneuve—whose name graces that race—became one of the very best on the circuit before his death in a tragic accident, and that his son Jacques subsequently fulfilled his father's dreams by winning the world championship in 1997, surely helped make this event very popular in Canada, Quebec in particular. This lends additional confirmation to our thesis regarding the potency of nationalism in the transformation of a sport from activity to culture.

Lastly, American sports feature and foster the American predilection for quantification and ranking: "The most. The biggest. The longest . . . The 100 greatest movies. The 100 greatest novels. The top 10 steakhouses. The top five sunsets."[62] In a society that anchors much of its legitimacy in meritocracy and achievement rather than in entitlement and ascription, "value free" numbers denote not only a sense of impersonal fairness but also a clarity of rank understood by everybody, regardless of cultural background and linguistic origins. Numbers are clear to all social groups, conveying a sense of universalism and measurability that has provided much-needed clarity to a multicultural society like that of the United States. America's number fetishism and obsession with rankings have made two ostensibly conflicting, yet essential, American values compatible: that of competition and of fairness. No team sports are more quantified than the American Big Three and One-Half. Indeed, soccer's lack of quantification and statistics has often been mentioned as one of the reasons for its lack of attraction to the average American sports fan.

America's sport space comprises the following three major team sports, with hockey most definitely worthy of more than an honorable mention: Historically the oldest in its institutionalized form, baseball—"America's national pastime"—is a game that evolved in both myth and reality as a consciously constructed contrast to English cricket. This sport captured center stage for roughly a century in America's sports culture primarily by becoming America's "people's game," thereby assuming an analogous position to that of soccer in England and later the rest of the industrial world. Next in line chronologically is football, whose entry into America's sports culture was through the colleges. Indeed, the college game remained far more important than its professional counterpart until the 1950s, when the latter assumed pride of place and in the process displaced baseball as America's most watched and followed team sport. Lastly, the game of basketball has—in notable contrast to the other two—an unchallenged American origin. Emanating from conscious invention by a single individual in 1891, the game soon became a major activity among working people and the children of immigrants, especially in the nation's inner cities. It also developed a major presence in America's YMCAs, high schools, and colleges well before the professional version of the game had attained much importance at all. Though basketball was nowhere near as popular as baseball, even football, until the emergence of the NBA's successful period in the 1980s and the NCAA's "March Madness" tournament in the course of the 1970s and 1980s, the cultural seed for this late proliferation had been planted precisely during the time period that we deem essential for the lasting success of a sport's mass appeal during the twentieth century. And, of course, there is the hybrid case of hockey. While not an American sport in its origins and not even in terms of its center of gravity for much of this century, hockey attained a sufficiently early and prolific exposure in the Northeast and Upper Midwest regions of the United States to render it a clear culture in these parts. That Canadian culture is geographically, linguistically, conceptually, and experientially very close to American, and that places like Detroit, Chicago, and Boston established a viable hockey culture throughout the twentieth century, allowed the game sufficient presence in America's sport space for it to expand all across the United States by the 1970s and 1980s, and to become an accepted junior partner to the Big Three in American sports culture. It is ice hockey's current position in the American sport space that soccer's advocates and fans hope and believe the game has a realistic chance of attaining in the first decades of the twenty-first century.

Two ....

The Formation of the American Sport Space
"CROWDING OUT" AND OTHER FACTORS IN THE
RELEGATION AND MARGINALIZATION OF SOCCER

Soccer failed to gain more than a marginal existence in American sports culture for three interrelated reasons, each of which can be conveniently and respectively labeled historical-sociological, cultural-anthropological, and organizational-institutional. The first—and certainly the most important and instrumental—is that soccer as both a recreational and spectator activity was "crowded out" in the nineteenth century from below by the prior emergence and success of baseball as a sport for the American masses in spring and summer, and from above by American football as a sport for the middle and upper middle classes in autumn. This chapter mainly focuses on these sociological roots for soccer's relegation by providing a brief account of the key junctures in the historical development of baseball, football, basketball, and hockey—the sports we have labeled the Big Three and One-Half. However, the other two reasons warrant mention here, as it will become apparent that each of these sports exhibited identifying and institutional features that soccer was unable to match or, in contrast to the cases of basketball and hockey, unable to adjust to the requisites for success in the American sport space.

Regarding the second reason, like the first modern British sport to be played and watched in the United States, cricket, soccer was perceived by both native-born Americans and immigrants as a non-American activity at a time in American history when nativism and nationalism emerged to create a distinctly American self-image. Soccer enthusiasts generally refrained from any attempts to integrate their sport into the culture of their adopted land, choosing instead to emphasize the game's non-American roots and features, often in an endeavor to retain their own pre-American identity. For the vast majority of immigrants looking to "fit in" in the new country, sports helped to unify ethnically diverse groups toward assimilation. "Immigrants saw sport as a socializing force, an 'Americanizing' force," according to University of Cincinnati archivist Kevin Grace, a sports specialist. "If you were a fan who loved baseball, you were American."[1] The same applied to basketball, football, and boxing. But if one liked soccer, one was viewed as at least resisting—if not outright rejecting—integration into America and its general ethos. For the typical

soccer-playing immigrant, as with the transplanted English cricketer, soccer served as a link to one's European roots in the midst of the inexorable
"melting pot" of America; hence, "Americanizing" the sport would have
negated its raison d'être. And unlike the early milieu of basketball, which
featured ethnically based teams advertised as such, soccer was clearly
identified as a non-American sport with foreign origins. Moreover, once
soccer gained converts among native-born Americans after the turn of the
century, it was almost exclusively as a recreational sport for college and
high school athletes who were often viewed as somewhat alien from the
American mainstream, "above"—or inadequate for—the accepted American sports of football, baseball, and basketball. Like the native American
game lacrosse, soccer came to occupy a certain niche at American universities that remained the domain of a small, though dedicated, coterie of
enthusiasts who were usually aloof from the mainstream of campus athletic activity that revolved around football and, later, basketball. Furthermore, those who regulated soccer with FIFA's sanction in the United
States pointedly ignored collegiate and scholastic soccer, and the colleges
and high schools reacted in kind, thus establishing a relationship of mutual recriminations, misunderstandings, disdain, and simple indifference
that persists to this day and has most decidedly harmed soccer's development in American sports culture.

This brings us to the third and final reason we have noted, that of organizational impasse and institutional obduracy, which amply informed the
failed development of soccer in America. Simply put, there is much evidence that soccer in the United States was cursed by an array of exceptionally poor leaders who failed miserably at developing any sort of comprehensive organizational framework that would have been able to promote
and represent the sport on American soil. Instead, they engaged in petty
rivalries and internecine organizational struggles that only helped to preserve their narrow fiefdoms and the status quo at the expense of creating
an institutional structure that might have been able to disseminate the
sport to the vast majority of the American public. As will be clear in the
next chapter, we believe that there was at least one critical juncture in
soccer's past where the game most certainly had a reasonable chance of
entering the American sport space, but failed to do so on account of the
organizational inadequacies that governed its existence in the United
States. American soccer did not develop the organizational characteristics
necessary to move beyond the cultural margins in a modern society.

This chapter provides the contextual and comparative basis for expli-
cating these three reasons for the marginalization of soccer in the United
States through a brief examination how baseball and football came to
occupy and dominate the American sport space, while basketball and
hockey established themselves on similarly solid—though initially no-

where near as wide or productive—a footing, all by the end of the key period (1870–1930) that we have identified as so crucial. Specifically, this chapter looks at the key junctures on the path toward hegemonic sports culture in the United States, as well as some of the essential institutional features that these sports developed and adapted, both at these junctures and along the way. We first examine the development and rise of baseball from a game for children to a sport played and watched by grown men, eventually to find its own hegemonic niche among the American middle classes and then industrial workers and the masses, thereby "crowding out" soccer from a social and cultural position in the United States parallel to what it would eventually occupy in much of the rest of the world. Next, we focus on the singular path of premodern football in America as both a "running" and a "kicking" game, and the juncture at which it permanently split along different lines of development. We proceed to the period when football became a defining cultural activity for American colleges and their supporters and a feature of middle-class American life, eventually experiencing its own "outward" and "downward" dissemination. The chapter concludes with brief accounts of the other two occupiers of the sport space in the United States, basketball and ice hockey, both of which succeeded despite featuring characteristics that would prove decisively debilitating to soccer in the United States: identification as a game for "ethnics" in the case of basketball, cultural and institutional origins clearly beyond the borders of the United States in the case of hockey.

Crowding Out from Below: Baseball As "the American National Pastime"

Almost from the very beginning of its modern development as adult recreation and entertainment, baseball owed a good deal of its successful proliferation among the American masses to its identity as "American." The creation of the Abner Doubleday myth served to squelch for future generations the British claim that baseball was a descendant of the children's game known as rounders, while baseball's devotees found it increasingly difficult to swallow the idea that their favorite pastime was of foreign origin.[2] Pride and patriotism required that the game be native, unsullied by English ancestry, while intense American nativism, already apparent during baseball's formative period in the 1850s, helped ensure the modern game's eventual success. Ties to rounders were consciously denied, and baseball was systematically defined in a favorable light against its first— and for many years only—rival, cricket. Above all, baseball's advocates proclaimed it more competitive and socially egalitarian than cricket and better suited to and more accurately reflecting life in the New World, boasting its bourgeois and indigenous qualities and contrasting them favorably to cricket's aristocratic demeanor and Old World origins.

By the eighteenth century, rules for games that somewhat resembled the baseball of modern times, such as rounders in England and poisoned ball in France, could be found in books for children.[3] The first written entry of such a game played in America is found in the diary of George Ewing, a soldier in the Continental Army at Valley Forge who wrote of playing "a game of base" on 7 April 1778.[4] Yet, it would still be many years before an adult man could regularly and comfortably engage in what most of society viewed as a child's pastime. The biggest factor in modifying the prevailing values was simply that burgeoning industrial capitalism allowed for more time away from work for many Americans, while a more tolerant and pluralistic attitude toward secular activities took hold.[5] In postcolonial American towns, groups of boys and/or young men might pass the time in crudely organized games called town ball, goal ball, round ball, or base ball.[6] Most relevant for the later success of modern baseball was that a great many American boys and young men were becoming familiar with batting, throwing, and catching a ball, though not within the context of an organized modern team sport. By 1820 some towns had passed ordinances banning ball play on the grounds that such activity was a threat to person and property and a disturbance of the peace. But town ball, variations of "old cat," cricket, rough versions of football and ice hockey, and other games managed to thrive as pastimes for young American males.[7]

As for adult men, the early American "sporting scene" was of a quasi-aristocratic nature. Besides participatory activities such as hunting or fishing, horse racing was the principal diversion for an American gentleman or would-be gentleman. Other "sporting" activities (that is, usually those open for wagering) included cockfighting and various parlor games, though these were not in very high repute among the well-to-do and those who aspired to upper-class status. Boxing, though it drew interest from some sporting gentlemen, was generally considered vulgar and lower class. It was banned in most of the United States and usually took place on the sly, attracting its own aficionados. Wrestling matches, boat races, and foot races also drew the interest of sporting spectators. Ball games in general were considered the province of the immature, though the idea of exercise for health was beginning to gain acceptability. Some upper-class and upper middle-class males in New York regularly played racquet games at organized athletic clubs.[8] By the late 1830s, cricket, though played mainly by recent English immigrants, began to attain popularity among some native-born Americans who viewed themselves as gentlemen. Cricket clubs were formed in New York in 1840, and Philadelphia in 1843.[9] The fledgling sporting press of the day took notice and actively encouraged Americans to embrace the game, though it was still not widely played. William T. Porter of *Porter's Spirit of the Times* played cricket and was a founder of the New York Cricket Club, that city's less exclusive answer to the St. George Cricket Club. Baseball was still mostly considered a child's game.[10]

In 1845, at the behest of Alexander Cartwright, a group of men mostly of middle-class means organized the New York Knickerbockers baseball club and secured a permanent playing site at Elysian Fields in Hoboken, New Jersey, to become the world's first formally organized baseball team, or at least the first on record.[11] Cartwright, a bank teller and volunteer fireman, is also credited with heading the committee that developed the first written rules of baseball, which, despite many changes since then, have provided the main contours of the game to this day. A significant modification from earlier baseball was the institution of the tag-out, eliminating the practice of "burning" a runner with a thrown ball for an out. As the Knickerbocker rules stipulated that the pitcher would have to serve to the batter underhanded, baseball through its early years would more resemble the slow pitch softball so prevalent throughout the United States today than the much more difficult game it would become in the course of its development.[12]

On 19 June 1846 (incidentally the same year that J. C. Thring organized the first football team at Cambridge, a milestone in the histories of soccer, rugby, and—almost as directly—American football), the Knickerbockers played their first game against another team, the New York Baseball Club, and lost, 23–1.[13] Also an elaborate social affair, the ensuing dinner assumed equal or even greater importance to the contest on the field, reflecting the values of the aspiring gentlemen of the respective clubs and the values of the early baseball teams that would soon emulate them. Though the Knickerbockers have often been portrayed as upper class in many accounts, they were mostly men of white-collar middle-class standing who aspired to upper-class status as gentlemen.[14] The tradition of recreational games followed by socializing over dinners or lunches continued into the next decade as other teams joined the Knickerbockers in New York (notably the Gothams, Eagles, and Empires) as well as in Brooklyn (the Excelsiors, Putnams, Eckfords, and Atlantics), though some of these teams, notably the Eckfords, included skilled workers among their members.[15]

Baseball eventually began to attract the attention of the press, which had been covering and promoting cricket in New York since 1840 and had done much to popularize that sport. By 1855 editorial space was regularly devoted to baseball, though cricket still commanded greater coverage.[16] The character and social standing of the players began to include more men whose aspirations were not necessarily inclined toward status as gentlemen, while the game was also drawing spectators. For players and spectators alike, the need to win was quickly gaining importance; bets by players among themselves, between players and spectators, and among spectators were not uncommon.[17] Concurrent with the growth of partisanship throughout the 1850s was a rapid "downward" social dissemination of baseball's popularity in the New York area and other parts of the East Coast, as policemen, barkeepers, schoolteachers, doctors, lawyers, and even clergymen would field their own teams. Skilled workers would soon become some of the game's most talented players and dedicated fans. The players of the Brooklyn Eckfords were mostly mechanics and shipwrights; the New York Mutuals—founded in 1857 by William "Boss" Tweed—were named for the Mutual Hook and Ladder Company, and the Manhattans consisted mostly of policemen.[18] Reflecting the changing values of the nation, the aristocratic-type milieu of the aspiring sporting ballplayer was quite soon superseded by the new ethics of egalitarian competition with victory as the goal. On the field, sportsmanship gave way to competition, a transition more or less completed by the eve of the Civil War. Hence, the central aspect of modern baseball, which dictated a fundamentally and structurally antagonistic relationship between the pitcher and the batter: The pitcher was no longer to "serve" the batter a "hittable" ball, but indeed just the opposite. As winning became all important, the press displayed less sympathy for losing teams, particularly those who appeared to shirk the practice time necessary to sharpen competitive skills.[19]

When a team of Manhattan all-stars defeated their Brooklyn counterparts at a race course in Flushing, New York, in 1858 (not far from the site of present-day Shea Stadium), a crowd of 1,500 paid fifty cents each to watch the contest and cheer for the team that represented their city. (Thus was inaugurated a rivalry that would last exactly one hundred years.) By 1858 there were approximately fifty clubs in the New York area with an additional sixty junior clubs that often acted as "feeder" teams for the seniors, a foreshadow of the farm systems of modern organized baseball. That year, twenty-six teams met and adopted the name of the National Association of Base Ball Players, though there was actually little to qualify it as "national" in character, since only a fraction of teams actually in existence were represented, with only a few from outside the New York area. Significantly, NABBP rules stipulated against clubs compensating players monetarily for their services, while club delegates voted to exclude the junior teams from membership, a signal of the growing separation of on-field competition from recreation. By 1860, sixty clubs were represented by the NABBP, seventy-four the following year. That number would jump to well over three hundred in the years following the Civil War.[20]

Baseball over Cricket

While the popularity of the New York game took off in its native area in the 1850s as more clubs were formed, clubs playing a variant known as the Massachusetts game also thrived in Boston and its vicinity, while a town-ball variation was popular in Philadelphia. Within a few short years, both the older game from New England and the Philadelphia variant would give way as adherents of the New York game spread their gospel.[21] Cricket was also gaining in popularity, but it increasingly had to compete as a pastime with what was viewed as the home grown American game. Both sports provided forums for partisanship and gambling, but baseball would soon prove more attractive to the general public, while cricket would turn insular.[22]

That baseball would eventually ascend as cricket declined was not preordained. Taking their lead from Australian sports historian Ian Tyrell, George B. Kirsch and Melvin Adelman discount as ahistorical the argument that the game's structural impediments and its disadvantage in being perceived as foreign led to its failure in the United States.[23] Instead, the key lies in the class position and national presumptions as well as aspirations of those who played cricket. Efforts to Americanize the sport were repeatedly denounced and thwarted by cricketers and their clubs. Structural changes that might have made the game more appealing to American spectators (such as shortening the usual three-day length of matches) were viewed as heresy, since the rules of England's Marylebone club were considered "perfect"; anything different was just not cricket. Allowing more native-born Americans a chance to play, and thus to improve their skills and excel on the field, would certainly have made the game more attractive to potential homegrown players and spectators. But for many cricket players, the greatest value of the game was to serve as a cultural link to the motherland. In direct contrast to baseball, most cricketers both desired and succeeded in keeping their game exclusive in terms of the class composition of the players and spectators and in the related way of its continued adherence to England instead of the New World. Except in Philadelphia, cricket would not experience the "downward" class dissemination that would make baseball a game for all Americans. There were exceptions, but as play on the typical baseball field evolved from sportsmanship to competition, American cricket decidedly and deliberately retained a more reserved style and an ethic of exclusivity. Furthermore, unlike baseball, efforts at organizing cricket clubs into a true umbrella organization in America never reached fruition. For the most part, the American cricketers were content to keep the game a gentlemen's activity, though not without gambling and professional players.[24]

That baseball might indeed be structurally more egalitarian and partici-patory (hence democratic) than cricket did not necessarily preclude the latter from gaining American adherents. The athletic skills needed for both sports are quite similar, though baseball provided much greater op-portunity to utilize those skills and, most important, the opportunity to improve them. A baseball player will have his turn at bat a minimum of three times in a full game—usually four or five—while a cricketer might bat only once in the course of a match lasting three days, five in the case of a "test match." If a cricket batsman is out quickly, he has little to do but sit and watch until his entire team finishes batting or "declares," both of which could take a long time, indeed days. But regardless of how he did at bat, a baseball player gets to play in the field at short intervals, minimizing the time spent sitting and watching. And regardless of skill, all who play baseball get a relatively equal amount of time at bat and thus equal opportunity to improve their game while engaged in a competitive contest. (Hence, when a team of top professional baseball players jour-neyed to England in 1874, they soundly defeated, at cricket, a team com-posed of the best cricketers in the world. Except for the English-born brothers George and Harry Wright, none of the Americans had ever played cricket before.)[25] In our view, baseball does indeed have an advan-tage of modern access over cricket from at least the standpoint of partici-pation. The comparative strengths and weaknesses of the two games in the context of spectatorship are really a matter of personal preference and aesthetics, which are completely subjective, and thus beyond proper comparison. However, it is not a cultural presumption to state that base-ball in America, like soccer in England, was better suited to the tastes of the masses than cricket, and thus captured their hearts and minds. But unlike their British counterparts, American workingmen of the latter nine-teenth century were emulating the bourgeois preferences of their middle-class countrymen in their sport of choice.

The blame for cricket's failure as a sport for the American public can be directly traced to those who played and controlled it within the historical context of the era, the timing of cricket's dissemination against baseball's emergence, and in lesser measure to the intrinsic structure of the game itself (always in opposition to baseball).[26] Whether or not cricket and baseball could have shared the American sport space became a nonissue and a moot point by the time the Civil War had ended, but this case corroborates our argument in chapter 1: Without active participation on the part of the working class and/or the commercial middle classes in adopting a sport as their own, the chance of that sport becoming part of the society's sport culture—of entering its sport space—remains minimal. Moreover, structure alone does not decide the outcome of a sport's fate in society. As the case of cricket in the United States demonstrates, agency

also matters a great deal. Indeed, the marginalization and eventual disappearance of American cricket represents something of a precursor to the
experience of soccer in the United States. Soccer—like cricket before it—
appeared to exclude itself from contemporary American culture, or more
precisely, it was perceived to do so by the vast majority of Americans.
Though the American-born would not be specifically precluded from
playing soccer (as was often the case with cricket), the lesson of American
cricket would be lost on those who would steward the game of soccer in
the United States for much of the next century.

In 1855, cricket was actually still ahead of baseball in terms of adherents and matches, and some clubs played both. Yet, by 1859 the *New
York Clipper* would state that "cricket has its admirers, but it is evident
that it will never have the universality that baseball will." That same year,
an American tour by the "All England Eleven," a professional all-star
team composed of that nation's best cricketers, generated much interest
and excitement. Crowds of over twenty thousand, the largest to date to
view a team sports event, attended a two-day match at Elysian Fields in
Hoboken; the "Eleven" also garnered much fanfare and big crowds in
Rochester and Philadelphia. Still tending to hold cricket in higher esteem
than baseball, the press saw the public's reaction to the tour as evidence
of a coming cricket boom. Indeed, some baseball players began to take
up the game.[27]

But ultimately the English tour would serve mainly as an example for
promoters on how to make money on a team sport, while providing a
model on how a crack baseball team might operate. After the Civil War,
baseball clubs from New York, Washington, D.C., and Philadelphia
would tour the rest of the country to spread the baseball gospel. The
expanding network of railways facilitated the expansion of baseball's
popularity, and both would accelerate after the war. Urban teams could
create a chain reaction of baseball interest when traveling the countryside.
A holiday atmosphere would usually envelope a small town when it was
visited by a touring nine from the big city, as farmers, townsmen, and
their families flocked to the designated field to root for the home team.
On the rare occasion when they could best the "city slickers," local pride
would swell; the connection between sports and civic "boosterism" became forever intertwined. By 1860, clubs playing the New York game in
Cleveland, Detroit, Chicago, Milwaukee, St. Paul, and smaller cities were
reporting on their matches to the New York sporting weeklies, while
teams playing by NABBP rules could be found in San Francisco, Stockton,
and Sacramento.[28]

In both myth and reality, the American Civil War extended baseball's
path toward its standing as "America's National Pastime." Anecdotes
abound of Union soldiers getting ambushed by rebel troops while playing

baseball, as do stories of southerners learning the game either from Union prisoners of war or as prisoners of the Union themselves. Meantime, the New York game continued to thrive on its original turf, though many players were away with their regiments. Most notable in this period was the appearance of professionalism, initially in "under the table" transactions. By 1868, with the proliferation of baseball clubs continuing exponentially, most top teams were paying some, most, or all of their players either directly or through high-salaried "regular jobs." Two years later, those favoring professionalism would permanently split from the "old guard" and form their own National Association of Professional Baseball Players.[29]

Baseball's first openly all-professional team, the Cincinnati Red Stockings, was also first in institutionally attaching a team to a city by linking a city's civic pride to the success of "its" team; that only one of the players hailed from Cincinnati itself was also an innovation. Forever after, the "home team" as an institution would represent the city while the respective hometowns of the individual players (or their respective class origins) were not an issue. Previously, a "home team" had meant just that: a team based on the geographic identification of the players themselves. The Red Stockings did indeed put Cincinnati on the map by winning fifty-six straight games over the 1869 and 1870 seasons, including total dominance over those previously considered baseball's best, the teams of New York and Brooklyn. But the team was disbanded, or in actuality transferred to Boston, after the hometown's hysteria subsided during its second season when the Red Stockings had finally lost a game, then two, then five. Maintaining a squad with such high salaries was not feasible without (in twentieth-century terms) a perpetual "big market" fan base. Yet, precedents had been set: A successful team composed of openly professional players, irrespective of their geographic origins, could quickly attain a following by becoming linked to a specific geographic locale. For the press, spectators, and the growing legions of "cranks" (i.e., fans), the best baseball now clearly meant the professional game. Additionally, a team playing the New York game of baseball had definitively demonstrated that the game could be played successfully and attract great interest far from the New York area.[30]

Baseball As a Business and Cultural Icon

In the years that immediately followed the success of the Red Stockings, the teams of the National Association of Professional Baseball Players would attempt to operate on principles similar to those utilized by the Red Stockings. These teams nominally resembled cooperatives in that they were generally run by and for the players with oversight and financial subsidies by trustees whose involvement usually derived from "sporting" and/or civic interest. However, Chicago's William Hulbert engendered the idea of exploiting baseball's institutional team charisma for the profit of businessmen through the revolutionary concept of harnessing the joint stock company as an essential instrument in the commodification of a sport. In the winter of 1876, Hulbert employed the personal charisma and business acumen of his first ally and partner, Albert Spalding, to form what was the first sports business enterprise and alliance in the world: the National League of Professional Baseball Teams. Still conspicuously in operation, the National League thus predates the English Football League (the world's second oldest sport league) by twelve years. Spalding himself would later portray the essence of the conception and founding of the new league as "the irrepressible conflict between Labor and Capital asserting itself."[31]

No longer were the players to run the enterprise of baseball, instead they would be employees of teams run by businessmen. Each team in the National League would have an exclusive territory in which to garner and nurture the allegiance of spectators for the team's profit. Hence, baseball's process of institutionalizing the charisma of a team could be extended to the institutionalization of an alliance of teams. Yet, by no means did the National League have a monopoly on the best baseball to watch in those years. Only by carefully and ruthlessly promoting their own interests did Spalding (who took over in Chicago after Hulbert's death in 1884) and his fellow owners achieve dominance over the sport. Their first task was to make and keep baseball "respectable," so as to attract and retain the higher-paying customer. Along with at least superficially rooting out the gambling elements, the National League insisted upon a minimum fifty-cent admission charge, as well as bans on ballpark alcohol sales and Sunday baseball. Hence, a space opened for a rival league, the American Association, to emerge by utilizing a twenty-five-cent fee, Sunday play, and beer at the ballpark so as to target fans from the lower economic strata, with considerable success. The American Association also found a fan base (and in some places club ownership) in the milieu of German immigrants to the Midwest whose custom of nourishing themselves with beer and sausages (i.e., hot dogs) while watching baseball became essential ingredients of modern American culture.[32]

Additionally many teams and leagues operated outside of the two "major leagues," usually in smaller cities and towns, but also in the same territory as that of the two major leagues. Emulating the examples set by the "robber barons" of the era, the National League would eventually impose its rule over the other teams and leagues (and over all professional baseball players) through the "General Agreement" and the "reserve clause." The reserve clause, initially a mechanism to keep clubs competitive by restricting wealthier teams from signing all the best players, gave a club the rights to a player's services permanently, or for as long as the club desired. Publicly, this was the declared antidote to the practice of players "revolving" from one club to another regardless of contract, a significant threat to a club's ability to attract and keep fans; but the result was the de facto institutionalization of a form of serfdom for the players vis-à-vis their clubs for nearly a century. The General Agreement bound all participating teams to accept the reserve clause and to respect the territory and player contracts of all other teams, both in and out of the National League. This effectively lent the National League and the American Association the institutional designation of "major league" while permanently relegating all others to "minor league" status, excepting the short-lived Union and Players leagues and the reform-oriented American League, beginning in 1901. In return, the minor league teams could obtain good revenue by selling player contracts to each other and to the majors. Within a short period of time, most of the "minor leagues" would submit to the hegemony of the majors, becoming an integral—though exploited and underappreciated—part of "organized baseball" itself.[33]

As the National League and the American Association thrived in the big cities while lesser leagues and clubs succeeded in the smaller cities and larger towns, baseball as a spectator sport crowded out any potential competition from other team sports. The nation's social elite, for a while at least, would still eschew baseball and denigrate its players, promoters, and fans while looking toward its demise and the resurrection of a "true sport" like cricket.[34] But the middle and working classes would embrace the game and echo the sentiments of those who promoted it on the field, in newspapers, and from boardrooms: Baseball was America's national game and pastime. Until the advent of television in the 1950s, no team sport—not even the other two and one half germinating in America's sport space—rivaled baseball as a cultural presence in American life. Most certainly, none did in the spring and summer.

In the late 1880s and early 1890s, the greed and hubris of the major league owners threatened the stability of the organized game. The challenge of the upstart Union League would be met at the cost of higher salaries and bitter intraleague acrimony. The imposition of a salary cap on individual players and the subsequent slashing of salaries, as well as the players' resentment of the reserve clause (which, in effect, made them the chattel of owners for life) would lead to the "players revolt" and the formation of the Players League. After utilizing numerous strike-breaking tactics, the National League owners decisively thwarted the ballplayers' quest for emancipation by inducing the financial backers of the "cooperative league" to betray the players. The cost of the Union League war and the players' revolt was the dissolution of the American Association and the absorption of its four surviving teams into the National League.[35]

Developments both on and off the field would threaten the National League as the nineteenth century drew to a close. The "respectable" fans whom the National League had initially attracted began to stay away as the professional game's reputation reached abysmal levels; the owners themselves engaged in sectarian power struggles while ignoring the weakening of their product on the field.[36] Into this situation stepped Ban Johnson, a former sportswriter who had founded the Western League, a circuit that initially operated as a minor league under the General Agreement. Adhering to a policy of supporting his umpires and quickly punishing any on-field transgressions by players and managers, Johnson established a league with a reputation for baseball "clean and proper." By 1901 Johnson had moved franchises into most of the bigger cities, changed the new league's name to the American, and waged war on the National League by raiding the older league's teams for talent, causing a substantial rise in salaries. By presenting major league–level competition without the disreputable on-field rowdiness, the American League quickly gained adherents, particularly among middle-class families looking for "clean" entertainment. The National League owners, still fighting among themselves, were in disarray and sued for peace. Depending on the point of view, it could either be said that Ban Johnson saved baseball for the American middle classes or saved the American middle classes for baseball.[37]

Thus was set the organization of Major League Baseball, which survives in expanded form to the present day. Johnson, though initially a self-proclaimed champion of the players, agreed to abide by the reserve clause and pledged to cooperate with the National League to preserve the territorial integrity of both leagues, each remaining separate but equal. Additionally, a championship series between the two leagues to be played at the conclusion of each season, known since as the World Series, was instituted in 1903. Initially accepted with trepidation by many owners and managers, the Series was a tremendous success and further promoted the popularity of big-league baseball.[38] The sixteen major-league teams (eight in each league) represented ten cities and constituted major-league baseball in an unchanged manner for fifty years until the Boston Braves of the National League transferred to Milwaukee in 1953, thereby sparking a period of relocation and the establishment of new franchises that continued into the late 1990s.

It is generally agreed that baseball's "modern era" began in 1901 with the establishment of the American League (the so-called "junior circuit"), and in 1903 with the first World Series. The two major leagues would coexist, rarely challenged, through to the present day. There would be minor leagues and minor-league teams that exhibited perhaps a fair number of players with skills comparable to those displayed in the majors. Most notable among these would be clubs in big cities bereft of major-league representation, such as some from the Pacific Coast League until the 1950s, and the independent Baltimore minor-league franchise prior to World War I. However, except for the short-lived Federal League of 1915, there would be no more serious challenges to the monopoly of Major League Baseball, comprised of the American League and the National League as devised by the structure of 1901/1903.[39] These two leagues, though constituting Major League Baseball, had remained separate in autonomy, rule making, and competition save for spring training exhibitions, the World Series, and, since 1933, the All-Star game. This separation was abandoned beginning in 1997, with limited interleague play during the regular season. Tellingly, this break with longtime tradition occurred precisely at a time when baseball's formerly incontestable place as a solid occupant in America's sport space was seen to waver in the wake of the 1994 players strike, which forced cancellation of that year's World Series.

However, there were no such signs at the beginning of the twentieth century. To the contrary: after the peace of 1903, the game became singularly popular with the American public. Daily newspapers devoted entire sections (within the newly instituted sports section) to baseball, as baseball writing gained in measure and stature. Many writers sought to plumb the depths of the game, creating a genre known as "inside baseball," which purported to reveal facets hidden from the casual observer.[40] Indeed, the game became so much part of American culture that many of its expressions entered the American vernacular, from which they have yet to disappear. In addition to "inside baseball," terms such as "off the bat," "ballpark figure" (as opposed to one "not even in the ballpark"), "making the majors," "in the big leagues now," "bush league," "out of one's league," "out in/of left field," "out in the bleachers," "down to your last strike," "extra innings," "step(ping/ed) up to the plate," "squeeze play," "going for home," "got/getting thrown a curve," "down and dirty," "high and tight," "screwball," "bean ball," "spitball," "switch-hitter," "pinch hitter," "heavy hitter," "batting cleanup," "getting shut-out," "swinging for the fences," "striking (struck) out," "caught looking," "three strikes and you're out," "on deck," "playing hard ball," "rhubarb," "caught on a (the) fly," "hitting it out of the park," "fair or foul," "covering all the bases," "way off base," "batting one's weight," "rain check," "relief pitcher," "coming in in relief," "in the bullpen," "warming up in the bullpen," "seventh inning stretch," "that's/it's a whole 'nother ballgame," "it's a whole/brand new ballgame," and "that's the ballgame" all corroborate the cultural ubiquity of baseball in American life. Perhaps nothing bespeaks the power of baseball metaphors in the

American vernacular more aptly than that innumerable American youths have been first made aware of the progressions of sex through baseball terminology: "first, second, and third base" and, of course, "making it home," "going all the way," or "scoring" (proving wrong all who said "you'll never get to first base")—or "striking out" as the case may be. That baseball expressions far outnumber their counterparts from football and basketball confirms that among the Big Three of the American sport space, baseball was the first, prevails in longevity, and—largely because of these factors—still qualifies as the "national pastime," if indeed in a significantly reduced manner.

Baseball had become an all-around success story throughout the teens (even during World War I) when the entire endeavor was almost derailed by a confluence of three related deficiencies: underpaid players, their accessibility to gamblers, and a dearth of decisive leadership and authority at the top of organized baseball creating the Black Sox scandal of the 1919 World Series. Suffice it to say that the Chicago White Sox, clearly the best team in baseball at the time, lost the series to the much inferior Cincinnati Reds, five games to two, because several key Sox players conspired to lose some of the games. When details of the fraud emerged through the investigations of journalists, legal depositions, and a trial (in which the players involved in the scandal were acquitted), the credibility and viability of professional baseball was threatened. To retrieve the game's tottering reputation with the public and thus protect their financial investments, the owners—desperate to present the public with evidence that the game's legitimacy would be safeguarded—offered Judge Kennesaw Mountain Landis the job of commissioner of Major League Baseball. Landis subsequently ruled over all of organized baseball as its autocratic "czar" for twenty-five years.[41] Henceforth, a single commissioner appointed by the owners would (at least nominally) be in charge, an executive framework that was to be adopted by all major American team sports (including Major League Soccer, founded in 1996), though no subsequent commissioner in any sport would hold such power as Landis. There is no doubt that the appointment of Judge Landis and his ensuing "clean-up" of the game helped restore the public's faith, though his role in bringing back the fans to the fold has likely been inflated.[42]

The "Sports Explosion"

The national prohibition on the manufacture and sale of alcohol, and its immediate effect of creating an illegal but celebrated milieu of hedonism and excess; the "emancipation of women" (as symbolized by the vote, the rising hemline, and the loosening of the old Victorian morality); the booming economy and the stock market; technological advances, and the ever-expanding consumer culture all converged to make the "Roaring Twenties" likely the most romanticized era of American history, a decade in which American optimism conveyed an ethos wherein all things appeared "larger than life."[43] Most important for American spectator sports was the expanding availability of cash (and credit) for a steadily increasing number of Americans who began spending regularly on entertainment, the boom in private and public municipal and university development that saw "stadiums" replace old "ballparks" and "ball fields"; as well as a proliferation of indoor "arena" venues; and, perhaps most important, the exponential growth of the American mass media, which rendered spectator sports in the United States truly available for mass consumption through film (especially newsreels), broadcasting (i.e., radio), newspapers, and magazines.

The decade saw a true "sports explosion" as a direct result of the demand by the American public for entertainment and the eagerness on the part of sports promoters to supply it. Other sports besides baseball and football benefited from the public's interest in sporting events and sports news. Indoor arenas seating thousands enabled boxing—now legal and only somewhat disreputable—to draw major crowds and interest while technological innovation made indoor ice hockey possible on a hitherto unprecedented scale. Though basketball played by schools, clubs, and touring professional teams was still in its formative stage at this time, games played by both amateurs and professionals—usually combined with postgame "socials" and "mixers"—gained substantially in their popularity as winter entertainment. Horse racing experienced a great expansion in venues, "action," and locales, while golf and tennis players—male and female alike—were receiving greater coverage in the sports pages than ever before. Indeed, as we shall see in the next chapter, the "sports explosion" of the 1920s also witnessed a definite proliferation of American soccer, though this potential "critical juncture" for the game's possible entry into the American sport space in a meaningful way was missed for reasons of agency and structure.

Nowhere was this elevation of American sports culture in the 1920s more pronounced than in America's number one sport, baseball, wherein George Hermann (Babe) Ruth single-handedly transformed the game with his prodigious home runs (in quantity and distance), in the process becoming the first athlete in the United States—arguably the world—to attain true supercelebrity status. Ruth's team, the New York Yankees, enjoyed great success on the field (though it was not immediately the "dynasty" it would become) and at the turnstiles in the nation's largest population center and its cultural, financial, and media-related capital. Ruth's instantly recognizable features were reproduced in more photographs in his heyday than those of any other human being on the planet, as he became known in places on the globe that had never seen a ball or bat, let alone a baseball game.[44] In short, Babe Ruth was baseball's first true "crossover star." Ruth's domination on the baseball field and his celebration by the public and media gave him a permanent place in American culture well beyond the confines of the game of baseball proper. To this day, an individual who achieves dominance and/or special success in a particular métier is often referred to as "the Babe Ruth of [fill in the subject]."[45] The phenomenon of Ruth also expanded another lucrative field for athletes: product endorsements. Though not new, like so many things during the Roaring Twenties, this assumed a hitherto unprecedented scale.

The booming economy of the 1920s provided ever-increasing numbers of paid spectators, while the mass media further extended interest in the game to a larger number of casual fans. The two major leagues enjoyed a relative harmony under the firm hand of Judge Landis, while the "lively ball" brought a crowd-pleasing offensive bonanza to the product on the field. Moreover, the game thrived in minor-league towns and cities (especially on the West Coast), as well as in semiprofessional and industrial leagues.[46] While the Great Depression financially ruined millions of Americans and limited the cash average Americans could spend on entertainment, baseball—like Hollywood movies—became, if anything, even more popular during these years of hardship. Technological advances, most notably the fine tuning of outdoor lighting, which permitted night games (enabling clubs to draw on fans who previously could not attend during the work week), and the wide availability of radio to most Americans (if not in the home, than in public places such as taverns or social clubs) helped the game attain a level of popularity in the 1930s that was likely the most widespread of its long history. Broadcasts of sports contests were commonplace by the middle of that decade (most successfully baseball, football, and boxing, though basketball and hockey were regular fare as well), while the reporting of scores during the newscasts also became routine.[47] By this time, baseball had long been the (almost) all-inclusive national pastime and cultural kit for everyone in American society.

As such, baseball served as a significant mechanism in assimilating the nation's huge and ever-present immigrant population and its native-born (male) offspring. Congruent with baseball's essential "downward dissemination" to skilled and unskilled workers in New York had been the game's appeal to Irish Americans, native born and immigrant alike, as players (including the Major League's first superstar, Mike "King" Kelly) and spectators. After the Civil War, the game witnessed an influx of German American players and a large number of fans of Germanic origin, especially in the midwestern cities that were home to American Association clubs (with German-born owners of breweries also owning baseball teams). There was scarcely a European immigrant group after 1870 that did not produce baseball players within a generation of landing in the United States, though Anglo-Saxons and Northern Europeans would generally be the most prolific and well known until the 1930s, when stars such as Joe DiMaggio and Hank Greenberg, an Italian and a Jew, respectively, attained the adoration of the American public.[48] Newcomers to the United States would usually become at least casual baseball fans, and their children, if they played any sports at all, would most certainly take up baseball or one of its variants (stickball being the most common in cities for many years). Those few who preferred playing soccer, or any other Old World sport, were generally ignored (even vilified in certain cases) by the prevailing zeitgeist for failing to meet the cultural and social requisites of the "melting pot."

Finally, African Americans played the game very well and with much enthusiasm, but were prohibited from playing on the same teams as whites, initially by the old amateur association, though a few teams did attempt to include blacks. In the fledgling years of the General Agreement, close to fifty blacks played for minor league teams, and one, Moses Fleetwood Walker, played briefly for an American Association club in 1884. But as Jim Crow laws were institutionalized in the United States, an unwritten rule prohibited African American participation in organized baseball. This was finalized by the late 1880s as Cap Anson, the game's most esteemed player and manager at the time, stated his unequivocal refusal to play on the same field as any team including blacks on its roster. Though they would field their own teams and leagues (most notably the National Negro League) and—on occasion—play on the same field against whites in exhibition games, African Americans would not play on any team in organized baseball until 1946.[49]

Early Games of Football: From American Colonial Streets to Harvard Yard

When the Pilgrims arrived at Plymouth Rock in 1620, they found the Indians playing a game called "Pasuckquakkohowog," which could best be translated as "They gather to play football."[50] This game, performed by entire villages on playing surfaces often a mile long, had much in common with the earlier games of kickball, football, and soccer that history records in ancient China, Greece, and Rome, and also in Renaissance Florence and medieval England.[51] It appears well established that kicking a ball of the most diverse shape and consistency, and for the most varied occasions, was—just like hitting a ball with some batlike object—common to many cultures in different segments of the globe. It is equally well established that the modern game of soccer had virtually nothing to do with any of these early incarnations. Instead, soccer and rugby had their origins in the England of the early to middle decades of the nineteenth century where both emerged from the milieu of England's elite private secondary schools (the so-called public schools) and its two venerable universities, Oxford and Cambridge.[52]

In the United States, it was not the indigenous game played by the Native Americans that eventually emerged as the modern sport of soccer. Instead, it was the colonists who brought this game with them that—just like in England—remained a highly unregulated and completely localized form of ad hoc activity involving a ball and a large group of boys or young men engaged in what was often a brawllike manner in pursuit and/or control of the ball. Thus, historians agree that a form of the game was played in Virginia as early as 1609. The game was so rough at times that in 1657 the Boston authorities issued an edict banning it from the streets of town, instituting a penalty of twenty shillings for any offenders.[53] As in England, the game mutated from an occasional street activity into a regularized event at institutions that housed the country's elite and whose raison d'être was to educate this elite to be leaders in a rapidly modernizing world. Unlike baseball, which—from its very beginnings—prided itself on its "American" origins, American football never denied its British roots, often invoking William Webb Ellis's alleged run at Rugby in 1823 as the inception of the game. Also similar to what had occurred in England, football did not attain any social respectability until the first half of the nineteenth century, when the nation's top colleges—led by Harvard, Yale, Princeton, and Columbia—started playing various versions of the game on an intramural basis. At Harvard, for example, the so-called Battle of the Delta, a humorous epic poem written by a college senior in 1827, offers the first account on record of a football game. Played between the university's freshmen and sophomores, this contest must have been mostly a brawl, as it did not involve a ball. While there seem to be no actual records of games played at Harvard in the 1830s, there is little doubt that the game continued to be played in some ad hoc fashion. By the 1850s the game had become so brutal that it entered Harvard lore as "bloody Monday," as it was played on the very first Monday of the fall semester between the entering freshman class and the returning sophomores. Though a ball had been introduced by this time, there were still no special rules. The aim was to kick a ball of uncertain shape and consistency—perhaps round (perhaps not), made out of rubber or out of a bladder in a leather case (or both)—over the opponent's goal "without being hampered by such modern restrictions as offside, holding, tripping, etc., but there is some evidence that the ball could not be carried: it had to be kicked." Suffice it to say that this annual "football" contest between freshmen and sophomores assumed such proportions of unruliness that the Harvard faculty outlawed the game, as did the staff at Yale and Columbia among other East Coast colleges where similar intramural events occurred in the 1850s.[54]

Just a few years later, in the early 1860s, football was to reappear on the campuses of America's elite universities in a much more organized and regulated fashion, thus experiencing the game's first steps toward routinization and institutionalization. Students and alumni from a number of elite Boston secondary schools united to form the Oneida Football Club, which remained undefeated—and even unscored upon—between 1862 and 1865, lending the "Boston Game" exceptional prominence in America's still small and motley football world. Allowing the use of hands and feet, the Boston Game soon became the most popular sport across the Charles River in Cambridge, home of Harvard University. Signally, it was at this institution that the rules of the Boston Game (which had never been written down, but only passed along by memory and tradition) were codified. "Kicking was the prominent feature of the game, but under a certain condition a player was allowed to run with the ball, 'baby' (i.e., dribble) it, or throw it or pass it to another, and these tactics were liberally used. A player holding or running with the ball could be tackled. On the other hand, striking, hacking, tripping and other rough play was forbidden."[55] With the benefit of hindsight, we can safely say that Harvard's embrace of the Boston Game, its preference for running the ball instead of kicking it, and its unique position among American universities and colleges in terms of stature and prestige congealed into a potent force that would eventually pave the way for the success of football in America's sport space and soccer's concomitant marginalization therein. Yet, at this stage, soccer's kicking game and football's running game were still united in one sport that had developed sufficient uniformity, by the late 1860s, to permit the widening of its competitive horizons from its previous strictly local intramural contests to those among colleges.

This intercollege uniformity led to the first college football game in American history, held on Saturday, 6 November 1869, in New Brunswick, New Jersey, between Rutgers and Princeton. Reflecting the proximity of football to soccer at this juncture, this event has been classified as both the first football game and the first soccer game in modern American history. Indeed, the game's roundish leather ball resides at the American Soccer Hall of Fame in Oneonta, New York, while the American Football Hall of Fame in Canton, Ohio, found it important to attach an asterisk to this contest so as to denote its closer relationship to what was later to become the global game of football—tellingly called soccer in America bespeaking this country's exceptionalism in sports culture—and decidedly not its American variant. The game was played according to rules somewhere between those of Association and Rugby Football. Columbia joined the original two in 1870, and by 1872 the group included Rutgers, Princeton, Yale, and Stevens. These schools played an Association-type kicking game. Even though local differences in rules persisted, all participants agreed that the ball could not be picked up with the hands, caught, thrown, or carried.[56] Soccer, in its rudimentary form, seemed to have assumed an important foothold among leading American colleges. However, most decisively, it failed to do so at the country's oldest and most prestigious institution of higher learning: Harvard persistently opposed the "kicking game," clinging tenaciously to its Boston Game, which it had "perfected" in the interim. While adopting some of the features of the kicking game played by the other colleges, a committee of Harvard student players declined to integrate the more important soccer-style elements that had become the essence of the game on the other campuses.[57] When the other schools uniformly adopted Association rules in 1873, they desisted from calling themselves a league due to the absence of Harvard, which did not attend the meeting for fear it would be outvoted by the other schools and thereby have to surrender its beloved running game. "If Harvard had not refused it is highly improbable that the modern game played today—the American Rugby—would ever have been evolved [sic]. Instead, all the universities, colleges and schools today would be playing Association rules—practically soccer."[58] A critical juncture if ever there was one.

In search of an opponent, Harvard turned north of the border to McGill University, which at the time played rugby. The two universities agreed to two matches in Cambridge on 14 and 15 May 1874, the first according to the rules of Harvard's Boston Game, the second following McGill's rugby rules. As expected, Harvard won the first encounter easily and was poised to lose the rematch to McGill but, surprisingly, played to a scoreless tie.[59] Most important for the future path of football and soccer in American sport culture was the Harvard team's unanimous enthusiasm for the game of rugby, which the students henceforth embraced wholeheartedly as their own. The Harvard players, the growing number of fans, indeed the Boston press, were all thrilled by this totally unexpected Harvard triumph, extolling "Yankee ingenuity" for the respectable result. So taken were the Harvard players by the rugby rules, that they accepted an invitation to Montreal, where they played McGill on 23 October 1874. This time, Harvard beat McGill at its own game, winning outright. Harvard's conversion to McGill-style rugby had been so thorough and heartfelt in such a short period of time that the two sides decided to forego playing yet another game in Montreal according to the rules of Harvard's Boston Game (analogous to the two games played at Cambridge in May).

Instead, the Harvard players opted to enjoy the lavish hospitality of their Canadian hosts, which included sumptuous meals, dances with young ladies of Montreal's society, and fox hunting.[60] Following these encounters with McGill, the Boston Game (having been a hybrid between rugby and soccer, and thus still including more kicking and foot-involved ball contact than rugby) was dismissed by Harvard footballers as "sleepy" and boring. In its stead, the "running game" developed in its then purest form as Harvard's unchallenged team sport. Harvard played Tufts in the new rugbylike game, but neither Tufts nor McGill—nor any other college for that matter—would satisfy Harvard as could the only opponent regarded its equivalent: Yale.[61]

Barely one year later, in 1875, the desire of Harvard and Yale to meet at football became so keen that in October two delegates from each university met in Springfield, Massachusetts, to set the so-called Concessionary Rules that were to govern their first game. While Harvard yielded to Yale by agreeing to disallow the scoring of a goal by the team that had just made a touchdown, it is clear that Yale made the much bigger concessions to Harvard in terms of the game's very essence and character.[62] The Springfield agreement paved the way for Harvard and Yale to play their very first contest in football on Saturday, 13 November, at Hamilton Field in New Haven, an event that eventually became an annual ritual known for years in American sport culture as simply "The Game." Harvard handily won this first matchup, since it was played by rules that favored Harvard and thus forced Yale to contest a game in a sport that it had never before played. Yale's well-established rivalry with Harvard proved much stronger than its membership in the loose association with Columbia, Princeton, and the other schools then playing the "kicking game." Yale still fulfilled its "soccer obligations" that year to Columbia and Wesleyan, but by 1876 Yale had dropped soccer and replaced it with rugby. The other universities soon followed, Princeton succumbing last in 1877.[63]

Rugby-style football's triumph over soccer-style football at American colleges was so thorough that soccer did not reappear on American campuses on an intercollegiate level until 1902. By that time American football—rugby's successor in the New World—had gained an unshakable prominence in American college life. Stigmatized as slow, boring, and devoid of action due to the relative paucity of scoring when compared to any of the "Big Three" American sports, soccer—since its reintroduction as a varsity sport—has languished in the giant shadows cast by the successor of the game Harvard embraced so wholeheartedly in 1874. At American universities, as in American society, soccer (until recently, at least) remained largely the domain of foreigners and recent immigrants, both as players and as spectators. Football, on the other hand, was to become a mainstay in America's enthusiastic sport culture, surpassing even baseball by the early 1960s. But the track for football's triumph had been set as early as 1873: "Thus it may be said that *as a final consequence of Harvard's refusing to enter the Intercollegiate Association of 1873 Rugby was adopted as a compromise as the game of American colleges though later evolved, after many changes, into the present American game.*"[64] Yet another confirmation of the critical juncture that led to the path of what was to become American—and not global—football.

Soccer's disappearance from America's college campuses proved a costly, perhaps a permanently disabling, handicap since it occurred precisely at a juncture (1870–1900) during which the sport spaces of the two most important industrial countries of the time—Britain and the United States—were occupied and thus "tracked" for the entire twentieth century. While this defeat at the hands (literally) of rugby football on America's college campuses meant that soccer had lost its most important institutional agent as the sport's disseminator among America's burgeoning middle class, it in no way meant that the game had completely disappeared from the American scene. Instead, it eked out a marginal existence on the fringes of the country's sports culture where it continued in different milieus and guises.

Crowding Out from Above: Football As a Cultural Icon of the Bourgeoisie

Once rugby had established itself as the sport of American colleges, it immediately began to evolve from a quasi-aristocratic English game to a quintessentially American activity. It was Yale that provided the game with its charismatic "founding father" and most influential modernizer, Walter Camp. Indeed, Parke Davis ("the Plutarch of early college football") explicitly equated Walter Camp of Yale to George Washington by stating that "what Washington was to his country, Camp was to American football—the friend, the founder, and the father."[65] Attaining legendary fame as a player and reformer during the game's most formative years, Camp "was said to have been the model for the fictional character 'Frank Merriwell of Yale,' " America's first and greatest fictional sports hero on whom a whole generation of American boys was raised after 1896.[66] Astute observers of American sports and culture, such as David Riesman and Michael Oriard, have drawn explicit parallels between Walter Camp and Frederick Winslow Taylor.[67] Both were simultaneously (though, presumably, independently of each other) engaged in the modernization, regularization, and systematization of their respective fields—football and factory production—which were undergoing far-reaching changes of bourgeoisification (and "Americanization") at the turn of the century. Walter Camp could be described as the leading figure in the "Tayloriza-tion" of the sport that undoubtedly emerged as modern football following the successful conclusion of this process.

Under Camp's leadership, rugby's ad hoc and free-for-all scramble for the ball—the unpredictable English "scrum"—became the clearly deline-ated American "scrimmage" in which the offensive and defensive teams directly confronted each other. Confusion and ambiguity still continued, however, with both sides simultaneously vying for possession of the ball at the beginning of each play, often tying up the ball and thereby impeding recommencement of the game. Therefore, further clarification was added by awarding what was to become the "center snap" to the offensive team. Undisputed possession of the ball thus established, Camp and his reform-ers subsequently "Taylorized" the field by drawing clear lines on it, mak-ing a team's progress, movement, and location perfectly measurable at any time during the game. The gridiron—in and of itself a Taylorist con-cept—set the stage for football's subsequent and lasting domination by statistics (yards per carry, total passing yardage, total running yardage, etc.). To regulate and encourage movement on the gridiron, and to counter the "block game" in which each team would keep the ball for "its" half of the game, Camp introduced a rule requiring a team to make five yards in three downs, extended to ten yards in four downs in 1912. Camp reduced the number of players per team from fifteen to eleven, and each player was assigned a specific position in which he was expected to excel and specialize.[68] He devised the arrangement that became standard for the offensive unit of a football team to this day: seven linemen, a quarterback, two halfbacks, and a fullback. As part of his "scientization" of football, in which game plans, strategy, and tactics assumed an increas-ingly central role, Camp also introduced a rule that permitted tackling as low as the knees. This maneuver to bring a man down was more efficient (though also more brutal) than the earlier method of wrestling an oppo-nent to the ground from the waist, chest, and shoulders. The dangerous "wedge" appeared, perfected by Harvard to become the more devastating "flying wedge," only to be countered by Camp's Yale teams with the "shoving wedge."

Play became increasingly more violent, routinely resulting in a great number of major injuries and occasional deaths. Finally, President Theo-dore Roosevelt—known to use football metaphors in his speeches ("don't flinch, don't foul, and hit the line hard!")—personally demanded that the game be reformed to eliminate such obvious brutality. Only thereafter did Camp and others institute changes that eliminated overt and willful maiming without, however, compromising the roughness of the game that was deemed so essential. Roosevelt's involvement led to the establishment

of the Intercollegiate Athletic Association in December 1905, headed by
Captain Palmer Pierce of West Point; it was renamed the National Collegiate Athletic Association (NCAA) in 1910. With Camp in charge of the
American Football Rules Committee, the last substantial changes were
undertaken, yielding a game by the eve of World War I that has basically
remained intact on both the collegiate and the professional levels to this
day (though football rules were—and are—tinkered with on a yearly basis
at every organized level of the sport.)[69] One of the most important reforms
was the forward pass, establishing the "aerial attack" as yet another
weapon in a team's offensive strategy.[70] That football rules would continually evolve into an increasingly complicated code has been seen by many
of the game's advocates as one of its attractions and a particularly apt
reflection of American culture and society, especially when compared to
the simple rules of soccer and rugby. American football thus represented
a peculiar but potent synthesis between "science" and intellect on the one
hand, and manly strength and daring on the other, convincingly mirroring
America's belief in the value of "brains and brawn." It is in this context
that football attained the image of being modern and urban in notable
and explicit contrast to baseball, which had acquired an allegedly rural
allure and a pastoral persona—images that have remained with these two
sports to this day.[71]

Baseball had become the sport of the lower classes by the 1880s, "enjoying" the social prestige of stage acting or gambling (at least until it
was "rescued" by Ban Johnson and the American League).[72] Football, in
contrast, developed into the most popular sport among America's college-
centered middle class between the 1880s and the turn of the century. (Tellingly, at exactly the same time that soccer was "crowded out" from America's sport space by its disappearance from the college scene, the game
had begun its triumphant conquest of the European continent and Latin
America on its way to becoming the world's most popular team sport
throughout the twentieth century.)[73] Initially dominant only in the elite
schools of the East Coast, football rapidly spread westward, establishing
itself at places such as the University of Chicago (coached by the legendary
Amos Alonzo Stagg), Oberlin, Michigan, and Notre Dame in the Midwest, as well as Stanford and the University of California at Berkeley on
the West Coast. The 1920s witnessed the proliferation of college football
in the South and Southwest, with both regions producing major powerhouses by the 1930s.[74] By that time, public and private high schools across
the nation had long been fielding football teams and regularly playing
each other in organized scholastic leagues, while a college subculture of
raccoon coats, frat parties, pennants, and pep rallies had been permanently linked to the game in the popular imagination of most Americans,
not least through its portrayal and celebration in Hollywood movies. Be-

ginning in 1880, the final game of the collegiate season was played on
Thanksgiving Day in New York City. In 1883 this contest, featuring Harvard and Yale, drew a crowd of ten thousand paying spectators.[75] And by
1887, the Thanksgiving game between Harvard and Princeton attracted
twenty-four thousand spectators to New York's Polo Grounds.[76]

Football's "outward" dissemination was concurrent with its appearance at educational institutions of somewhat lower and broader academic
and social standing than that of the well-known colleges noted above.
The Carlisle Indian Industrial School in Pennsylvania (which fielded its
first football squad in 1895) would furnish football with two legendary
heroes, one a player and the other a coach: Jim Thorpe and Glenn "Pop"
Warner. This trade school for Native Americans provided a squad of Indians capable of competing on an equal footing with whites. Youth football
in the United States (that is, organized football for boys of pre–junior
varsity scholastic standing, i.e., under the age of fourteen) is still named
after Warner, while Thorpe is considered America's greatest all-around
athlete of all time (he won both the decathlon and pentathlon at the 1912
Olympics in Stockholm and played Major League Baseball for eight years,
though he made his initial reputation and was most celebrated as a running back in Warner's single- and double-wing offenses in 1911 and
1912).[77]

That football remained the virtual prerogative of collegiate America
underscored the middle-class nature of the sport's first four decades. Football games on Saturday afternoons in the fall, especially around Thanksgiving, became essential ingredients of American bourgeois culture. That
football had become an integral part of American culture is once again
illustrated by the numerous expressions the game has given to the American vernacular. Whereas perhaps not quite as numerous as the aforementioned baseball expressions—once again confirming the primacy of the
earliest arrival in a country's sport space in terms of influencing its popular culture—phrases such as "blind-sided," "thrown for a loss," "piling
on," "clothes-lined," "the old college try," "the old end-around," "making an end run," "picking up the ball and running with it," "got/getting
caught off-sides," "huddle(ing)-up," "running to daylight," "running
against the grain," "the triple threat," "the Hail Mary," "quarterback
sneak," "mis-direction," "the bootleg," "grinding it out," "throwing the
bomb," "making a goal line stand," "hold(ing) the line," "block(ing) that
kick," "fourth quarter action," "Monday morning quarterback,"
"punt," "punted," or "punting it" (as in "skip," "skipped," or "skipping
it," i.e., giving up or "flaking out"), "getting/making it to/past the goal
line," "dropping the ball" (as in, "management really dropped the ball"),
and "when in doubt, punt" all attest to football's presence in American
culture well beyond the confines of the gridiron. College football attained

such a hegemonic position in American middle-class culture that it succeeded in "crowding out" the professional game—as well as soccer—at least until the founding of the National Football League in 1920, but more likely well into the post–World War II era.

However, professionalism did not remain excluded from the world of American football. One aspect of the mens sana in corpore sano ideology of the American bourgeoisie was the perception of football as a bastion of amateurism; yet, professionalization of the college game had clearly set in by 1900, while gate receipts provided welcome revenue, even to the wealthiest universities. Yale was the first university to professionalize its coaching staff, and its rivals—after initially protesting this allegedly vulgar betrayal of amateur ideals—proceeded to follow suit, hiring their own professional coaches.[78] The ethos of the student athlete was often corrupted—though almost always covertly—by such practices as under-the-table cash payments or lower academic standards. Yet, the ideal of college football as bastion of true masculine sportsmanship retained its image through much of the twentieth century, while at the turn of the nineteenth century it provided a striking counterpoint to the excesses of professional baseball. Unlike the professional athlete—which for many years generally meant the baseball player to most Americans—football's student athlete was presumed to epitomize the sportsman at his best: Playing for the thrill, competitiveness, and pleasure in the sport for its own sake within the confines of a manly code. Like his on-field representative, the football fan was viewed as an enthusiastic "booster" for the spirit and pride of his school, a respectable university student or alumnus himself (while baseball fans of this era were often portrayed as roughnecks, gamblers, and yahoos). Whereas the baseball player or owner was out for himself and lowly profit, those who played or coached football were seen as being concerned solely with the good and glory of the team and school. In short, football was perceived as providing an opportunity to build character, while baseball had the image of simply providing characters (including many of ill repute). For most of the American public, in turn, the heroic and idealistic image of college football did not extend to the nascent professional game, nor to those who played it. It would take many years for professional football to be considered "respectable."

The Birth and Rise of the Professional Game

All those involved in football (the players, fans, coaches, and team owners) came to view the game not only as profoundly American, but also as fundamentally modern, contrasting it favorably to that other American sport, baseball. This led to the erroneous, but still powerful, myth that continues to glorify baseball as a rural game. Baseball, having developed into America's "pastime" and populated by the country's masses, seemingly lacked the vigor and drive of modernity associated with football's "scientific" aura. Rather than cultivating the leisurely image of a "pastime," football prided itself on replicating the tough, strategic, determined, and ultimately victorious side of American life. Football prominently featured all the values central to bourgeois capitalism in the United States: British elite origins to provide the necessary historical legitimacy coupled with American "robust manliness" to clearly distinguish it from its "soft," disorganized, Victorian predecessor; individual effort combined with intricate team work; hierarchical control in tandem with corporate cooperation; and equality of opportunity and access accompanied by the survival of the fittest in competition against a dangerous foe.[79]

Just like American capitalism, so too was football made bearable by the "rules of the game." In notable contrast to both soccer and rugby, American football—like baseball—developed a mass of intricate rules that served as a lingua franca for the sport in a multiethnic and multicultural society dominated by bourgeois values of individualism, rather than the noblesse-oblige collectivism of the British aristocratized sports world. Whereas a common culture among players—and between players and spectators—permitted British sports to develop with a minimal system of policing, a similar self-regulating approach was impossible in a country with a constant influx of new immigrants who had the importance of being number one impressed upon them on arrival. In addition to providing a common ground of understanding, rules helped systematize and quantify American sports. The performance of a team, as well as of the individual, could be more "objectively" measured than was the case in the murky, collectivist British team sports. One could thus tie remuneration, advancement, or demotion to a player's "numbers," analogous to the reward system in a Taylorized form of industrial production. The existence of written—as opposed to culturally internalized—rules also fostered an atmosphere in which a premium was attached to devising "trick plays" consciously designed to mislead the opponent by staying just this side of what the rules permitted or, indeed, by violating them outright in the hope that the policing authorities would not notice. "Trick plays"— basically unknown to soccer, rugby, and cricket—became woven into the fabric of American football and baseball. Lastly—as in politics—clearly stated, written, and universalistic rules had an equalizing effect on football by enhancing its attraction to otherwise disparate social groups. Rules thereby enhanced participation and contributed to the popularization—if, perhaps, less to the democratization—of this sport.

The explicitly professional game of American football originated in the cultural peripheries of America's steel and coal regions, such as Pittsburgh and the surrounding areas of Allegheny County.[80] The first pro teams were initially sponsored by athletic clubs ostensibly upholding the values of amateurism, but in reality paying for the services of a few "ringers," a practice already in evidence regarding certain "student athletes" at some colleges (as noted). By 1900 professionalism outside the college ranks was no longer denied (and winked at), but now openly acknowledged. Initially, most players were local working class members with an occasional college graduate hired as the special star, as was the case with the legendary William Walter (Pudge) Heffelfinger, generally cited as the first player to receive payment from a club—in this case, "the astonishing amount" of $500 for playing one game with the Allegheny Athletic Association in November 1892.[81] Spreading to the industrial regions of Ohio by the early 1900s, professional clubs were established in towns such as Akron and Canton (now the location of the Professional Football Hall of Fame). Most teams were owned by wealthy businessmen who liked the game and wanted to provide some entertainment to the local population (which often included a disproportionately large number of their own employees) and make some money in the process.[82] With the gradual growth of the professional game and its departure from America's hinterlands into the country's cultural centers, college graduates (or at least those with college football experience) would eventually furnish the majority of the players. By the 1930s a situation developed whereby American universities served as professional football's farm system, a function that they still perform. However, through the first three decades of the National Football League, the best college players did not necessarily go on to professional careers when their school days were over. Indeed, most utilized the fame and reputation gained on the college gridiron to land full-time positions in the business world.

The college game maintained its preeminence vis-à-vis its professional counterpart until the 1950s. This remained the case even in the wake of the "sports explosion" following the successful conclusion of World War I when professional football's disorganized barnstorming days were mitigated by the establishment of an institutionalized league: The National Football League (initially named the American Professional Football Association) made its debut in 1920. Though there was little about this league to render it national in the true sense of that word—its four charter teams were all remnants of a loosely affiliated regional league in Ohio— the founding of this organization furnished the nucleus of an institution that was to begin the massive dissemination of football away from the country's colleges and into the working classes and mass culture. This "downward" dissemination of the game provided entertainment to spectators and fans outside the realm of the collegiate world, sometimes as a direct outgrowth of machinations on the part of corporate management to co-opt the loyalty and attention of their employees away from union activity. Several of the early NFL teams were directly sponsored by firms in the midst of labor disputes and strikes, particularly the Green Bay Packers, the Decatur (soon to be Chicago) Bears, the Dayton Triangles, the Rochester Jeffersons, and the Columbus Panhandles. In each case, strikes and labor strife at the sponsoring company—and in the town in which its team was based—markedly declined. The new league was pressed for the financial resources to keep teams in business, hence "factory-sponsored teams had a critical role" for the viability of the nascent NFL. For the sponsor, the team was simply a way "to buy off labor unrest."[83]

The meeting of these two worlds—that of nominally amateur middle-class collegiate football with its explicitly professional, industrial, and working-class counterpart—was fraught with conflict, rivalries, and repeated attempts to draw clear boundaries. Since amateurism was such an essential ingredient of the bourgeois perception of college athletics—the student-athlete syndrome, the mens sana in corpore sano phenomenon—the American public disapproved of players who joined professional clubs while still active on college rosters. The owners of the new NFL attempted to address this issue by proclaiming a rule that forbade the use by a professional team of any player whose class had not yet graduated. This was generally abided and uniformly enforced by the end of the 1920s and, eventually, provided a model for all professional football and basketball leagues in their relations with the colleges until the 1970s. In 1936 the NFL conducted the first "college draft" whereby each team selected the "rights" to a college player in reverse order of the won-lost record from the previous season. This institution was eventually emulated by all professional leagues in all American team sports.[84] The worlds of college and professional football—though related—would remain institutionally separate to this day.

Largely due to the college game's preeminence in the eyes of the American public, both in the game's overall legitimacy and in its superior quality at the college level at the time, the NFL encountered difficulties in the routinization of its institution. Its teams, though present in such major markets as Chicago (with the Bears) and New York (with the Giants), featured such ephemeral "floating franchises" as Pottsville, Pennsylvania; and Duluth, Minnesota. In order to stay afloat, NFL teams continued their barnstorming, playing teams not in the league and whose existence was precarious at best. This constant "exiting" from the league by its teams rendered "loyalty" to it and "voice" within it very difficult, impeding the NFL's successful institutionalization until the late 1930s, or arguably the postwar era. To be sure, when the Chicago Bears played the New York Giants at the Polo Grounds in 1925, seventy-three thousand paying spectators turned out to see the Bears' Red Grange (the "Babe Ruth of football"), an event that saved the Giants from bankruptcy. But until the

1950s, the professional version of football remained deep in the shadow of the college game.[85]

Many fans were only interested in the professional game because of its annual contest with its collegiate counterpart, beginning in 1934 when the National Football League champion confronted a team of college all-stars. Even though the college players won nearly half of the first fifteen of these meetings (which were discontinued in the mid-1970s), such annual contests helped legitimate the professional game. Over the years, the league would survive challenges from three separate entities each called the American Football League, while a fourth would operate as a minor league in the East in the years immediately after World War II. (The fifth league of that name would finally prove successful.) Professional "minor league" football and semiprofessional football (with a very unclear delineation between the two) would proliferate throughout the nation, but nearly all of these leagues and teams would prove ephemeral.[86] By the late 1930s, the League had managed a few pockets of "major market" success, particularly in Washington, D.C. (where the Redskins, led by Sammy Baugh, had forty consecutive sellouts and a large radio following) and Chicago (where the reconstituted T-formation proved both successful on the field and exciting to watch), though it still played a marginal role in the consciousness of the average American sports fan. World War II halted the NFL's ascent, as it barely managed to hang on during the war.[87] Football in the America of the 1940s still meant the college game.

Basketball: "The Liberal's Game"

While it could be argued that in many ways basketball represents the smallest, newest, hence least significant of the "Big Three" on the iconic level of American sport culture, it should also be pointed out that the game "attracts more spectators on the high school, college, and professional levels than baseball and football combined. Baseball may be the national pastime and football the national mania, but basketball is the national game."[88] Though perhaps the most authentically American of the Big Three by dint of its indisputable American origins, basketball—in notable contrast to baseball and football—captured the rest of the world's sports imagination to such a degree that today the game ranks only behind soccer as the most popular team sport on the globe, with the pinnacle of its expression, the National Basketball Association, being the most recognized sport entity in the world. Gridirons remain exclusively confined to the North American landscape (and we are certainly correct by including Canadian football in our categorization, while discounting the NFL's recent export, now called NFL Europe, and NFL exhibition games in England, Japan, and Mexico), and baseball diamonds are still only featured on the playgrounds of the United States, some countries of the Caribbean basin, Central America, Japan, Taiwan, South Korea, Canada, Venezuela, Mexico, and, on occasion, Australia. In Europe, baseball has made limited inroads only in Holland and Italy, remaining completely esoteric to the rest of the Continent. But basketball hoops—like soccer goals—grace the parks, playgrounds, and gymnasiums of virtually every country in the world. Among the Big Three, only basketball has succeeded in reaching an audience extending well beyond its immediate American origins. And it has done so not only on the level of activity all over the world, but also as culture in many places where the game (though still subordinate to soccer or, in some cases, hockey) is a major part of that country's sport space. Among such countries are Brazil, Lithuania, Russia, Germany, China, and the Mediterranean rim with Spain, Italy, Croatia, Serbia, Greece, Turkey, and Israel. In addition, the game gained immense popularity in the course of the last decades of the twentieth century in some African countries, notably Nigeria, South Africa, and the Congo, as well as in several Arab nations. Another interesting feature that distinguished basketball from baseball and football from the very beginning: Women played the former on an organized level as early as 1892 and have continued to do so to this day to a degree completely unknown in baseball and football (though many American women and girls play baseball's "close younger sibling," softball).

Unlike baseball, football, hockey, soccer, and just about all other modern sports—all of which had premodern origins and precursors—basketball originated in a definite time and place, solely the invention of one man. In the fall of 1891, James Naismith, a thirty-year-old Canadian well versed in the games of soccer, rugby, and lacrosse, was the physical education instructor at the School for Christian Workers in Springfield, Massachusetts, and he needed an indoor game to keep his students physically active during the long winter months so common to New England. Bored with the a regimen of calisthenics, gymnastics, and various children's games, Naismith's "incorrigibles" were young men in their early twenties who required the daily fitness course for accreditation as secretaries for the Young Men's Christian Association. As something akin to indoor soccer had already been attempted in the gym only to result in a number of smashed windows, Naismith devised a game in which the ball was thrown and passed, yet in a controlled fashion. Since the janitor did not have the boxes Naismith had originally requested for this purpose (a coincidence that might otherwise have lent this new sport the name of "boxball"), Naismith decided to affix two peach baskets to the lower rail of the balcony on either end of the gym. By a matter of chance, the baskets were affixed at exactly ten feet from the ground (the reach of the janitor's ladder). A few other Naismith rules are also still in use, but to a much greater degree than with football, baseball, soccer, and hockey, most of the original rules governing the early game of basketball have been superseded and substantially revised in the course of the ensuing one hundred years, so much so that it is safe to say that the contemporary game of basketball is much further removed from its origins than these other major team sports are removed from theirs.[89] For one thing, basketball in its early years often took place within a wire mesh or rope net cage (hence the term "cage game" for basketball, and "cagers" for its players), which allowed the ball to be continually kept in play while avoiding a scramble for it by the players among the spectators. The cage was still used at some professional venues into the early 1930s, long after the widespread institution of the rule that awards possession to the team not touching the ball before it goes out of bounds.[90]

The Springfield students embraced the new game after initially playing it, sometime in early December 1891. Some reportedly introduced the game at various YMCAs over the ensuing Christmas break, while the school newspaper—distributed to all Ys—included an account and illustration of the game that Naismith, in his modesty, vigorously opposed to calling "Naismith-ball," as some had suggested. Basketball was soon "the rage" for physical education classes at YMCA gyms, which at the time numbered fewer than two hundred nationwide. Within a year of the game's inception, inter-Y competitions were drawing a fair turnout of spectators, often in the hundreds.[91]

The World of Ys, Colleges, and Barnstorming: Basketball's Surreptitious Entry into America's Sport Space

Only a few years after its invention, basketball had spread rapidly from local YMCAs to other venues that attracted people seeking indoor athletic recreation and/or entertainment. In the winter of 1896–97, the YMCA team of Trenton, New Jersey, became the first professional basketball team after severing its Y connection. By 1900 there were scores of teams playing for money around New England and the mid-Atlantic states, competing in gyms, dance halls, theaters, and armories. While these professional players held other jobs, the game had developed a sufficient following by 1910 that some of its professional stars—playing four or five nights a week—could earn as much as some major league baseball players, then the undisputed elite of the American professional sports world. Even more than the turmoiled infancy of every major American team sport, basketball was beset by a proliferation of competing leagues that played the game by slightly different rules, witnessed the sudden appearance and disappearance of teams, exhibited a destabilizing and debilitating player mobility, and for decades ultimately failed to consolidate the game under one all-powerful institution.[92]

The plethora of these leagues meant that none attracted national attention. Moreover, none were "major" in the sense of offering a single, clearly delineated, and uniformly accepted institutional framework to showcase the sport's absolute pinnacle, at least on the national, if not the international, level, à la the various first divisions in the world of soccer outside the United States and the two major leagues for baseball in the United States. The proliferation of these leagues on the local level and in a relatively narrow geographic area meant that professional teams played in venues also open to amateurs, thus blurring the distinction between the two and fostering an atmosphere that diminished the distance between the organized game and its recreational variant. The complete decentralization of basketball's organizational structure allowed the game to grow on the grassroots level long before it became part of the country's hegemonic sport culture on a par with baseball and football.

The professional game garnered local press attention, but nothing close to that of baseball, football, and boxing. However, as a competitive sport that could be played and watched indoors during the winter months, basketball found an immediate niche in gymnasiums, dance halls, and, occasionally, armories (which could seat as many as fifteen hundred spectators) in the nation's Northeast and Midwest.[93] This indoor winter niche was crucial for the game's expansion, popularity, and success (in terms of both participation and spectatorship), as basketball did not have to compete directly with either baseball or football, the two sports now firmly established in the American sport space. Additionally, unlike football and baseball within the context of recreation and activity, basketball could (and still can) be played competitively by as few as two individuals ("one on one") while, also unlike baseball (with the exceptions of hurling a ball against a wall or facing a machine in a batting cage) or football, it could (and still can) be meaningfully practiced by an individual alone, just like soccer.

In addition to the numerous professional teams populating the aforementioned leagues, there were a number of independent touring teams not affiliated with a specific league that barnstormed across the Northeast and the Midwest, occasionally even traveling as far west as Wyoming and Idaho, playing local teams and drawing substantial crowds numbering in the hundreds, sometimes in the thousands. The "social" or "mixer" (i.e., dance) that usually followed most games was just as popular a draw as the games themselves. Through the 1940s many teams became identified with towns, neighborhoods, civic organizations, or corporations, as well as individual owners, sponsors, and promoters. There were teams specifically composed of—and affiliated with—various ethnic groups (hence basketball's reputation as the "liberal's game"), usually in the context of the inner cities. (Yet, as with many soccer clubs in the United States, the ethnic lines were often blurred between clubs so designated.) Jews were closely associated with the game, but most other ethnic groups were also well represented. A fine case in point were the Buffalo Germans, who enjoyed a string of 111 consecutive victories between 1908 and 1911, a feat unmatched before or since in any major team sport. Bespeaking the motley nature and porous boundaries of the game, the Germans' opponents included professional teams, college teams, YMCAs, town teams, and semiprofessionals playing under National Guard colors.[94]

The proliferation of ethnically identified teams in the formative years of basketball was similar to that experienced by club and professional soccer in the United States for much of the twentieth century. But for several reasons—not applicable and/or in direct contrast to soccer—this did not prove a drawback and obstacle to the acceptance of basketball on the part of the American public, nor to the eventual success of basketball within the culture of the American sport space. Most important, basketball was an explicitly American invention and always identified as such; and while those who played for ethnic teams were often so identified, all were usually American born and American citizens and viewed themselves (and were generally viewed) as Americans. Unlike soccer (and cricket before it), basketball was not considered a mode for perpetuating an insular ethnocultural identity, nor as a connection to one's "old country." Additionally, as noted above, basketball had the indoor winter niche pretty much to itself (with the possible exception of hockey, which, however, requires special ice-making equipment for it to be played and presented indoors), as baseball and football were not played in the dead of winter, or usually indoors. Soccer, on the other hand, was "crowded out" by those two sports. Finally, unlike with soccer, basketball players, teams, and leagues did not require the imprimatur of any sort of overarching governing institution (save, where applicable, of the American Amateur Association and the NCAA), nor, of course, approval or regulation from any sort of international organization. Soccer leagues, teams, and players, on the other hand, were regulated by the United States Football Association (eventually the United States Soccer Federation), which, for much of its existence, was run by immigrants. The USFA, in turn, represented FIFA, a decidedly non-American organization. Indeed, it is quite likely that the lack of a formal organizational structure actually proved beneficial to basketball's early mass proliferation.

The free-for-all continued as barnstorming attractions captured the basketball world's attention. First and foremost of these teams—of which the most successful were on the road from late September to April, playing more than one hundred games in the East, Midwest, and South—were the Original Celtics, yet another reference to an ethnic identity (though few, if any, of this team's players were of "Celtic" origin). Drawing crowds of ten thousand or more on a regular basis during the 1920s and 1930s in venues of such major reputation in the sports world as New York's Madison Square Garden, the Celtics constituted the first group of basketball players to escape obscurity. In this era, America's sports fans knew their names, even if the rest of the general public might not have.[95] Two key barnstormers represented the African American community's entrance into this sport culture: the New York Renaissance Five (better known as the Rens), and the Harlem Globetrotters. The Rens reached their prime in the early 1930s, winning what was considered the 1939 professional world championship in a Chicago tournament, defeating the Harlem Globetrotters along the way.[96] The Globetrotters, founded in 1927 by Abe Saperstein, went on to win the 1940 Chicago championship tournament (defeating the Rens in the process) and proceeded to become a worldwide attraction after World War II.[97] Globetrotting throughout the postwar period to the tune of "Sweet Georgia Brown," the Trotters have to be credited—without any doubt—as basketball's most potent global ambassadors, performing in front of more people throughout the world than any other sports team in history.

Despite the continued organizational anarchy of professional basketball, the American Basketball League (ABL), founded in 1925, was the first truly national basketball league in the sense that it featured franchises in major cities such as New York, Boston, Washington, and Chicago. (Just as in football and baseball, "national" in basketball meant east of the Mississippi until the advent of easy cross-continental travel following the end of World War II.) Players were signed to exclusive contracts while rules were standardized to conform with those of the Amateur Athletic Union. Even though the ABL was to fail in 1931 after a number of permutations, the entry and exit of teams, and the burdens of the Great Depression, its presence gave the professional game a new and much more visible forum in the American sport space.[98] Hence, beginning in 1939, the *Chicago Herald-American* sponsored a yearly "World Tournament" in Chicago Stadium contested by twelve to sixteen of the best professional teams in the nation. This tournament, which lasted until 1948, often drew crowds of over twenty-thousand for single games that would determine the recognized professional "World Champion" of basketball.[99]

The National Basketball League (NBL), based in the Midwest, was founded in 1937. Catalysts for this professional league were the Goodyear and Firestone Rubber companies of Akron, Ohio, and the General Electric Company of Fort Wayne, Indiana. Like many of the early NFL clubs, most of the league's teams were either owned or heavily sponsored by companies whose names they often bore. However, virtually every NBL season witnessed the departure, entrance, relocation, and/or renaming of teams before the NBL passed from the scene in 1949. Its six surviving members merged with the Basketball Association of America (BAA), a rival to the NBL throughout the mid-1940s, now an eleven-team professional basketball league comprised of teams whose owners were often first and foremost proprietors of professional hockey teams in the National Hockey League or the American Hockey League in search of yet another indoor sport to fill their arenas. The resulting seventeen-team league was renamed the National Basketball Association (NBA).[100] Though disorganized, chaotic, and ultimately unsuccessful, these early professional basketball leagues (the ABL, NBL, and BAA) provided useful building blocks upon which the professional game of basketball was to flourish in America's postwar sport culture.

The College Game

It was the colleges that occupied basketball's center stage in America's prewar sport space. Just as in the case of football, but decidedly not in baseball, basketball quickly witnessed a bifurcation between the play and rules of the professional game and the version supervised by the Amateur Athletic Union and practiced mainly by the country's colleges under the auspices of the NCAA; this bifurcation has remained intact over the century of the sport's existence in the United States.[101] There are records from as early as 1892 denoting basketball's appearance at a few colleges. (Interestingly, the game was also played at two women's schools, Vassar and Smith, in that very same year). A considerable number of colleges began playing the game barely two years after Naismith's invention of it; Iowa, Ohio State, Temple, and Yale were all playing the game by 1895.[102] By the turn of the century, intercollegiate basketball games had become a common feature of campus life. In 1915, the AAU agreed to meet with the YMCAs and the NCAA to standardize the rules for amateur play everywhere, streamlining the college game and providing an institutional structure for its proliferation. Even though professionals and amateurs of all ranks—including those from the colleges—competed against one another in tournaments and exhibitions, the bifurcation of the two worlds was evident by the fact that professionals had to register with the AAU before playing amateurs. Once an athlete was declared a professional, he forever lost his amateur standing and Olympic eligibility in all sports at the time, a sanction that provided the AAU's ultimate power.[103]

Beginning in the 1920s, the college version of the game easily surpassed that of the professionals in terms of spectator attendance and press coverage, and like in football, this remained the case until the 1950s. A number of excellent teams in New York developed intense rivalries throughout the 1920s and 1930s to attract the city's attention and enhance college basketball's popularity and national prominence. A benefit triple header organized by Mayor James J. Walker for the city's unemployed, in January 1931, involved six New York–area colleges and drew sixteen thousand spectators to Madison Square Garden; it was a rousing success both financially and in terms of popularizing college basketball with the American public. By 1933 schools of the Big Ten Conference in the Midwest were drawing crowds that averaged eight thousand spectators, while several eastern colleges were consistently attracting over five thousand per game.[104]

As the sport proliferated throughout the United States, its Mecca would remain New York City. On 29 December 1934, Ned Irish organized his first college basketball doubleheader at Madison Square Garden, drawing 16,180 spectators. Irish went on to promote seven more very successful doubleheaders at the Garden within the next year, beginning three decades of major promotional activities featuring basketball in New York and other locales by the former sportswriter. Irish can safely be viewed as perhaps the key conceptual modernizer and organizational "nationalizer" of the college game—and thus basketball in general. Irish realized that the game had to be extracted from the armories, dance halls, river barges, and poorly lit gymnasiums and placed in modern arenas, viewing this not only as an issue of money, but also of image. Toward that purpose, the college game was accelerated and rendered more fluid through rule revisions that increased the game's speed, movement, overall flow, and strategy. Meantime, Irish organized the game's first truly national tournament in which the best colleges from across the country competed against each other in a single-game elimination. For many years, this New York–based event, the National Invitation Tournament (NIT), determined college basketball's national champion. The regular-season basketball tournaments at Madison Square Garden and the NIT tournaments provided college basketball its first truly national profile, while Irish "exported" his New York successes by presenting double- and triple-headers in other parts of the country. In 1937 the NCAA inaugurated its own season-capping tournament that would eventually rival, and then surpass, the NIT. (The AAU also had its own tournament, but it faded in significance as the NCAA expanded its domain.)[105] For some years, schools were allowed to compete in both the NIT and NCAA tournaments in the same season. Of the many who did, only the ill-fated CCNY squad of 1950 ever won both in the same year.

Unpaid athletes earning huge revenues for their schools—while gambling on college games was just as widespread as betting on professional sports—had been a given since the Harvard-Yale football contests of the

1880s. Yet the "amateur ideal," as promoted and enforced by those who purported to regulate major college athletics, made the idea of a Black Sox–type scandal unthinkable to most. However, the CCNY basketball team that won both the NIT and NCAA tournaments in 1950 was one of several teams to unleash just such a calamity. Unlike the Black Sox, who had thrown games outright, CCNY and other "tainted" college teams manipulated the scores of games so that the final tally would fall under the "point spread." (It has been noted that the CCNY players involved in this scam were indeed extremely talented in terms of basketball skill and teamwork, for not only could they win all key games, but they did so while concurrently ensuring that the score was just right—i.e., a margin of victory within the point spread—against teams not in on the fix trying their best to win.)[106]

The "point-shaving" scandals of 1950 portended the end of New York's reign as the Mecca of college basketball, as most of the sporting public, including coaches and athletic administrators, began to view the big city as a corrupting influence, even when it was revealed that teams across the nation—including such perennial powerhouses as Kentucky, Bradley, Toledo, and Akron—had also manipulated scores for several years at the behest of gamblers. Put bluntly, the consequences of this scandal were eventually to eliminate New York as the locus of first-rate college basketball to this day. Most of the players involved in the point-shaving scandal of 1950 were subsequently banned for life from both the college and professional games, while some of the gamblers involved served time in jail. A short-lived resurgence of college basketball in New York was short-circuited by yet another gambling-related scandal in 1961.[107]

Madison Square Garden and the NIT were now considered tainted and off limits by many schools, and the NCAA tournament assumed the NIT's place as the sole forum for determining the nation's college basketball champion. Even though the NIT continued to attract some excellent teams through the 1960s, it remained in the NCAA's permanent shadow, becoming something of a second-rate venue by the 1970s, where teams not selected for the NCAA tournament would compete for an increasingly lackluster trophy. The point-shaving scandal of 1950 provided additional impetus to efforts on the part of the NCAA to formulate and implement its own regulatory powers over all of college sports. From 1951 through 1953, the NCAA enacted a series of measures that combined to constitute its "sanitary code," transforming that organization into the hegemonic governing body of all college athletics, which it remains to this day.[108]

More than baseball, football, soccer (in the world outside the United States), and hockey, basketball has experienced an immense transformation in all its aspects during the course of its first century of existence. It began the twentieth century as far and away the weakest of the Big Three (even trailing hockey) and ended it as one of the major representatives of American sport culture. That basketball is clearly junior to baseball and football in terms of its historic importance to American sport as culture is demonstrated by the fact that only a few basketball expressions have entered the American vernacular compared to the many that have done so from baseball and the fewer, but still considerable number, from football. Indeed, the only basketball expressions common to contemporary American parlance are "scoring a slam dunk" or "it's a slam dunk" (denoting a clear-cut case or decisive achievement), "one on one," "taking (you/them/him/her/us) to school," "no harm, no foul," "putting on a/the full-court press" (as in applying maximum pressure or making an all-out effort), "the sixth man," and "in your face." But while basketball might have been less present culturally in the America of the early decades of the twentieth century than baseball and football, it was most decidedly present at the grassroots level and middle ground of America's sport space at its formation. Hence, while basketball could not compete with Major League Baseball and college football in terms of its cultural visibility in the early decades of the twentieth century, it was most certainly quite present on the local level, which, in turn, provided the foundation for its emergence as a major cultural phenomenon on the college level by the late 1930s, and on the professional level by the 1950s (discussed in chapter 4). Basketball offers a fine example of our thesis that a clear-cut presence—no matter how disorganized, chaotic, and organizationally weak—on a mass level was required in the early part of the twentieth century for a sport to have become a major cultural icon by the century's end. Basketball was widely played and followed in the America of the 1900s, 1910s, and 1920s, whereas soccer was not. This made all the difference for their respectively divergent paths in America's sport space of the twentieth century, and it will most likely continue to endure.

Hockey: The Success of a Canadian Import

The reason hockey provides such a fascinating—and indispensable—case for our study is manifold: First, unlike any of the Big Three, hockey *never* claimed American origins. Moreover, it became popular and part of the American sport space as an openly foreign sport in terms of its origins, practitioners, stars, and organizational framework. Thus, like soccer—but unlike the Big Three—hockey is decidedly a non-American game.

Second, crucially different from soccer, hockey developed as Canada's game. And Canada's very special relationship with the United States, we submit, makes all the difference as to why hockey entered the American sport space successfully and developed therein to become part of America's sport culture, whereas soccer did not. For the purposes of our argument, Canada—though politically apart from the United States throughout its history, first as a British colony, then as a British Dominion, and subsequently as a completely independent sovereign country—exhibited sufficient cultural similarities and featured sufficiently close ties in economy and society with the United States as to render it if not formally part of the latter, than very close to it. The dense and constant social exchanges between these two neighbors created an affinity in their respective cultures that—though clearly different and separate—shared sufficient markers and fundamental bases to render them very permeable, if not necessarily interchangeable. And while it is undoubtedly true that the general path of cultural dominance has migrated from the more powerful United States to the weaker Canada, it is also true that this was never a simple one-way street. As in all hegemonic relationships, the weaker of the two partners also exercises considerable influence on the stronger. While less true in politics, this is certainly the case in culture, particularly if the dyads—as has been clearly the case with the United States and Canada—share many common bonds, notably those of history, religion, and, most important, language.[109] The famous adage that the American-Canadian border has been the longest nonguarded border between any two countries in the world—both historically and geographically—says it all.

The cultures of these two countries developed in such an intertwined manner via such a close geographic proximity that neither perceived inventions of the other as "foreign" or "alien" and thus undesirable. The level of comfort and familiarity between these two countries fostered a situation in which not everything developed by the culture of one was guaranteed automatic acceptance by the other, but where most certainly all the structural requirements were present for precisely such an acceptance. In short, the cultural affinity between the United States and Canada has offered a sufficient, but not a necessary, condition for the easy mutual transfer and adoption of innovations, trends, and ideas, and this remains rather exceptional in the world. Hockey is precisely such a transfer and yet another example demonstrating that no matter how the cultural dominance of the stronger prevails over the weaker—and indeed shapes their mutual relationship—it is never a one-way street. Thus, in our case at hand, it was a Canadian game with its Canadian culture that was found so attractive in the United States, where it was adopted with vigor and enthusiasm regardless of its "foreign" origins. For the purposes of our argument, the sports cultures of Canada and the United States have been virtually identical. The longest unguarded border in the world might as well not have existed in terms of hockey's presence in these two countries.

Third, though a Canadian game in origin, hockey successfully entered the United States in the key formative period between the turn of the century and 1930. Indeed, hockey's presence in the American sport space was arguably more advanced in the 1920s than that of basketball's. (Recall that in the 1930s and 1940s owners of hockey teams and indoor hockey arenas looked to expand their ownership into basketball to utilize their arenas more fully.)

Fourth, just like basketball and soccer—and unlike football and baseball—hockey has successfully entered the sport spaces of many countries beyond the confines of the North American continent and its immediate vicinity. Hence, hockey—like basketball and soccer—can claim to be a global game. Indeed, in the course of the late 1980s and early 1990s, hockey in North America developed far and away the most international character of the major league sports that comprise the American sport space, specifically in terms of including players from overseas. But precisely because of its North American origins and its early cultural proliferation in the United States, hockey does not have the burden of being seen as "foreign" and "alien" and "strange" the way soccer always has and continues to have (albeit to a lesser extent today than in former times). The reason for this lies in history: having first established a considerable toehold in a crucial—and at that time—dominant geographic area of the United States (i.e., the country's Northeast and upper Midwest), hockey could easily expand west and southward in the 1960s, 1970s, 1980s, and 1990s. In other words, for hockey to flourish in places like Anaheim, Dallas, Phoenix, San Jose, Tampa Bay, and Miami in the 1990s, it had first to have established cultural roots in places such as Boston, New York, Detroit, and Chicago many years earlier.

Fifth, representatives of Major League Soccer and others hoping to see soccer finally become established in the American sport space have repeatedly referred to hockey as an example to follow, and as an aim whose attainment was certainly within the realm of the possible for soccer. Hence, in terms of hockey's presence as the weakest—yet decidedly extant—culture among America's dominant team sports, it exhibits certain structural affinities that might represent an optimistic harbinger of soccer's future in the North American sport space.

The Canadian National Pastime

By the 1880s a sufficient number of hockey clubs existed in Montreal to warrant competitive tournaments, and the game had spread to a sufficient degree in Canada that one can begin to speak of an early institutionalization of hockey as Canada's premier sport. By the late 1880s, the so-called "McGill Rules" developed into a lingua franca that allowed teams from diverse localities to compete among each other. The *Gazette* in Montreal called for the creation of a "Dominion Hockey Association" to develop hockey as a "national pastime" and give it "a higher standard of excellence, both as a game and in the eyes of the public."[110] (That the *Gazette* had already, in the 1880s, labeled hockey the "national pastime" speaks volumes as to how the game was cherished above others and how it was to enter Canada's sport space as a mighty and virtually unchallenged hegemon and remain so to this day. The parallels to baseball as America's "national pastime" are striking.) Just as in the case of all modern team sports at a comparable stage of their development, hockey at this time was at least as much a social event for middle-class gentlemen as it was a competitive game. Again, corresponding to all bourgeois cultures of the time, gentlemen played the game for fun, recreation, physical activity, and socializing, but never for money.[111] By the 1890s the game had proliferated throughout much of Canada with a myriad of teams comprised of amateurs, professionals, and semiprofessionals playing each other in a cacophony of ad hoc arrangements. Two leagues were the first institutions to offer the game an important organizational coherence: the Montreal-based Amateur Hockey Association of Canada, and the Ontario Hockey Association.[112]

Competition between the champions of these two leagues was made possible by Lord Stanley of Preston, the sixth governor general of Canada and a keen hockey fan, who—in honor of his retirement in 1893—donated a cup (which he had purchased for less than fifty dollars) to serve as a challenge trophy for which any team in any league was to be permitted to compete in order to establish the acknowledged dominion champion. Of equal importance was Lord Stanley's proviso that "the games [be] fairly played under generally recognizable rules." The new trophy was not to be controlled by any one association; rather, it was to be a permanent challenge cup awarded by an independent committee of Cup trustees. The Stanley Cup, the second oldest sports trophy in the world (the America's Cup in yachting being the oldest), preceeded the Davis Cup by seven years. As one of the most prestigious trophies in the sports world, it helped streamline the game of hockey into a nationally recognized pastime with a true national championship. The first Stanley Cup game was played in Montreal on 22 March 1894, ten months after Lord Stanley's departure from Canada (meaning that he never got to see any game played for the trophy that bore his name). Six years later, nearly eighteen thousand fans attended a four-game Stanley Cup series in Montreal. At this time, the Stanley Cup was a temporal free-for-all, with virtually no calendar structure, in which teams challenged the incumbent immediately after the latter had won the trophy. Since 1910, when the National Hockey Association took control of the trophy, the Stanley Cup has symbolized supremacy in professional hockey. As of 1926, the coveted trophy has been limited to teams in the National Hockey League.[113]

Establishing an American Presence

Already, at the turn of the century, a significant number of Canadian players had migrated to Michigan and Pennsylvania in the hope of earning a
living from hockey skills acquired and developed by playing for amateur
teams in Quebec and Ontario. Characteristic of the greater—and earlier—
commercialism of American sports (as well as American culture in general) in contrast to the more staid and less commodified atmosphere in
Canada, professionalism in hockey was more acceptable in the United
States than in Canada at the time.[114] Pittsburgh was an especially popular
place for Canadian players, since teams there provided "regular jobs" in
addition to hockey salaries of fifteen to twenty dollars a week.[115] In addition to Pittsburgh and other towns in western Pennsylvania, clubs
emerged in St. Paul and Duluth, Minnesota; St. Louis; Detroit; and Michigan's Upper Peninsula, in particular Sault St. Marie; indeed, there developed an Upper Peninsula League. Many of these American teams not only
played each other, but also Canadian clubs. For the purposes of the establishment of a hockey culture in these parts of the United States (and at
this critical temporal juncture in the development of modern team sports
in all modern societies), the political border separating the two countries
was all but nonexistent.

As witnessed at the comparable stage in the other team sports, this early
period of hockey was characterized by many rival leagues, regular player
raids, and an organizational pluralism bordering on anarchy. The first
major institutional regularization of the sport occurred in 1910 with the
founding of a new league in Montreal, the National Hockey Association
(NHA), the direct forerunner of the National Hockey League (NHL).
Comprised entirely of professional teams, this league evolved into a six-
team circuit by 1917 and included the Montreal Canadiens, who were to
become hockey's most storied and victorious franchise throughout the
twentieth century. The NHA introduced six-man hockey (from the previous seven-man teams), added numbers to the players' jerseys, and
changed the former two thirty-minute halves to three twenty-minute periods. Assists were added to the increasingly meticulous record-keeping that
characterizes all modern organizations.

Parallel to the development of the National Hockey Association in the
East, the Patrick brothers (Lester and Frank) founded the Pacific Coast
Hockey Association (PCHA). An agreement was worked out for the two
respective champions of the NHA and the PCHA to meet in a contest for
the Stanley Cup. In 1915 a decisive development occurred for the future
of hockey in the United States: The PCHA's New Westminster team was
moved to Portland, Oregon, for the first time making an American-based
team eligible to play for the Stanley Cup. One year later, a new PCHA

franchise was established in Seattle, Washington. The next year, the Stanley Cup trustees officially confirmed that an American team was indeed eligible to contest for the Stanley Cup, since the trophy was meant to signify global supremacy in hockey. The Stanley Cup became, in essence, a North American instead of a purely Canadian trophy, most certainly including the United States in hockey's culture. More important was the obverse: the inclusion of a Canadian game in America's sport culture and sport space. Sure enough, barely one year later, in March 1917, the Seattle Metropolitans defeated the Montreal Canadiens, to win the Stanley Cup. However, Seattle's Stanley Cup—while important in terms of legitimizing hockey as sport in the United States—was not an especially abrupt and unusual event. Hockey had established its American roots well before 1917; the Seattle victory merely solidified and legitimated it. The nominal internationalization of hockey began with its first appearance at the Olympic Games of 1920 when—predictably—Canada won the gold medal and the United States the silver. Beginning with the first Winter Olympics in 1924 (1920 still featured a single competition rather than the subsequently separate Summer and Winter Olympics), Canada won the gold medal for hockey in every Olympic tournament until 1952, with the exception of the 1936 games when Great Britain won gold, Canada silver, and the United States bronze (the United States would win the silver medal three times behind Canada's gold). However, the true internationalization of hockey would not start until immediately after World War II.

From its very beginning, violence and fighting were endemic to the game. In 1907 Charles Masson of the Ottawa Vics hit Owen McCourt of Cornwall over the head with a hockey stick, killing him in the process; Masson was subsequently acquitted.[116] And nearly one hundred years later—on 21 February 2000—Marty McSorley of the Boston Bruins whacked Donald Brashear of the Vancouver Canucks over the head with his stick. Only a miracle prevented Brashear from dying or incurring a serious injury. These are but two extreme examples of the constant violence that has been an integral part of hockey on all its levels (amateur and professional, junior and senior, minor league and major) and in every era of the game's existence. Hence, blaming (as many do) the game's expansion into the United States—its Americanization, so to speak—as the primary cause for the continued presence of violence in the game is simply not accurate. Violence has deep historic roots in the game's Canadian origins and is constantly reproduced on every level of the Canadian pastime. Indeed, with the internationalization and "Europeanization" of the NHL, many Canadian traditionalists feared the game's violent character might change and that hockey's internationalization might mean its "sissyfication." To be sure, there have been a number of important voices in hockey—notably Wayne Gretzky's—that have decried the constant violence in the NHL (to little, if any, avail).[117] The Canadian culture of hockey found a welcoming home in the United States, where for many years it maintained its ways and means largely unencumbered by a different country's milieu through the monopolization of virtually every spot on every roster with Canadian players. The NHL, the game's pinnacle, remained largely a Canadian league performing to American audiences and in American cities.

It should be noted that hockey's presence in America's sport space has also been fostered by the game's popularity on the high school and college level in the country's Northeast and Midwest. Particularly after World War II, when the NCAA began to organize annual championship tournaments to determine a U.S. national champion analogous to the Association's year-end championship tournament in many other sports (most notably basketball), hockey on the college level has become quite popular, rivaling college football and basketball in parts of New England, Michigan, the Dakotas, Minnesota, Colorado, and upstate New York. American colleges have recruited players from Canada as well as the United States to represent their colors. In Boston, the hockey teams of Harvard, Boston College, Boston University, and Northeastern are much more popular in the city's sports culture than any of these universities' basketball or football teams (with the arguable exception of Boston College football); the annual Beanpot Tournament, held every February among these four schools, is clearly one of the city's most celebrated cultural icons.

The National Hockey League was officially founded on 22 November 1917 when the owners of the National Hockey Association held a meeting to organize a new entity that was exactly like the old one, but without the ornery and difficult owner of the Toronto club.[118] Frank Calder, who had originally come to Canada from Britain to play soccer but in the process had fallen in love with hockey, became the NHL's first president. The Roaring Twenties witnessed the first radio broadcast of a hockey game (in March 1923), catapulting the sport into a new level of communication that was to create a common bond among Canadians from coast to coast that few, if any, other cultural phenomena attained—in terms of thoroughness, enthusiasm, and popularity—to the same degree. The twenties also saw the game's major arrival and exposure in the United States.

Though experiencing the entry and departure of several teams, the NHL sported two divisions by the 1926–27 season. Significantly, the league established a strong presence in New York with two clubs, one of which (the Rangers) survives to this day. Additionally, several minor league hockey teams operated in New York City and the surrounding areas (some of these teams would compete for fans with the Rangers well into the 1940s). The boom period of the 1920s also saw the construction of major indoor arenas such as the Boston Garden, Madison Square Garden, Maple Leaf Gardens, Chicago Stadium, and the Montreal Forum, all of which offered seating to approximately fifteen thousand spectators.

With the onset of World War II, the league continued its operation with the blessing and encouragement of the Canadian *and* the American governments, both of which—and this confirms our argument about hockey having become an integral part of American culture—declared hockey essential to national morale, as baseball and football were so deemed. Just like the other three American sports, hockey also flourished during the war years and offered a welcome diversion from the worries of the conflict overseas.[119] However, the war did indeed take its toll on the viability of some teams, if not on the game itself, since by 1942 the NHL was reduced to the so-called Solid Six (Montreal Canadiens, Toronto Maple Leafs, Chicago Black Hawks, Detroit Red Wings, Boston Bruins, and New York Rangers). These clubs would form the core from which the league would expand most prolifically, beginning in the late 1960s.

There can be no doubt that at the end of the twentieth century, hockey could legitimately be classified as a significant occupant of America's sport space. Be it in terms of newspaper coverage of every aspect related to the sport—that is continuous and regular stories that went well beyond the actual games; regular presence on local and national television; iconographic presence of the game's stars in America's culture well beyond the confines of sport; and the following that the sport engendered on a popular basis—hockey had successfully entered the American sport space as culture, far exceeding its existence as a mere activity, though still quite subordinate to the Big Three of football, baseball, and basketball. This subordinate position in American culture vis-à-vis the Big Three is demonstrated by the paucity of hockey terms to have found their way into the American—as opposed to, tellingly, the French Canadian—vernacular: "hip check(ed)," "hat trick" (as in a group of three successes and/or accomplishments, or three-in-a-row), and "in the penalty box" (akin to "in the doghouse") are perhaps the only such phrases to attain status similar to the many terms derived from baseball, football, and even basketball.[120]

Three ....

Soccer's Trials and Tribulations
BEGINNINGS, CHAOS, "ALMOSTS," OBSCURITY, AND COLLEGES

DESPITE ITS overall existence on the fringes of American sports culture, the history of soccer in the United States has indeed been "long and varied."[1] This chapter presents the motley patchwork of respectable marginality—ranging from the beginnings of soccer's discernible presence in the late 1800s through the years immediately following World War II—by first delineating the world of club and semiprofessional soccer in the United States, offering a taste of this world's organizational disarray and including an account of the early attempts to organize the sport in the United States. Subsequently, we turn our attention to the professional game, where the organizational and institutional inadequacies besetting this sport in America will become even more obvious. This includes an account of the first American Soccer League—a successful, yet ultimately ephemeral, establishment of a first division venue for the sport and a missed opportunity to put the sport on firmer footing in the American sport space. We also offer a brief account of the performance of American national teams on the international stage and present a few highlights of European and Latin American clubs visiting the United States. We then turn to a discussion of soccer's presence at American colleges in the course of the twentieth century, arguing that the very structure of college soccer has continued to impede the development of the game's overall quality, thus adding to its marginalization in America's sports culture. In short, this chapter deals with most of soccer's historical era, which Chuck Cascio has appropriately labeled "the dark ages in Yankeeland (1900–1968)," while noting a few subsequent developments.[2] Two essential aspects of soccer in contemporary America—youth soccer and women's soccer—are discussed in chapter 5, which will analyze the game's massive proliferation in the United States as an activity, if still not quite as culture, in the wake of developments that occurred in the late 1960s and in subsequent years.

Club and Semiprofessional Soccer in the United States and the "Organization" of American Soccer

In the last quarter of the nineteenth century, soccer was played by many immigrants to the eastern parts of the United States—initially most from the British Isles—who formed amateur teams almost always composed of members of a specific ethnic group, as demonstrated by the teams' names: Brooklyn Celtics, Anglo-Saxons F.C., Clan McKenzie F.C., Spanish-American F.C. and Over-Seas F.C.[3] To be sure, there were teams composed of American-born players, such as the one from St. Louis, Missouri, which defeated a team of Irishmen in 1881. Some neighborhoods in cities and towns that retained strong first-generation cultural identification with particular nationalities became "soccer islands," mostly throughout the eastern United States, sometimes in entire towns such as Fall River, Massachusetts, and Kearny, New Jersey, longtime soccer strongholds and spawning grounds for talent and fans to this day. Ethnic social clubs often created the basis for soccer in large metropolitan areas, such as New York City, Philadelphia, Pittsburgh, Chicago, Boston, and, most notably, St. Louis, which later would nourish numerous native-born American players.[4]

The American Football Association (AFA) was formed in Newark, New Jersey, in 1884, the first soccer league ever to be organized outside of Britain. Indeed, this association predates the formation of the English Football League, the two-tiered organization of English professional soccer clubs, by four years. The AFA gave uniformity to the rules of play on the field, though bickering among the clubs commenced almost immediately, soon to be exacerbated by the depression and labor unrest of the 1890s. Much of the conflict revolved around the axis of professionalism versus amateurism, though there were virtually no soccer players in the United States at the time earning a livelihood solely by the game. Similar to baseball in its formative years, many players would "revolve" among teams according to convenience and payment. Meantime, other regional associations of varying stability and stature also emerged. One, the New York State Association, was fairly well organized and remained separate from the AFA, which, after several years of dormancy, was resurrected in 1906, this time incorporating some clubs that aspired to professional status. In 1912 the New York State Association would form the germinal for the formation of the American Amateur Football Association (AAFA), with the stated purpose of expanding regulation and promotion of the sport on a national basis.[5]

Members of the AFA and the AAFA, each representing both amateur and semiprofessional clubs, would travel to Stockholm independent of each other to request recognition from FIFA at its 1912 congress. Rather than choosing one or the other, FIFA told the two rivals to consolidate. After settling the inevitable turf war, they did so in 1913, thus forming the United States Football Association (USFA), an organization that was controlled by amateurs ("in the pejorative sense of the word," writes Paul Gardner).[6] In addition to incompetence in running their operation, these soccer officials further alienated the sport from the mainstream of American society by not only identifying themselves as immigrants but, more important, by priding themselves on consciously maintaining the foreign flavor and European origins of the game, certainly a drawback at a time in American history when nativism and the creation of an American identity in clear opposition to Europe was culturally hegemonic. Further emphasis on soccer's foreign ties and on the game's allegiance to a distinctly non-American body came from the fact that it took the intervention and imprimatur of FIFA, soccer's international ruling body headquartered in Zurich, to mediate and validate the organization and regulation of American soccer. In retrospect, this did not bode well for the sport's position in the United States because, yet again, it underscored soccer's foreign character to the American public (or at least those paying attention). Moreover, it was to demonstrate emphatically something completely unthinkable to any of the major American team sports: a lack of complete sovereignty and total control on the part of American organizations who instead remained subservient and subordinate to a foreign entity.

The USFA never achieved its goal, as stated by its English-born and German-educated first president, Dr. G. Randolph Manning, of making "soccer the national pastime of the winter in this country." The USFA proved inept at organizing and promoting the sport to the vast majority of the American public and it also failed to accumulate financial capital for its stated purpose, while never moving beyond the ethnic insularity that consistently hindered soccer's meager advancement into American culture throughout the 20th century. Additionally, the USFA completely ignored college and high school soccer, thus adding to its isolation and depriving itself of any sort of influence among native-born players and potential fans. As for the professional game, here too, the USFA did more to impede than help its development until, perhaps, the USSF—as the federation was later called—was co-opted by Alan Rothenberg and his associates prior to the 1994 World Cup in the United States.[7] The evolution in the changes of the Federation's name helps illustrate two related difficulties that have consistently confronted America's soccer leadership from the beginning: first, the longtime resistance and reluctance to recognize American realities in which "football" has denoted a completely different game from what the rest of the world and America's soccer enthusiasts have understood it to mean; and second, to find a distinct identity for soccer that was American, yet also apart from the behemoth of American football. To wit: Not until 1945 did the federation add the word "soccer" to its title, when it was renamed United States Soccer Football Association (USSFA). This was changed yet again in 1974 when the word "football" was finally completely relinquished, thus yielding the current United States Soccer Federation (USSF).

One of the USFA's first acts was the creation of the National Open Cup Competition in 1914, renamed the National Challenge Cup in 1923. This democratic competition—in clear opposition to the much more exclusive league play—aligned the United States with most soccer-playing countries in the world, whereby teams of all levels of proficiency and organizational character—amateur and professional, major league and minor league— enter a year-long single-elimination tournament to establish the eventual victor who, for that season, holds the nation's cup. To be sure, professional clubs with much greater playing skill than their amateur counterparts consistently dominated these tournaments throughout much of the twentieth century. So, too, in the United States, where from the very beginning professional and semiprofessional teams, such as the legendary Bethlehem Steel F.C. (which won the Cup in four of the first six years of competition), dominated play. Still, bespeaking the relatively unspecialized and undifferentiated nature of American soccer—especially in contrast to countries featuring soccer as hegemonic sports culture—the lack of clear distinctions among amateurs, professionals, and semiprofessionals pertained for the first decade of the tournament. A separate national competition for amateurs was inaugurated in 1923, after the initial success of a professional league in the eastern United States, the first American Soccer League.[8]

The list of winners for the Cup through the years reveals an overwhelming ethnic flavor to the American soccer scene. However, native-born Americans were often included on most or all of these teams. Moreover— and this is an important point because it is so quintessentially American since it affirms the "melting pot," even in the very attempt of its denial— club composition was never limited by ethnicity. Hence, for example, Italians regularly played for German clubs, Irishmen played for Italian-named teams, and Gentiles of all kinds played for Jewish sides. But American-born players were usually the children of immigrants playing for clubs with a definite ethnic identity and affiliation, often from towns where ties to the Old Country created and maintained the game's local popularity. The consistently overwhelming self-identification of American soccer with ethnicity clearly reinforced its separateness for most Americans, especially when viewed against the indigenous nature of the Big Three and ice hockey.

Throughout the twentieth century, regional club leagues would proliferate in the United States, most notably in the New York region, but elsewhere as well. As a result of a concerted effort on the part of local enthusiasts to promote the sport as recreation for youth, St. Louis developed into a city that could well be labeled America's soccer Mecca or unofficial soccer capital by dint of its extensive amateur leagues, club networks, and fan involvement, which burgeoned in that city's ethnic communities, particularly in Italian neighborhoods where soccer rivaled baseball as the most popular sport. Organizations like the German-American League in the New York area, founded in 1923 with five clubs, and consisting of over fifty when its name was changed to the Cosmopolitan League in the 1970s, provided competition for clubs and players from a wide range of ethnic backgrounds. However, historically speaking, most of the club soccer played in the United States by adults was through affiliation with various ethnic organizations, and the most successful teams—amateur and semiprofessional alike—were almost always based on ethnicity even if such a base was never exclusive, such as the membership of the Maccabees of Los Angeles, four-time Challenge Cup champs in the 1970s.[9] Since the soccer explosion of the 1980s, adult club and recreational leagues without specific ethnic affiliation, designation, or character have become much more common than ever before in the history of American soccer, though many clubs and leagues, particularly those popular with Hispanics, continue to have a significant ethnic orientation and composition.

ASL, APSL, CISL, CSL, NPSL, ISSL, NESSL, USISL, NSL, HASL, LISFL, IASL, EDSL, CJSL, LIJSL, PSAL, NASL, NESL, NJSL, NCJSL, NDASA, NCSA, NHSA, TSL, FSSL, DSA, ISL, MSL, MISL, MLS, MSC, EPSA, PSA, ENJSA, CSA, SCSL, OSL, OJSL, SCSL, SDSI, CSSA, ENYSSSA, GAL, MSSA, MASS, MDCVSA, PWSA, RISA, VSA, WVSA by no means provides an exhaustive list of all the soccer leagues that have existed in one form or another—and at one time or another—in the United States.[10] The total chaos and cacophony besetting this world could not be in starker contrast to the monopolistic organization and pyramidal structure of soccer's existence in most countries where the game maintained its preeminent cultural position throughout the twentieth century. To this monopolistic pyramid on the domestic level, one could add the global uniformity and total monopoly exacted and carefully policed by FIFA's ubiquitous power; soccer's institutional presence in the world could not be more different from its chaotic and haphazard structure in its 100-plus years in the United States. Organizationally speaking, the logic of American soccer has always much more resembled the quintessential business orientation of other American team sports—including the Big Three and hockey—than it has soccer's institutionalization in continental Europe, the British Isles, and Latin America. Simply put, while soccer and all other sports have had to be primarily profit oriented and commodified businesses in the United States, they assumed a much more etatist, para-public, and decommodified status in the countries where soccer was to dominate the sport space for the twentieth century. This bespeaks the primacy of the market in the United States as the main construct of most aspects of social life, including culture and sports, as well as the key role of the state in Europe and Latin America, especially in matters of culture and sports. Though soccer's organizational anarchy and instability have considerably changed in the United States since the middle of the 1990s (as discussed in chapter 5), it is probably true "that all of soccer in America will never be under the direction of one Association or Federation."[11] The country is simply too big, too diverse, too decentralized, and ruled by too strict a set of market-oriented and competition-encouraging antitrust laws to make such an all-encompassing and all-inclusive organizational pyramid possible.[12] This creates a built-in problem, since any and all soccer entities must still meet the approval of FIFA. As noted above, this is an alien concept to the popular construction of sports for most Americans.

Professional Soccer in the United States: A Few Highlights amid Domestic Disarray and International Marginality

Until the establishment of Major League Soccer (MLS) in 1996, it would be no exaggeration to argue that for over a century, very few Americans could ever earn a full-time living through the game of soccer in the United States. Moreover, it is also safe to say that with the exception of a few ephemeral periods that witnessed first-class professional soccer played on American soil almost exclusively by imported players (indeed, imported teams)—in addition to the "friendlies" played by visiting European and Latin American sides—the world's most popular team sport never reached beyond mediocrity, at best, on American soil. Confirmation of American soccer's marginality, even on the professional level, has been the fact that—again until the arrival of MLS—nearly all players, coaches, managers, administrators, and promoters had to hold "regular jobs," sometimes through affiliation with corporate sponsors, to make ends meet. The very best American professional soccer players might have earned a living wage by playing for different clubs in various formats—sometimes concurrently—in a wide range of locales, including overseas. Further bespeaking the amateur and haphazard nature of this professional world was that, typically, many of the better paydays emanated from "extra-curricular" exhibition matches that occurred apart from the competitive schedule of a given league or association. Until the advent of MLS, only a handful of American soccer players ever earned a regular form of remuneration equivalent to that of a Class A minor league baseball player. Hence, the term "professional" has to be understood quite generously when used in reference to much of soccer's history in the United States.

There were several overtly professional soccer ventures—some with legitimate qualifications for "the big time"—attempted in the United States. The first, a poorly planned venture on the part of some National League baseball owners in 1894, lasted less than three weeks. The most recent and, without a doubt, most solidly financed, committed, and organized, has been Major League Soccer, which began play in April of 1996. The century bracketed between these two ventures witnessed a wide array of associations and leagues that ranged in scope from the second American Soccer League—a mostly regional and ever-changing association, founded in the 1930s, which still exists on a continuing minor league level to this day—to the overambitious North American Soccer League (NASL), which lasted from the late 1960s until 1984 and experienced huge, but ultimately ephemeral, fanfare during the mid-1970s as a direct result of the relatively brief American career of the world's greatest soccer player of all time, the legendary Pelé.

The Ill-Conceived and Ill-Fated ALPFC

The first professional soccer league in America was established in the fall of 1894, only six years after the inauguration of the professional game in England, thereby making the United States—at least in terms of historical record—the second country in the world to witness professional soccer. Alas, from the very beginning of this venture, called the American League of Professional Football Clubs (ALPFC), organizational incompetence and avarice on the part of management permitted no institutional foundation upon which the game of soccer could build its American future. Owners of baseball's National League franchises in Baltimore, Boston, Brooklyn, New York, Philadelphia, and Washington, D.C., joined in a scheme to utilize professional soccer so as to attain revenue from their otherwise idle ballparks and managerial staff during baseball's off-season. Field managers and team names mirrored those of their baseball sponsors, while players were contracted away from teams in immigrant communities to fill the rosters; none of these players were native-born Americans. The exception was the Baltimore club, which hired eight top professional soccer players directly from Manchester, England, as well as an experienced soccer coach. The American League of Professional Football Clubs began play on 6 October 1894.[13]

The Baltimore team was by far the most successful on the field and at the gate, winning all of its games while drawing eight thousand enthusiastic spectators to its opener against the Washington, D.C. club. However, a 10–1 trouncing of Washington in a rematch raised the ire of both the other team owners and the *Washington Post*, which complained that Baltimore's players were direct British imports, among the best the "home of the Association game" had to offer.[14] This attracted the interest of United States immigration authorities, who launched an investigation that, along with public carping by the other clubs, created a "cloud that hung over" the embryonic league. Adding insult to injury, this incident not only tarnished soccer's image in an increasingly nativist America, but also caused quite a commotion back in England, where the defection of soccer stars to the disdained New World simply for purposes of higher pay was met with contempt and anger.[15]

In light of what is known about the business acumen and practices of the National League baseball owners of the day, it should come as no surprise that an attempt by half of them to establish a major league soccer venture was poorly conceived from start to finish and ended an abysmal failure. (It may be recalled from the last chapter that at this time [c.1890–1900], the owners of the National League were establishing a well-deserved reputation for fecklessness, incompetence, and greed that would lead to the successful challenge by the American League.) That the owners, their administrative staffs, and their baseball field managers knew next to nothing about soccer was reflected in the lack of anything resembling a comprehensive plan for the formation of teams, and in the lack of proper marketing and presentation of the sport to the local publics of the respective cities (with the possible exception of Baltimore). Though the admission fee of twenty-five cents (half the standard for NL baseball) was within reach of a good number of the American sports public, the ALPFC scheduled all of its games for weekdays, thus precluding the attendance of virtually all potential spectators who were most familiar with and appreciative of soccer: immigrants, almost all of whom, of course, had to be at work. Soccer matches on Saturday afternoons, accessible to the working public near the turn of the century, would have conflicted with college football, already immensely popular at this time. Whether or not this would have mattered regarding the attendance of immigrants at ALPFC matches was, apparently, not an issue for the owners. Given that all the players were foreign, it is most likely that the owners—with typical lack of aplomb—never gave a thought to the issue of conflicting class positions among spectating publics (i.e., whether immigrants would chase away more "respectable" spectators.)[16]

Prior to the first contests, the press had been enthusiastic about soccer and the creation of this league. After all, newspapers featuring the related preferences of Anglophilia and elitism—the *New York Times* in particular—still devoted the bulk of the editorial space in their sports pages to horse racing and the increasingly obscure cricket and polo, while barely tolerating baseball, ignoring boxing, and criticizing American football and those attending its games. These initially positive press reports failed to stimulate attendance for ALPFC matches, which, except for Baltimore, remained in the hundreds, dipping to "fewer than 100 fans" for New York's Polo Grounds on Thursday, October 18. By this time, the league's directors (unbeknownst to Baltimore's ownership and over the objections of the Washington club) had already decided to abandon their ill-fated venture. The final match of the ALPFC occurred in Baltimore on October 23 before a crowd of approximately six hundred.[17] Thereafter, America's first truly professional soccer league—and the world's second—disappeared into complete oblivion.

There can be little doubt that this abysmal organizational failure hurt soccer's chances to make its mark on America's sports culture. It is quite possible that soccer's subsequent trajectory in the United States might have been significantly more successful had the baseball owners of 1894 committed more thought, better planning, more professional execution, more skilled marketing, and—most important—more money to their soccer enterprise.[18] However, it would have required much greater patience and guile than these owners possessed, as evidenced by the poor management of their baseball interests. Additionally, a more committed approach would have required a direct appeal to—and likely identification with—immigrant communities in the midst of the overt nativism displayed by a sizable portion of the American public and the press in the 1890s, when anti-immigrant sentiments were commonplace.[19]

More significant, perhaps, was that the position of American football required, engendered, and solidified the subsequent development of the uniquely American genre of collegiate athletics. Any "top-down" process for soccer in the United States was, forever after, a very unlikely scenario, not least from the direction of committed professionalism in the 1890s. Football had already crowded out soccer from the sport space of the American middle classes, and it is therefore highly doubtful that soccer could have overcome the overriding tendency on the part of the American mass public—native born and immigrant alike—to adopt American bourgeois preferences and values. In short, it is not likely that soccer could have successfully competed with football, let alone displaced it as the autumn sport for the American masses, which football would eventually become. This path, though still underdeveloped, had clearly emerged by the 1890s, thus placing soccer in a difficult, though not necessarily hopeless, predicament.

Meantime, the promotion of what was already widely known as Britain's most popular sport—at a time when that country and its culture instilled a great ambivalence in many Americans—would likely have created some sort of backlash against soccer. The ALPFC owners' publicly stated rationale for abandoning their soccer venture was the desire not to compete with college football (which was expanding exponentially in America's sports culture in this period). A partisan public debate on the merits of the American version of football versus those of the Association game—tinged with a much higher degree of nativism and nationalism vis-à-vis the old colonial "Motherland" than that experienced by the "contest" between baseball and cricket a generation earlier—would likely have ensued if the ALPFC had persisted, with or without matches on Saturdays. This was the era, after all, that witnessed the organized effort to "prove" baseball's complete "Americanness" apart from any relations to British rounders, eventually enshrining the Doubleday myth.

In retrospect, it seems highly unlikely that soccer could have overcome all these formidable hurdles at this juncture in American history and thus enter America's collective sports culture for the twentieth century. That the point was moot, as far as the owners were concerned, was not for public consumption, as they stated their intention to resurrect professional soccer in the near future. They did not. In 1901 a plan for a professional soccer league based in such Midwestern cities as Chicago, St. Louis, Detroit, and Milwaukee appeared on the drawing board of Charles Comiskey, the legendary owner of the Chicago White Sox. This league was to be financed and managed by baseball owners of the upstart American League. Not surprisingly, the idea never materialized on account of inadequate financial backing for such a risky venture. We prefer to interpret the lack of money for soccer as a telling mirror of the zeitgeist, which was rather inimical regarding soccer's proliferation and firm establishment in the United States, precisely in those crucial twenty five years—1890–1915—when the game's foundations were laid in virtually every country where it was to dominate sports culture throughout the twentieth century. The Spanish-American War of 1898, as well as major labor unrest in New England and other mill districts at the turn of the century (which found thousands of newly arrived immigrants out of work in what would have constituted prime real estate for soccer's American home) further stacked the deck against soccer in America. "In fact the war and labor strife had a depressing effect on the entire soccer scene and stymied the progress of the American Football Association. The American Cup Competition, emblematic of the national soccer championship, was abandoned from 1899 to 1906."[20] To be sure, the organizational and managerial incompetence of the owners further exacerbated a bad situation, adding an institutional handicap to an already powerful historical one. Soccer's sad fate in those crucially significant formative years was seriously "overdetermined" in the United States.

More Organizational Chaos and the Missed Opportunity
of the First ASL

The first two decades of the new century witnessed an exacerbation of
the already chaotic and motley organizational framework that had come
to characterize soccer's institutional presence in the United States. This
era was typified by indistinct boundaries between amateurs and semiprofessionals, the absence of full-time professionals; and the continued identification by way of ethnicity in the formation of clubs and their followings,
as well as the perception of the game as separate from American sports
culture by both its practitioners and enthusiasts on the one hand and
the vast majority of the American public on the other. Aside from the
organizational turf wars, which (as noted) were only settled at the behest
of FIFA—thus creating a weak federation that, at least in principle, was
to exercise some officially sanctioned authority over parts of soccer in
America—the most significant development in this period was the corporate sponsorship and financing of several clubs, notably the aforementioned Bethlehem Steel, often featuring some of the best players recruited
directly from the British Isles (mostly Scotland). Most of these clubs were
the direct representatives of factories and mills, including the immigrant
workers of these firms as players and fans.[21]

Meantime, several semipro leagues and associations continued to exist,
mostly in New England and the mid-Atlantic states. An attempt to form
a professional league composed of the "best clubs in the East," in 1909,
lasted one season. The years preceding this effort saw several tours of the
United States by two top amateur all-star teams from England—Pilgrim
F.C. in 1905 and 1909, and the Corinthians in 1906 and 1911—which
helped spread the game to the college scene as a recreational alternative
to football, while also engendering the incentive to bring some sort of
comprehensive organization to the sport in the United States similar to the
way it was being institutionalized in many European and Latin American
countries at this time. A semiprofessional successor to the failed Eastern
League, known as the National League, was organized prior to World
War I, though—in typical American soccer fashion—this entity had split
into several sectional leagues by 1921.

Soccer continued to thrive in the St. Louis area, where a team of native-
born Americans, the Kensingtons, had emerged as the best in the city,
capable of regularly defeating teams of immigrants and foreigners. Other
clubs based in St. Louis—most significantly those composed largely or
wholly of native-born players—thrived locally, as did the St. Louis Professional League in the 1920s, experiencing relative success with spectators

and on the field against prominent clubs from other regions, including the top team from the newly formed American Soccer League in the first of two "championship matches" in 1925.[22]

The Roaring Twenties was a particularly auspicious time to give soccer one more chance to attain a substantial presence in America's sport space; all the more so, because in this "Golden Age of American Sports" this space expanded and its major participants reached a prominence in American culture heretofore unprecedented. Heroes such as Babe Ruth, Red Grange, and Jack Dempsey became American icons and helped catapult their respective sports way beyond the immediate confines of the ballpark or the arena wherein they occurred. Recall from the last chapter that this was exactly the time when American football entered the professional ranks in an organized, meaningful manner with the founding of the National Football League in 1920. Making matters for soccer's renewed effort at entering the "majors" all the more promising was the complete coincidence of the British football associations' four-year withdrawal from FIFA (in 1920, and lasting until 1924), thereby freeing many first-rate players to join clubs anywhere in the world, even in leagues and teams not necessarily FIFA approved. Enter the American Soccer League in 1921, a well-financed and well-organized professional soccer league anchored in eight such traditional soccer centers of the Northeast as Philadelphia, Jersey City, Pawtucket, Fall River, Harrison, Holyoke, New York, and Brooklyn and sporting a regular schedule of games to be played on Saturdays, Sundays, and holidays.[23] The ASL owed its existence to Thomas W. Cahill of St. Louis and New York City, a native-born soccer devotee who had been the executive secretary of the United States Soccer Football Association from its inception in 1913, and whose dream was to place soccer on a plane in the United States comparable with its standing in Britain and Europe and to establish the game as the national pastime for the baseball-free months of the fall, winter, and spring.[24]

Even though the usual instability of the initial stages of any American professional sport's league formation—tellingly, though, that of soccer in particular—befell the ASL in terms of continuous roster and franchise changes, the first few years were very promising. Far from fleeing this endeavor, financiers generously supported it, most notably Horace Stoneham of baseball's New York Giants, who sponsored an ASL franchise of that name. Along with the arrival of Bethlehem Steel F.C.—without a doubt the only American soccer club with any kind of pedigree and general name recognition—in the league for the start of the 1924–25 season, as well as respectable attendance figures, things appeared to look reasonably auspicious for soccer's future in America's sport space, perhaps for the very first time. The ASL expanded to twelve clubs for the 1924 season, while the aforementioned temporary withdrawal on the part of the British federations from FIFA, as well as the Irish Civil War, sent a wave of top players, mostly Irish and Scottish, to the league's teams. Additionally, tours by top teams from continental Europe would bring players of various non-British nationalities to the ASL, where they could earn better money than on the continent. This included players from the legendary all-Jewish Viennese Hakoah club that toured the United States as reigning Austrian champions in the spring of 1926 after having won the Austrian league championship of the 1924–25 season.[25] When Hakoah played a team of players combined from Indiana Flooring and the New York Giants at the Polo Grounds in New York City on 1 May 1926, the game attracted a crowd of forty-six thousand. This attendance figure—impressive by any country's soccer and sports standards—was the largest ever to watch a soccer game in the United States, a record that would stand until the glory days of the New York Cosmos of the North American Soccer League in the 1970s.[26] Several eminent soccer historians concur that some of the best soccer in the world was regularly played in the United States at the time, primarily in the ASL as part of its regular season, as well as in exhibitions that ASL teams and combined ASL all-stars would play against first-rate European touring clubs.[27]

At its zenith, the ASL experienced success at the gate as well, averaging around six thousand spectators in New York and even more in the New England locales, impressive numbers when viewed in the context of the cold winters of the eastern United States, which is when and where much of the ASL's season occurred. Except for the Red Grange phenomenon, the ASL was more successful in terms of attendance and press coverage than the then fledgling National Football League, a notion that seems nearly incredible from the vantage point of the different trajectories taken by soccer and football in the United States during the ensuing seven decades.[28] But, of course, football had a complete and long-established lock on the collegiate scene and thus a secure place in America's sport space.

The ASL garnered its most significant press coverage where it experienced its best crowds, which, alas, happened to be in its lesser, but all the more enthusiastic markets, such as Fall River. Media attention in the large markets of New York and Boston, though respectable and constant, never attained the prominence of the smaller ones. The success of the ASL in the 1920s belied one inherent weakness that would be duplicated fifty years later by the NASL: a dearth of native-born talent and, by extension, native-born fans. To be fair, there were a respectable number of ASL players who were native-born Americans, as well as many who had arrived in the United States as children and subsequently developed their soccer skills on American soil, such as Archie Stark, a prolific goal scorer who had immigrated to the United States from Scotland at the age of ten and was without any doubt the best soccer player in America during the 1920s.[29]

Though the ASL's spectatorship was overwhelmingly immigrant in composition and ethnic in orientation, the league had generally managed to attach club allegiance to geographic identifications—an important first step in the modernization of any team sport on its path toward attaining major league status—thus partly overcoming the ethnic insularity that has plagued soccer throughout its American experience (perhaps even today). In the wake of the economic expansion, media explosion, and cultural revolution of the 1920s, the ASL might have eventually rectified soccer's reliance on immigrants for both players and fans. Additionally, the severe restrictions on immigration to the United States at the time could also have required a response on the part of the league's management that might have helped in "Americanizing" the game. However, the traditional bickering and the destructive intraorganizational rivalries so typical of American soccer would not spare the ASL. Add the terrible calamity of the stock market crash in October 1929 and the ensuing Great Depression of the early 1930s, and soccer would once again become completely marginalized in the United States as a consequence of ineptitude endogenous to the soccer world's leadership, and bad luck exogenous to its control.

In 1928, as a likely attempt to garner national publicity for the league and attain legitimacy for soccer in the eyes of the American public, the owners of the ASL decided to emulate Major League Baseball by appointing Bill Cunningham, a nationally known sports columnist from the *Boston Morning Post* and a former All-American football player from Dartmouth College, as "National Commissioner" of the league. Unfortunately for the ASL—and all those with an interest in the fate of professional soccer in the United States—Cunningham knew little about the sport and most definitely even less about the arcane and internecine relations of its American organizational governance. Hence, the ASL exhibited a significant deficiency in its leadership when a usual skirmish with the USFA over what should have been a minor dispute led to what Jose correctly calls "the soccer war . . . that destroyed much of the progress that had been made over the past seven years."[30] At the heart of the dispute was the ASL's objection to the playing of games in United States Open Cup competition during the league season. Previously, the ASL had been temporarily suspended by the USFA in the 1924–25 season for refusing to allow its teams to enter the competition, as the league claimed that this disrupted its schedule and caused confusion. Now the ASL wanted the cup competition played at the end of the ASL season, or its teams exempt until the season was over. (However, one might suspect that in both instances the issue of revenue sharing with the USFA, as well as the perception that promoting and participating in Cup matches lessened the value

of ASL competition, were significant, though not publicly voiced, con-
cerns of the league.) The USFA refused and the league, in turn, ordered
its teams not to enter the competition, as it had done in 1924–25.[31] Three
successful franchises—the New York Giants, Bethlehem Steel, and the
Newark Skeeters—were suspended from the ASL after they had ignored
the league's ruling and opted to enter the Open Cup tournament. Cunningham, the ASL Commissioner, fined the renegade teams and suspended
all franchise privileges until they would agree to withdraw from Cup competition. On their part, the teams appealed to the USFA, whose president,
Armstrong Patterson, threatened the ASL with "drastic action" were it
not to revoke the penalties issued against the three teams. The ASL refused
to rescind its punitive action and was subsequently suspended by the
USFA, automatically depriving the league of FIFA sanction and recognition. The ASL was now an "outlaw" soccer league. It continued to play as
such, minus the three teams that now formed their own USFA-sanctioned
"official" league, called the Eastern Professional League, joined by five
other clubs, all of whom had a distinct ethnic flavor to their names—such
as the New York Hispano, New York Hungaria, New York Hakoah, and
Newark Portuguese—as well as in their followings and personnel. Meanwhile, citing infringement on its territory by this new entity, another soccer organization, the Southern New York State Association, sided with
the ASL and withdrew from the USFA. Talk of a new organizational challenge to the USFA, in alliance with the renewed British boycott of FIFA,
did not result in any action on the part of the ASL and its New York-
centered appendage.[32]

A "peace" was negotiated on 9 October 1929—just as the stock market
teetered on the precipice—but the damage had become irreversible. Both
leagues experienced constant fluctuations in teams during the middle of
the season. Some of these disappeared overnight, others changed cities or
switched leagues, as was the case with the New Bedford team that jumped
from the ASL to the Eastern Professional League late in the 1927–28 season. Suffice it to say that after seven years of relative stability, continuity,
and success, chaos once again became the regular modus operandi of soccer in the United States. Not surprisingly, the sport's most important financial backers in the United States—precisely those who would have
been crucial to maintaining a viable professional league as the Depression
unfolded, as well as giving soccer a chance to attain anything close to a
serious presence in America's sports culture—had withdrawn from this
disorganized scene in disgust. With its stability and legitimacy severely
impaired, and with most of its clubs and their followers suffering serious
financial hardship, the ASL would not recover. Foulds and Harris put it
best: "The American Soccer League prospered for almost a decade but
dissension, the impending depression of the 'thirties,' a lack of sufficient

foresight and a modicum of imagination spelled the end of a period of transition during which the United States seemed to be emerging as a major world soccer power."[33] At a juncture when soccer could have possibly taken off and become a major presence in America's sport space, the habitual internecine battles that had so handicapped soccer's evolution in the United States set it back for decades. Routinized professional soccer of first-division quality would not reappear in the United States until the 1970s, and never again in the autumn, forever after the undisputed prerogative of collegiate and, eventually, professional football.

America's "golden age of sport" of the 1920s might have furnished soccer with some sort of permanent niche in which to establish itself as a legitimate and major spectator entertainment for the broad American public. The undeniable, though still sporadic, success of the ASL in the 1920s could have conceivably provided the foothold necessary for the Americanization and proliferation of the sport on the professional level in the United States and its acceptance by the public beyond the marginalized province of "hyphenated Americans" and foreigners. Instead, the demise of the ASL of the 1920s highlights the ephemeral experience of soccer in the United States, and the self-destructive tendencies of those who purportedly sought to elevate the game's status in America from an immigrant activity to one of popular culture. The ASL's struggles and its final demise in 1931 augmented soccer's aura of obscurity for most Americans who—at least until the 1980s, possibly even the 1990s—continued to view soccer as the sport of foreigners, immigrants, school-children, and those student athletes as well as weekend "jocks" who saw themselves in some fashion "above," "not fit," or otherwise disinclined toward the homegrown North American sports of baseball, football, basketball, and ice hockey.

The Second ASL (ASL II): A Representative of America's Soccer History

The next attempt at a professional soccer league in the United States came soon after the ASL's demise in 1931. The so-called second American Soccer League began its existence two years later, though it had little in common with the first ASL besides the name. Generally limited to the Northeast until the 1970s, and playing from September through April until 1969 when the league adopted a spring/summer schedule, this second ASL could at best be called a minor league endeavor, in all senses of the term. Much closer to a semiprofessional association than to a professional sports league, this outfit managed to survive in various guises, with a variety of ever-changing franchises, virtually no serious financing, poor attendance, almost nonexistent promotion, and the habit of fielding ethnic-based teams that further guaranteed the league's obscurity to the American public. Similar to the semiprofessional baseball, football, and basketball teams that represented many athletic clubs in the late nineteenth and early twentieth centuries, ASL II franchises exhibited characteristics much closer to those of social clubs than professional sports organizations. Indeed, it might be misleading to call the second ASL a professional sports league, since virtually none of its players earned their living solely through ASL II competition; most played concurrently for various independent and regional clubs, while also working "regular jobs" away from soccer. For example, Walt Chyzowych, one of the most talented goal scorers of the 1960s and the star player with the ASL's Ukrainian Nationals, received three dollars for practices and six dollars for matches on Sundays.[34]

The second ASL was often beset by conflicts with other soccer organizations, most notably the German-American League in the New York area. Beginning in the 1950s, the two organizations engaged in a rivalry that fluctuated between petulant acrimony, which sometimes resulted in deliberate scheduling conflicts, to negotiations for merger, which briefly came to pass (in 1964) only to unceremoniously dissolve, conforming to the organizational history of American soccer. Making an already marginal life even more difficult for ASL II was its persistently rocky relationship with the USSFA, still the nominal body in charge of soccer's official FIFA-dictated sanctification in the United States. The machinations that lead to the eventual formation and ascension of the North American Soccer League (NASL) in the 1960s and 1970s brought the ASL to what was likely its nearest brush with extinction in its long history of marginal existence.

However, despite the dominant position attained by the NASL by the middle 1970s, ASL II was able to survive until 1983. In fact, under the leadership of Eugene Chyzowych (Walt's brother), ASL II actually expanded its operations into the Midwest "and changed from a club–conscious–type organization into a business-related sports enterprise."[35] In an effort to lend credence to this change of heart and to underscore the league's serious attempts to professionalize its image, garner more attention from the national sports media, and—most important—attract possible investors, the second ASL hired basketball legend Bob Cousy as its commissioner in 1974. Cousy held the job for five years during which ASL II expanded to the West Coast, for the first time converting what had been mainly an Eastern entity into a nationwide soccer league. Just like his predecessor, Bill Cunningham, commissioner of the "original" ASL in the 1920s, Cousy was a fine person with immense name recognition and a deep knowledge of mainstream American sports. Alas, like Cunningham, he knew little about soccer as a game, its culture, history, institutions, and traditions. But even if Cousy had been a knowledgeable "soccer man," it remains quite doubtful that he would have been able to turn this ill-fated entity into anything resembling a success. By the time Cousy became commissioner, ASL II faced formidable competition from an NASL that was riding its crest. Of the two leagues, the NASL clearly had the far better product, superior locations, sounder financial backing, more sophisticated marketing, and more extensive media coverage. Merger between the two leagues never went beyond the stage of speculation. But even without the presence of the NASL, it is quite certain that no man's abilities and aura—even those of Bob Cousy—could have altered the second ASL from what it had essentially always been: a semiprofessional outfit with an ever-changing lineup of regionally based clubs of varying quality, whose basis for team identification, though primarily ethnic for decades, had mutated to a postethnic mix in the course of the 1960s and 1970s based mainly on location, provided teams stayed put long enough to establish that kind of identity and allegiance in this world dominated by constant flux and instability.

ASL II went under in 1983, but a number of its teams joined the United Soccer League, which played until 1985. Its successor, ASL III, emerged in 1988 but soon merged with the Western Soccer Association (WSA) to form the American Professional Soccer League, which was subsequently absorbed by the USISL Select League that adopted the A-League name in 1996, the founding year of Major League Soccer (MLS). Remnants of ASL II exist as part of the A-League, thus—as will be discussed in chapter 5—forming an integral part of America's newly streamlined soccor establishment. While the second ASL represented a world of American soccer that in many ways has ceased to exist, the league's legacy continues by dint of having some of its teams participate in the newly constituted A-League.

There are three areas in which the second ASL's contributions to American soccer remain undeniable: the development of some fine players who represented the United States in international competition, the introduction of indoor soccer in 1939 (which engendered an enterprise four decades later that will be discussed in chapter 5) and of televised games in 1952, and the steady import for two decades of the world's finest club and national teams from Europe and Latin America for exhibition matches, thus offering the American public some soccer at its very best.

While the second ASL clearly could not match the overall quality of play routinely exhibited by its predecessor and namesake, it did sport a handful of superb individual players, some veterans of the first ASL and quite a few American born. First and foremost among these was William "Billy" Gonsalves, a native of Fall River, Massachusetts, and arguably the best American-born soccer player of all time, who also played for teams in semiprofessional leagues outside the ASL's purview. Earning a variety of nicknames in the course of his 27-year career, Gonsalves was often characterized as the "Babe Ruth of Soccer," an unsurpassable accolade in American sports, denoting the unique brilliance of his overall play as well as his uncanny ability to score goals, of which he amassed over a thousand.[36] Following Gonsalves's appearance with the American team at the second World Cup in Italy, he was not only received by the pope but was offered $10,000—an incredible sum at the time—to play for a number of Italian clubs. But Gonsalves opted to return to the United States, where he ended up winning a record eight National Challenge Cup championships with a variety of teams before concluding his career, appropriately, with Brooklyn Hispano of the second ASL.[37]

Other eminent ASL II players who performed ably with the American national team over the years included Walter Bahr, Harry Keough, John Souza, and Edward Souza. A Philadelphia native and one of the finest American-born halfbacks, Bahr had a long and outstanding club career and then turned to coaching soccer at Penn State.[38] Bahr's most important claim to fame in the small world of American soccer lore was his shot that hit the English goal's right post and then bounced back to Joseph Gaetjens, who then scored the American goal (a diving header) in the game against England in the 1950 World Cup, still the biggest upset in World Cup history (see below). Bahr's sons, Chris and Matt, were also fine soccer players, but both attained much greater fame and fortune as place kickers in the NFL. Keough, a St. Louis native, followed his illustrious playing career by proceeding to win five national titles as head coach of St. Louis University's soccer program. Though unrelated to each other, the Souza boys—John and Edward—both hailed from Fall River, where they further enhanced that town's already considerable soccer reputation by their attractive and effective play over many years.

In October 1952, local station WPIX in New York televised several ASL doubleheaders from Yankee Stadium, soccer's first exposure on American television.[39] Poor attendance at the games and even poorer viewership in front of television sets put a quick end to this ill-fated experience. Still, soccer had appeared pretty much simultaneously with the major forces of baseball, football, basketball, and hockey in the forum that was soon to become far and away the most eminent in the dissemination and reproduction of America's sports culture for the remainder of the twentieth century and beyond.

Another arguably even more important legacy that the ASL bequeathed to soccer's existence in the United States, was its frequent and continuous import of top-flight foreign clubs and national sides for "friendlies" with ASL II teams, ASL II all-stars, and, perhaps most important, for matches among these visitors themselves, thus giving American audiences the opportunity to enjoy world-class soccer in the United States. Beginning in 1946, with a visit by Liverpool FC (a famous English team that was to return three times for such occasions), ASL II sponsored exhibition matches on such hallowed baseball grounds in New York as Ebbets Field, Yankee Stadium, and the Polo Grounds. One of the best matches of that era was played under the floodlights at Ebbets Field on 15 June 1948 when Liverpool defeated Djugaardens of Sweden in a 3–2 thriller that was billed as the very first encounter between two top-tiered foreign teams on American soil.[40]

Throughout the 1950s, an average of six foreign teams a year came to the United States to take part in similar events, among them clubs with pedigrees such as Real Madrid, Manchester United, Celtic Glasgow, Rapid Wien, and Vasco da Gama from Rio di Janeiro. On 12 May 1957, a game between Hapoel of Israel and an ASL All-Star team attracted 22,609 spectators to Brooklyn's Ebbets Field, many of whom presumably came to see Marilyn Monroe perform the honorary kickoff to a game that was in part a fund-raiser for Israel.[41] In 1958 at Downing Stadium on Randalls Island (which had become a somewhat regular venue for such matches), Liverpool FC and the German club 1.FC Nürnberg played before twenty-three thousand fans. These sorts of matches brought top quality soccer to New York City as well as some other places in the United States through the 1950s and early 1960s, though the ethnic angle remained a major component of the events. These matches demonstrated that soccer—when played at its highest level—was capable of drawing significant numbers of American spectators while earning good revenue for the promoters. In 1965 ASL II staged three well-organized major soccer events in New York that were to prove significant for the near future of soccer in America. In June, AC Milan, one of the most pedigreed clubs in Italy and the world, played the Brazilian team Santos FC at Downing Stadium with twenty-five thousand fans in attendance. In August, thirty thousand people returned to that very same venue to revisit Santos, which now opposed Benfica from Lisbon. And one month later—this time at Yankee Stadium—41,598 soccer fans came to see Santos perform yet again. The Brazilians' opponent was Inter Milan, AC Milan's bitter crosstown rival, and a club of equal prominence and excellence.[42] These three clubs were the very best that Europe had to offer at the time, with Benfica having won the European Champions League Cup in 1961 and 1962, AC Milan being its successor in 1963, followed by Inter Milan in 1964 and 1965. These teams boasted some of the world's finest players, such as Eusebio (Benfica) (often called the European Pelé), Gianni Rivera (AC Milan), and Sandro Mazzolla (Inter Milan).[43] But far and away the greatest attraction in all three events was Santos's superstar, Pelé, who at the time was without any doubt the finest soccer player in the world and, above all, the only global soccer star with genuinely broad name recognition among American sports fans. Pelé's appearances at these three matches in 1965 paved the way for his subsequent recruitment by the New York Cosmos of the North American Soccer League nine years later, an event that would give a boost to soccer in the United States and provide something of a lasting legacy.

The success of ASL II in presenting foreign teams to American spectators engendered the creation of a venture based on a similar concept. The International Soccer League, initially affiliated with ASL II and beginning play in 1960, was the brainchild and vehicle of William Cox, a former owner of the Philadelphia Phillies of baseball's National League. Cox conceived of a setup whereby eleven teams from overseas and one team of American "all stars" would compete in a league for an eventual champion. The teams that Cox brought from overseas—like West Ham United of London and Dukla Prague—were by no means top quality, but they were most certainly respectable and usually on an upward trajectory in their home leagues.[44] The International Soccer League played most of its games at New York's Polo Grounds, consistently showing attendance in "the five figures."[45] Despite poor organization, the ISL "was still incomparably better than anything the local ethnic leagues had to offer." The ISL lasted until 1965, at which point, arguably for the very first time in America's soccer history, the sport had garnered the serious interest of truly wealthy businessmen who were keen to invest in it.[46] The story and outcome of this venture are discussed in chapter 5.

The United States in World Cup Competition through 1950

Bill Gonsalves anchored the American team that participated in the very first World Cup, held in Montevideo, Uruguay, in July 1930. Though this tournament featured only thirteen teams, the Americans proved rather successful by first impressively beating a strong Belgian side, 3–0, and then defeating Paraguay four days later by the same score, with Bert Patenaude, Gonsalves's teammate from the Fall River Marksmen, scoring all three goals. (Indeed, Patenaude was the first player ever to score a hat trick in a World Cup tournament.) These impressive wins put the United States into the semifinals, in which an injury-plagued American team (down to eight fit men in the second half) lost to the eventual runner-up, Argentina, 6–1.[47] Of the sixteen-man roster comprising this team, ten players were American born, five originally hailed from Scotland, and one from England. With the American national team performing respectably on the international scene, the failure to include soccer in the 1932 Olympic games at Los Angeles was yet another significant setback for the progress of the game in the United States. Exposure at such an internationally visible and prestigious venue on American soil—with the home team having a good chance of playing well, perhaps even attaining a medal—might have sparked the dormant plug of nationalism and created an interest in soccer on the part of an otherwise apathetic public.[48] In May 1934 the second World Cup in Rome saw the United States defeat Mexico, 4–2, in the opening game (which was technically not yet part of the competition but a qualifier for it). But the Americans were subsequently relegated from the tournament by a humiliating 7–1 loss to the tournament host and eventual champion, Italy. No American team attended the third World Cup, held in France in 1938 (won yet again by Italy), and the tournament was not held in 1942 and 1946 on account of World War II; the fourth World Cup was played in Brazil in 1950.

Four of ASL II players noted above—Walter Bahr, Harry Keough, John and Edward Souza—were members of an American national team that was to make soccer history on the global level at this fourth World Cup tournament. However, quite representative of soccer's complete marginalization in the United States, this event made headlines virtually everywhere in the world except the United States, where it was barely noticed, if at all. We are of course referring to the miraculous American upset victory over mighty England in Belo Horizonte on 29 June 1950. This event received such low attention on the part of the American public that no American newspaper other than the *St. Louis Post-Dispatch* sent a reporter to cover it. Dent McSkimming, the only American reporter among over four hundred sportswriters from all over the world covering the event could only travel to Brazil by paying all expenses out of his own pocket.[49] The Americans lost their first game to Spain, 3–1. Next up was mighty England, which had finally settled all its disputes with FIFA and was contesting its very first World Cup (after opting to stay out of the first three) as one of the heavy favorites (together with host Brazil and neighboring Uruguay). The English team, sporting such soccer greats as Billy Wright, Alf Ramsey, Tom Finney, Stan Mortenson, and the legendary Stanley Mathews had just demolished Italy, 4–0, after humiliating Portugal, 10–0, in preparation for the tournament. Indeed, the English were so confident of an easy victory over the lowly "Yanks" that their manager, Walter Winterbottom, decided to leave Mathews in Rio de Janeiro so as to spare the superstar the tiring journey to Belo Horizonte and thus save his energy for future, more exacting games. The English players and English public, as well as the entire soccer world, presumed the American team—a pushover for the powerful English side. Yet, the Americans walked away with a 1–0 victory that continues to stand as the most unanticipated result in World Cup history (even more than West Germany's comeback victory against a hugely favored Hungarian team—the famed "arany csapat" [golden team]—in the 1954 World Cup final in Bern, Swit-zerland).[50] Sadly for the American players, their immense accomplishment of relegating the heavily favored English from the tournament remained largely unknown by the American public, let alone appreciated. Even such internationally minded papers of record as the New York Times men-tioned this event only in a short story obscurely buried on the fourth page of its sports section. Adding insult to injury was the fact that in the soccer countries where this amazing achievement could have been appreciated, it was not. False accusations that most of the American players were in actuality not Americans were widely circulated—especially in the English press, but elsewhere as well—and believed. This was simply a misrepre-sentation that tarnished the American team's accomplishment, since only three players—Edward McIlvenny (a Scotsman); Joseph Maca (a Bel-gian); and Joseph Gaetjens (a Haitian), the goal scorer—were not Ameri-can citizens; they were American resident aliens, a perfectly acceptable and FIFA-sanctioned status for international play at the time.[51] While underdogs are always the darlings of the world, the overall power and political might of the United States simply preclude that any of its repre-sentatives—even its weak soccer team—be accorded this affect and ap-preciation. Instead, their achievements are habitually met with derision, suspicion, and disdain.

Still Another Exceptionalism: Soccer at American Colleges and Universities

Conforming to the chaotic nature of soccer's existence in the United States, it is important to note that the sport has enjoyed an institutional presence at America's colleges and universities at all times completely in-dependent of any other soccer organization in the United States and, in-deed, the rest of the planet (which almost always means that guided and/or sanctioned by FIFA). In other words, soccer at America's institutions of higher learning represents a world unto itself, with its own rules, regu-lations, and norms, as well as formal and informal values. These have not only been quite different from those of the other two soccer worlds just noted, but have indeed greatly contributed to the "Balkanization" of soc-cer in America and—so our argument—have impeded its development, both in terms of its quality on the field and in its presence in society and culture. While there have been certain changes since the advent of MLS in terms of trying to integrate the separate world of college soccer into that of America's premier professional soccer league, soccer at Ameri-ca's universities still remains an entity all its own, just as it was when it first appeared on the nation's campuses at the beginning of the twentieth century.

As we left off in the middle of the last chapter, once the "running game" had solidly triumphed over the kicking version of football on the American college scene in the 1870s, soccer disappeared from American campuses until 1902. At that time, amid a rising criticism of American football for being too rough and causing too many injuries, a few wealthy Philadelphia-area secondary schools as well as Haverford College began fielding teams and playing games in the Philadelphia Cricket Club League. Recall that it was during this time—in 1905 to be precise—that the escalating brutality in football had led President Theodore Roosevelt to threaten to ban it from the nation's campuses. The wealthy secondary schools that had begun to play soccer initially did so after prohibiting their students from playing what they preferred to call "American rugby." This certainly did not help soccer's reputation, as it provided Americans yet another negative view of the sport: a game for those too elite and/or effete to play the "manly" (and dangerous) game of football.

Although the hope among soccer enthusiasts that college authorities would elevate their game to a place of prominence on college campuses never materialized, football's temporary crisis of legitimacy and the renewed—though limited—interest in soccer did lead to the creation of the Intercollegiate Soccer League in 1906, to which Columbia, Cornell, Harvard, Haverford, and the University of Pennsylvania belonged. Until 1914 the league played its games in the early spring in order to avoid competing directly with football and baseball. Thereafter, all matches were played in the fall, as they have been in college soccer to this day.[52]

By 1910 soccer had also emerged at Midwestern colleges and even reached the West Coast, where the University of California, Berkeley, defeated Stanford, 1–0, in a match in which the teams of both schools were composed mostly of foreigners. These early years revealed a pattern of sporadic growth in college soccer: "Soccer could live or die at any institution depending on whether one man or a group of students pushed for its acceptance, whether they remained zealots or eventually departed. Soccer still was lacking a solid foundation at this time." While the game appeared at one college, it disappeared at another where it had already been played. Thus, for example, "as quickly as it came, soccer was forgotten in Minnesota, passing like a comet. At Columbia, the sport was dropped because of a lack of a playing field."[53]

The overall rationalization and modernization of American sports during the 1920s also reached college soccer, as in the course of the decade it developed into a regular team sport on most of the nation's better-known campuses. By 1926 there were two college conferences for soccer. This number had increased to six by 1936, eight by 1954, and ten by

1959, when the NCAA inaugurated its championship tournament for soccer. The massive growth of college soccer as an integral part of college athletics began after World War II: Whereas in 1946 there were 86 colleges in the United States playing the sport in an organized manner, the number had mushroomed to almost one thousand by 1978, with the current figure at nearly twelve hundred—more than the number of colleges offering American football as a varsity sport.[54]

With very few exceptions, soccer at the college level attracted very few spectators and drew minor interest on campus. Soccer was generally viewed as a recreational activity that could be enhanced through interschool competition, and an alternative for those students who might not have had the athletic skills or physical size—or both—required for football and basketball. Simply put, college soccer never attracted the most athletically gifted students since its status as an activity never attained the aura of culture that football and basketball had so long enjoyed in American campus life. Many who played soccer did so only as a way to remain active and have some fun in the off-season of the sport of their first choice. Soccer was often the game for the football and basketball rejects, those whose athletic ability or size simply did not enable them to make those more exalted squads. Moreover, soccer players attained the image on campus of being either foreign, aloof, snobby, or simply odd. Though soccer had become much more popular with spectators on some campuses in the course of the 1990s than it ever used to be, it is still—at best—on the level of volleyball, lacrosse, and wrestling, nowhere near the status of football and basketball.

By the 1960s, colleges were regularly awarding athletic scholarships in the sport, and some developed into real powerhouses. The most notable have been St. Louis University (which won the NCAA title a record ten times in the 1960s and 1970s), the University of San Francisco (winner of four NCAA titles), Indiana University, the University of Connecticut, the University of Southern Illinois–Edwardsville, and Hartwick College. The University of Virginia dominated college soccer in the first half of the 1990s under the brilliant coaching of Bruce Arena, who would later lead D.C. United to the first three MLS championship games (winning the first two in 1996 and 1997, losing the third in 1998) before becoming head coach of the United States national team in 1998.

By the 1970s, a few college players were being touted as good enough to play in the North American Soccer League, the first true upper division major league in American soccer since the demise of the first ASL in 1931. Alas, most were not. However, in the years to follow, American colleges did produce some players who have been sufficiently skilled to play, on occasion, for first-division teams in Europe. Among these have been Tab Ramos, John Harkes, Eric Wynalda, Claudio Reyna, Alexi Lalas, John

O'Brien, Landon Donovan, Brad Friedel, and Kasey Keller, the core of
the U.S. World Cup squads for the 1994 and 1998 tournaments, as well
as the most recognized American players in MLS. With the possible exception of the goalies Friedel and Keller, who had assumed leading roles for
one solid (Leicester City) and one outstanding (Liverpool) club of England's Premier League before—in Keller's case—becoming one of the
best goalies in Spain's top division, Claudio Reyna's becoming a fixture
with Glasgow Rangers, and John Harkes's making three appearances on
the hallowed pitch of Wembly, most American players were little more
than journeymen on their respective teams, most of which were of average
quality, with little chance of winning either a league championship or
national cup, let alone anything on the international level. America's 1990
World Cup team—composed almost exclusively of college players and
coached by Bob Gansler, an NCAA man with no coaching experience at
the time outside the world of college soccer—was woefully outclassed by
its opposition of Italy, Austria, and Czechoslovakia, respectively, whose
victories over the American team would not even begin to capture the gap
separating American college all-stars from the skills and experience of
top-level professional teams in Europe and Latin America.

There are a number of reasons that college soccer—as presently constituted, in full conformity with its tradition and the rules imposed on it by
the NCAA—will not lend itself to produce American players capable of
attaining the skills and experience necessary to be competitive at the
sport's premier professional level. Moreover, we also believe that the very
structure of college soccer still remains a serious impediment to the overall
improvement of American soccer as a whole. Here are some of the factors:

The college season: Simply put, the biggest handicap that American
college players have in acquiring and developing the necessary skills for
the professional level is the brevity of the scholastic playing season. Current NCAA rules prohibit the playing of any competitive contests in a
sport out of its designated season at the Division I, I-A, and II levels. (Yet,
a student athlete may participate in a second or third sport during the off-
season of a first.) Hence, all NCAA soccer is played only in autumn, with
a typical schedule of about twenty-five games over a three-month period.
Additionally, NCAA rules stipulate that a student athlete loses eligibility
(usually including athletic scholarship) in a sport if he participates in that
sport at any professional level. (Though, interestingly, an athlete may be
a professional in one sport and still retain college eligibility in another.
More than a few college football and basketball players, such as John
Elway [Stanford], Danny Ainge [Brigham Young], and Drew Henson
[Michigan], have played professional baseball during the summer breaks
of their NCAA careers.) This precludes soccer-playing student athletes
from honing their skills in the summer and/or during school breaks

through higher-level competition. Hence, the short NCAA-imposed fall season has two drawbacks: It precludes the yearlong steady competition required to improve one's soccer abilities to levels of international excellence, something that simply cannot be replaced by practice, no matter how thorough and conscientious; and it exacts such a large number of games in so short a time—a minimum of two games per week on average, often more—so that, with practice and travel, the players are under constant physical pressure and thus exposed to a high risk of injury.[55]

The college rules: Since college soccer represents a world all to itself, apart from FIFA and the USSF and only beholden to the NCAA, it has adopted rules that have been all its own, not conforming to those of the FIFA-sanctioned global game. For example, it was not until the 1972 season that the NCAA switched to two 45-minute halves from the previous method of playing four 22-minute quarters. While this particular NCAA rule had no tangible effect on the development of the game's actual quality as played in American colleges and merely served to highlight the independent ways of the NCAA and its realm in American university sports, another rule—namely that of unlimited substitutions during a game—most certainly did, in our opinion. Concretely, NCAA rules allow, with some restrictions, players to leave and return in the course of any contest. The basic idea behind this rule was to render the game more aggressive and exciting—above all, to increase the number of goals—by not permitting fatigue to slow the action on the field. Yet, the net effect has been that physical prowess, speed, and conditioning have been consistently favored over ball handling and the overall sense of the game that comes with playing entire contests. With few players allowed to play complete games, and by relying on athletic ability over a general "feel" for the game, college soccer has consistently emphasized technique, athleticism, and patterned (i.e., "learned") play over improvisation and a certain playfulness that cannot be taught in a systematic manner, but can only be acquired on the field itself. The generous substitution allowed by NCAA rules also fosters a culture of specialization that has become an integral part of the set-patterned system of American football, but has always been somewhat alien to the much more fluid and improvised nature of soccer. In a way, our objection to college soccer is somewhat unfair because what we bemoan is, in fact, its complete reliance on athletic activity instead of on an expression of cultural tradition. But with the latter mostly absent in American soccer, it should come as no surprise that there has been an excessive emphasis on the former at all levels of the game, though most prominently at the collegiate one. This brings us to a discussion of another reason that in our opinion renders college soccer not so much inferior but just different from soccer played in leagues around the world.

The college coaches: Very few college coaches have hailed from the world of professional soccer, and fewer still have played the game at a level performed by the top leagues and teams in the world. Indeed, signaling the college game's American insularity has been that very few of the NCAA-licensed coaches have hailed from Europe or Latin America. Americans such as Walter Bahr, Harry Keough, and Bruce Arena have been few and far between, with the result that American college players are rarely, if ever, coached by former soccer greats or simply players with experience in countries such as Germany, Italy, England, Argentina, or Brazil, or even in less prominent soccer countries such as Austria, Bulgaria, Peru, or Portugal. So it is not surprising that most American college coaches compensate their deficient cultural feel for the game with excessive emphasis on "play book" soccer dominated by athleticism and learned mechanics.[56]

The very existence of colleges per se as major loci of sports in America: While football and basketball have thrived through college athletics as a particular expression of American exceptionalism (as demonstrated and discussed in the previous chapter), soccer's marginality in this sphere will, in our view, continue to impede its progress toward attaining a status approaching that of the Big Three and One-Half in the United States. It is universally accepted that the years of age between eighteen and twenty-two are totally critical in the development of skills necessary for playing soccer at its highest level. Spending those years in NCAA soccer simply does not suffice for establishing those skills. Indeed, for the aforementioned reasons, we believe that college-level soccer actively hinders instead of fosters the experience and playing competence necessary to perform at the game's premier level. After graduating high school, high-caliber soccer players faced with the choice between a free college education or rolling the dice on a career in professional soccer have, for reasons of pragmatic self-interest, opted for the former. Until there is enough bonus money available to make the latter choice worthwhile for much of the best young American soccer talent—as has been the case with professional baseball, football, basketball, and hockey—as well as the creation of organized venues similar to baseball's farm system, hockey's junior club system, or the intricate and deliberate pyramidlike network of the European clubs (that weans players from their childhood onto the professional level), elevating the skills of a large number of American players to "first division levels" will remain an elusive endeavor. Additionally, the NCAA's continued refusal to change eligibility restrictions as well as to allow for a spring soccer schedule in addition to the one in the fall, will significantly contribute to soccer's marginality in America's sport space. Unlike in the culturally dominant sports such as football and basketball, where the college and the professional tracks have furnished a smooth continuous line, the tracks have remained virtually incompatible and mutually exclusive in soccer.[57] A promising young American soccer player has had to choose between one or the other. Until the upper echelon of American high school players are somehow accorded the possibility of attaining both a college education and a professional soccer career (as has been the case with football and basketball, but also increasingly with baseball and hockey), the game of soccer will continue to experience a dearth of top-flight American players. Hence, it will continue to be limited in its appeal to the American public by lack of identifiable American heroes in what is still, for most Americans, a peculiar and somewhat unfamiliar game, and/or a game that presents a boring low quality of play. And that was precisely the catch-22 that hastened the demise of the NASL (as we will argue in chapter 5).

There are two further points, which we deem relevant to our presentation of soccer at American universities, that we will discuss in chapter 5: The first pertains to an immense success story for American colleges. We are, of course, referring to the phenomenal advance of women's soccer in the United States, quite arguably the very finest in the world in whose development the colleges have been totally central. The second relates to the so-called Project 40, begun in 1996–97 at the behest of MLS precisely to counter the inevitable bifurcation between a college education and the uncertainty of a professional soccer career that all eighteen-year-old soccer talents have had to confront. For the very first time, an organizational mechanism has been put into place in the United States that is explicitly designed to eliminate this stultifying dead end.

Four ....

The Formation and Rearrangement of the American Sport Space in the Second Half of the Twentieth Century

ABOVE ALL other factors, there are four key developments that defined and shaped the American cultural sport space in the second half of the twentieth century: modern and mature organizational stability, racial integration, geographic and franchise expansion, and, most important, the ubiquitous presence and effect of television. The first development noted here—the maturity of modern sports leagues in terms of their political economy—meant that the professional venues of the Big Three and One-Half had all achieved a level of stability that ensured their permanent existence and modern institutionalization.[1] Major League Baseball had attained this level of economic and institutional maturity by 1903, when its organizational framework became set; no franchise in either the National or American League has since ceased to exist (though some might relocate). Since at least the early 1950s, the same could be said of the teams in the NFL, NBA, and NHL; the only exceptions are teams in leagues that would seek to challenge the hegemony of the established entities in their respective sports. One of these challengers would prove immensely successful: In the 1960s, the American Football League ensured the survival and permanence of all its franchises by successfully forcing a merger with the NFL. Other challengers, such as the All-American Football Conference, the American Basketball Association, and the World Hockey League, attained some success as a few of the teams from these now defunct enterprises were incorporated into their more established rivals. Two challengers to the NFL in the 1970s and 1980s, the World Football League and the United States Football League, would completely fail and all their teams vanish. It goes without saying that no soccer league in the United States had ever attained this level of maturity and stability until, apparently (as of mid 2000), the advent of Major League Soccer.

The breakdown of "color lines" in the professional Big Three began immediately after World War II, a process essentially complete—at least on the playing fields and in the locker rooms—by the mid-1960s. (The NHL has been open to players of all races since at least that time, but there have been only a few black professional hockey players.) The last barrier to the complete participation of African Americans (and all other minorities) in American team sports fell in 1966, after an all-white University of Kentucky basketball squad was defeated by an all-black team representing Texas Western University in that season's NCAA finals. From that point forward, no serious athletic program at the college level could fail to recruit black athletes. Soccer in the United States has historically experienced a dearth of African American players and spectators. However, the case of hockey demonstrates that this is not a fatal deficiency, just a handicap (though hockey, as "the sport of white guys," might attain some tangential benefit in terms of the interest and identification on the part of some of its core American spectatorship by dint of this unintentional feature of the game's milieu and culture). The lack of African American participants in soccer is examined in the context of participation and recreation in the next chapter.

Two other major changes in American sports were direct functions of technological advances: The introduction of coast-to-coast commercial airline travel allowed the location of professional major league franchises in any American geographic market that team and/or league management deemed profitable, large enough, and/or worthy (most significantly, those on the West Coast and in the Southwest). Initially, the advent of television substantially affected all out-of-home activities in the United States: Restaurants, night clubs, stage and movie theaters, concert and dance halls, and amusement parks all experienced substantial losses in patrons and revenue. Television also brought about the demise of another longtime institution of American entertainment and culture: vaudeville. The use of television in presenting sports to the public would result in numerous changes in the ways each of the Big Three and One-Half operated and how each was perceived by the public. Television changed American (indeed, the world's) culture so intrinsically, that this is easily taken for granted. Ultimately, since at least the 1960s, it is television that has determined the presentation and perception of a major sport in the United States, its financial success, as well as its popularity and position within the American sport space.

Since the 1950s, sport spectatorship for most Americans has usually meant time spent in front of a television, and it is within this realm that soccer is at a distinct disadvantage vis-à-vis the Big Three and One-Half. From the point of view of television networks and stations, and their advertising clients, the continuous play of a soccer game is an impediment to the routinization of the sport as television programming (as opposed to a "big event" like the World Cup). Unlike games in each of the Big Three and One-Half—wherein opportunities for commercials exist within the ebb and flow of the contest (such as the time between innings and half-innings in baseball, and time-outs, as well as intermissions between quarters, halves, and/or periods in football, basketball, and hockey) or can be imposed (i.e., "television time-outs")—a soccer match provides no such opportunities, save for intermission at the half, generally the least desirable time for an advertiser in basketball or football. Except for those directed at Spanish-speaking audiences, few television (or radio) networks and stations or advertising agencies can attain the same level of revenue from regular broadcasts of soccer games—wherein most advertising is limited to the display of a company or product "logo" in the corner of the picture and/or its verbal mentioning by the announcer as in, "this portion of the game is brought to you by product X or company Y"—as that gained by running a series of thirty- or sixty-second commercial spots during regular entertainment and news programming, as well as in sport telecasts besides soccer.

From the perspective of a typical American television sports viewer, many of the obstacles to watching soccer derive from its lack of familiarity (though this matters little to the viewer not knowledgeable regarding the game who simply finds it boring to watch on television). As in other team sports on television, some degree of knowledge on the part of the viewer is necessary, so as to presume and/or anticipate the position of players and action off camera. But with players spread out all over its large field, soccer faces a greater deficiency in this context than any of the Big Three. Quite simply, soccer (like hockey, which has experienced its own problems with television) does not translate from in-person spectatorship to the small screen as well as basketball, baseball, and football. Indeed, in some ways, watching these latter sports on television can sometimes be preferable to a seat (especially a poor one) in the stadium or arena, at least in terms of getting a better view of the action. Few would ever make this claim about soccer.

This chapter examines the critical junctures experienced by the Big Three and One-Half in the second half of the twentieth century that have formed the modern American sport space. As with chapter 2, it is not our intention to present a full history of these sports (as there are many works by fine sports historians that do so). Rather, we seek to provide the contextual and comparative basis to further explain soccer's continued marginalization in the American cultural sport space. Hence, this chapter highlights some of the key junctures and features that defined the evolution of that space, particularly in terms of the developments noted above (institutional and organizational maturity, racial integration, geographic and franchise expansion, and, most important, television) as well as some related outgrowths, notably the rise in player salaries and the establishment of player free agency, and some changes on the field, court, or ice. Professional football ascended to the primary position in American sports culture in the second half of the twentieth century, while basketball also ascended and baseball declined. Above all, it was the advent of television that was most instrumental in this reorganization of the American sport space, and television that continues to define this space. Ultimately, the success or failure of soccer to attain the level of culture in the United States will be determined by and on television.

Baseball and the "New Order"

The conclusion of World War II brought the issue of segregation in American sports—baseball in particular—to national prominence. That an African American could risk his life for his country in war, yet was prohibited from participating with whites on an equal footing on the sports field seemed to many a cruel injustice. In particular it was Branch Rickey, the general manager of the Brooklyn Dodgers, who felt so strongly about righting this wrong that he proceeded to sign players from the Negro Leagues. Rickey found an ally in Happy Chandler, the former governor of Kentucky, who had succeeded Landis as commissioner of baseball after the judge's death in 1945. Despite a vocal and vigorous opposition by many in and out of baseball, Chandler supported Rickey's decision to sign Jackie Robinson, a gifted athlete, though not necessarily the most accomplished player of the Negro Leagues.[2] Robinson first played for the Dodgers' top farm team, the Montreal Royals, in the 1946 baseball season, and then made his major league debut on opening day the following year. Fortunately, Robinson excelled on the diamond even beyond Rickey's expectations, winning that season's Rookie of the Year award (the very first such award in the history of the game) and the hearts and minds of the fabled "bums" on the field and in the stands of Brooklyn's Ebbets Field. Robinson's accomplishments—all the more phenomenal because he had to perform in an environment of extreme hostility and hatred perpetually directed his way—proved to the American public that African Americans were indeed worthy of inclusion in organized baseball and could compete on an equal footing with the very best white players at the game's highest level.

In retrospect, the story of Jackie Robinson could rightly be seen as the inauguration of the modern civil rights movement in American society; many have since called it "baseball's finest hour." Following Robinson, Larry Doby debuted in the outfield for the Chicago White Sox later in the 1947 season to become the first black to play in the American League. To be sure, the floodgates of integration did not immediately open wide for African Americans in organized baseball, but a defining moment had occurred, a precedent had been set—a critical juncture that was to change the racial composition of America's leading sport institution, irrevocably paving the way for a major shift in American culture as a whole. Robinson and Doby were soon followed by Satchel Paige, Roy Campanella, Willie Mays, Henry Aaron, Ernie Banks, and many others who would change the institution and culture of baseball forever. The last club to sign a black player was the Boston Red Sox, in 1958, by which time the National Negro League had ceased to exist.

Nineteen fifty-eight also witnessed the sudden departure of the Giants and Dodgers from New York and their relocation to San Francisco and Los Angeles, respectively. This move not only deprived New York—however temporarily—of a National League presence, but it also heralded the true nationalization of baseball by dint of its presence on a major league level in California, about to become the nation's most populous state.

Above all, the fifties witnessed the arrival of the medium that was to revolutionize sport culture in the United States and the world. Television nationalized American sport culture and transformed it to a degree unimaginable before the 1950s, causing a major rearrangement of the American sport space whereby baseball was to lose its long-held preeminence to football. The World Series was first televised nationally in 1947, making an immediate impact as crowds gathered in public places across the nation to watch the games. By 1950 most baseball clubs were regularly televising games locally, though it would take Federal passage of the Sports Broadcasting Act in 1961 to allow routine national broadcasts by NBC of the *Game of the Week* (which attained solid ratings). Meantime, major league baseball had landed a firm and lucrative national television contract that included the World Series.[3] Television was to change baseball as an institution and culture in the following two decisive ways. First, it devastated the minor leagues, as fans in formerly lucrative minor league markets stayed home to watch televised games of the majors (or regular television programming). By the middle of the 1950s, over half of the minor league teams had folded and very few that remained could operate independent of major league sponsorship. The Pacific Coast League, perhaps the most successful minor league since Ban Johnson's old Western League, saw its status as the premier baseball venue west of the Mississippi disappear as part of the game's nationalization through television and the presence of the Dodgers and the Giants in the Golden State.[4] By June 1977, Major League Baseball was producing *This Week in Baseball*, which kept sports fans abreast of the "best" (i.e., most exciting) plays of baseball, thus helping the casual sports viewer (those not "inside baseball") stay in touch with the game by emphasizing its highlights and providing a faster-paced look.

Second, this new medium seemed particularly well suited for the transmission of baseball's main rival in America's sport space, football. In 1958 the NFL's nationally televised championship game between the

Baltimore Colts and the New York Giants at Yankee Stadium—subsequently labeled "the greatest football game of all time"—provided the critical juncture in what was to become football's television triumph over baseball, and the former's concomitant displacement of the latter as America's most watched and followed sport, if perhaps still not its "national pastime."

Baseball's Unexpected Fortunes and Unwelcome Struggles

That baseball had entered an era in which it was to lose its leading position in America's sport space to football, while struggling with basketball for the runner-up spot, was not apparent to the American sports world of the late 1950s and early 1960s. The move by the Dodgers and Giants to the West Coast—though deeply mourned by New Yorkers, especially in Brooklyn—proved a boon to the game. Game Five of the 1959 World Series witnessed the all-time attendance record for a Major League Baseball game when 92,706 fans crowded into the Los Angeles Coliseum (the Dodgers' temporary home and a venue ill suited for baseball).[5] In 1961 the American League expanded to ten teams, which entailed lengthening the schedule from the traditional 154-game season to one comprising 162 games. That same year, Babe Ruth's hallowed home-run record of 60 in one season was challenged by the Yankee teammates Mickey Mantle and Roger Maris, with the latter prevailing and breaking the record with 61 (a record long denoted by an asterisk to acknowledge that Maris had hit his sixtieth and sixty-first home runs after the season had passed the old 154-game mark). The following year saw the National League add two teams, and Ty Cobb's record of 96 stolen bases (set in 1915) fell to the Dodgers's Maury Wills, who stole 104. But though the 1960s witnessed some amazing feats on the baseball field, particularly by such singularly talented pitchers as Sandy Koufax, Don Drysdale, Bob Gibson, and Denny McLain, the game had lost a good deal of its appeal. The legendary Yankee dynasty disintegrated in a span of two years, and batting averages declined precipitously, reaching an all-time low in 1968. (Carl Yastremski won the American League batting title that year with a .301 average, while .290 was good enough for second place. The National League produced but five hitters with averages over .300.)

Hoping to reinvigorate itself, baseball expanded again for the 1969 season, engendering the split of each league into two divisions and inaugurating two intraleague divisional championship series (initially three out of five, expanded to four out of seven in 1985) prior to the World Series. Major League Baseball also chose a new commissioner, Bowie Kuhn, partly in hopes of emulating the innovative leadership displayed by the

NFL's Pete Rozelle. To address the dearth and decline of offense, several modifications to the standard rules were made, most notably the lowering of the pitching mound from fifteen to ten inches, the narrowing of the strike zone, and an active ban on the "spit ball." American League teams, in particular, had suffered such an alarming decline in attendance at their venues and in the all-important medium of television that they instituted a further innovation in 1973 to boost the offensive dimensions of the game: The designated hitter allowed a team to use a player of its choice to bat in lieu of the pitcher for an entire game without affecting the status of the pitcher in the field. While 1969 witnessed a popularity boost for the game with the totally unexpected National League Pennant and World Series victory of the underdog "Miracle Mets" in the nation's media capital, there was no question that by this time baseball had lost to football its position as America's favorite spectator sport. Indeed, baseball had been in the process of losing ground to basketball in the United States, particularly in New York City, which would soon boast of featuring the concurrent champions in each of the country's Big Three sports—the Mets in baseball, the Jets in football, and the Knicks in basketball—a feat unattained before or since by any other city in the United States. By all accounts—particularly those of the *Sporting News*, the "bible of baseball"—the game was in trouble. An increasing number of young people found the game "too slow and boring," particularly when compared to football and basketball. Sometime in this period, basketball surpassed baseball as the country's most popular recreational team sport, though this was not immediately reflected in terms of spectatorship and viewership for either sport. (Although basketball has indeed remained America's most favored recreational team sport over the past quarter century, the popularity of slow pitch softball—baseball's "younger sibling"— likely allows baseball to retain its position as the "national pastime," at least in terms of total participation for both males and females of all ages.) Though baseball attendance would rise dramatically for most franchises in the 1980s—following the serious decline of the 1960s and early 1970s—football and, eventually, basketball would experience much greater success than the national pastime in the increasingly more significant and lucrative venue of television.

Yet another event occurred in 1969 that was to change fundamentally the structure of labor relations in baseball and in all major American team sports: Curt Flood, a talented outfielder for the St. Louis Cardinals, challenged the legality of baseball's reserve clause in the courts by arguing that it robbed players of the freedom of movement accorded to most Americans in the labor market, while artificially restricting the players' salaries. Though the U.S. Supreme Court upheld baseball's exemption from antitrust laws (a situation unique to baseball and not applicable to football, basketball, and hockey) thereby defeating Flood's challenge and upholding the reserve clause, the die had been cast.[6] Through another court challenge, Marvin Miller, the energetic president and lead negotiator for the Baseball Players Association, won a subsequent agreement that the reserve clause issue would be decided by legal arbitration.[7] In 1977 arbitrator Peter Seitz ruled in favor of the players, declaring the reserve clause invalid and raising the specter of all major league player contracts being void. But Miller shrewdly negotiated a deal with the owners whereby only unsigned players with at least seven years of major league experience could become free agents (which the owners mistakenly viewed as a concession on Miller's part), thus creating a seller's market for the services of a select few on a yearly basis. The result was the unprecedented movement of players among franchises and an ever-upward spiral of players' salaries that continues to this day. Another contributing factor to the escalation of salaries has been the institution of salary arbitration, to which the owners also agreed in the 1977 settlement. Baseball—and American sports as a whole—would never look the same. The average annual salary of a Major League Baseball player was $29,303 in 1970; by 1994 it had catapulted to a whopping $1,200,000.[8] Parallel explosions in player salaries accompanied the worlds of football and basketball (and hockey to a lesser extent).

Free agency not only exploded the level of players' salaries in baseball, it also permanently changed the former continuity of team rosters. Players now move about freely after the expiration of their contracts, offering their services to the highest bidders (a situation not limited to baseball). This has hurt teams in small markets and favored those in larger and/or wealthier ones, as the owners of MLB have rejected revenue sharing among clubs (à la the NFL) while the players have successfully prevented salary caps (à la the NFL, NBA, and NHL). The ownership structure of the game changed as well. Since the late 1970s, all major league owners have been required by circumstance to have made their wealth in businesses other than baseball. The last of the old-fashioned baseball owners who made his living solely through the game was Calvin Griffith of the Minnesota Twins which he sold in 1980.

By the mid-1980s, baseball had reached a stage of antagonism and uncertainty in its system of industrial relations reminiscent of the conditions that had beset the game almost exactly one hundred years before. Several work stoppages hampered the game, often curtailing or canceling spring training; the beginning of a few seasons was postponed and—in the two worst cases—full-scale strikes interrupted the 1981 season for a long period and canceled the end of the 1994 season, including the play-offs and World Series. The unthinkable had happened: What two World Wars, the depression, the Korean War, and other calamities could not bring about,

severe disharmony at the pinnacle of the national pastime had finally accomplished. An American institution—the World Series—had been severely damaged, perhaps in an irrevocable manner. Indeed, this sad event
had become symptomatic of baseball's general malaise after over one hundred glorious years at the apex of the American sport space. Yet, as witnessed by the fabulous and memorable 1998 season, the often mentioned
and much expected demise of baseball in America might be terribly pre-
mature and plain wrong, proving yet again that the sports cultures that
managed to occupy a country's sport space between 1870 and 1930 can
be much more resilient than other aspects of our fast-paced world. All
Americans, not just regular baseball fans, were riveted by the home run
competition between Mark McGwire of the St. Louis Cardinals and
Sammy Sosa of the Chicago Cubs, who, in a memorable hourly duel in
August and September, not only surpassed Roger Maris's hallowed home
run record of 61 by hitting 70 (McGwire) and 66 (Sosa) respectively, but
did so in an almost moving spirit of mutual admiration and true sportsmanship. With rejuvenated interest in the game conspicuous across the
nation, including the all-important New York market—where the Yankees' exceptionally impressive collective accomplishment as a team and
the continued success of interleague play between the Yankees and the
(now contending) Mets captured the city's heart—the American public
and media seemed far from ready to turn their backs on "the grand old
game."[9] Meantime, the prodigious home-run-hitting of McGwire and
Sosa, and the Yankees' brilliant success as a team continued to enthrall
fans during the 1999 season, though not to the same extent experienced
the previous year. Early in the 2000 season—as McGwire reached the
milestone of 20 home runs faster than any other batter in history and
double-digit scores seemed commonplace—baseball officials considered
the possibility of returning the pitcher's mound to the height of fifteen
inches.

Football's Triumph over Baseball: The Major Effects of Television on the Reorganization of the American Sport Space

The Cleveland Rams' relocation to Los Angeles in 1946 was the first of
many significant new developments in professional football that occurred
after the war; this move opened up the nation's West Coast to professional
sports on the major league level.[10] That same year, the NFL received the
first of several truly competitive challenges in the form of a well-financed
rival league. By signing the best available players to much higher salaries
than the NFL owners had ever contemplated, the All-America Football
Conference presented a brand of football decidedly superior to that offered by the NFL and the best college teams.[11]

During its four-year existence, the AAFC was dominated by the Cleveland Browns, so named for their innovative coach and general manager, Paul Brown. Among the players whom Brown invited to his inaugural training camp were two African Americans, Marion Motley and Bill Willis. At the same time, the Rams signed the first NFL black players, Woody Strode and Ken Washington. Motley, a talented fullback, teamed with quarterback Otto Graham to present the greatest offense that football had yet seen (though the Browns were just as dominant on defense), convincingly demonstrating—as in baseball—that African American players could indeed be an asset to a professional team.[12]

Unlike baseball, football had not historically been completely segregated. Some colleges admitted a small number of African Americans, and some had allowed black students to compete on the football field—though almost always as linemen, rarely in the marquee positions of the backfield. One notable exception was all-purpose back Fritz Pollard, who, in the 1920s, became the first black to attain the status of head coach in the NFL—and the last until the late 1980s. In the 1920s, several black players had made the college All-American team, such as Pollard, Paul Robeson, the Rutgers end (whose name was erased from the prestigious All-America list—as if he had never existed—in the late 1940s as punishment for his communist sympathies, long after he had achieved fame as an entertainer), and tackle Duke Slater of Iowa. Additionally, black colleges, such as Grambling and Tuskegee, competed against each other on the gridiron, occasionally playing white schools. However, as the opportunity to attend college was severely restricted for minorities, so too were their opportunities in football. Meanwhile, an "unwritten rule" had kept African Americans out of the NFL since 1933.[13] But World War II and the subsequent postwar economic boom in the United States had set the stage for numerous changes in American society.

The AAFC drew more spectators than the NFL by a wide margin for three years, until the dominance of the Browns was so overwhelming that it discouraged attendance and interest in AAFC cities other than Cleveland. In addition to this qualitative imbalance in the composition of the AAFC's teams, the financial pressure engendered by the bidding war for players took its toll on both leagues, which, as a consequence, initiated merger negotiations in 1949. Three AAFC teams—the Browns, the Baltimore Colts, and the San Francisco 49ers—were absorbed into the NFL for the 1950 season, while the other AAFC teams were disbanded, their players allocated to the NFL by draft. The Browns dominated the NFL until Graham's retirement in 1955 and remained one of the league's premier clubs through the 1960s, led by another Brown—Jim, arguably the greatest running back ever to have played the game. Two final major innovations to the game occurred in the late 1940s and early 1950s: free substi-

tution and face masks. Traditionally, players had been required to compete on both sides of the ball, with substitution generally limited to one
player per play or time-out, or as a replacement in case of injury (which
sometimes engendered fake injuries). However, the new system of pla-
tooning between offensive and defensive squads allowed for finetuning
the specialization—now such a hallmark of modern football—while
allowing players to maximize their own particular skills within one realm
of the game (offense, defense, or special teams) without detracting from
the others. Additionally, it completely relegated the kicking aspect of football (i.e., kickoffs, punts, extra points, and field goals) to specialists (by
the 1970s, usually former soccer players). Meanwhile, the use of face
masks significantly reduced injuries, though some of the "old-guard"
players (last, and most famously, Bobby Lane) continued to use the old
style helmets for the remainder of their careers. Both innovations, after
fits and starts, were eventually utilized by the colleges.[14] With the benefit
of hindsight, one can classify this period as the maturation of professional
football and the game's entry into its "modern era" of true major league
status. Professional football was on its way to challenging the college
game as the foremost representative of the sport in America's sport space.

NFL clubs began to experiment with regular local television coverage
of games in the late 1940s, quickly discovering the necessity of "blacking
out" all home games to protect gate revenues. By the early 1950s, most
NFL clubs had local television contracts (the New York Giants, for example, put together a regional network of stations to carry their games
throughout the Northeast), while the league's championship game was
being broadcast nationally. In 1956 CBS contracted to provide national
coverage of some regular season games; NBC paid $100,000 for the rights
to televise the championship game, won that season by the New York
Giants, who were subsequently discovered by Madison Avenue, which—
like much of the American economy in the 1950s—was experiencing a
boom. Once again, the centrality of New York (as the nation's most populous city, its media capital, as well as its cultural and financial center)
played a crucial role in launching the popularity of a sport beyond its
immediate confines into the nation's overall culture. As with the New
York Yankees in baseball, a successful New York franchise facilitates a
sport's—and its league's—"crossover" potential, meaning that it develops awareness and popularity of its product and its stars well outside the
world of sport. The Giants' success began to offer the NFL prominent and
consistent national press coverage. It also yielded respectable television
ratings for the league, thus helping it break into the collective national
sports consciousness in places and with segments of the public that had
previously paid little attention to the professional game. The Giants became the professional game's first "media team," as many of the team's

players (particularly stars Frank Gifford, Kyle Rote, and Charlie Con-
nerly) attained fame through product endorsements, television appearances, and radio shows—in other words, activities apart from the football
field. College football also found a home on television, both locally and
nationally. However, the NCAA—now firmly in the driver's seat regarding the national regulation of all college sports—was not initially aggressive in pursuing a national television contract for the college game, resting
on the laurels of the game's pretelevision popularity. This complacency
was to change by the early 1960s.[15]

Enter another critical juncture in American sport culture: The NFL's
1958 championship game between the Baltimore Colts and the New
York Giants at Yankee Stadium provided the watershed for professional
football's standing vis-à-vis the college game, as well as for football surpassing baseball as the premier representative in America's sport space.
Previous national telecasts of the annual NFL championship had witnessed games dull and lopsided in competition. However, 1958 was the
year of the television quiz show scandals and NBC, perhaps looking to
reingratiate itself with a particularly important segment of the American
public (i.e., middle class males with spending power), promoted the game
well beyond anything the NFL had yet experienced. Additionally, the
game enjoyed a buildup engendered by the recent rivalry between the
two contesting teams, as well as the trials and tribulations each had undergone in getting to the championship game. Whereas the Colts fit the
part of the underdogs from the small city facing the big brash New York
powerhouse, their quarterback, Johnny Unitas (soon to be the NFL's
first true "glamour" star, "straight out of central casting"), provided a
dramatic counterpoint to the Giants' defense led by linebacker Sam Huff,
a name to become synonymous with football violence and toughness.[16]
The contest was exciting beyond a football or television executive's
wildest dream, as the Colts tied the game with seven seconds left and
then proceeded to win in "sudden death" overtime on a run by Alan
Ameche.[17]

The evening after the Colts' victory, Unitas and Ameche appeared on
the *Ed Sullivan Show* (already a CBS institution at the time and a major
launching pad into American culture for many a performer and entertainer), and Unitas would claim his MVP award—a new Chevrolet Cor-
vette—on that week's *Pat Boone Show.* [18] The NFL had finally made the
American "bigtime," and from this point onward professional football
would permanently surpass the college game in overall popularity. In the
course of the next decade, it would decisively do the same regarding baseball. As noted by Allen Guttmann, this is demonstrated by examining
which sport was featured on the cover of *Sports Illustrated* (considered
by many the foremost American sports magazine) in these years: From

1955 through 1958, baseball was featured on forty-one *Sports Illustrated* covers, football on twenty-two; from 1959 through 1962, baseball had twenty-eight covers, football twenty-five; from 1963 through 1966, baseball had thirty, football fifty-two.

The NFL's rise to the dominant position in America's sport space commenced with television and continued under the shrewd guidance of Pete Rozelle, the league's commissioner beginning in 1960. The NFL was able to produce heroes on a weekly basis and romantic images for some of its teams, most notably the Green Bay Packers (the only publicly owned major league franchise in all of North American team sports), who dominated professional football for much of the 1960s. As broadcast technology progressed, professional football proved almost perfect for television in both its presentation and scheduling. CBS signed the first exclusive contract for the rights to broadcast all of the league's games for the 1962 and 1963 seasons. Rozelle guided the NFL owners in marketing their product, securing the most advantageous television deals (recognizing the primacy of television over selling seats), sharing the revenue so attained, and expanding the league into new markets while making (and keeping) key political and legal connections that allowed the league to avoid several legislative and judicial antitrust challenges. Rozelle also projected personal and league authority in carefully choosing to take stands against players associating with gamblers or publicly criticizing league officials; he conceived and initiated a long-running United Way campaign to burnish the league's public image.[19] Meantime, the rapid and formidable success of the NFL had led to the formation of a new rival league in 1960, the American Football League (AFL).

The AFL's strategy was to occupy niches in the country left uncovered by the NFL. Hence, it based franchises in markets bereft of NFL representation, as well as New York and the San Francisco Bay area (Oakland), while securing a television contract with ABC. However, this deal was not very lucrative for either party, and the network chose to promote its weekly slate of college games ahead of those of the upstart professional league. Kept afloat mostly through the funds of some of its well-heeled owners, notably Lamar Hunt of the Kansas City Chiefs—a name to figure prominently in the world of American soccer—the AFL gradually began to compete with the older league for the best talent in professional football. Some of the NFL's rejects, such as George Blanda and Jack Kemp, developed into major stars in the AFL, the world of professional football, American sports, and—in Kemp's case—even American national politics. Just as the NFL gained in popularity vis-à-vis the college game for its greater emphasis on the passing game, the AFL attracted fans to its brand of football by presenting a more offensive-minded contest than that played in the NFL.[20]

The breakthrough for the AFL came in 1965, when the league signed a firm national contract for exclusive coverage of its games with NBC. This provided the New York Jets the necessary funds to outbid the NFL for the services of University of Alabama quarterback Joe Namath, signed to a four-year guaranteed contract of $427,000.[21] This was an unprecedented sum of money in professional sports, let alone football, which no NFL player was close to receiving at the time—though things would soon change on that front, too. (Baseball superstars such as Mickey Mantle and Willie Mays, as well as basketball "franchise players" such as Bill Russell and Wilt Chamberlain, received similar salaries, though none had ever garnered a multiyear deal as enjoyed by Namath.) Namath and the NBC deal gave the AFL instant credibility, particularly in the all-important New York market, at the time bereft of a contending club in any of the major American sports (though the Knicks were respectably competitive) with the decline of the football Giants and the baseball Yankees, both of whom had been perennial major contenders just a few years before. Whereas Johnny Unitas of the crewcut and "all-American boy" image had been a perfect football hero for the 1950s, "Broadway Joe" Namath soon embodied the glamorous football "antihero" and sex symbol typifying the turbulent 1960s. Sporting a "Fu Manchu" mustache (which he publicly shaved for $10,000) and a full-length fur coat, Namath was anything but low-key or humble; instead he was prone to making inflammatory and brash remarks directed at opponents, while his public social life was reminiscent of the high-living Babe Ruth of the Roaring Twenties. In New York, the Joe Namath Fan Club boasted its own song and large constituency of teenage girls, as this football player received the kind of idolization previously reserved for movie and rock stars. Namath undoubtedly became professional football's most successful crossover star up to that point and, arguably, ever since.[22]

The two competing leagues had warily coexisted under an informal agreement not to sign each other's players, though competition for players out of college had grown intense, creating an upward spiral of salaries. The "truce" was broken in early 1966 when the New York Giants signed kicker Pete Gogolak (the very first of the soccer-style place kickers now standard in both the colleges and pros) away from the AFL's Buffalo Bills. Hence, both leagues began to bid for those players whose contracts had expired. John Brodie, a talented quarterback for the San Francisco 49ers, used an offer from the AFL to win a huge NFL contract, while the AFL found fair success in signing many of the best college players, often at higher salaries than those offered by the older league. In June 1966, the NFL agreed to a "peace" with the upstart league that—though far from finalized—included the following crucial arrangements: the immediate implementation of a combined college draft and a permanent truce on the "raiding" of players, and the creation of a "world championship" game between the two champions of the respective leagues to be held at a "neutral" warm-weather site. Thus was born the Super Bowl, which in the course of its history has become far and away the single most important one-day event in American sports, and regularly the most successful television spectacle in all American public life, including sports, culture, and politics.[23] The Super Bowl has been regarded as a national holiday by many Americans, and it garners the highest television ratings of the year with consistent regularity, while featuring by far the highest-priced advertising spots of any sport event in the world. Indeed, next to soccer's quadrennial World Cup championship game and certain events in the summer Olympics, the Super Bowl has developed into the world's most widely watched single event, and the most watched on an annual basis.

That its first two occurrences were hardly taken seriously by the American sports public was evident by the fact that neither was sold out, nor was television viewership particularly impressive. Lopsided victories by the Green Bay Packers over the AFL champions (the Oakland Raiders and the Kansas City Chiefs, respectively) appeared to confirm, for most of the public, the NFL's contention that the newer upstart AFL and its teams were markedly inferior to the product offered by the older league. This would change with a bang in early 1969, when the AFL's New York Jets were to meet the NFL's Baltimore Colts in the third world championship game of professional football. However, the 1968 season that preceded that contest proved that the AFL was garnering a television audience to rival the older league, while also demonstrating to the networks that football was indeed worth their investment. The key televised event that season was the famous "Heidi game": NBC cut away from a Jets-Raiders contest with a minute and five seconds remaining and the Jets ahead, 32–29, in favor of the scheduled showing of "an expensive musical production of Heidi." A few seconds later, the Raiders scored a touchdown, then recovered the ensuing kickoff to score another. Calls from outraged viewers flooded the switchboards of NBC and its affiliates at an unprecedented rate. "In a sense, NBC never quite realized what it had or was able to make the most of it, as the famous 'Heidi game' of November 17, 1968 suggests."[24]

After winning the AFL championship for the 1968 season, the Jets were handicapped as 16-point underdogs to the Colts, the biggest pregame disparity between any Super Bowl contestants before or since. The game received a huge buildup while providing several elements of melodrama. Adding fuel to the fire, Namath "guaranteed" a Jets victory to a doubting but enthralled national media. For a storybook ending, the Jets soundly defeated the Colts, 16–7, proving that the AFL had indeed become the

NFL's equal, perhaps even its superior.[25] To dispel any doubts that the Jet's (and the AFL's) victory had been a fluke, the next Super Bowl (by now the event's official name) was again won by the junior league's representative, in this case the Kansas City Chiefs, who trounced the NFL's Minnesota Vikings.

With the AFL proving its total parity with the NFL, the merger proceeded for the 1970 season with both leagues as equals. It included full regular-season play among teams of the formerly separate leagues, while three NFL teams (the Pittsburgh Steelers, Baltimore Colts, and Cleveland Browns) received compensation to join the AFL teams in the newly named American Conference of the NFL. This so-constituted National Football League (since supplemented with several expansion franchises) had already surpassed baseball in terms of the popularity of its product before its actual inception, and it has remained the mainstay of American professional sports to the present day.

Football's success was propelled and consolidated by its ubiquity on television. In the first season of the newly configured league, ABC presented three highly successful NFL games during prime-time hours on Monday night, joining NBC and CBS in televising professional football to the American public. The following season, Monday Night Football became a regular weekly feature of ABC programming, quickly developing into one of the most consistently popular staples of American television culture and a weekly ritual for millions of Americans.[26] Monday Night Football has remained among the top-rated shows of all American television, frequently attaining the weekly number-one spot in overall national viewership. It has easily been television's highest-rated regular sports program of all time. A typical Monday night broadcast has garnered ratings equal to or surpassing those of a second or third World Series baseball game, or virtually all NBA basketball playoff contests. Indeed, cumulatively speaking, Monday Night Football is quite likely the highest-rated regular television show of any kind for all time.

Football's immense popularity with the American public can be further gauged by its centrality to the viability of any major television network. When the fledgling new FOX network succeeded in outbidding CBS for the rights to telecast all NFC games for a four-year period beginning in 1994, this alone instantly established FOX as a major contender among the networks and aggravated the troubles that CBS had been experiencing for quite some time. The negative effects of losing the NFL were so detrimental to CBS, it appeared willing to pay virtually any price to regain the rights to televise some NFL games once the old television contract with the league was renegotiated in 1998. CBS led the charge in creating an eight-year network television package with the NFL that amounted to $17.6 billion and included FOX, the Disney-owned ABC (as the continued guardian of Monday Night Football), and ESPN, in addition to CBS.[27] This has been far and away the largest amount of cash paid by any television consortium for the rights to televise any sport event, including the Olympics and the World Cup in soccer.

With such riches offered by the game of professional football, it is not surprising that others—in addition to those privileged by a stake in the NFL—tried to cash in. A number of rival leagues were formed, such as the World Football League in 1974–75 and the United State Football League (USFL), 1983–85. Both of these leagues succumbed rather quickly, despite their attempts to differentiate their product from that of the NFL, such as the USFL's spring schedule. The challenges of these leagues to the established NFL failed in the market as they did in the courts, where a jury awarded but three dollars to the USFL in an antitrust case against the NFL, sealing the challenger's doom. Still, professional football's financial attractiveness is so immense that—at the time of this writing—NBC (the network owned by General Electric, and the one left with no football in the television contract of 1998) and Vince McMahon (the flamboyant owner of the World Wrestling Federation, WWF) had entered into a 50-50 partnership in owning a new professional football league called XFL, which was to begin playing in the spring of 2001.[28]

The players have been among the major beneficiaries of these league formations and lucrative television contracts. Whereas the average salary in the NFL was $25,000 in 1967, this figure had ballooned to $650,000 by 1994.[29] During the same period, strikes, lockouts, and other industrial actions rendered management-player relations in football as complex and controversial as they were in baseball, though the NFL Players Union has proved nowhere near as powerful or cohesive as its baseball counterpart, nor has its leadership been anywhere near as shrewd. "Salary caps" and other measures by the owners attempted to slow the rise in player compensation, while the players and their union eventually were able to utilize the U.S. judicial system to gain concessions from the owners—such as free agency—after the failure of two players' strikes. Just like the other two sports of the American Big Three, professional football has experienced developments since the 1970s that have completely changed the playing field between management and labor regarding the overall stakes at hand, the size of the compensatory packages for the players, and, of course, the profits for the owners.

There is yet another dimension that bespeaks the fortuitous marriage between professional football and television. While football has clearly become the most popular of the Big Three in the United States and is far and away the most dominant representative in contemporary America's sport space, the game itself is played by relatively few Americans in the fashion most approximate to the version exhibited in its college (and high school, or even Pop Warner) variant, let alone that of the professional level. Most Americans have not played football in its organized form—that is, beyond the casual and "safe" games of "touch" or "flag" football, or the rough youth games of sandlot tackle football without coaches, rehearsed plays, and proper equipment. While it is clearly a judgment call to argue that the distance between the professional game and its daily "piker" variant is larger in football than it is in baseball, basketball, hockey, and soccer—or any other sport for that matter—we are on safe ground, we believe, in stating that the very essence of football on a competitive, organized level (professional, college, high school) is fundamentally different from the game played in schoolyards or on playgrounds, and at picnics, company outings, and weekend retreats to a degree that is not the case with basketball, soccer, and baseball (even in its softball variant). In the latter cases, elements of the "big league" game are all there, even if performed on a woefully low level when compared to the routine feats of the professionals. Touch or flag football, on the other hand, in its very essence constitutes a completely different game from that performed by high schools, colleges, semiprofessional teams, and the professionals. Augmented by the fact that most Americans rarely (if ever) attend an NFL game in person, it is clear that between activity and following, in the case of American football—between active playing and participation on the one hand, and passive spectatorship on the other—the gap is immense. Football in the contemporary United States more resembles the cultural icons of entertainment than of sports. And television is the medium that continued to drive this metamorphosis, as it still does.

At the end of the twentieth century, the position of professional football at the apex in the American sport space was unchallenged, despite fluctuations in the NFL's television ratings in the late 1990s. That any potentially successful soccer venture in the United States—at this point, MLS—must play its games in the summer is implicit recognition of football's current and likely future dominance, as well as its successful "crowding out" of any newcomers and potential rivals.

The World's Game and "March Madness": Basketball's Journey from the Periphery to the Center of America's Sport Space

While the official annals of the NBA list 6 June 1946 (the founding date of the Basketball Association of America), and 1 November 1946 (the first game played in the BAA) as the founding of the NBA, it was really not until 3 August 1949—the merger date between the six remaining National Basketball League clubs with the BAA—that the new league truly emerged. The league initially was dominated by the Minneapolis Lakers, the last BAA champions and five-time NBA champions (counting their 1949 BAA title) by 1954. The Lakers relocated to Los Angeles in 1960, thereby making professional basketball truly national in scope.[30] There were several major innovations instituted by the new league in the course of the 1950s. In a quest to "open up" the game to enhance its appeal to the fans, the NBA engendered several rule innovations. The most important: widening the foul lane from six to twelve feet, prohibiting zone defenses, awarding a penalty shot following a team's fifth foul in any one period, and—far and away the most decisive new feature—introduction of the 24-second clock, thereby revolutionizing professional basketball and ushering in the game's truly modern era. "The shot clock that saved the NBA" guaranteed that fans attending an NBA game would witness continuing action, with honest attempts by both teams to score at least every twenty seconds or so, instead of what had derisively been called "stall ball" in which teams essentially engaged in foul-shooting contests, particularly in the third and fourth quarters of a game when the team with the lead would simply refuse to part with the ball.[31] Stalling had become so endemic to the game that fans stayed away from professional basketball, finding it much too slow and boring, while those who did attend often headed for the exits well before the conclusion, since the element of excitement was missing. The results of the new shot clock were dramatic and immediate: In 1954–55, the first season with the new rules, average team scoring per game jumped by 13.6 points—from 79.5 to 93.1.[32]

The other revolutionary change for the NBA occurred in 1950 with the first appearance of African American players in a major organized basketball league. That the league was slow to integrate (recall that baseball had done so in 1947, and professional football in 1946) is attributable to two factors. First, the league's precarious financial situation caused the owners to pursue a cautious and hesitant course, so as not to alienate fans whose allegiance to the game was still potentially shaky. Second, and perhaps more important, the most highly attended NBA games at the time were those preceded by Harlem Globetrotter exhibitions. Hence, the NBA refrained from pursuing black stars in fear of alienating the Globetrotter's owner, Abe Saperstein, while Saperstein, whose Globetrotters had long established their fame as the premier entertainers in the game, could still outbid the NBA for a player's services.[33]

The first black players in the NBA were not stars, though most helped to improve their teams and were generally popular with fans. In terms of on-court dominance and fan appeal, the first black players to make a significant impact on the NBA were two former teammates from the University of San Francisco (NCAA champions of 1955 and 1956, 55 consecutive victories) who became teammates with the Boston Celtics, Bill Russell and K. C. Jones. Russell, arguably the greatest center ever to play the game (at least in terms of rebounding, defense, and championships) and his Celtics would dominate the NBA until his retirement in 1969, as Boston became basketball's equivalent of the New York Yankees, football's Green Bay Packers, and hockey's Montreal Canadiens. Not only did the Celtics amass eleven NBA titles during Russell's thirteen-year career with the club, but Russell's style of play revolutionized the game. While still in college, Russell's shot blocking and leaping ability changed the way defense was played and led him to garner the NCAA tournament's MVP for four consecutive years. Indeed, the NBA's "goaltending" violations were formulated and enforced by the league with Russell in mind.[34] Russell would also become the first African American to attain the status of head coach or manager in any American professional major league (with the exception of Fritz Pollard in the early years of the NFL, which, at that time, was hardly major) when he was named player-coach of the Celtics in 1966.

Adding to Russell's greatness and permanent contributions to the professional game was his rivalry with an equally important and brilliant African American center, Wilt Chamberlain. A star player at the University of Kansas and for a year with the Globetrotters, the seven-foot-one-inch Chamberlain joined the Philadelphia Warriors of the NBA's Eastern Division in 1960, guaranteeing many a memorable showdown with his Celtic counterpart during the regular season, as well as in the play-offs. Four inches taller than Russell, Chamberlain was as prolific an offensive player as Russell was the unquestioned master of defense; they were both kings of the rebound.[35] Chamberlain and Russell became an inseparable tandem in the history of professional basketball, with contribution to the game's growth and development rivaled only by another tandem twenty years later. Two other African American contemporaries of Russell and Chamberlain require mention here because of their major influence on the game and immense contributions to its attractiveness: Oscar Robertson, one of the greatest guards and finest all-around players ever to step on a basketball court, and Elgin Baylor, whose incredible moves to the basket began a lineage of spectacular players that would include Connie Hawkins, Earl "The Pearl" Monroe, Julius Erving ("Dr. J."), Michael "Air" Jordan, Clyde "The Glide" Drexler, Kobe Bryant, Grant Hill, Vince Carter, and Kevin Garnett.

There can be no doubt that by the 1960s, the NBA had firmly established itself as a major league in the topography of American sport institutions. What it lacked at this time was consistent exposure via the medium that had transformed American culture and sports viewership since the middle 1950s: On the national level, professional basketball's television contract with ABC provided only a few Saturday broadcasts throughout the league's regular season, with only spotty play-off exposure. Most teams had only local television coverage that broadcast their away games while blacking out home games, lest television reduce gate receipts. In 1969 the NBA finally obtained a lucrative television contract that offered the professional game national coverage on a regular and fairly extensive basis. However, the league still retained the rights to continue blacking out games in the market in which they occurred. Though this policy did indeed protect gate receipts, it actually represented a short-sighted policy that deprived the NBA of the full dissemination of its product, limiting exposure for contests that could have provided the greatest potential television audiences. Hence, when the New York Knicks defeated the Los Angeles Lakers in the final game of the play-offs for the 1969–70 season in a game of storybook drama (with Willis Reed, the New York team's center, dragging his numb and mangled leg onto the court to confront the Lakers' Chamberlain in one of the more inspirational efforts in the history of professional sports), New Yorkers not privileged to attend or without access to pay-television (minimally available in those years) were relegated to listening on the radio, or foregoing the contest altogether.

By 1967 professional basketball had attained sufficient popularity with the American public that the phenomenon so common to all major American sports in such circumstances occurred yet again in basketball: The American Basketball Association (ABA) inaugurated play as a rival challenge to the NBA. Though the ABA presented a brand of basketball that initially was clearly inferior to that offered by the NBA, by the early 1970s the newer league had attracted sufficiently good players in great enough numbers to offer a product that boasted good crowds and a decent television viewership in its strongest markets. The ABA raided several players from the NBA (most notably Rick Barry), but it found greater success signing top talent from the college ranks, including Spencer Haywood, Artis Gilmore, Dan Issel, George McGinnis, George Gervin, and Julius Erving. In 1974 Moses Malone became the first professional basketball player of the modern era to go directly from high school to the professional ranks when he signed a contract with the ABA's Utah Stars (an occurrence that would become relatively commonplace by the mid-1990s). The ABA followed the model of all organized challenges to an established professional league in America's major team sports, which was to force a merger with its more established rival. Owners of four of the five most viable and financially stable ABA teams—the New York Nets, Denver Nuggets, Indiana Pacers, and San Antonio Spurs—were willing to pay the steep entrance fee for membership in the NBA when the ABA collapsed in 1976. (The owner of the last ABA champions, the Kentucky Colonels—likely the most talented ABA team, and one that had been well supported by its hometown fans—would not pay the cash and folded the team.) The ABA players not belonging to any of these four teams were dispersed throughout the NBA by a special draft. Aside from the refugee teams and players and the practice of signing college underclassmen, the ABA left one lasting legacy to the NBA, indeed to all of basketball: the 3-point shot. This innovation, first introduced in the ABA, is now used in virtually every organized form of basketball at virtually every level of the game worldwide.

Despite its triumph over and absorption of the ABA challenge, the NBA was experiencing a difficult time during the second half of the 1970s. The disappearance of the Celtics dynasty; weak teams in the league's major markets of Los Angeles, Chicago, and, especially, New York; a proliferation of black players that rendered the rosters of some teams exclusively African American in a society where most paying sport fans are white; and a never-admitted (but generally known or suspected) drug problem among many players were noticeably and negatively affecting the appeal of the NBA for many sports fans, including those most interested in the game of basketball. On the court, NBA play was seemingly typified by the athletic sizzle of "run and gun" without reciprocal efforts toward playing defense or, at times, emphasis on actually winning the game. The fan base for professional basketball stagnated, indeed receded in some places. Whereas the college game attained new heights in popularity as the NCAA received a huge television contract for the rights to its March tournament, the NBA was not able to garner a firm national television commitment when its deal with NBC expired in 1979. By 1980 the NBA hit a low when some games of its play-off finals between the Los Angeles Lakers and the Philadelphia 76ers were not televised nationally, or even shown on tape delay. Such was the case for the clinching game six of that series in which a twenty-year-old rookie named Earvin "Magic" Johnson scored 42 points, while adding 15 rebounds and 7 assists, in a spectacular display of talent exhibited while playing all three positions: center, forward, and guard (the last, his usual position).[36]

In a curious affirmation of the dialectic process at work, it was at precisely this nadir in the league's recent history when the nucleus of its future success of hitherto unimaginable proportions was initiated. Together with the aforementioned Magic Johnson, an equally talented young player named Larry Bird had joined the league and been named its top rookie of the 1979–80 season. The two had first crossed paths in the 1979 NCAA championship game between Bird's Indiana State (the loser) and Johnson's Michigan State (the winner), which to this day has remained the most widely watched college contest in basketball history. Bird, the white player in Boston, and Johnson, the black player in Los Angeles, created a rivalry between their two respective teams and each other that engendered newfound interest in the league, and, most important, among younger sports fans. Johnson and Bird would garner eight NBA championships

between them (five for Johnson, three for Bird), while their teams dominated the 1980s in a competitive relationship that captured the imagination of the public. Bird and Johnson—Larry and Magic—became a tandem that significantly benefited the game of professional basketball, even
more than the 1960s tandem of Russell and Chamberlain.

Into this much improved situation of a reinvigorated and exciting
league now offering an attractive product to an increasingly interested
public stepped two men in 1984 who were to take the NBA and basketball
to heights unimaginable only a few years before: David Stern succeeded
Larry O'Brien as the NBA's fourth commissioner, and Michael Jordan, a
young player from the University of North Carolina's 1982 NCAA championship team and the 1984 gold medal U.S. Olympic team, joined the
Chicago Bulls. In separate ways, Stern and Jordan propelled the NBA to a
level in the American sport space where the league and its product equaled
and—by some measures—surpassed the position of Major League Baseball. Perhaps more impressively, they succeeded in making the NBA into
a globally known league whose teams and players became internationally
admired and followed to a degree unprecedented by any other American
team sport. The newly won interest in, and status of, basketball as culture—which has clearly expanded way beyond its former stage of mere
activity in many countries across the globe—was initiated by three related
developments. First, Michael Jordan became the most popular athlete in
the world, reaching dimensions even beyond those formerly attained only
by soccer's Pelé and boxing's Muhammad Ali, and never before even re-
motely reached by any superstar of any of the other American team
sports. Second, the institutionalization of the annual McDonald's open
tournaments that (beginning in the fall of 1987) regularly pitted an NBA
team against the very best club teams from such international basketball
powers as Spain, Italy, Russia, Lithuania, and Greece. Finally, the first
appearance of professionals at the Olympic games in Barcelona during
the summer of 1992 created and presented the American "Dream Team,"
featuring Michael Jordan, Magic Johnson, and Larry Bird (all three playing on the same team for the first and only time, excluding meaningless
exhibitions), placing its unique skills on a global stage to the delight of
millions of new basketball fans around the world.

The significant pioneering contribution of the Dream Team to the
global popularization of basketball cannot be overestimated (not least in
terms of merchandising opportunities); the NBA has yet to look back.
This pertains to the two immensely lucrative television contracts that the
league signed with NBC in the course of the 1990s, as well as with cable's
TBS and TNT, giving the NBA superb exposure both during the regular
season and in the all-important play-offs. It also pertains to the boom in
salaries that has rendered NBA players the wealthiest athletes in the world

(on average), far surpassing their colleagues in football and baseball. The average NBA player's salary for the 1967–68 season was $20,000; by the 1994–95 season this figure had increased to $1.8 million, substantially exceeding comparable figures in football and baseball.[37] By 1996 and 1997, average salary in the NBA had reached the amazing sum of $2.5 million, while young superstars such as Shaquille O'Neal and Kevin Garnett had signed multiyear contracts in the range of $120 million.

In marked contrast to its three major-league rivals in baseball, football, and hockey, the NBA had prided itself on never having lost one single minute of play on account of any kind of industrial action (be it a lockout or strike) in its history of more than fifty years; but suddenly it experienced three lockouts in short order. The first two—in the summers of 1995 and 1996—were settled in time not to affect the schedules of the two respective seasons. However, contrary to the belief of the American sports public that the NBA's contending factions would never indulge in a work stoppage that would collectively cost them hundreds of millions of dollars and—worse still—cause immeasurable loss in image and goodwill for the league and its product the way baseball, hockey, and football had done in the past, the lockout of 1998 lasted slightly over six months. All preseason games were canceled, as were all regular games for November, December (1998), and January (1999), as well as that season's annual All-Star game. Both sides made compromises that salvaged at least parts of the 1999 season and a slightly delayed, but regular, play-off competition. Yet even before that truncated season could commence, another calamity befell the NBA: Michael Jordan, its marquee player and most illustrious representative, announced his retirement from the league. Jordan's retirement accomplished the unprecedented: For at least two days it eclipsed soccer in the world's media, clearly demonstrating that Jordan, the individual, was perhaps the international cultural equivalent of the world's most popular sport, if the NBA and basketball surely were not.[38] So, while it is one of the telltale signs of modernity that institutions always outlast any individual, regardless of personal charisma, there can be no doubt that Jordan's departure will diminish the NBA's global luster and weaken, even if temporarily, basketball's prominence in America's sports culture.

The College Game

On the other hand, NCAA basketball has experienced no problems comparable to those that have potentially threatened the continuous success of the NBA. The only significant negative developments for college basketball in recent years have been the annual loss of the most talented underclassmen to the NBA and seemingly frequent violations of the NCAA's byzantine rules regarding the recruitment and compensation of student athletes by various coaches, administrators, and alumni (a perennial problem in college football as well).

Bespeaking the great popularity of the college game on campus and its standing as a part of American middle-class culture almost since its invention by Naismith, college basketball as an institution hardly suffered during the gambling-related scandals of the early 1950s and early 1960s. Even though the game never returned to its prescandal prominence in New York City, the rest of the nation's enthusiasm for college basketball continued unabated. In contrast to the professional game, college basketball experienced no problems in getting its games televised by the country's three television networks in the 1960s or 1970s. Indeed, by the middle of the 1960s, the NCAA tournament had developed into one of the premier sporting events on television, regularly surpassing even the most coveted NBA games (including the play-off finals) by a considerable margin. The NCAA tournament's place in the pantheon of American sports has, if anything, increased over the past thirty years, rendering its sobriquet, "March Madness," part of the American vernacular. That the NCAA tournament as a whole no longer surpassed the NBA finals in terms of television ratings by the early 1990s merely means that the NBA's product (mainly due to the immense drawing power of Michael Jordan) has attained a general level of popularity formerly reserved for the college game and its championship rounds alone.

Though on a completely different level, the final game of the 1966 NCAA tournament between Texas Western University (later renamed University of Texas at El Paso—UTEP) and the University of Kentucky (one of the most prominent representatives of college basketball in the game's history) was of equal importance to the sport's dissemination. Providing the real (i.e., social and cultural) significance to this event, Texas Western fielded a team in which all the starters were African Americans, whereas Kentucky appeared with an all-white team as a consequence of the failure (or refusal) of Adolph Rupp (Kentucky's legendary coach) to recruit a single black player to that university's basketball squad. When underdog Texas Western soundly beat the heavily favored Kentucky Wildcats, the last vestige of overt segregation in a major American team sport had ended, at least on the field of play.[39]

The Women's Game

As noted in chapter 2, one salient characteristic distinguishing basketball from both baseball and football has been the participation of women as players, virtually from the game's inception. However, women played by markedly different rules (initially, no dribbling at all was permitted for certain players on the court, later amended to allow one bounce of the ball, two bounces in the 1950s, and three bounces in the 1960s, with six players to a side); a standardization of the rules for the women's game (generally in line with those for the men) did not occur until 1970. However, not until the middle of the 1970s could one really speak of women's basketball as resembling the modern game that it has since become. In the wake of Title IX of the 1972 Federal Education Amendments to the Civil Rights Act of 1964, colleges began to take women's basketball seriously, which, in turn, meant that girls across the country began to play in organized summer leagues and on the high school level to an unprecedented degree qualitatively and quantitatively. A real breakthrough for women's basketball occurred in February 1975, when some twelve thousand fans paid to see the first women's game ever played at Madison Square Garden, as national champion Immaculata College of Pennsylvania, the winner of the first three AIAW (Association for Intercollegiate Athletics for Women) championships, defeated Queens College.[40] The NCAA did not sanction these tournaments until 1982, the year it began keeping statistics and official records for the women's game as it had for the men for nearly a century. In barely one decade, NCAA women's basketball blossomed in quality of play and popularity, with numbers in spectatorship that had previously been simply unimaginable. Players such as Lynette Woodard, Nancy Lieberman, Anne Donovan, and Cheryl Miller attained star status on the firmament of American team sports and gained the recognition and respect of a public that had hitherto only accorded it to female star athletes in individual sports such as tennis, skiing, figure skating, and gymnastics. However, in the late 1970s and early 1980s, two women's professional leagues that featured many of these players failed miserably at the box office, ending up defunct.[41]

By the 1990s, the women's NCAA tournament—featuring such powerhouse teams as Tennessee, Old Dominion, Stanford, the University of Texas, the University of Connecticut, and the University of Southern California—had become a major attraction with a serious national following, regularly covered by the national sports press while garnering respectable television ratings on network television. A galvanizing moment occurred at the 1996 summer Olympics in Atlanta, when the U.S. women's basketball team won the gold medal. This event not only helped consolidate the women's college game as an indispensable part of America's modern basketball world, it also spawned another attempt to establish the professional game. As has repeatedly been the case in the development of all American team sports, success fosters emulation. Again, not one, but two rivalrous women's professional leagues opened for business in 1997: The

American Basketball League (ABL) and the Women's National Basketball Association (WNBA). The ABL, which became defunct in January 1999, had better players and higher salaries than the WNBA: The average ABL salary was $80,000, and top players earned $150,000, while the WNBA range has been between $40,000 and $90,000.[42] Yet, it seemed that the ABL was always the weaker of the two by dint of its field of teams in places such as Hartford, Columbus, San Jose, and Long Beach; the scheduling of its season in the winter and early spring (when the NBA and both men's and women's basketball at the college level are in full swing); and—most important—its possession of only a precarious television contract offering very little exposure. In contrast, the WNBA carries the NBA brand name; piggybacks on the NBA's immense popularity and marketing; plays its season in NBA venues during the summer months when the men's game is in recess; operates in prime markets such as New York, Los Angeles, Houston, and Chicago; has boasted consistent average attendance over ten thousand per game; and—notably (and potentially most crucial)—telecasts games on the NBA's primary network, NBC (as well as ESPN on cable). Whatever the future fate of this league may be, there is no doubt that, in its own way, it will have helped to establish the women's game well beyond the point of its former marginalization. Whether it will ever attain the status of cultural ingredient in the American sport space remains to be seen.

The "One-Half": The "Continentalization," "Internationalization," and "Americanization" of Hockey

In the 1950s the Montreal Canadiens won five Stanley Cups in a row to become hockey's equivalent to professional baseball's New York Yankees. The 1950s also witnessed the introduction of hockey to television; by 1957 games in all six cities (Montreal, Toronto, New York, Chicago, Boston, Detroit—the Solid Six, as mentioned in chapter 2) were telecast.[43] Indeed, as of the 1956–57 season, CBS began televising games on Saturday afternoons from the League's four American cities. In Canada, the Canadian Broadcasting Company's *Hockey Night in Canada* on Saturday evenings created feelings of commonality and national identity (at least among the country's male population) that few, if any, other institutions could approximate.[44] In Canada, television widened, as well as deepened, the hockey (and sports) community created by radio in the 1920s and 1930s to a hitherto unprecedented level.

Hence, it was solely due to the potential reach and riches of television that a number of American cities became prime markets for new NHL clubs. In 1967—the NHL's fiftieth anniversary—the league expanded its product coast to coast by signing a $3.5 million contract with CBS for *Game of the Week* coverage and by placing new teams in six cities. Overall, the NHL added twelve new teams to the Solid Six (tripling in size between 1967 and 1974) in a span of seven years, while its lengthy playoff schedule now extended well into late May, often even early June. Professional hockey had truly become an American national game that—in terms of sheer geographic presence and reach, though not in stability, popularity, or revenues—rivaled the Big Three. But just like in the case of the Big Three, success for hockey also entailed new challenges, in this case, on both the global and the national fronts.

On the global front, the best of the NHL finally had an opportunity to set the record straight once and for all as to who were the real world champions and the best hockey players, the NHL professional stars or the Soviet state "amateurs" who had dominated the Olympics and the yearly international world championships of hockey since the mid-1950s, events barely noticed by the average North American sports fan. An eight-game series was set for September 1972, with the first four held in cities across the Canadian continent and the next four in Moscow, that mobilized patriotic interest among Canadians like no other cultural event before or since. So it was nothing short of a national shock to Canadians—and to a lesser, but still considerable, extent to American hockey fans—when in the series' first game, Team Canada suffered an ignominious 7–3 defeat in Montreal at the hands of the Soviets, who outplayed the Canadians in every aspect of the game. Adding insult to injury, the entire Canadian as well as Quebecois political elite—beginning with Prime Minister Pierre Eliot Trudeau—were present at this event, fully expecting the NHL stars to trounce the Soviets. Canadian flags were lowered to half mast to mourn this completely unexpected and "shameful" defeat on the part of the Canadian NHL stars. Even though Team Canada rallied in the end and narrowly won the series, four games to three (with one tie), the NHL's alleged invincibility had been tarnished, if not completely shattered: It was clear that the Stanley Cup winner was not an automatic world champion, that skating around with the Cup trophy did not automatically anoint one the very best in the world. That the top Soviet teams—especially Red Army and Dynamo Moscow—were every bit the equals of NHL squads was emphatically demonstrated in late December 1974 and early January 1975, when both played a number of NHL clubs on a quick tour of North American cities. After destroying the New York Rangers, 7–3, in Madison Square Garden, Red Army then tied the Montreal Canadiens, 3–3, in a classic game on New Year's Eve at the Montreal Forum, only to lose to the Philadelphia Flyers a few days later, 4–1. In the meantime, Dynamo also held its own against other NHL teams. In 1976 Canada barely won the first newly installed Canada Cup tournament featuring the world's best hockey nations. Three years later, the NHL All-Stars met the Soviets in a three-game Challenge Cup series at New York's Madison Square Garden, losing the series, two games to one. In the 1981 final of the second Canada Cup tournament, the Soviets humiliated the NHL's best with an 8–1 thrashing. Three years later—in what was to be the third and last Canada Cup tournament—the Canadians redeemed themselves by defeating the Soviets, two games to one, in competition that many still consider the very best hockey ever played on this planet. All told, of the 140 games played from 1972 through 1991 between Soviet teams and various Canadian and U.S. units—NHL All-Stars, Team Canada, Team USA, and a range of NHL clubs—the Soviets won 83.[45] Throughout these many contests, nobody could have predicted that with the fall of the Soviet Union, the NHL would become home to all of the best Russian players by the mid-1990s—in effect, now constituting the top Russian hockey league. When the Detroit Red Wings won the Stanley Cup in the spring of 1997, five of their best players were Russian. By the late 1990s 20 percent of all NHL players hailed from Europe (Russia, Sweden, Finland, and the Czech Republic, in particular), and 20 percent were American, as compared to the 1974–75 season when barely 1 percent of the NHL's players were Americans and none, with the exception of Toronto's Borje Salming, hailed from Europe. The NHL's top scoring leaders for the 1998 and 1999 seasons were European, while every team in the league employed at least a few European players. In barely two decades, the league had gone from an exclusive Canadian fraternity to an international institution.

Concomitant to the Soviet (i.e., international and global) challenge, the NHL also faced one from North America: the formation of a rival league. The World Hockey Association announced its existence in 1972 by signing Bobby Hull, the great Chicago Black Hawks star, to a $2.75 million contract to become the WHA's Winnipeg Jets player-coach, giving the new league instant credibility. At the time, salaries of this sort were virtually unknown, even in the Big Three, let alone in hockey. In rapid order, star players jumped from the NHL to the WHA, defections that hurt many NHL teams. For example, the newly franchised New York Islanders lost 7 of their 20 expansion draft choices to the WHA and subsequently set an all-time record for futility with 60 losses.[46] One year later, 46-year-old Gordie Howe, the Detroit Red Wings legend, joined the WHA's Houston Aeros to play alongside his two sons, Mark and Marty. This was more than a publicity stunt for the new league, as the elder Howe played in 419 WHA games, collecting 508 points while twice being named the all-league right wing and garnering an MVP award.[47]

The WHA lasted for seven years, embracing thirty-two teams in twenty-four cities at one time or another, twenty of which were eventually abandoned. Reliable estimates put the combined losses of league owners at $50 million, while the 803 players who performed in the WHA earned $120 million.[48] Almost every player in professional hockey benefited in some way from the WHA, as average NHL salaries, which had hovered in the middle of the five-digit range until the WHA's arrival, reached the six-digit mark by the late 1970s and early 1980s. In the 1984–85 season, the average NHL salary was $149,000; by the 1994–95 season, the average NHL salary had reached $600,000, a hefty increase, but still below the corresponding figure in baseball and basketball. To be sure, NHL superstars like Wayne Gretzky earned ten times the average annual League salary.[49] Perhaps even greater beneficiaries of the WHA's seven-year presence than the players were their agents, a completely unknown entity in the world of hockey prior to the WHA and a fixture since then. Four teams from the crumbling WHA entered the National Hockey League in the fall of 1979, including the Edmonton Oilers, the dominant team of the middle and late 1980s with five Stanley Cup victories and the showcase for Gretzky, the greatest player in hockey history, and a true global sports star in the vein of Michael Jordan and Diego Maradona.

One additional and recently nascent feature of hockey needs to be mentioned: In 1990, eight nations held the first hockey World Championship for women in Ottawa, offering entertaining and competitive play. A more significant moment in the quite short history of women's hockey occurred eight years later, when women's hockey was admitted as a medal event at the winter Olympics in Nagano, Japan. The two best teams and erstwhile rivals—the United States and Canada—met in a final game to decide who would go home with the gold and silver medals. The decisive American victory to win the gold boosted hockey's profile in the United States and the world and helped gain some new fans for the game. However, in between winter Olympics, women's hockey garnered virtually no attention, and it is not likely to rise beyond the level of activity for a few players(except for a brief stint every four years) anytime soon.

As we argued in chapter 1, nationalism plays a crucial role in the popularization of all sports, and hockey is no exception. Two American victories in Olympic games represented important galvanizing moments for the sport's growing presence in the United States. First, the U.S. gold medal at the 1960 winter Olympics in Squaw Valley needs to be noted in this context. Much more important was the U.S. gold medal garnered exactly twenty years later, when a group of college all-stars defeated the mighty Soviet Union's Red Machine in the 1980 Winter Olympics at Lake Placid,

New York, before millions of viewers watching what was essentially a David and Goliath story on ice. Hockey's popularity in the United States experienced impressive growth as a direct result of this victory, reaching into constituencies that had been hitherto oblivious to the sport.

Lest the reader presume an overly sanguine view of the growth and position of hockey and the NHL in the United States and its sports culture, one must note the implicit instability represented by the peripatetic nature of some of the league's franchises. Indeed, several have moved more than once since the mid-1970s. Though this has sometimes been the result of management seeking better deals and newer arenas, it also highlights the weakness experienced by some NHL teams in what should have been supportive and lucrative markets for hockey. Additionally, the NHL has not fared anywhere near as well on national television as any of the Big Three. Through the 1970s and 1980s, the NHL experienced great difficulty in attaining and maintaining a long-term commitment from any American national television network. Many have noted that hockey (like soccer) on television is much less compelling and attractive than in-person spectatorship, and that this is the case to a far greater degree than the disparity between television and in-person spectatorship with the Big Three. Just like in soccer, enjoyment on television presupposes a far greater knowledge and appreciation of the sport than that possessed by a majority of Americans.

The wider dissemination of cable television in the 1980s gave the NHL a boost, as it found something of a home on ESPN (which it later abandoned for a deal with FOX, only to eventually return to ESPN). When the New York Rangers ended a fifty-three-year drought by winning the Stanley Cup in 1994 (on the eve of that year's World Cup to be held in the United States), hockey experienced a lift in both television ratings, level of press coverage, and, apparently, popularity with the public. However, this was not sustained, as television ratings for both NHL regular-season and play-off games (on both FOX and ESPN) have since been decidedly "flat." Ratings for the NHL play-offs in 1999, shown exclusively on ESPN, were disappointing, less than those usually garnered by regular-season baseball games. If one were to deconstruct the Big Three and One-Half into its six components (i.e., the NFL, Major League Baseball, the NBA, college basketball, college football, and the NHL), the NHL decidedly ranks sixth.

Finally, hockey has failed to appeal to the African American community in terms of either participation or spectatorship. To be sure, the NHL now includes a handful of black players, but hockey as sport and culture continues to remain as overwhelmingly white as ever. As in the case of soccer, the all but total absence (with a few exceptions) of hockey in America's black community will remain a serious impediment in the game's becoming a nationwide rival to the Big Three. But the shortcomings of hockey in the United States should not detract from the major strides the game has made in the post–Cold War era of the 1990s to enhance its international visibility and prominence. It is more than idle talk to envision a global hockey league at some point in the future, or to have the North American champion play the European champion for the Stanley Cup, which would constitute something of a "World Cup for Hockey." Though this would most certainly violate the letter of Lord Stanley's bequest, it would honor the spirit of his trophy by making its winner the truly undisputed world champion of professional hockey. The position of hockey in the American sport space has been cited as a level toward which soccer in the United States could aspire; American soccer enthusiasts would be quite satisfied with such a place for their sport at some point in the twenty-first century.

The Big Three and One-Half As Institutions of Primacy, and Soccer's Related Problems

That Major League Baseball and the NFL, NBA, and NHL all represent the ultimate in their respective sports is a given for Americans as well as sports fans in the rest of the world (especially since the demise of the Soviet Union). Indeed, athletes in baseball, basketball, and hockey anywhere in the world must by necessity aspire to play in these American venues if they want to "reach the top." (In terms of the NFL, this really only pertains to Canada, as American football is confined to North America, and the few football players born and raised on other continents—mostly place kickers—were introduced to the game on American soil). As far as the fans of these sports (as well as those who promote and purvey their product) are concerned, any competition occurring outside these primary sports institutions in the United States is considered decidedly minor and inferior to the North American product. Though another example of American exceptionalism in sport, this is mostly an outgrowth from the ways in which these sports initially developed in relative geographic and cultural isolation from the rest of the world, long before their dissemination beyond the confines of the United States and Canada.

The situation for soccer is exactly the opposite. Soccer players worldwide (including those from the United States) must aspire to play their game and ply their trade in one of the elite four leagues in Europe (English, Italian, German, Spanish), a singular difference from an athlete in any of the Big Three and One-Half, indeed, the exact opposite. Additionally, soccer itself is exceedingly diffuse in terms of its institutionalization. Unlike any of the aforementioned major leagues in the Big Three and One-

Half, there is no single pinnacle in soccer. Instead, there are several competitive forums and institutions that could make a claim for primacy: each of the elite four, the European championship tournaments (annual club or quadrennial national), or the World Cup tournament (every four years). Indeed, arguments and debates among soccer fans as to which venue makes for the best soccer or soccer team ("the world's greatest") is something of a hallmark of soccer culture.

Hence, on top of all the other seemingly alien aspects of soccer presented to the American sports fan, one can add the diffuse dissemination of soccer in all of its organized venues, particularly in terms of what might be seen as the sport's summit. This presents a twofold problem for soccer in the United States. First, the institutional structure of soccer—because of the nature of its historic global dissemination, which makes for a diffusion of its primary venues—creates something of a "dissonance" for American sports fans. However, just as important: The best soccer in the world is not played in the United States, which simply makes the sport less attractive to American fans. In recognition of this reality, Major League Soccer—the latest and best attempt to establish professional soccer as a major sport in the United States—seeks to provide an ambience for its product that will appeal to particular fans of the game while attracting new fans. As stated by Sergio del Prado, general manager of the Los Angeles Galaxy of MLS: "Unlike in other sports, where the best basketball players are playing in the NBA or the best baseball players in the world are playing major league baseball, and so forth, I don't think that the public feels that about MLS. So what we have to do is try to make it a very attractive buy for the fans as far as getting their money's worth for their entertainment dollar. . . ."[50]

Indeed, the contrast to hockey and the NHL—perhaps the optimal level of attainment for the future of soccer in the United States—could not be starker: Whereas the NHL—regardless of all its difficulties—represents the pinnacle of the sport in the eyes of American fans as well as hockey connoisseurs all over the world, MLS decidedly does not. Indeed, instead of a case where the world's best players flock to the United States, America's best soccer players (if seeking the highest levels of remuneration and competition) continue to aspire to play in England, Germany, Italy, or Spain. This represents a huge difference and constitutes a major handicap for soccer's image in the United States.

More provocative and exceptional (especially when examined in the context of overall sports history and culture), the best women soccer players in the world hail from the United States and may actually represent soccer's best chance in this country to traverse the vast divide between activity and culture. The female aspect of the game might present an opportunity to utilize both the requisite institutionalization of primacy briefly described above, as well as harness the forces of nationalism to find a "shortcut" for establishing soccer on firm footing in the American sport space. Women's soccer, MLS, and these points are discussed in further detail in the following chapter.

Five ....

From the North American Soccer League to
Major League Soccer

UNLIKE *the* NASL, by omitting the definite article and calling itself "Major League Soccer," this new league wanted to convey to the world that—just like Major League Baseball—it stood for the apogee of the sport of soccer in the United States: alone, uncontested, unchallenged, at the very top, (perhaps even) permanent. This nomenclature can be seen as signification of the very first time that soccer in America had assumed at least a modicum of organizational rationality and institutional clarity, in which Major League Soccer embodied the apex of a pyramidal structure whose subordinate parts had a direct relationship to each other, as well as with the top.

Whatever the eventual outcome regarding the establishment of soccer as a fifth major sport in the United States, there can be little doubt that the thirty-year period under consideration in this chapter witnessed an immense metamorphosis in soccer's American presence from the sport's previous century-long existence in the United States; providing organizational clarity was a major step. During these three decades, soccer experienced a quantitative growth in America that—as is always the case—had major qualitative implications whose eventual destiny remains completely unclear at the time of this writing. To be sure: Soccer failed to rival baseball, basketball, football, and hockey in terms of presenting any serious challenge to the hegemonic positions that these four continue to enjoy in America's sport space at the turn of the millennium. Yet, at the same time, soccer has entered the American vernacular to a degree not known in the United States until the late 1980s and early 1990s. The term "soccer mom" became accepted American parlance during this period, while the usual banter that has come to characterize nightly newscasts on local television often includes exhortations directed at the weatherman to bring blue skies for the kids' soccer game on the weekend. The word "soccer" no longer evokes foreignness, as it had for a century. Instead, it has managed to become quite American in the course of these thirty years, mainly associated with kids, women, moms, dads, recreation, participation—in short, wholesome activity. The most convincing fact of soccer's complete acceptance by the American vernacular in the course of the last two decades of the twentieth century has been its ubiquity in advertising, where—tellingly—it features youth. Whether soccer's firm presence in the realm of activity will at some point translate into an equally respectable presence in the realm of culture remains unclear at this time. Yet, one thing is certain: The game's solid existence in the increasingly crowded catalogue of physical activities pursued by Americans at the end of the second millennium cannot but help give soccer a chance in the new century to become the fifth sport in America's sport space. This offers no guarantees, but without its presence on the level of activity, soccer would most certainly stand no chance at all of entering American sports culture.

   This account begins with a description and analysis of the North American Soccer League (NASL) which incorporates much of the old, but also highlights some of the new. In particular, it was this league and its legacy that laid the groundwork for soccer's entrance into the American vernacular, even if only as activity instead of culture. By examining the NASL's rise and fall we revisit a number of themes that we have come to see as so detrimental to soccer's presence in the United States. But we also highlight some of the NASL's features that we believe contributed to soccer's metamorphosis in America after the league's demise. After a brief account of indoor soccer in the United States (itself an exceptionalism of sorts), we next focus on soccer's meteoric rise as an activity of choice for youngsters and women within the framework of an account of the game's substantially altered and more prominent presence in American society in the late 1990s compared to any other time in American history. The game's particular appeal to American women and the excellence attained by the best of these women in the global game offers yet another dimension of American exceptionalism, not least as a potential path and shortcut for soccer's entry into American sports culture. Lastly, this chapter concludes with a detailed account of Major League Soccer, the latest and perhaps the first truly successful professional soccer league in the United States, or perhaps the last possible vehicle for eliminating soccer's marginalization in America's sport space.

The North American Soccer League (NASL): 1967–85

Recall (from the last chapter) that the mid-to-late 1960s were quite auspicious in terms of serious growth in the number of franchises and, in the case of football and basketball, nominally successful rival major leagues, with hockey to follow suit in the early 1970s. Times seemed favorable to the establishment of a new soccer league as well. In a fine study of the NASL, Phyllis Marie Goudy Myers demonstrates how the general environment of this era was auspicious for the formation of sports leagues in general, and a soccer league in particular: The cultural environment in the United States at this time featured leisure as an ethic and a commodity that would soon see the business community and the American vernacular coin the phrase "leisure industry." Economically speaking, unemployment was at a record low, the stock market was performing extremely well, and the nation was experiencing a lengthy boom that facilitated increased consumption of leisure goods and recreation. The demographic environment featured two developments particularly favorable to the expansion of existing sports leagues and the creation of new ones: the coming of age of the baby boom generation, whose early cohort had just reached its late teens and early twenties at the time; and a seemingly irreversible trend toward the formation of major urban centers surrounded by large and generally prosperous suburbs (where a majority of Americans would live by the mid-1980s). Finally, Myers notes that the legal environment of the time was favorable to the formation of sports leagues.[1]

Another auspicious development for the establishment of a substantial new soccer league at the time was the interest in soccer on the part of a number of wealthy American businessmen and major corporations, most of whom had been successful owners of Big Three and One-Half professional sports teams, including Lamar Hunt, Jack Kent Cooke, Judge Roy Hofheinz, Madison Square Garden Corporation, and R.K.O.-General.[2] Some were hoping to attract large crowds to fill their stadiums while their football or baseball teams were out of town or out of season, while others had been alerted by the huge crowds and immense popularity that soccer enjoyed in Latin America and Europe; still others simply liked the game. Whatever the case, there is no doubt that the World Cup final between West Germany and England at Wembley in the summer of 1966 enhanced soccer's attractiveness to members of a predisposed public. This contest—won by England in a thrilling overtime, with the perennially controversial and still contested go-ahead goal by Geoff Hurst—was televised all but live (on a slight delay) by NBC, and received a favorable reaction across North America.[3] Surprisingly, such seasoned businessmen as these failed to commission any sort of market analyses regarding the viability of soccer as a major league sport, relying instead on their optimistic view that there were enough "ethnics" in the United States who could sustain such an endeavor, provided it offered a product of excellent quality. The average American sports fan would soon follow, they reasoned. In the completely uncoordinated manner so well known to the history of American soccer, three distinct groups of wealthy investors emerged in the latter half of 1966 seeking approval from the USSFA to gain FIFA sanction for a new professional league. Two of the groups soon merged to form the National Professional Soccer League (NPSL) and landed a television contract with CBS. But the NPSL balked at the demand of the USSFA for a percentage of both gate receipts and television money, thus incurring the

Association's wrath and its refusal to sanction the nascent league. This made the NPSL a "pirate" organization outside the purview of FIFA's global monopoly, rendering its players, owners, and entire organization soccer "outlaws." The other group, headed by Jack Kent Cooke, went along with the antiquated, self-serving, and self-important USSFA, thereby gaining the Association's—and by extension FIFA's—authorization. It entered the world under the name of the United Soccer Association, giving it the catchy and recognizable acronym USA.[4] Hence, the spring of 1967 produced two competing coast-to-coast major league professional soccer organizations where there had previously been none.

Despite its "outlaw" status, the NPSL was able to sign enough foreign players to field ten teams while it filed an $18 million lawsuit for restraint of trade against FIFA, the USSFA and the USA; its two-year national television commitment from CBS called for weekly telecasts. Meanwhile, the USA rushed into the 1967 season with twelve hastily assembled teams of its own, all brought over in their entirety from South America and Europe to now represent a USA franchise for the summer.[5] While these were respectable teams from internationally established leagues, they most certainly were not their respective countries' best. Moreover, most players viewed their summer stint in the United States as an extended vacation and an easy way to make a little extra money before heading back to the "real" competition of their home leagues in the autumn. Needless to say, the quality of play in the USA was mediocre at best, and no better in the outlaw NPSL, whose television ratings were abysmal. By the end of that season, both leagues had run up huge financial losses, made little, if any, impact on the American sports public, and were headed for yet another disaster in American soccer history. Yet, in an unusual act of cooperation for a sport with a history replete with self-destruction, the two leagues decided to merge for the 1968 season after the NPSL agreed to drop its lawsuit against the USA and its organizational allies. The two leagues then formed the seventeen-club North American Soccer League (NASL), which began play in the spring of 1968 and was to last until 1985. If anything, the NASL's first season proved even more disastrous than 1967 had been for its two predecessors. CBS bowed out of its contract, everyone lost money, and by the beginning of the 1969 season, the NASL had shrunk to five teams. The league managed to hang on over the next six years largely on account of the committed presence of two men: league commissioner Phil Woosnam and Lamar Hunt, owner of the NASL's Dallas franchise (Dallas Tornado) and, much more significant for the credibility of the league and soccer in general, the NFL's 1970 Super Bowl champion Kansas City Chiefs. The presence of Hunt, a highly respected businessman from an extremely wealthy family, gave the shaky league its sole anchor of legitimacy and hope. Yet, highlighting the ephemeral nature of professional soccer in America and the completely unconventional—even weird—manner of building its teams, Hunt's Tornado embarked on a global odyssey that carried the team to twenty countries, playing forty-five games of which it won ten, lost twenty-seven, and drew eight before the team had played its very first game in Dallas. "This bizarre event saw a US club team waving the flag without even an American player on the roster and made up of players who had never even set foot in the United States."[6]

Still, despite the bleakness of the situation, there were two developments during these lean years that were to prove decisive for soccer's proliferation in the United States: The first was that Pelé, without a doubt the world's best soccer player and the only one widely recognized in America, twice toured the United States with his club, Santos, in 1968, playing a number of NASL teams all over the country. During the first tour, Pelé—very much at the top of his game—wowed audiences in St. Louis, Kansas City, Boston, and Washington, D.C., where the visiting Brazilians beat all local opposition quite handily. In New York and Cleveland, however, the NASL teams defeated Santos, proving yet again that in professional soccer—just like in baseball, football, basketball, and hockey—even a mediocre team has a decent chance of beating a top side on any given day. Later that season, Santos returned yet again, defeating the Atlanta Chiefs (who were to win the first NASL championship) and the Oakland Clippers (winners of the NPSL title the previous season).[7] It was during these two trips that Pelé first became acquainted with American soccer, since his earlier visits to Randalls Island and other New York venues (see chapter 3) had seen his club play European and Latin American sides on American soil, rather than American teams per se. The visits in 1968 and the games played against NASL teams ignited Pelé's own pioneering spirit and his lifelong optimism regarding the future of American soccer.

The second development entailed the introduction of respectable, if not world-class, professional soccer to cities in the United States where the game had generally never been played and where it had no history at all: Dallas, Kansas City, and Atlanta. Hence, roots were established that were to yield impressive results twenty-five years later, as when Dallas became the regular host of what has arguably developed into soccer's most prestigious and sought-after youth tournament in the world.

The NASL was reinvigorated in 1975 when the New York Cosmos signed Pelé to a three-year contract worth $4.5 million, bringing soccer by far the most media coverage it had ever enjoyed in the United States. CBS made a point of broadcasting Pelé's first NASL game, and attendance skyrocketed. Pelé's presence gave the league instant legitimacy in the world of soccer, and like a magnet, his presence attracted other major stars from around the world. In short order, such living legends as Germany's Franz Beckenbauer and Gerd Müller, Italy's Giogio Chinaglia, Holland's Johan Cruyff and Johan Neeskens, Northern Ireland's George Best, Peru's Teofilo Cubillas, Poland's Kazimierz Deyna, Brazil's Carlos Alberto, Yugoslavia's Vladislav Bogicevic, England's Gordon Banks, and Portugal's Eusebio (often called "the European Pelé")—among many other excellent European and Latin American players—entered the NASL, thereby raising soccer in the United States to a level not previously approximated since the first ASL in the 1920s, and not since attained, with the exception of a month-long interlude during the World Cup tournament in 1994 (see chapter 6).[8] With Pelé, the Cosmos became the league's glamour club, moved from dusty and decrepit Downing Stadium on Randalls Island to the newly completed Giants Stadium in the New Jersey Meadowlands in 1977, and rapidly assumed a prominent place in the crowded firmament of the New York sports scene. New York media reported on the Cosmos with the prominence accorded the New York teams in the Big Three and One-Half, and some of the club's home games became the "hot ticket in town," attended by such prominent celebrity fans as Henry Kissinger, Mick Jagger, Rod Stewart, and Elton John.[9] As many as 77,691 fans crowded into Giants Stadium on 14 August 1977 to witness a play-off game between the New York Cosmos and the Fort Lauderdale Strikers, providing soccer a genuinely world-class ambience while enjoying a superbly played game in which the home team defeated the visitors, 8–3. This game, as well as others during the NASL's play-offs in the late 1970s and early 1980s, matched the quality of play attained by the very good, if not perhaps the very best, professional soccer leagues in the world. That the New York Cosmos could indeed compete with the very finest club teams in the world was amply demonstrated in the team's repeated global tours, during which it regularly defeated some of the world's most prominent sides. (To be fair, these games were all "friendlies," so it is questionable whether the Cosmos's opponents exerted the same level of energy and effort as for contests that "meant something.") When ABC signed an extensive contract with the NASL in 1979, the league's future looked rosy beyond anybody's expectations and it seemed like soccer was finally going to make its long-delayed entry into the American sport space. Alas, once again things would not turn out that way.

In 1982, ABC—dissatisfied with perpetually low ratings for soccer on television—did not renew its contract with the NASL. In short order, it became clear that the league's success was all glitter with little substance, and the house of cards soon came tumbling down. After losing three franchises in 1981, the League lost seven more in 1982, including Lamar Hunt's Dallas Tornadoes. Even for Hunt, the cumulative losses incurred by the league and his team had become too much to bear. It was revealed that no NASL team had ever turned a profit; instead each had steadily lost vast sums of money. The remaining franchise owners scapegoated and fired NASL Commissioner Woosnam, hiring New York politician Howard Samuels as a replacement. Appalled by the league's financial disarray, its past spending sprees, and its poor prospects, Samuels instituted massive reforms, such as cutting roster sizes while also negotiating a salary-cap agreement with the NASL Players Association. The league was down to nine franchises in 1984 when Samuels suddenly died of a heart attack, leaving the job of trying to save the NASL to Clive Toye, without a doubt the third most meritorious member in the NASL's leadership triumvirate alongside Hunt and Woosnam. Toye held the title of "interim president," as no move was made to find a new league commissioner. But it was simply too late, as the moribund NASL was out of business by the following year. On Father's Day of 1985, the Cosmos played Lazio of Rome at Giants Stadium. Gone were the crowds of years past; only nine thousand fans attended, a sadly low number given the prominence of the visiting team and its hailing from Italy, surely a major draw in the New York metropolitan area. "The sad ending to the Lazio game, and to the shining Cosmos adventure, was the spectacle of both teams in an all-out brawl on the field. The Cosmos were finished, they would never play again."[10] Another professional soccer league had attained its untimely demise in the United States.

In retrospect, there were several factors that ruined the NASL, only some of which were financial. Foremost, the league found itself in several catch-22 situations. Realizing that only top-quality soccer would draw major-league-type crowds to matches, the owners of the NASL competed with each other in lavishing huge contracts on players from abroad. Revenues never matched the salary outlay for these players, though without these players there would have been no revenues at all, as the quality of play on the field would have not drawn spectators or have attracted a network television contract. That there were very few American players in the NASL was a powerful factor in limiting spectatorship, both in person and on television, once Pelé had retired from the world of soccer (in a memorable farewell game at Giants Stadium in 1977).[11] But American players were simply not good enough to provide the league with the necessary quality of play. So the NASL's appeal would be limited with a majority of players from the United States, just as it had been with a majority of players from overseas. The only alternative would have been to build slowly from below, from the grass roots, with limited revenue and expenditures, while emphasizing homegrown talent playing below first division quality. But there had long been soccer on that level in the United States— as in the second ASL, as well as many other leagues—with the obvious result of always remaining confined to inferior quality and a minor league level and appeal. Besides, once committed to major league status, the NASL owners could not expect to downgrade their product and still recoup their huge financial losses. Additionally, the NASL had succumbed to what had always kept soccer out of the mainstream in the United States: the complete absence of a soccer culture in relation to the culture of the Big Three and One-Half in American sports. Simply put, most Americans were not sufficiently interested in watching soccer in a sustained manner beyond the occasional glimpse of Pelé. As for the "hyphenated Americans" who traditionally comprised the bulk of the sport's constituency in the United States, most apparently lost their enthusiasm for home teams not composed primarily of their ethnic or national brethren. This was reflected in the poor television ratings and the ever-declining number of spectators in the stands.

Ostensibly, the post-NASL period merely reverted to the status quo of soccer in the United States in an array of regional amateur and semiprofessional leagues playing on the local level, more or less ignored by the American sports public. In 1985, the Western Soccer Alliance was formed on the West Coast, while yet another incarnation of the American Soccer League emerged in the east in 1987. Indoor soccer (see below) assumed some of the slack left by the defunct NASL, but, on the whole, the overall soccer scene in America was yet again splintered, localized, and largely irrelevant. From this vantage point, the NASL's presence was little more than a chimera, a shiny flash-in-the-pan with no lasting effect. But this was clearly not the case, as a completely new constituency would emerge in American soccer during the course of the 1980s and 1990s that was to give the game a grassroots and indigenously American dimension hitherto not experienced in its century-long existence in the United States. To clarify: While there were clearly antecedents in terms of a soccer presence in places like St. Louis, Kearny, New Jersey, and Fall River, Massachusetts, where soccer had cultural dimensions, the NASL, greatly flawed as it was, spawned a nationwide awareness of the sport that it did not have before. There is no way to prove a direct connection, but greater numbers of American youth and, notably, American women began to take up the sport as the saga of the NASL wound down; the number of participants have continued to increase steadily in subsequent years. Both women's soccer and youth soccer emerged in the wake of the NASL's brief but conspicuous presence in the United States. As such, they are the NASL's most lasting legacy and arguably Pelé's most important institutional contribution to the game of soccer in the United States. A discussion of these two quintessentially American phenomena in the context of soccer's changed position in the United States of the 1990s follows a short digression on another unique feature of soccer in the United States.

Indoor Soccer

As noted in chapter 3, the second ASL pioneered indoor soccer in the United States as early as 1939.[12] Madison Square Garden became a crucial forum for the proliferation of boxing, ice hockey, and (mainly college) basketball as sports culture throughout the New York metropolitan area in this era (and, by extension, the larger American sport space at this time), and it hosted indoor soccer games in an attempt to harness another viable winter sport. With five players plus a goalkeeper to a side, a special emphasis on dribbling skills, quick passing, and the use of the boards all around the arena, indoor soccer seemed a hybrid between traditional soccer and ice hockey. As a spectator sport, it never took off in this initial experimental period.

Played periodically at various venues throughout the United States in an ad hoc fashion, this form of the game attained a prominent, though temporary, institutionalization via the Major Indoor Soccer League (MISL), inaugurated in 1977 by sports promoter Earl Foreman, initially with the full support and backing of the NASL. Featuring sixteen teams in major American markets, Foreman was confident that this fast-paced mixture of soccer and hockey was "the game that Americans want." In complete accord with the internecine history of soccer in America, the MISL soon actively challenged the NASL (which at the time was, of course, at the crest of its popularity). Indeed, lucrative contracts from the MISL lured some of the NASL's best players to forsake the regular game of soccer for its indoor American variant. The defection of Rick Davis—captain of the United States national team and the leading American-born player of the day—from the NASL's flagship Cosmos to the MISL's St. Louis Steamers in 1983 was a serious loss for the former, in many ways heralding its impending demise. But the MISL itself could not elude the chronic institutional instability endemic to American soccer. After changing the location and quantity of its teams virtually on a yearly basis, the league folded in 1992, with Foreman admitting that indoor soccer was "unable to attract new owners."[13]

But this American experiment did not fade into oblivion, as two new indoor soccer leagues emerged: the Continental Indoor Soccer League (CISL) and the National Professional Soccer League (NPSL). Both introduced indoor soccer in the summer months, the off-season period for teams of the NBA and NHL. So it is not surprising that some of the owners of the seven CISL teams have illustrious names from the boardrooms of major American sports: Jerry Buss (Los Angeles Lakers), Jerry Colangelo (Phoenix Suns), Donald Carter (Dallas Mavericks), and Jim Thomas (Sacramento Kings). "People also visit movie theaters in the summer, so we figured they would visit indoor arenas as well," said the coach of the CISL's San Diego Sockers, aptly characterizing the mindset that has led to the fair (though obscure) success of indoor soccer in the United States.[14] Indeed, on the very evening of the World Cup's opening day in June 1994 (the second game of the most prestigious soccer tournament in the world, and the very first ever in Dallas), nearly seven thousand fans chose to attend a CISL game in the Mavericks' arena rather than attend (or watch on television) the match between South Korea and Spain in Texas Stadium played at exactly the same time.[15] Perhaps there is no clearer example of the often separate worlds of American and global soccer than this rather revealing incident.

Indoor soccer's quite limited and modest, but undeniable, popularity has also tangibly improved the quality of the game, as best gauged by the American team's second-place showing in both the 1992 and 1996 indoor soccer World Championships. This is no mean feat, considering that these tournaments were also contested by fifteen other teams all hailing from premier soccer powers. Yet, the huge difference between indoor soccer's presence in the United States and in many European countries testifies to the completely different history and gestalt of the game in these respective environments. In Europe, indoor winter tournaments during the league break offer a welcome entertainment for fans, a good way for players to stay in decent shape and hone their skills, and a bit of extra cash for players and owners alike. In short, indoor soccer in Europe complements and confirms the overall presence of soccer culture on the Continent. But in the United States, this version of soccer undermines the still precarious culture of the "game proper" itself by offering an alternative and a competitive threat.

The State of American Soccer, 1970s into the late 1990s: A Major Activity in Search of a Hegemonic Culture

As argued, it was the NASL that planted the seeds for soccer's subsequent emergence as a recreational activity in the United States by attaining a high profile and a concurrently respectable level of media coverage in the 1970s. This provided a sort of legitimation for the game among the American professional and commercial managerial classes (i.e., "yuppies") who desired a game their children could play that was allegedly nonconfrontational, nonviolent, often coeducational, and noncompetitive (it does not matter who wins "as long as everyone has a good time"), and apart from what many of the upscale and educated viewed as the crass and crude milieu of the Big Three and One-Half. Additionally, soccer appealed to segments of the educated classes in the United States who

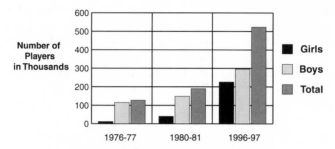

Figure 5.1. Gender participation in high school soccer over time.

viewed the sport as some sort of conduit for "multiculturalism" by way of its international appeal and separateness from the culture of American team sports. Again, it was the NASL that provided the initial legitimation of soccer in the eyes of what would develop into a "soccer constituency" for the game as an activity (as opposed to a "soccer constituency" for the game as spectatorship and culture—as we have defined the term—in the United States). Hence, it is mostly the children of these "soccer-yuppies" who currently comprise the sport's participants in the United States and who would presumably provide the basis for making soccer a major sport in the United States and part of the nation's sport space.

By virtually every measure, soccer's recreational surge in the United States has been truly impressive, if not indeed meteoric, since the early-to-mid-1980s.[16] According to the Soccer Industry Council of America, an organization that has accumulated detailed statistics in virtually every conceivably related category, there existed 18,226,000 so-called total participants in soccer in the United States for 1997. (The category of total participants is defined as members of the United States population six years of age or older who have played soccer at least once per year.) This number has steadily increased since the 1970s: from 15,388,000 in 1987 (the first year for which such figures are available) to 15,945,000 in 1990, 16,365,000 in 1993, and 18,098,000 in 1996, an impressive increase of 18.4 percent in the ten-year period ending in 1997. In terms of gender, there were 11,081,000 males (60.8 percent) and 7,145,000 females (39.2 percent), the latter yielding a proportion nearly eight(!) times larger than the corresponding figure in any advanced industrial country comparable to the United States in social structure and economic development (say, Sweden, Germany, Britain, and other West European countries). Simply put, women—as discussed in the next section—participate in and excel at soccer in the United States, whereas they do not in countries where the game has traditionally formed the backbone of hegemonic sports culture and often assumed a monopolistic pride of place in their respective sport spaces (see figure 5.1). Regarding age, in 1997 six- to eleven-year-olds

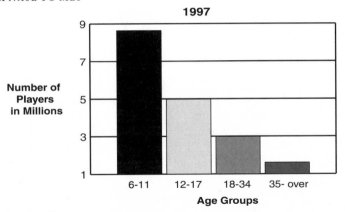

Figure 5.2. Soccer participation by age groups, 1997.

comprised 8,646,000 (47.4 percent), twelve- to seventeen-year-olds
4,981,000 (27.3 percent), eighteen- to thirty-four-year-olds 2,985,000
(16.4 percent) and the thirty-five and over category 1,614,000 (8.9 percent), impressive confirmation of the notion that soccer in the United
States is undoubtedly, though perhaps not exclusively, a favorite activity
for children and adolescents in particular, and that its popularity as activity considerably decreases as age increases (see figure 5.2).[17] (See the appendix to this chapter for a more detailed look at the demographic character of soccer participation in the United States.)

These figures are a most impressive demonstration of the growth and
breadth of participatory soccer in the United States—especially for youth.
However, they do not reveal the particular character of this participation
for kids: organized teams and leagues purveying structured play, completely dependent upon the efforts and resources of adults (parents,
coaches, referees, recreation league administrators) for the entire endeavor, in contrast to the spontaneous and casual "street" activity in
which most sports attach themselves to a culture in grassroots fashion. In
other words, the millions of American kids playing soccer rarely play the
game or its variants (i.e., "one on one," "two on two") on their own,
away from the well-kept fields to which they are driven by their soccer
moms. This poses a twofold problem for the sport in the United States.
First, soccer is a game in which spontaneity and improvisation make for
the best and most exciting play and players, and the complete reliance on
structured play in organized forums inhibits the quality of both, which
means that American players continue at a decided disadvantage vis-à-vis
their European and Latin American counterparts. Second, the dearth of
soccer at the "street level" inhibits the sport's wider dissemination beyond
its white middle-class constituency in the United States.

To be sure: baseball—still considered the national pastime—is not often seen in its sandlot form in the United States these days, and offshoots like stickball are now almost nonexistent (though softball—both in organized leagues and in casual sandlot games—is quite prevalent). Most kids play their baseball in institutional structures like Little League, Babe Ruth, and Pony Leagues; the days of the mass proliferation of casual sandlot and playground games are long gone. Yet, baseball as culture still thrives by virtue of its long tradition and history (as discussed in chapters 2 and 4); soccer, on the other hand, lacks a similar cultural conduit. Though soccer's proliferation at the recreational level in the United States has been quite prolific, its deficiencies in this context prevent its full utilization for complete entry into American hegemonic sports culture.

The limitations of recreational soccer seem to have confined its competitive qualities to the level of activity in the case of most of the boys, adolescents, and young men who play it. However, as to the women, the game has succeeded in attaining such a level of global excellence that it offers a whole new dimension to the sport in the United States and worldwide. This new stature might just perhaps help transcend soccer's now undisputed presence as an American activity into the realm of sports culture. It is to this new and fascinating world of women's soccer that we now turn.

Women's Soccer in the United States and the 1999 World Cup

Simply put, America has once again assumed an exceptional role, in two ways, in terms of its soccer experience: By involving the country's women in the game to a degree unprecedented anywhere else in the world, the United States has become the very best soccer nation in a sport in which its men have remained marginal, at best, throughout the twentieth century. Signally, American women became the very best in precisely the team sport not so contested and claimed by their countrymen.[18] The U.S. women's national team has dominated this sport on the world level and has been far and away its most consistent, impressive, and successful performer: The team won the first women's soccer world championship in China in 1991, took third place in the next tournament played in Sweden in 1995, won the very first Olympic gold medal awarded in women's soccer at the summer games at Atlanta in 1996, attained the gold medal in the Goodwill Games in New York in July 1998, was not beaten by anybody but arch-rival Norway (the world champions of 1995 and Olympic gold medalist in 2000) in four years, and—to top it all—won the title in the 1999 Women's World Cup, played in the United States, in what proved far and away the most popular and successful event in the entire history of women's team sports, while garnering the highest American television audience ever attained for any soccer game, male or female. Above all, this Tournament, culminating in the dramatic victory by the American team, created a moment when for the very first time soccer enjoyed a genuine popular following in the United States, as a large number of Americans truly cared about and *followed* this event to an extent never before experienced by soccer in this country. If still merely for a limited time, soccer had finally made it to the popular world of office talk around the watercooler. It did so once again during the two-week tournament of the Sydney Olympics in the fall of 2000, in which the American women lost the gold-medal game to Norway in what arguably has been thus far the best match in women's soccer history.

Though not getting anywhere near the media attention devoted to either men's sports or individual women's sports, the American national team had drawn decent numbers of spectators in its recent past prior to the 1999 World Cup. Some regular matches, such as the one between the United States and England in San Jose on 9 May 1997, attracted crowds in excess of seventeen thousand enthusiastic fans. The gold medal game between the United States and China at the Atlanta Olympics attracted seventy-seven thousand spectators, far and away the highest attended public event in the history of all women's sports up to that time.[19] Figures approaching and surpassing that were garnered for all the appearances of Team USA in the 1999 tournament, though contests between other teams did not fare anywhere near as well.

All the U.S. national team's players are products of the nation's college soccer world. Indeed, in marked contrast to men's soccer where—as we argued in chapter 3—the college game has been an impediment to the development of first-rate American players who can compete successfully at a professional major league level, colleges have fostered the women's game and developed into the loci for producing the world's finest female soccer players. As with the proliferation and growing popularity of women's basketball, this is a direct legacy and consequence of the institution of Title IX of the 1972 Federal Education Amendments to the Civil Rights Act of 1964. In this context, it would be remiss not to mention the incredible record of the women's soccer team for the University of North Carolina, Chapel Hill, which won sixteen NCAA Division I titles in nineteen years (a feat unparalleled by any Division I college in any team sport, male or female); average home attendance for these Tar Heels was 2,401 in 1997, far surpassing that of men's college soccer.[20] Hence, the promise of the women's game in the United States becomes all the more evident in contrast to the increasing problems on the men's side.

As has been the case with most advances in modern feminism, the United States has been way ahead of Europe and other countries of the advanced industrial world. Just as laws against sexual harassment and gender discrimination and other recent advances in gender equality, equal opportunity, and nonsexist behavior are still met with derision on the part of Europeans, so too does the rest of "the real football world" (as opposed to "that American abomination") scoff at soccer played by women. As Julie Foudy—one of the stars of the U.S. team—said so clearly: "Everyone plays soccer here [in the United States]. Girls are encouraged. But you travel abroad, and the game is considered a man's world in so many cultures. A girl is considered a freak if she plays. We've been to Spain, and jumped into a men's game and been looked at like we were crazy."[21]

German, English, and Brazilian newspapers, for example, either ignored the 1999 Women's World Cup or ran articles making fun of it. Some saw it as yet another American aberration in which vulgar materialism and Hollywood-style commercialism—phenomena that these countries routinely associate and conflate with their negative views of the United States—had altered their hallowed game of soccer. In other words, the women's game was either seen as a sort of blasphemy or as a kind of comedy performed in a country where soccer had become a "yuppie" activity apart from the "authentic" sports culture of the game found in its major "home" countries. In Europe some of the more serious pieces on the tournament and/or women's soccer ran in the human interest sections of newspapers rather than on the sports pages. German television, for example, only broadcast the second half of the final between the United States and China (begun at 11:00 P.M. local time), preferring to air its usual late-night Saturday soccer talk show, which featured the manager of Hertha BSC Berlin discussing his club's unexpectedly fine showing the past year and his views on the forthcoming Bundesliga season. Quite revealing of hegemonic sports culture, in this case, talk attained preference over action.

However, any soccer aficionados who chose not to watch the 1999 tournament final missed out on a contest with all the energy, excitement, and tension that only a World Cup final (as in the men's game) can produce. This match was the crown of a tournament that slowly but surely made its way onto the radar screen of the American media and public, in the end providing women's soccer newfound esteem, status, and dissemination. The tournament featured sixteen teams, up from the twelve that had contested the first two cups in China and Sweden, respectively. Total attendance for the tournament topped 650,000, while the U.S. team attracted NFL-level crowds to its matches, including 79,972 at the New Jersey Meadowlands, 65,080 in Chicago, 50,484 in Foxboro, Massachusetts, 54,642 in Landover, Maryland, and 73,123 in Palo Alto, California. As noted, matches not including Team USA, though respectable in terms of attendance, did not fare nearly as well; Germany-Mexico at Landover, for example, drew 20,129.[22]

The games were televised by ABC, ESPN, and ESPN2, and ratings generally increased over the course of the tournament. Team USA's opening match had a 1.7 rating on ABC, while ESPN averaged a 1.45 for all its telecasts of the tournament; not exactly stellar numbers, but both well exceeded the best ratings ever attained by Major League Soccer in its four-year existence.[23] Additionally, the 3.8 Nielsen cable rating for the U.S.-Brazil semifinal (played on a Sunday afternoon) was the highest rating soccer had ever achieved on ESPN, or any other cable network, and surpassed ESPN's telecast for Game 6 of the NHL Stanley Cup playoffs a month earlier (a Dallas-Buffalo triple-overtime affair played in prime time, which had a 3.51).[24] And as noted, the U.S.-China final played before more than ninety-two thousand spectators at the Rose Bowl in Pasadena, California—won by the United States in a shoot-out after the teams had played to a scoreless tie—attracted more American viewers than any previous soccer game, with a 11.4 national rating and a 31 share, surpassing the previous television best for soccer in the U.S. (the 1994 World Cup final played in the same stadium, see chapter 6) while enjoying numbers close to Game 1 of the 1999 NBA Finals (11.5 rating) and Game 1 of the 1998 World Series (12.3).[25]

Perhaps most impressive of all, the women's national team attracted and attained media coverage—which started slowly and steadily increased toward the crescendo of the final, then gradually subsided over the next two weeks—that could easily rival what is routinely directed at the Big Three, and in one month far surpassed all the cumulative media coverage garnered by MLS in four years. On each night of his television show during the tournament, talk-show host David Letterman displayed a women's national team photo in which the players appeared to be wearing nothing but *Late Show* T-shirts, while Letterman himself transformed the term "soccer moms" into "soccer mamas" (which progressed into "the babes of summer," a play on "the boys of summer" of baseball). This highlighted an aspect of women's team sports heretofore avoided or actually suppressed: An image of femininity and wholesome sexual appeal was purveyed—quite willingly on the part of the players themselves—as a message "that women can be both athletic and feminine in an endeavor that, in many countries, still carries the stigma that women who play are somehow unwomanly." Indeed, a side-angle photo in *Gear* magazine featuring U.S. defender Brandi Chastain "crouched behind a soccer ball wearing only her cleats and her rippling muscles," drew the attention of journalists, pundits, and reporters, as well as many people with little previous interest in soccer.[26] When Chastain threw off her shirt—to reveal a sports bra—after scoring the clincher's final shoot-out, some speculated that this was either an act of wanton exhibitionism, an instant of "momentary insanity" (as Chastain herself claimed), a blow for gender equality (as shirt shedding by male players in celebration of a victorious moment is something of a tradition in soccer), or a shrewd and calculated marketing ploy (since the sports bra in question was a Nike prototype planned for mass production).[27]

The players of Team USA and their World Cup triumph were the cover stories for *Time*, *Newsweek*, and *Sports Illustrated* (the latter two covers featuring Chastain's now famous flexing-in-sports-bra moment) the week after the final, and also graced the cover of *People* magazine (with glowing personal profiles on all eleven starters inside) the following week. Meanwhile, the post-tournament public appearances of the players en masse— at Disneyland and the WNBA All-Star game, on NBC's *Today Show* (and outside the studio), meeting President Clinton (who had attended two tournament matches, including the final) at the White House—also rated coverage in both the sports and main news sections of nearly all daily newspapers and on local television news reports. All these developments bespoke qualities of culture that went well beyond the public indifference usually accorded to activity.

By virtue of their consistent achievement of excellence steadily portrayed for a solid month in newspapers and television—peaking with the final game and its well-publicized aftermath—the U.S. national team's most prominent members became nationally known sports figures. Players like Foudy, Chastain, Mia Hamm, Michelle Akers (likely the greatest female player in the history of the game), Kristine Lilly, Tisha Venturini, and Briana Scurry (the goalie, and only African American member of the sterling eleven) had attained star status in the sense that their names and faces have become recognizable to the larger American public beyond the narrow confines of the soccer world. Though opportunities for marketing 1999 Women's World Cup merchandise and advertising tie-in sponsorships were for the most part neglected, several of these players netted product endorsement deals before (most notably Hamm's well-known Nike spot with Michael Jordan), during, and after the tournament. [28] The respective images (and career highlights) of Akers, Chastain, Hamm, Lilly, and Scurry were featured on five special-edition box designs of Wheaties cereal, perhaps the ultimate benediction the world of American commerce and marketing can bestow upon an athlete. Though not a first for women athletes, it was indeed a first for soccer: No soccer player ever had graced a Wheaties box in the 75-year history of this popular General Mills product.[29]

Most important, these superb and very successful athletes have become the role models and heroes for millions of young American girls who now aspire to be players, just like these stars. (And perhaps not so surprising, the women of Team USA have also engendered a following among adolescent soccer-playing boys.) The exceptional success of the American women's game—in notable contrast to the status of their male counterparts— fulfills two key conditions essential to making any sport popular in the

United States or, for that matter, in most places: attractiveness for being the very best (i.e., quality as a means), and attractiveness for winning and making their fans feel proud for being American in a sport where being American had certainly not been a major source of pride and satisfaction (i.e., quality as an end).

As this competition showcased exciting games, featured American stars who helped make the game known to people—particularly women—beyond the soccer community, and culminated in a highly watched American victory on home turf, it provides some hope and promise for the founding of a women's professional league that (like the WNBA in basketball) may indeed help institutionalize women's soccer on a level that clearly exceeds the competence and purview of the country's colleges. A successful Women's World Cup was not a sufficient condition for the establishment of a women's professional soccer league in the United States, but it most definitely constituted a necessary one.[30]

As suggested at the end of the previous chapter, women's soccer may present an opportunity to utilize the institutionalization of primacy and global excellence that has so far been a requisite for the successful entry of any team sport into America's sport space. This could indeed provide a "shortcut" for soccer toward a position in that space. A professional women's soccer league would not only feature the victorious athletes of Team USA but also attract the best women soccer players from abroad (à la the NBA, MLB, and NHL). With adequate financial backing, such a women's league would likely attain unchallenged recognition as the sport's pinnacle (outside the World Cup), its highest representative of routinized competition, something no soccer league in the world—including the elite four of Europe, whose respective followers regularly debate over such a designation—can boast. However, for such a venture to succeed—in terms of revenues and as a legitimate entry into American hegemonic sports culture—a fundamental shift would have to occur in the ways in which women and girls relate to sports and sports culture, not so much as participants but as followers.

Demographic analysis of the audience for the 1999 World Cup reveals that prior to the final, "women made up only 34 percent of the World Cup audience on ESPN and 35 percent on ESPN2, compared with 39 percent for ESPN's WNBA games and 40 percent for the NCAA women's basketball championship tournament."[31] (Indeed, these figures for women's basketball reveal something of a weakness in the female fan base for that sport.) Title IX and other developments during the last quarter of the twentieth century have opened the door for women as athletic participants, but this has not engendered the concomitant establishment of a large female constituency for women's team sports as culture. That significant numbers of young women and girls have adopted sports as one of their activities but not as one of their interests points to a fundamental difference in how males and females relate to sports: Countless millions of boys have dreamed of becoming professional athletes in one of the Big Three and One-Half (or soccer outside the United States) but instead have grown up to find other livelihoods. Yet, the vast majority of these males retained their interest in these sports as followers long after acknowledging that they themselves would not be "big-time" participants. Hence, success (in terms of cultural entry) for a women's professional soccer league is dependent on large numbers of those girls now playing soccer growing up to become fans and followers long after they no longer participate on the field. A culture of sports following and affect—an overwhelmingly male preserve—has so far not been adopted by women for women's sports. For the most part, women do not immerse themselves in the culture of being fans and followers of a team and its sport as do so many men. Until there is some sort of change in this context—when women routinely watch women's soccer, ordinarily and routinely talk about it "around the water cooler," and develop affect and attachment to particular teams—the opportunity for the women's game to act as the conduit for soccer's entry into the American sport space will likely be precluded.

Of course, such a change in the relationship of women to team sports (in this case soccer) requires an institutional structure—as in a professional sports league—to begin the process. Plans for just such a venture were announced in February 2000. The Women's United Soccer Association (WUSA) is slated to begin play in April 2001 with the backing and involvement of corporate magnates, including John Hendricks and James Kennedy (the respective chairmen of Discovery Communications and Cox Enterprises), Amos Hostetter Jr. (a former chairman of Continental Cablevision), Brian L. Roberts and Amy Banse (president and a vice president, respectively, of Comcast Corporation), and Joseph J. Collins (chairman and chief executive officer of Time Warner Cable). "A minimum of $40 million is to be provided by the initial investors to fund a minimum of eight teams, plus league administration, during the first five years of operations."[32] Of course, with the history of American soccer what it is, plans for any sort of new soccer enterprise could not go uncontested. The owners and executives of MLS sought to form and promote their own women's league, and applied to the USSF for just such approval. Meanwhile, most of the players from the U.S. 1999 Women's World Cup team announced that they would only play in the WUSA, not in any MLS-sponsored venture. Yet another debilitating "turf war"—such a recurring theme for soccer in the United States—seemed inevitable.[33]

But this time the plot took a different turn. After six months of negotiations, MLS and WUSA worked out an agreement whereby "there will be cross-investment and broad cooperation between the leagues in the areas of marketing and promotion, scheduling and stadium development." Players from Team USA are to form the core for clubs located in Atlanta, Boston, New York, Orlando, Philadelphia, San Diego, San Francisco, and Washington, D.C., with plans afoot for expansion. And a full year ahead of presenting a single game, the WUSA garnered a four-year television contract with Turner Broadcasting.[34] Hence, the most important legacy of the Women's World Cup of 1999 will likely be the establishment of a highly viable and visible women's professional soccer league. Guarded optimism seems in order, though we again must emphasize the changes in the relationship between women and team spectator sports that must occur for women's soccer (or any women's team sport) to effect any significant changes in the American sport space. It is to a discussion of Major League Soccer—a direct mandate of the 1994 World Cup held in the United States—that we now turn.

Major League Soccer: A Work in Progress

After four full seasons, the overall tally on MLS is such that supporters and enthusiasts of the sport have plenty of evidence to be pleased with its past accomplishments and to look toward the future with optimism and hope. Conversely, the league's detractors and those much more skeptical of its achievements and future promise can equally find plenty of numbers to support their negative prognostications. In our assessment of MLS, we will cautiously err on the side of optimism for one simple reason: Whatever MLS's television ratings may be and regardless of how low the attendance figures of some of its franchises have been during the first four seasons, the league has consciously—and conscientiously—tried to right the traditional lethal wrongs besetting American soccer. Only time (quite likely at least one generation) will tell whether it will prove successful in its endeavor to establish soccer as a solid fifth (and profitable) major league team sport in America's sport space and become part of American sports culture, in addition to its existence as mere activity.

Perhaps the best way to begin a short analysis of MLS is to see it as an "anti- (or most certainly non-) NASL"—in other words, as a conscious attempt to avoid the mistakes that ultimately doomed its predecessor. To be sure, the NASL operated in an era when soccer was nowhere near the activity it had become by the time MLS emerged, but still, the errors of the past could not be repeated if this latest attempt to establish professional soccer at the major league level in the United States is to succeed. The origins of MLS hail back to one of FIFA's explicit conditions for agreeing to hold the World Cup in the United States in 1994: "One of the principal reasons that prompted FIFA to assign the 1994 World Cup to the United States . . . was FIFA's desire to help a professional league get off the ground as soon as possible. A World Cup final competition is a golden opportunity for providing traditional football with potent publicity at the professional level in a country like the United States, where three popular ball games of American football, basketball and baseball already predominate."[35] To be sure, FIFA's stated requisite to have such a professional league established in the United States has to be taken with a grain of salt, especially since it was FIFA that had vehemently opposed staging the 1986 World Cup in the United States, thereby contributing to—though far from causing—the NASL's disappearance and soccer's American setback. In hindsight (as well as at the time, actually) it seems quite obvious that FIFA's primary goals in placing the 1994 World Cup in the United States were financial, as the Association well knew that holding such a tournament in the United States could not be anything but immensely lucrative for itself. Yet, FIFA's actions in this context eventually spoke louder than its words: World Cup '94 did indeed prove the germinal for MLS.[36]

From the very beginning of FIFA's considerations to put the World Cup in the United States, with the desire to have such a tournament followed by the launching of a serious professional soccer league in America, one man assumed central importance through all steps of the Association's plans, short and long term: Alan I. Rothenberg, a Los Angeles lawyer who was not only a devotee of soccer but also a superb organizer and manager. Rothenberg had been an owner of the Los Angeles Aztecs of the NASL from 1977 until 1980, and the general manager and counselor of the Los Angeles Wolves of the United Soccer Association (USA) before that. But most significant as far as FIFA was concerned, Rothenberg proved immensely efficient and successful in organizing all the soccer games at the Los Angeles Olympics in 1984, which attracted the largest number of spectators among all events featured in the Games. The gold medal contest between France and Brazil drew more than 100,000 spectators to the Rose Bowl, an amazing figure by any standards for any tournament anywhere in the world.[37] FIFA empowered Rothenberg both to organize the World Cup and to set up a professional soccer league to follow in the wake of that event. Fully cognizant of the long history of constant internecine warfare among various professional leagues and the U.S. Soccer Federation, FIFA (which had done its share in the past to contribute to such conflict) wisely supported Rothenberg's bid to become president of the USSF in 1990, a position that he held for two terms, until August 1998. By uniting the leadership of the Federation (still the sport's single most important body of legitimation and sanction domestically and—perhaps more important—internationally) and of the newly developing professional league in one person, FIFA and American soccer were blessed—for the first time in one hundred years—with a situation whereby the sport's foremost adjudicating body in the United States and its professional entities were not at odds.

On 17 December 1993 Rothenberg revealed the new league's name as well as its logo. He also announced seven cities that would have MLS franchises, five fewer than the originally planned twelve teams that were to form the new entity.[38] Even though American businessmen were enthusiastic about the World Cup's appearance in the United States, past experience had taught them to be quite cautious about investing in yet another professional soccer league whose future remained uncertain at best.

Lest mistakes that contributed to the demise of earlier leagues—the NASL in particular—be repeated, MLS was to be organized in a very different manner from the get-go. At the core of this new organizational approach was the so-called single-entity concept, a sort of socialized soccer structure, as it were. As the league's media guide states: "MLS features a unique ownership and operating structure. Unlike other professional sports leagues, which are a confederation of individual franchise owners, MLS is structured as a single limited liability company (single-entity). In a single-entity league, each team operator owns a financial stake in the league, not just their individual team. In addition, player contracts are owned by the league rather than by individual teams. The single-entity concept allows teams to operate autonomously in their markets, but with the incentive to see that all teams are financially successful. MLS believes this single-entity structure enables it to avoid many of the pitfalls that have plagued other professional sports leagues. The single-entity design provides MLS and its member teams with the ability to: Limit the disparity between large and small markets; Offer commercial affiliates an integrated sponsorship and licensing program; Decrease the opportunity for sponsor ambush; Gain economies of scale in purchasing power and cost control; Make decisions in the best interest of the entire league rather than just one team."[39]

Though MLS failed to begin play in 1994 (or even 1995), as originally planned—thereby missing a golden opportunity to utilize unexpectedly easy access to America's sports viewers on account of the strike that prematurely ended the 1994 baseball season and continued to haunt the "national pastime" throughout all of 1995—the league's inaugural season was finally announced on 17 October 1995. Following the MLS Player Combine in January 1996 and the league's first player draft one month later, each of the ten clubs entered its first-ever spring training. "An overflow crowd of 31,683 at Spartan Stadium witnessed San Jose forward Eric Wynalda score the league's historic first goal in a 1–0 victory over D.C. United. The ultimate goal—to launch a world-class professional soccer league with 10 teams—had become reality."[40] Setting aside MLS's understandable self-promoting hyperbole regarding its "world class" status, there can be no doubt that professional soccer had made yet another—and perhaps lasting—comeback on the American sports scene, if not quite yet in its sports culture and sport space (as we have defined and used those terms in the course of this book).

The first two seasons were contested by ten teams divided into an Eastern and Western Conference. The former comprised the MetroStars (playing at Giants Stadium), the New England Revolution (Foxboro Stadium), the Columbus Crew (Ohio Stadium, [Columbus Crew Stadium as of 1999]), the Tampa Bay Mutiny (Houlihan's Stadium [Raymond James Stadium as of 1999]), and D.C. United (RFK Stadium). The Western Conference consisted of the Colorado Rapids (Mile High Stadium), the Dallas Burn (Cotton Bowl), the Kansas City Wizards (Arrowhead Stadium), the Los Angeles Galaxy (Rose Bowl), and the San Jose Clash (Spartan Stadium). For the 1998 season—MLS's third—the Eastern Conference was joined by the Miami Fusion (Lockhart Stadium) and the Western Conference by the Chicago Fire (Soldier Field). Several cities—including but not limited to Seattle, Charlotte, Cincinnati, Pittsburgh, San Diego, Houston, Portland, and Atlanta—have expressed interest in bringing Major League Soccer to their respective regions. MLS plans to add two more expansion teams in either 2000 or 2001, followed by an additional two clubs in 2002 or 2003 to bring the league to sixteen teams, a size league management believes ideal.[41]

The goal for most of the MLS franchises is to move eventually from their current stadiums—where a crowd of ten or twenty thousand "gets lost" among the cavernous building and the empty seats, and the playing fields are sometimes too small or oddly shaped—into venues specifically built for soccer. The first such structure—seating 22,500 and financed by the ubiquitous Lamar Hunt for his Columbus Crew team at a cost of approximately $28 million—opened in May 1999.[42] The creation of such venues is deemed essential for a league that will depend on the "ambience" of its product and the "atmosphere" in which it is presented so as to attract a particular audience, specifically families with children.

MLS is the only Division I professional outdoor league in the United States, as sanctioned by FIFA and the USSF. It plays a spring-to-fall schedule in which each team plays thirty-two games—sixteen home and sixteen away—followed by the play-offs (best-of-three Conference Semifinals, best-of-three Conference Finals), which culminate in the MLS Cup for the league's championship in October. In terms of a solid commitment to the league's success, there can be no doubt that MLS has attracted a number of serious investors who combine the following positive characteristics: deep pockets; continued experience and involvement with major league sports in the United States; a proven interest in, knowledge of, and loyalty to soccer in America; and a cogent sense that soccer is the world's only truly global team sport and the world's most popular form of entertainment, a crucial factor for investors who think globally. Among MLS's financial backers and owners are Rothenberg himself, John Kluge and Stuart Sobotnick of Metromedia Company (one of the largest privately held companies in the United States), the aforementioned Lamar Hunt (perhaps soccer's most consistent and reliable backer in the United States [see chapter 3]) and his sons Clark and Lamar Jr.; Philip Anschutz (railroad/real estate industrialist and co-owner of the NHL's Los Angeles Kings); former investment banker Marc Rapaport; Kennetz Horowitz (a communications entrepreneur and wireless telephone pioneer); and the Kraft family (owners of the NFL's New England Patriots), led by father, Robert, and son, Jonathan.[43]

Perhaps the most important difference between MLS and all previous attempts to establish professional soccer on a major league level in the United States has been the presence of some of the world's most successful corporations as the league's commercial affiliates. Firms and product names such as AT&T, Bic, Bandai, Budweiser, Fujifilm, Honda, MasterCard, Pepsi, Snickers, All Body Sport Quencher, Avis, Kodak, Chevrolet, Nike, Reebok, Umbro, adidas, and Kellogg's have joined as official sponsors, suppliers, or corporate partners in long-term deals worth more than $80 million. For these global companies, it seems important that the United States, with its huge market, join the global community via international venues such as soccer. Conversely, they realize that a major presence in American soccer will help enhance their position in global soccer, which they correctly perceive as a crucial medium in world markets.

Lastly, a special deal with Disney's Wide World of Sports helped ensure MLS's legitimation in the all-important world of high finance and corporate capitalism. MLS and Disney organized all kinds of joint features during the league's third year, such as holding the third annual MLS All-Star game in the Citrus Bowl in Orlando, which involved the Disney city in the entire All-Star week as well as other MLS activities such as spring training and a "kick-off campaign" with all twelve MLS teams.[44] Most important in the Disney deal has been MLS's multiyear television package with ABC, ESPN, and ESPN2, all owned by Disney. Among these three English-language networks and the Spanish-language Univision, MLS had sixty-nine regular-season and play-off games televised during the 1998 season (in addition to games televised by local stations in their home markets), a record number in terms of soccer's exposure in America's most potent—and singularly influential—communication medium.[45] MLS has been the beneficiary of having its games broadcast by some of the finest soccer commentators in the United States, perhaps even worldwide. The duo of Andres Cantor and Norberto Longo have handled Univision's national game of the week, while on the English-language side, American audiences have had the opportunity to enjoy the commentary of Seamus Malin, and play-by-play accounts by such veteran broadcasters as Bob Ley, John Paul Delacamera, Tommy Smyth, and Derek Rae.

Until the middle of its fourth season, MLS enjoyed what appeared to be able leadership from its commissioner and deputy commissioner, Douglas G. Logan and Sunil Gulati, respectively. Among Logan's assets were his extensive experience in the communications and entertainment industry and his complete fluency in Spanish. (The realization by the league that the Spanish-speaking community in the United States forms one of its most important constituencies is best manifested by having all its communications and materials published bilingually. MLS is a completely bilingual and bicultural entity, which, as will be discussed below, has both advantages and disadvantages.) Immensely knowledgeable about the game and its players all over the world, Gulati was undoubtedly the "soccer man" of the two. Born in India, Gulati is a young Columbia University–trained economist who worked for the World Bank before returning to New York to teach economics at Columbia and help oversee MLS. In August 1998 Gulati experienced the first of two setbacks. He narrowly missed becoming vice president of the USSF by a few votes after a very contentious campaign. The victor was John Motta from New Hampshire. These two men represented different constituencies in American soccer—Gulati the professionals, and Motta the amateurs, roughly speaking—whose past internecine conflicts proved nothing short of catastrophic for the game's overall presence in the United States.

Then at the beginning of MLS's fourth season, Logan summarily dismissed Gulati for alleged interference in some contractual disputes between Tab Ramos and the New York/New Jersey MetroStars. Whatever the merits of the case, there was absolutely no doubt that the young league had lost its most talented executive and perhaps the only one at league headquarters who really knew the game of soccer as culture, not only as activity or entertainment. Logan himself would subsequently lose his job by August 1999, leaving the implication that MLS was hurting.[46] The league owners then appointed Don Garber as MLS's second commissioner. Like Logan before him, Garber is not a "soccer man," as his previous job was senior vice president and managing director of NFL International, where he worked closely with NFL Europe and managed business activities for the NFL outside of the United States.[47]

Despite the difficulties reminiscent of American soccer's troubled history, MLS represents a change from all previous attempts to establish major-league professional soccer in the United States in arguably the most important area of the game, that of the players. In notable contrast to the NASL—which relied almost exclusively on the import of aging foreign superstars such as Pelé, Beckenbauer, and Cruyff to gain the attention of the media and public, while American players were accorded a subordinate (usually bench-warming) position on the teams—MLS features American players much more prominently, mixing them with very good foreign players who, however, are not superstars. Among these have been players like Colombia's Carlos Valderama, Bolivia's Marco Etcheverry and Jaime Moreno, Mexico's Jorge Campos, El Salvador's Raul Diaz Arce, Sweden's Thomas Ravelli, and Switzerland's Alain Sutter. However, some of these foreign players have shown little regard and loyalty to their MLS teams and little respect for the league. Campos, for example, has twice abandoned MLS clubs in midseason to return to his club in Mexico. Clearly, to most foreign soccer players, MLS represents a livelihood but not a cultural identity.

This has been most evident with Lothar Matthäus, one of the game's true giants and the most "capped" male player in the world (meaning that he, more than anybody else, had been accorded the honor to represent his country—in this case, Germany—by playing for its side). After lengthy negotiations, Matthäus decided to leave Bayern Munich to end his playing days in the New York metropolitan region, helping to lead the MetroStars to a better place from the woeful existence that the team had led in the previous two years in MLS. But from the get-go of Matthäus's arrival in New York, it was clear that his heart never left Germany, that he was reluctant to play in the United States, and that he used every possible opportunity to jet back to Europe, not only to continue playing for the German national team in the European national championship in June but also for various other reasons, many of which were only tangentially related to soccer. Matthäus made it clear by his demeanor and behavior, if not by his explicit language, that he regarded his gig with MLS as a stop-gap measure to earn some extra cash and see whether he still had the ability and desire to continue his soccer-playing career in a "real" soccer league such as the German Bundesliga, perhaps for a different club than his old side. While Matthäus's mercenary approach to MLS and soccer in America was particularly obvious and egregious, it seems far from unusual. Many an aging superstar from a soccer country regards MLS good enough to be a fine source of income when the player's talents might be in declining demand in the prime leagues of the game. These players come to MLS not for the commitment to help a fledgling league get much-needed legitimacy or—better still—to help soccer make it as culture in the United States, but simply to make money. And with MLS's signing of players such as Matthäus and the former Mexican superstar Luis Hernandez, the league is dangerously approaching the strategy pursued by NASL with such adverse consequences for the game's development at the top level in the United States: the neglect of local American talent and the long-term investment in the game in the United States in favor of immediate benefits yielded by the presence of well-known foreign superstars. It was precisely this pitfall that MLS set out to avoid. To be sure, MLS finds itself in a dire predicament. As a business, it needs to make money in the here and now to survive. This logic dictates that it resort to the hiring of well-known players, regardless of their commitments to the league and soccer's fate in the United States. But as the obvious premier league of professional soccer in the United States, MLS also has the mission to wean American soccer players to a level that will provide international respectability and competitiveness to the game played in the United States.

The latter is all the more important since for the very first time in American soccer, the very best American-born players have an opportunity to pursue their professional soccer careers at home, in the immediate presence of their countrymen and -women. MLS has been able to retain and feature the best American soccer players and virtually the entire squad of the United States national team, helping to boost the game's presence. While names such as Tony Meola, Alexi Lalas, Eric Wynalda, Eddie Pope, John Harkes, Tab Ramos, Marcelo Balboa, Mike Burns, and Cobi Jones have not reached anywhere near the visibility and recognition accorded to star players in the Big Three and One-Half, they have attained some respectable presence in local markets and—through national advertising campaigns for a number of products—on a nationwide level. Indeed, with the exception of a handful of American athletes including Claudio Reyna, Chad Deering, Jovan Kirovski, Kasey Keller, Brad Friedel, Frankie Hejduk, and Tony Sanneh (all of whom have played for respectable European clubs), most of America's top soccer player have chosen and found gainful employment in MLS. As such, MLS is well poised to fulfill the same role for American soccer that other major soccer leagues have consistently accomplished in their respective countries throughout the twentieth century: being the routinized forum and steady institution that the country's best players can safely call home.

"Major and Minors" and "Project 40"

In the long run, two reforms associated with MLS may prove the most essential ingredients in terms of reforming American soccer to a degree where it could become world class. Both address the issue of institutional continuity, something woefully absent through all of soccer's history in the United States. The first is the establishment of a three-tiered system of professional soccer that for the first time makes the structure of American soccer very similar to that of Europe, South America, and the rest of the world. The twelve MLS teams serve as America's first-division professional league. Teams from the 1996 A-League and the 1996 United Systems of Independent Soccer Leagues' professional and premier leagues (USISL) formed a 24-team second division that has been administered by USISL under the moniker of A-League. (By 1999, the A-League had expanded to thirty teams, with a maximum capacity envisioned at thirty-two.) As of 1996, the USISL has also run a third division, a professional league called United States Division III Professional Soccer League (D3 Pro), and what amounts to an amateur fourth division called the Premier Development Soccer League. For the first time, the United States has three organized and firmly affiliated divisions of professional soccer leagues, plus an amateur league.

Unlike most professional leagues in Europe and Latin America, the American system does not include the practice of promotion and relegation between the first division (MLS) and the second division (A-League). However, each MLS team has been affiliated with a minimum of two A-League teams, as well as three to four D3 Pro teams. Within the affiliated USISL clubs and their "parent" MLS teams, there exists a system of player movement whereby MLS teams can "call up" USISL players and conversely send them down to USISL clubs for professional seasoning, rehabilitation of injuries, or simply to further the relationship between MLS and the USISL.[48] In other words, this soccer structure is very similar to baseball's farm system, where major league teams have clearly defined relationships with their affiliated teams at each level of the minors (AAA, AA, and A) from which they promote and demote players on a regular basis but—unlike soccer structures elsewhere—do not relegate or promote teams from one level to the next. Hence, the A-League's Rochester Raging Rhinos remain stuck in their A-League Division though they performed better at the gate than four MLS teams (Dallas, Tampa Bay, Miami, and Kansas City), averaging 11,498 visitors in 1998 and playing arguably better quality soccer than some of the MLS clubs.[49]

The parallel in baseball also happens to hail from upstate New York, where Buffalo's AAA club, the Bisons, has on occasion rivaled some of MLB's weaker clubs in terms of attendance and civic support, but—except for hope of attaining an expansion franchise—with absolutely no chance of advancing into the majors. (Denoting America's sports exceptionalism, such an elevation would seem rather odd—or likely ridiculous—to most Americans. That no such vertical interleague movement exists in American sports, in a land of alleged opportunity and meritocracy, seems quite strange to the rest of the world.) That this system of continuity has worked is best proven by the 143 transactions that occurred between MLS clubs and USISL teams, involving a total of 132 players, during the first season of play.[50] In 1997 twenty-seven USISL players were called up to MLS teams, while fifty MLS players were loaned out to USISL clubs, demonstrating that the interaction between these two leagues—as well as the other two below them—had become institutionalized, offering a clear path of continuity to an aspiring young American player.[51] Simply put, for the first time in America's soccer history, a talented young soccer player who starts on the amateur level and excels at the game now has the concrete institutional possibility, as well as the structural clarity, in which to advance his soccer career all the way to the "majors." This had never been the case before 1996.

The second reform attempts to address a problem we have repeatedly noted in this book: The college experience, an essential expectation of middle-class American life, and absolutely crucial to the future career of almost every young man and woman, happens to be detrimental to the development of the soccer skills necessary to play the game at a world-class level. Enter Project-40, a joint venture between Major League Soccer and the United States Soccer Federation—in and of itself a novelty in the history of American soccer—aimed at providing America's young soccer-playing talent with the valuable training and playing opportunity "at the level needed to enhance the United States' international success."[52] This "industrial policy" aims to reconcile an American college education with the acquisition of world-class soccer skills, with the explicit aim of leading the United States to a higher level in the world of international soccer. The very concept and its implementation have been totally unparalleled in the history of American soccer. Indeed, this arrangement as a whole—with its explicitly stated goal of "excellence"—remains a rarity in the laissez faire, market-driven, and chaotic world of America's sports establishment. "Project-40 signees earn the minimum annual MLS salary ($24,000) and are awarded a five-year academic package covering tuition (not to exceed $37,500) by the United States Soccer Federation. Project-40's eventual goal is to provide each player with the opportunity to participate in 40–60 quality contests each year, on various professional levels, enabling the player to develop at a faster pace than ever before, during the extremely important years when he is 18 to 22 years of age."[53]

Approximately thirty players had joined Project-40 by the 1998 season, some of whom were assigned to MLS clubs where they stayed for much of the season, such as, for example, Brian Dunseth (New England Revolution), Joey DiGiamarino (Colorado Rapids), Nino Da Silva (Kansas City Wizzards), Barry Swift (MetroStars), and Eric Quill (Tampa Bay Mutiny). Others formed the roster of a team called U.S. Pro-40 Select that competed in the A-League. Monday through Thursday of each week, Project-40 individuals trained with their MLS clubs before embarking on a Friday-to-Sunday A-League period that saw the team play either two A-League games, or one A-League game and a scrimmage against a nearby MLS team. With twenty-eight road games during a six-month A-League season, the Project-40 players were confronted with a challenging schedule that approximated the demands placed on soccer players at the top levels of the game. In addition to playing with and for MLS teams, some Project-40 players also joined fine European clubs, such as the Glasgow Rangers (Scotland's most frequent league champion), Sunderland of the English First Division, and Latin American teams such as Atlas F.C. of the Mexican First Division and Catolica of the Chilean First Division. Project-40 thus established an environment, as well as a structure, able to expose talented young American soccer players to the world of the professional game without foreclosing their college education.

Some colleges initially perceived Project-40 as a direct threat to college soccer. Though still in its infancy, Project-40 has already taken players into MLS who would otherwise be seen on college sides. "Joey DiGiamarino and Brian Dunseth went Pro-40 in 1997. They would have been seniors for Cal State Fullerton in 1998. And Josh Wolff was playing in the MLS Cup with the Chicago Fire instead of taking on UNC Charlotte that weekend with South Carolina, the school he left after his junior year. Pro-40 has already affected the approach college coaches take when recruiting. They explain options to the players and the parents, and also get a feel for where education fits in their priorities. College coaches expressed their concern about Pro-40 in a meeting . . . when they confronted MLS commissioner Doug Logan and deputy commissioner Sunil Gulati about what they felt were, in essence, poaching tactics." In a sense, then, Project-40 has engendered a relationship between college soccer and MLS not dissimilar to that of college basketball to the NBA. The very best soccer players—like their counterparts in basketball—now have an option they previously did not have: to turn professional. Just as the two worlds in basketball learned to coexist without being a major detriment to each other, it is likely that college soccer will not suffer in the long run on account of the presence of MLS. Indeed, they might even come to complement each other. One thing is certain: " 'College soccer is not going anywhere,' (Bob) Warning (St. Louis University's soccer coach) said. 'It will be around forever, so we better make it the best it can be.' "[54] MLS would like to make the same claim for itself.

The Public Response So Far

As far as attendance at MLS games and television viewership are concerned, the tally lends itself just as easily to a positive as it does to a negative interpretation. Attendance at games was nothing short of sensational in the first season: 2,786,673 spectators attended 160 regular season games, an average of 17,416 per game, eclipsing the projected 10,000–12,000 per game by a handsome margin. The 1996 MLS playoffs drew 300,455 fans to 17 matches, an average of 17,673. Notable highlights include the 31,683 fans at the league's aforementioned inaugural game in San Jose on 6 April 1996; the 78,416 who crowded into Giants Stadium on July 14 to watch the first MLS All-Star game between the Eastern and Western Conference all-stars (though it should be noted that this game was followed by the "real" show, an exhibition match between 1994 World Cup champion Brazil and a FIFA World Star team); and the 34,643 who defied a driving rain storm (six inches in twenty-four hours) to watch the first-ever MLS Cup in Foxboro Stadium between D.C. United and the Los Angeles Galaxy on 20 October 1996.[55] To be sure, even in MLS's first season, major disparities emerged between the league's "good" markets such as Boston, Los Angeles, San Jose, and New York and its laggards such as Kansas City, Tampa Bay, Dallas, and Denver. By 1997, the league's second season, the figures looked a bit more sobering: 2,338,653 people attended the 160 games of the regular season for an average of 14,616 per game. As in the previous season—and as expected—the numbers were higher for the 13 play-off games, with a total of 208,194 and a 16,014 average per game.[56] The decline occurred in all MLS venues, with those previously strong remaining on top and the weak ones—like Kansas City and Dallas—sinking into the four-digit area, and thus below the psychologically (let alone financially) important 10,000 mark. The worrisome downward trend continued into the third season as the league's average per-game attendance declined to 14,312; and if one eliminates the two expansion teams that joined MLS in 1998, the annual average would be lower still, at 13,617. Of the two new teams, the eventual MLS rookie champion Chicago Fire proved a success story, not only by its victorious performance on the field but by averaging 29,413 per game in the stands at Soldier Field. Things looked a lot more sobering for the Miami Fusion, the other expansion team, whose average per game attendance was 12,764.[57] The 1999 figures declined ever so slightly. The league average tallied at 14,282 with the strong markets in Columbus, Los Angeles, Washington, D.C., and New England averaging around 17,000, but the weak markets of Dallas, Miami, and Kansas City declining precipitously, the latter two falling into the 8,000 range.[58]

Downward trends in spectatorship are never good signs. Yet, put in an optimistic light, the attendance average of the League's fourth year is still above what was originally projected for the first five years of MLS's existence. Moreover, if compared to other first-division soccer leagues around the world, the MLS average—though not stellar—is very respectable, given that MLS was merely four years old when these numbers were compiled. To be sure, MLS does not come close to the European "Elite Four," led by the German Bundesliga with a 32,951 attendance average for the 1997–98 season, followed by Italy's Serie A with 30,704, England's Premier League with 29,184, and Spain's Primera Division with 29,987. Scotland follows in fifth place with 17,937, and France in sixth with 16,087; and then comes MLS with 14,282, followed by average league attendance in such soccer powers as Brazil, Holland, Russia, Portugal, Austria, Belgium, the Czech Republic, Switzerland, Hungary, Norway, Denmark, Sweden, and Poland. The following major countries were omitted from this research, but it is expected that Mexico (estimated at 35,000), Argentina (approximately 30,000), Chile (25,000), and Colombia (20,000) would place ahead of MLS in terms of average spectatorship for their respective first divisions.[59] All in all, MLS's attendance numbers were not bad when gauged in comparison to league attendance in long-established soccer countries, again considering that the American venture was but four years old. Of course, when measured against the average 55,000-plus attendance of NFL games and the 30,000-plus of MLB games, the MLS record appears rather meager.

As can be expected, MLS conducted extensive research to ascertain the profile of its audience. Survey results, broken down into three categories—overall, Hispanic, and non-Hispanic—found that 77 percent of the respondents were between the ages of eighteen and forty-four, of which 29 percent were between twenty-five and thirty-four. Since one stated objective of MLS has been to bring "the spirit, passion and intensity of the world's most popular sport to the United States" by "featuring competitive ticket prices (average in 1997: $13.38) and family-oriented promotions such as the interactive 'Soccer Celebration' theme park at the stadium" and, crucially, by creating an atmosphere in the stadium and its environment that appeals "to the children who play and the families who support soccer," it seems evident that data related to families and children among spectators have been of particular interest to the League.[60] Hence, it must have been satisfying to league officials that 38 percent in the overall category said that they attended MLS games with children under eighteen years. As expected, the Hispanic number for attending with children was slightly lower, at 36 percent, than the non-Hispanic (39 percent) but, in all likelihood, still much higher than in soccer-dominated Latin American countries where going to games remains a predominantly adult male preserve. Giving some indication that this tradition has continued for Latin fans in the United States, a greater proportion of Hispanic respondents (40 percent) than non-Hispanics (32 percent) indicated that they attended MLS games with someone aged twenty-five to thirty-four, most likely a male friend. That non-Hispanics—as expected—see MLS soccer much more in terms of family entertainment than Hispanics is borne out by yet another datum: 49 percent of non-Hispanics indicated that they attended MLS games with someone between the ages of thirty-five and forty-nine (in all likelihood parents, guardians, or relatives) whereas only 27 percent of Hispanics did so.

The gender data further bear out the fact that Hispanic MLS spectators are culturally and demographically closer to soccer fans in countries where soccer forms the core of sports culture than they are to the non-Hispanic MLS supporters: Seventy-eight percent of the Hispanic respondents indicated that they were male, as opposed to 67 percent of non-Hispanics. Overall, 70 percent of MLS spectators were male and 30 percent female, yet again confirming the recent American exceptionalism in terms of soccer's considerable feminization in the United States in notable contrast to soccer-dominated countries in Europe and Latin America, where female presence at soccer venues hovers around the 15 percent mark at most, but usually lower. Regarding the ethnic composition of the fans, 54 percent considered themselves Anglo, 36 percent Latino, and 10 percent "other." Columbus (89 percent) and Kansas City (87 percent) reflected the greatest Anglo attendance, whereas Los Angeles (82 percent) and Washington, D.C. (78 percent) had the greatest Latino presence. New England (19 percent) and New York/New Jersey (16 percent) featured the largest number of "other" respondents. (As noted, the large presence of Latino fans and MLS's utilization thereof present a double-edged sword that will be discussed at the conclusion of this chapter.)

Confirming the dichotomous nature of the MLS fan base are the following data concerning household income (above $50,000 per year) and college graduation: Regarding the former, 26 percent of the Hispanic respondents but 57 percent of the non-Hispanics indicated that they lived in households with an income of $50,000 or more per year. Not surprisingly, Kansas City (59 percent) and San Jose (57 percent) had the richest fans, while Los Angeles (21 percent) and Dallas (35 percent) were the two clubs with the poorest spectators, as determined by the lowest percentage of respondents who indicated that they had an annual income of $50,000 or more. Indeed, these were the only two cities to score under 40 percent in this category, confirmation that MLS fans—non-Hispanics for certain, but Hispanics as well—are generally financially comfortable. Education data further corroborate the overwhelmingly middle-class nature of MLS's spectatorship, even among Hispanics. In terms of the proportion of college graduates among MLS fans, 57 percent of non-Hispanics indicated that they held a college degree, as opposed to 39 percent among the Hispanics. Tampa Bay and Washington, D.C. (both at 57 percent) were at the top of the education scale, while Los Angeles (35 percent) and New England (43 percent) were the only markets to have fewer than 50 percent of respondents without a college degree.[61]

As illustrated in the last chapter, the television audience is of much greater importance than the spectators at the venues for the long-term viability of any sports league in the United States, and MLS is certainly no exception to this iron rule. Once again, the tally of the first four years can be seen in an optimistic and a pessimistic light. To begin on the positive side, MLS's ratings on ESPN2 were only slightly below those for that network's college basketball presentations and NHL regular season broadcasts. MLS's games on the Spanish-language network Univision outdrew on average that network's coverage of the Mexican First Division. However, we fear that the negative interpretation might be the more realistic: Being close to ratings of regular season NHL games on ESPN2 is as close to a ghettoization and marginalization on American television as one can possibly get, short of beach volleyball, tractor pulling, and curling. During the 1997 season, not one MLS broadcast on ESPN2 or ESPN attained a 1.0 rating, not even the MLS All-Star game, by far the highest rated of a regular season MLS game that year with an 0.8. Most MLS games hovered around the 0.2 and 0.3 mark, not at all encouraging. The numbers were not much better for the play-offs, during which no match attained a 1.0 on either of the two ESPN channels. The picture for MLS's first season in 1996 was nearly identical. With the exception of the League's opener in San Jose on April 6 (a 1.0 rating), no game broadcast on the two ESPN channels that season garnered ratings even close to 1.0, with most hovering again in the 0.1 to 0.4 range. The ratings for the 1996 play-off games were not much better. To be sure, a few ABC-televised MLS games reached a 1.0 rating or inched even a few decimal points beyond that, but on the whole the television picture remained as bleak in 1998 as it had been in the league's first two seasons.[62] If anything, the 1999 figures were even a tad below those of 1998. Thus, for example, MLS Cup '99 between D.C. United and the Los Angeles Galaxy—two of the league's marquee clubs—attracted 17 percent fewer viewers on ABC than in the previous year's MLS Cup.[63]

The MLS on-the-Field

The quality of play in the first four MLS seasons has been mixed. The first of two MLS on-the-field objectives to "encourage attacking and entertaining soccer with dynamic players and coaches" was fulfilled, at least statistically speaking. MLS games averaged 3.3 goals per game, one of the highest per-game averages of any professional soccer league in the world and certainly higher than in any of the elite four of Europe or the averages attained at World Cup competitions since the late 1970s.[64] The other MLS on-the-field objective to "assist and improve the performance of U.S. soccer teams in competition, on an international scale for club, national and youth sides" has also been partly fulfilled, despite the national team's abysmal performance at the World Cup competition in the summer of 1998, a topic amply featured in chapter 7. On the negative side, there can simply be no question that the overall level of MLS play has not come close to replicating that offered by the top professional soccer leagues in the world. While comparisons of this kind remain subjective and very vague by definition, it would be not unfair to characterize the quality of MLS soccer as being akin to that played in the second divisions of established soccer powers in Europe and Latin America.

On the positive side, one should note D.C. United's six championships in four years, two of which occurred in the international arena against top-level competition. Playing not only efficient but also very attractive soccer, D.C. United won the double—MLS championship and U.S. Open Cup championship—in its very first year. In 1997 D.C. United repeated as MLS champion, but fell short in defending its U.S. Cup title by losing to the Dallas Burn in the final game. One year later, United made it into its third consecutive MLS Cup game, where it was favored to beat the surprise finalist Chicago Fire, a first-year expansion team. D.C. United lost and the new MLS Champion, Chicago Fire, stepped into its shoes by beating the Columbus Crew a few days later in the U.S. Open Cup championship game, thus becoming holder of the now-coveted "double." United, however, expanded its earlier successes to the international arena. As MLS champions—thus the United States champions of first-division professional soccer—D.C. United represented the United States in the championship tournament of the CONCACAF region (which includes all the FIFA-affiliated soccer federations of the countries in North America, Central America, and the Caribbean). United won that tournament, thus becoming CONCACAF champion, a region that—after all—does include such established soccer powers as Mexico and Central American countries such as Costa Rica, El Salvador, and Honduras. Subsequently, United impressively proved its CONCACAF title no fluke by defeating the world-class Brazilian and South America champion Vasco da Gama to earn the coveted Interamerican Cup, a trophy no previous U.S. soccer team had ever held. Defeating even a jet-lagged Vasco was no mean feat.[65] This victory capped D.C. coach Bruce Arena's brief but successful MLS coaching career for which, along with his NCAA championships, Arena was awarded the most difficult challenge of his coaching career: to reshape and rebuild the United States men's national team as its coach after its debacle in France. The early results were impressive: Two victories over mighty Germany, one against Argentina, and a narrow loss to Brazil (though two of these matches were "friendlies"). These early successes carried over into June 2000 when this Bruce-Arena-managed Team USA beat South Africa and Mexico by the impressive scores of 4-0 and 3-0, respectively. D.C. United continued its winning ways after Coach Arena's departure by regaining its MLS crown in 1999 and by adding yet another U.S. Open Cup championship to its short but illustrious pedigree as American soccer's best club team.

On the negative side, the success of D.C. United in the CONCACAF tournament appeared to take place in complete obscurity, as far as the American media and broad sports public were concerned. The former provided almost no coverage—save for that found in the weekly space provided to the soccer columnists of some newspapers—while the latter demonstrated absolutely no interest, save for the small niche of soccer fans. The same can be said for the success of both United and the Fire in the U.S. Open Cup competition in 1999 and 1998, respectively..

Perhaps the most encouraging sign after four MLS seasons was that slowly but surely, more American players were beginning to emerge as important players for their respective teams. While there still were relatively few American-born playmakers and goal scorers in the league, improvements at all positions were clearly discernible to spectators and professionals alike. " 'Americans are increasingly playing a more important role . . . ,' says Bruce Arena, 'In terms of quality, the American players are better and there are more of them than in the past.' "[66] If true, this might as well be the highest praise so far for MLS's achievements and contributions to soccer's future in the United States.

The Paradox between Identification and Affect for Soccer in the United States

As discussed in chapter 1, nationalism and affect are two potent forces in the sports culture of any nation. In terms of the potential elevation of soccer into the American sport space, these represent both opportunity and danger, especially in their conflation. In terms of affect, a successful professional team in any modern sport must gain the allegiance of a fan base, specifically, "the home crowd" (in the stands and on television). If it succeeds in this realm and demonstrates excellence on the field of play, it may then possibly—as in the case of some of the more successful franchises throughout the history of team sports, such as the New York Yankees, Dallas Cowboys, Los Angeles Lakers, and (for that matter) Manchester United—proceed to gain the affect of legions of fans outside of the home market and reap the profits thereof. This points to an American first (if not an exceptionalism): the modern organization and appeal of professional team sports that goes back to the founding of the first openly professional baseball team, the Cincinnati Red Stockings and, subsequently, the establishment of the National League (see chapter 2). Well over a century later, fans of the successful Yankees and Cowboys—as well as those for the perennially disappointing Chicago Cubs and Tampa Bay Buccaneers—do not care about the geographic (or occupational, class, ethnic, and, roughly since the 1950s, racial) origin of the players who perform for their teams; what matters is that they perform well for the team the fans consider their own. Thus, it matters little that many a New York Yankee now hails from the Dominican Republic and Panama, or that one-third of the rosters of the three New York–area hockey clubs has a European background. The fans' affect for or disapproval of these top-level professional teams remains independent of the players' ethnic or geographic origins. While the players' composition on teams has become global, the fans' affection for them has remained local.

But once again, history matters. This globalization has no detriment in terms of the fans' feelings for and interest in the team and the game as long as both have enjoyed hegemonic cultural presence throughout the twentieth century. Thus, it matters little, if at all, that the pedigreed London club Chelsea fielded teams in recent years without one English player on its side. Nor has it been to the detriment of Arsenal, Chelsea's North London rival, that a majority of its players hail from outside the British Isles. Chelsea, Arsenal, CF Barcelona, AC Milan are the soccer equivalents of the New York Yankees and the established clubs of the NHL. But they are the distinct opposites of the new teams in MLS who are yet to find their identities in their respective local communities in a game that has been burdened by the stigma of being foreign, indeed downright un-American. In MLS's case, the plethora of foreigners on the league's respective teams might yet again work to the disadvantage of soccer's cultural acceptance in the United States.

For MLS, the next challenge lies in attaching its teams' geographic identifications to the affect of a solid local fan base—of making the MetroStars "New York's team," the Burn "Dallas's team," the Galaxy "L.A.'s team," and so forth. We believe that we are on safe ground in predicting that it will take at least one full generation for MLS teams to attain such affect, which is why it will likely take that long—if it happens at all—for MLS to fulfill its goal of joining MLB, the NFL, NBA, and NHL as the foremost institutional representative of a fifth major team sport in the American sport space.

In the meantime, however, MLS faces the pitfall of reattaching to itself precisely that potentially detrimental phenomenon that greatly contributed to the marginalization of soccer throughout its American experience and helped to bring about the demise of the NASL: the reliance on "ethnic" players to draw immigrant or "ethnically identified" soccer fans out to the game to root for a team that comprises—at least in part—their countrymen or ethnic group, while the sport itself retains (or regains) the image in the United States as the game for—and by—foreigners and "ethnics." In Los Angeles, crowds upward of forty thousand have consistently turned out at the Coliseum for exhibition and tournament appearances of the Mexican national team and other clubs from Latin America (including a 1998 Mexico-U.S. match that witnessed ninety thousand Mexicans—most of them residents of the United States—booing the American national anthem and flag, an incident discussed in chapter 7). Such appearances at the Coliseum by teams from Latin America have dwarfed those for Galaxy games at the Rose Bowl. The milieu at the well-attended Coliseum events is reminiscent of soccer throughout most of its marginal American existence, albeit on a larger scale: "For many immigrants, soccer is a nationalist lifeline to their homelands. . . . For Marina Fietes, a native of Nicaragua at the Mexico-Argentina game . . . and her friends the game is a trip, if only for an evening, back to hometown life. 'An American flag doesn't mean much here,' Fietes said, gazing at the overwhelmingly immigrant crowd at the Coliseum."[67]

The temptation to field a team that appeals to specific ethnic and/or immigrant groups is alluring to the Galaxy: "If the Coliseum crowd is mostly immigrant, the Galaxy attracts the more established, U.S.-born children of immigrants, its marketers say. . . . But though the Galaxy is a U.S. team, its promoters amplify their fan base by wooing Latin American soccer gods. A few years ago the Galaxy featured goalkeeper Jorge Campos [who, as noted, subsequently abandoned the Galaxy in mid-season for his club in Mexico] . . . 'It's a no-brainer,' [Galaxy vice president Michael] Arya said. '[Latinos] are much more likely to come to a Galaxy game if we have a Salvadoran player. It's more than that he is a great player—he's one of them. . . .' For the 40% of the Galaxy audience that is not Latino, the Galaxy has featured stars of Iranian, Armenian, Nigerian and other soccer-loving backgrounds."[68] This might work in Los Angeles, for a while at least, but fielding ethnically based teams (and leagues) has proved extremely detrimental to soccer in the United States throughout the sport's mostly obscure history.

Almost three years since D.C. United traded Salvadorian forward Raul Diaz Arce after the 1997 season, "there have been fights in the stands whenever visiting teams that feature Salvadorian players come to RFK [stadium]. The Salvadorian fans cheer for the visitors, which sparks trouble with the home fans."[69] On the plus side, this shows that D.C. United has established something of a base of loyal fans willing to stick up for their team. But on the down side, this demonstrates how interest and loyalty to a major league professional team based on the ethnic or national identity of its players will prove ephemeral, as the teams of the NASL found out. Perhaps just as important, such incidents serve to reinforce the negative image (violence engendered by ethnic allegiance) that soccer often projects. This is particularly acute for an enterprise—MLS in this case—that is seeking to attract to its games American families wanting "good clean" entertainment.

However, this does not preclude the utilization of nationalism on the part of American soccer, which could easily occur within the context of the women's game, as discussed. The success of the American women's national soccer team provides an avenue through which the sport may be promoted to a whole new level. A professional women's soccer league in the United States could potentially be in an excellent position to utilize the institutionalization of global primacy and unchallenged excellence discussed at the end of chapter 4. While MLS—barring some phenomenal otherworldly event, such as the U.S. (men's) national team winning a World Cup, or at least legitimately contesting it into the advanced rounds with superb play—will have to build slowly over the course of a generation, the women could conceivably offer a shortcut for soccer to enter the American sport space, providing that changes occur regarding the relationship of women to sports culture.

There can be no doubt that America's soccer landscape had vastly changed between the advent of the NASL in the late 1960s and the establishment of MLS in the late 1990s. From soccer's vantage point, one should almost talk about two different countries when describing the respective milieus that created and shaped these two professional soccer leagues. To be sure: With all these immense changes that have reshaped soccer's American environment in thirty years, there have also been some major continuities. Indeed, we have argued that without the NASL there would not have been a "soccer explosion" at the recreational level, without which there would in turn have been no MLS or two-time U.S. Women's World Cup Champions. The 1994 World Cup played in the United States—another major event that made definite contributions to soccer's changed and evolving persona in American sports—is the subject of the next chapter.

Six ....

The World Cup in the United States

*The United States was chosen, by the way, because of all the
money to be made here, not for any soccer prowess. Our
country has been rented as a giant stadium and hotel and television
studio for the next 31 days—and that's fine. I have no illusions
about this World Cup being the breakthrough for American soccer,
but for the next month we are the center of the universe.*
—George Vecsey, New York Times, 12 June 1994

*The sporting equivalents of uppity vegetarians, wine tasters,
cineastes, dog snobs, will be telling us that soccer is a world
language we simply must learn, as cognoscenti, as decent blokes
and as international business dealers. . . .*
*Let's reflect on this before the T-shirts and the Cup cups arrive.
Do we have to care because most of the rest of the world cares?
Is there space in our crowded spectator sports schedule for more
games? Is there room in our hearts for more heroes? What's in this
World Cup for us?*
—Robert Lipsyte, New York Times, 27 November 1993

THE WORLD CUP USA organization, responsible for staging the 1994
World Cup in the United States, had set several specific goals for the event.
Foremost was the maximization of profits for itself, the USSF, FIFA, television networks, and the nine World Cup host cities. This required making
each match successful in terms of attendance, security, and logistics, as
well as television and press access. Additionally, arrangements with corporate sponsors and retailers, based on advertising sales and product licensing, brought in substantial revenue.[1] Another goal was to attain a
respectable American television audience by utilizing a strategy that
sought to attract the casual American sports viewer (as in someone who
might not watch weekly NFL telecasts but watches the Super Bowl).[2] This
included the requisite of bringing World Cup soccer to the attention of an
American public that, on the eve of the games, was woefully uninformed
regarding the event.[3] Finally, there was the stated objective of using the
World Cup as a vehicle to launch a new professional soccer league that
would eventually showcase first-division soccer in the United States, with
mostly American players.[4]

The 1994 World Cup was a singularly unique and financially successful event that managed to put soccer at the forefront of the American sports agenda for a short period of time. As a result, future World Cups may draw the attention of the American public comparable to that of the Olympics: a sensational event to be watched and talked about every four years, so long as there is a U.S. team Americans can cheer. Indeed, as we will see in the next chapter, there can be no doubt that the 1998 World Cup held in France attracted substantially more attention from the American sports public than it otherwise would have had the preceding tournament not been played in the United States in 1994.

The World Cup in the United States helped propel this tournament onto the front pages of the country's leading newspapers. There is much evidence that the tremendous success of the World Cup tournament in the United States has indelibly given this event a clearly recognizable profile among America's elite newspapers and a considerable segment of its sports fans. At the same time, it remains evident that recognition of a "big event" has little, if anything, in common with the development of affect and appreciation for a sport as culture on a continuing basis. In other words, while the World Cup in the United States had tangible positive results for the awareness of future World Cups on the part of the American public—particularly the country's cosmopolitan and first-generation ethnic sports fans—it remains less clear how much direct influence the tournament had on love and/or appreciation for the game of soccer among Americans on a day-to-day basis. This is not to say that the effect on the enhancement of soccer as sport culture was negligible or nonexistent. It is merely to say that the impact of World Cup '94 on this aspect of the game remains much more murky and will only materialize in the long run, if at all. However, the direct impact of World Cup '94 on the future of soccer as part of hegemonic sports culture in the United States remained marginal in the course of the 1990s, as the attention it provided for the sport was very short-lived for most of the American public. The World Cup succeeded in the United States as a big sensational event, but it failed to provide the desired impetus for the advancement of soccer into the American sport space. Though Major League Soccer finally emerged in 1996 as a directly mandated legacy of the World Cup, whatever opportunities for marketing and promotional advantages the new soccer league may have gained from the World Cup were long gone. After World Cup '94, most Americans remained disinterested in the world's most popular spectator sport, and, except perhaps for World Cup tournaments such as the one in France in 1998 and the Women's World Cup in the United States in 1999 (which presents its own exceptions and possibilities), that is unlikely to change anytime soon.

That the World Cup was a successful event in the United States is cor-roborated by record attendance figures, good television ratings, and the substantial amount of coverage provided by the American press. All of the matches took place without any major problems. Most of the games sold out, and only a few were attended at less than 90 percent capacity, in stadiums ranging from just under sixty thousand to over ninety thousand spectators. Morocco played Saudi Arabia in New Jersey's Giants Stadium before a near-capacity crowd of more than 72,000 on a Wednesday after-noon in June.[5] It is not presumptuous to assume that this contest would not have drawn one-fifth of that figure in Italy in 1990, or Mexico in 1986, the sites of the preceding two World Cup tournaments, countries where soccer forms the core of the respective sport spaces and where knowledgeable and discriminating fans would have found it beneath their interest to attend a game contested by two such mediocre soccer teams. Americans attended such a game for two reasons: first, because Americans love "big events" and are open to such experiences; and second, because Americans—as relative novices to the game of soccer—do not carry the discerning perceptions and collective memories that for decades have in-formed international soccer culture, wherein a clear hierarchy of teams has developed in which neither Saudi Arabia nor Morocco rank near the top. Clearly there was great interest by Americans, as well as international "soccer tourists," in watching World Cup soccer in person regardless of the particular game and the quality of its contestants. Cumulative televi-sion ratings for the tournament ranked above the 4.0 to 4.3 that Alan Rothenberg, president of World Cup USA, had predicted. Overnight rat-ings initially peaked at 10.4 for the second-round match between Brazil and the United States on the Fourth of July, to be surpassed two weeks later by the Brazil-Italy final at 12.4.[6]

The 1994 World Cup was a fine financial investment for almost all concerned, while it also succeeded as a big-time sports spectacle and event. However, World Cup '94 and its aftermath ultimately illustrate the continued absence of a soccer culture in the United States, especially in comparison to the Big Three and One-Half. While the immediate aims of World Cup USA were handsomely realized, the long-term goal of estab-lishing soccer as a "big-time" spectator sport in the United States was not, well past the tournament and into the late 1990s. In demonstrating how the 1994 World Cup succeeded as an event in opposition to its shortcom-ings in making significant inroads for soccer into America's sport space, this chapter focuses upon an analysis of how the World Cup was pre-sented to the American public by both print and television media, and how soccer and its foremost event were perceived by the American press. Additionally, this chapter explores the levels of awareness and interest by the American public in the World Cup, the varied impact the World Cup had on each of the nine American cities that hosted tournament matches, and the short-term success the World Cup experienced in terms of advertising and marketing. While identifying clear successes derived from World Cup '94, we will also address the tournament's failures in terms of the goal to promote soccer as a major sport in the United States. Moreover, we will analyze the implications that World Cup '94 and its aftermath provide for our overall thesis: the perpetuation of soccer in its historical position as a marginal phenomenon in American sports culture. The surprising success of the U.S. team and the significant effect this had on the ways in which the American public and the American media reacted to World Cup '94 are unifying factors throughout this analysis, providing further corroboration of our premise—discussed in chapter 1 and in subsequent chapters—that nationalism can provide a powerful impetus for any sport and its attendant culture, though it may also prove ephemeral.

An examination of World Cup '94 also reveals the differences between those Americans who might be interested—by a wide range of degree—in soccer and a good part of the majority with little or no interest in the sport. America's "soccer constituency," excepting those of specific ethnic or immigrant groups, tends to be mostly suburban, white, fairly well educated, and relatively affluent. As we briefly noted in chapter 5, the typical member of this "constituency"—often the parent of one or more soccer-playing offspring—finds a supposed antithesis to the Big Three and One-Half in soccer: less emphasis on competition with greater emphasis on play for its own sake, nonviolence, coeducational participation, marginal professionalism, and little partisanship. Additionally, soccer provides identification with a quasi-elitist notion of sophistication by way of internationalism, multiculturalism, and iconoclastic nonconformity in relation to American sports and their cultures. (Ironically, the appeal—both real and imagined—that soccer has for many of these people serves to undermine the potential success of pro soccer in the United States. Highly competitive play and partisanship, both occasionally violent, are staples of first-division soccer throughout the world. Similarly, the absence of big business and highly paid professionals—with the attendant hubris commonly exhibited by American athletes and soccer stars worldwide—is to a large extent what many find so charming about American soccer.) Though caricatures are simply that, and always an exaggeration, they do reflect some perception of reality; in this instance they also illustrate the way American soccer fans and non–soccer fans often view each other. Hence, as opposed to stereotypical American male sports fans who supposedly argue, beers in hand, about the NFL or baseball from their bar stools, stereotypical American soccer fans—male and female alike, and together—supposedly segue from a discussion of Mozart to one on

Maradona over cappuccino at the café or smoothies at the health club juice bar.

America's lower middle classes and working poor (excepting many of Latin origin, and first generation immigrants), who comprise a huge chunk of the fan base for the Big Three and One-Half, generally ignore soccer. This "class bifurcation" in American sports culture regarding soccer is reflected in the different ways that the World Cup (and soccer in general, both before and since the tournament) was covered by the American press and in the overall demographic makeup of those Americans interested in soccer and the World Cup. Ultimately, an examination of how the American media covered World Cup '94 and how the event was perceived by the public provides a case study that further explicates the American exception in sport.

The American Media and World Cup '94

The American media in general—not only in the sports pages and sports news shows—devoted a considerable amount of editorial space to World Cup coverage by reporting events on the field, describing the sometimes carnival-like atmosphere in the nine host cities, and exploring various aspects of soccer and its culture both internationally and domestically.[7] It is safe to say that no World Cup had ever received anywhere near the amount of coverage in the American media accorded this unique event in 1994. While the form and substance of this coverage varied widely according to the particular forums and topics involved, there can be no doubt that for slightly more than a month the World Cup registered an impressive presence in America's media. Occasionally the sports segments on some local network news shows slightly truncated their highlight clips of other sports to make room for World Cup coverage. A few newspapers that traditionally limit the editorial space of their sports sections, most notably the national edition of the *New York Times*, may have moderately curtailed coverage of ancillary sporting "events" like the NBA and NHL drafts to make room for World Cup coverage. Otherwise, no World Cup coverage came at the expense (in terms of newspaper space and air time) of any other sport, including baseball, basketball (which saw the conclusion of the NBA play-offs the same day the United States upset Colombia), football, and hockey (the former in its off-season, the latter just having concluded its Stanley Cup play-offs), or professional golf and tennis (which held major tournaments as the World Cup competition unfolded). Instead, the sports pages of newspapers were expanded. A few matches— some specific to the host city where they occurred, as well as those of the U.S. team and the semifinal and final matches—did occasionally manage to crowd out other sporting events, but only in terms of priority in the placement of headlines and stories. Many American sports columnists wrote pieces debating the merits of soccer, most identifying positively with the World Cup, some with the game itself. Most were noncommittal on the prospects for professional soccer in the United States, though a few became quite enthusiastic. There were some columnists who were quite negative, and a few who were downright nativist and chauvinistic (though the latter attitude was sometimes a reaction to similar sentiments expressed by foreign journalists concerning the alleged inferiority of American sports compared to soccer).[8] However, many U.S. sports magazines, most notably the *Sporting News* (long one of America's foremost weekly sports publications), completely ignored the World Cup, thus reinforcing the notion that to many American sports fans, as well as the public at large, the World Cup—even when hosted by the United States—remained at best a marginal event.

There was a "four-day soccer boom" in the United States, beginning with the U.S. team's upset of Colombia (still the only American World Cup victory since the miraculous defeat of England in Bello Horizonte in 1950) and ending with its loss to Romania. Media coverage of the U.S. team, as well as of the World Cup itself, was most extensive in this brief period, and U.S. players such as Alexi Lalas, Cobi Jones, and Tony Meola became recognizable to the American public at large (not least because of their hair styles). Press coverage, and the interest of the average American, began to decline after the United States loss to Romania and dropped substantially after the United States was eliminated from the tournament. Television ratings nothing short of spectacular (well more than double the quantity expected before the tournament by media experts and U.S. soccer officials, particularly for the matches played by the U.S. team) receded noticeably after the elimination of Team USA. Once the tournament narrowed, newspapers in host cities no longer staging games also significantly decreased their World Cup coverage. Two days after the final match, soccer coverage in almost all American newspapers returned to what it had always been before the World Cup: occasional (and marginal) to nonexistent. (Exceptions to this overall trend have been *USA Today*, the *Los Angeles Times*, the *Boston Globe*, and the *Miami Herald*, newspapers that had established something of a tradition in soccer coverage prior to the 1994 World Cup, as subsequently noted.) Reader complaints to sports editors that there was not enough coverage of soccer also returned to that of pre–World Cup levels: a few very strident and loud, but lonely, voices amid the dominant majority consisting of football, basketball, baseball, hockey, golf, tennis, and boxing fans.

The "Buildup"

In June 1993, some newspapers ran columns and stories examining soccer and World Cup issues as sort of a general note and, perhaps, reminder for a mostly apathetic American sports readership that World Cup USA was exactly one year away. The first of what would become many pieces by sports columnists speculating on the chances for soccer to gain a foothold on American soil began to appear, and the potential for Team USA to play a significant role in attracting the interest of the American public in the World Cup was clearly identified by all. For the most part, soccer coverage in the American media was not significantly expanded until just a few days immediately prior to the World Cup. Exceptions were newspapers that had previously established soccer as a regular staple in their sports sections, specifically the *Los Angeles Times* (which would consistently devote far more editorial space to the World Cup than all other U.S. dailies), the *Miami Herald* (whose readership, like that of the *Los Angeles Times*, includes a large Hispanic population), the *Boston Globe*, and *USA Today*. This comprised coverage of qualifying matches in Europe in November 1993, U.S. exhibition matches featuring the German national team in Miami and California in December 1993,[9] and the Joe Robbie Cup tournament of February 1994 in Miami that featured the United States, Colombia, Bolivia, and Sweden.[10]

It should be noted that the sports departments of some newspapers may be predisposed toward a favorable view of soccer, while some may tend to have a more negative or ambivalent view of the sport. While these predilections may often be completely random and the consequence of the particular preferences and tolerance levels of individual editors and managers as well as the inclinations of the personnel of a newspaper's sports department, there is no doubt that the particular paper's readership milieu and the social standing of its clientele also played a large role in determining whether and to what extent the paper would cover the World Cup and soccer. For example, George Vecsey, a leading sports columnist at the *New York Times*, has been an unabashed soccer fan who has written that he considers football—particularly as played in the NFL—boring. This is nothing short of heresy for an American sportswriter (but, perhaps, not incongruent with the presumed upper-echelon milieu of readership for the *New York Times*). In comparison to most American sports columns (again excepting those found in the four papers just noted), a fair number by Vecsey focus on soccer, thus giving the *New York Times* readers an angle not generally found in most other sports sections. The *Times* generally projects a favorable view of the sport, occasionally giving

it a relatively generous share of its usually limited sports section compared
to that of other major daily newspapers. To be sure, not all *New York
Times* sports columnists are soccer enthusiasts and proselytizers à la Vecsey. As one of the epigraphs headlining this chapter demonstrates, Vecsey's colleague Robert Lipsyte clearly is not. Moreover, it is telling that
the *Times* soccer coverage has always concentrated on the international
aspect of the game. Tellingly, the *New York Times*—as behooves its image
as the country's premier cosmopolitan paper of record covering international news—always carries the league standings of the German Bundesliga, the Italian Serie A, the English Premier League, the Scottish League,
and the Spanish First Division in its Tuesday editions. It also covers major
international matches both on the country and club level, and devotes
solid space to the American national team.

   However, in terms of covering the local soccer scene in the New York
metropolitan area, the *New York Times* has been woefully tardy, as it
does not have a regular beat reporter covering the New York/New Jersey
Metrostars of MLS. But with its image and self-perception as the nation's
"paper of record," it was evident from the very beginning that the *New
York Times* would provide first-rate World Cup coverage. *USA Today*,
which has arguably the most comprehensive sports section of any newspaper in the country, has always included soccer coverage on a daily basis;
it would also provide a good deal of space to the World Cup. Similarly,
excellent coverage emanated from the team of sports writers at the the *Los
Angeles Times*, led by Grahame Jones, arguably one of the finest soccer
journalists in the world. Anne Killion at the *San Jose Mercury News* has
also expressed an enthusiasm for the sport, which she fully brought to
bear in covering the World Cup. Among the very best were Frank Del-
l'Apa and John Powers of the *Boston Globe*, superb soccer reporters by
any measure. A number of newspapers, including the *Boston Globe* and
the *Miami Herald*, ran daily Spanish-language World Cup sections that
featured translations of articles from their regular sports pages, as well as
specially commissioned pieces penned by some of Latin America's most
renowned soccer columnists.

   The sports sections of tabloid newspapers, presumably in recognition
of their readership (lower middle class and urban working poor), generally tend to give less prominence and space to soccer than newspapers
with a presumably more suburban, upscale and well-educated readership.
Compared to the *Times*, soccer has always been proportionally a less
prominent feature of the tabloid *New York Post* and *New York Daily
News*. The sports sections of these papers, both attracting a readership
composed largely of lower-middle-class and working-class Whites, urban
Blacks, Caribbean (i.e., baseball-oriented, not soccer-loving) Hispanics,
and mass-transit commuters of all socioeconomic groups, devote the bulk

of their coverage to the Big Three and One-Half, boxing, horse racing, auto racing, tennis, and golf. But here, too, there have been some striking exceptions. Few American newspapers have had a better soccer coverage on a regular basis than the *Boston Herald*, most definitely a tabloid by any measure, whose soccer writer, Gus Martins, excelled in his World Cup reporting. This is all the more remarkable because—with exceptions to be sure—negative views of soccer and a general indifference, sometimes even hostility, toward the game and the World Cup were more commonly expressed in these forums of localism than in the more cosmopolitan broadsheets. On the whole, the World Cup coverage in the American press was at least as detailed, thoughtful, and sophisticated as in virtually any European newspaper that we surveyed. Indeed, in terms of sheer quantity, some American newspapers devoted much more substantial space to the World Cup than did their European counterparts. With the exception of *L'Equipe* and *La Gazzetta dello Sport*, two explicit sport dailies, no European paper offered as fine a World Cup coverage as found in the *Los Angeles Times*, the *Boston Globe*, and *USA Today*, to mention perhaps the very best in the United States. It was not unusual for the *Los Angeles Times* to offer thirteen pages of Cup coverage, compared to two pages in the eminent *Times* of London.

The drawing held in Las Vegas on Sunday, 19 December 1993 to determine the seeding and venues of the World Cup teams was the first noteworthy news coverage created by the World Cup in the United States. This took place during a full day of NFL games, thus limiting both American viewership and press coverage. Most reports noted that of the estimated 500 million people watching the draw worldwide, fewer than 1 million were American. The results of the draw were featured prominently in the sports sections of most newspapers, though quite secondary to football, basketball, and hockey coverage in all cases. The entertainment that accompanied the draw—where celebrities like Faye Dunaway and Robin Williams took part in the actual drawing, and performers like Barry Manilow and James Brown sang—was overwhelmingly dismissed as glitzy farce and triviality. Many writers speculated that the draw itself was fixed to ensure that particular teams would play at certain venues (which, by a complicated formula, it was), and to create advantages for certain teams (which has long been suspected of all World Cup draws). The feud between FIFA czar Joao Havelange and Pelé, still the only soccer superstar and legend recognizable to the American public, was widely noted, as Pelé was forced to sit unobtrusively in the audience, not a part of the official festivities. However, that one of the world's best female soccer players, Michelle Akers, was on the podium with such soccer icons as Franz Beckenbauer led many a European commentator to see this as nothing short of blasphemous, furthering the prevalent view from Europe that this event was yet another example of America's sullying of a tradition that it simply did not—and could never—appreciate, and whose premier event it therefore most decidedly did not deserve to host. Contrast this to the admiration the same European journalists accorded Sophia Loren, who performed a parallel function at the drawing for the World Cup in Italy in 1990. Overall, the World Cup drawing did not engender an increase in the American media's typically meager coverage of soccer beyond the following day. That the event occurred at 11 A.M. Pacific time to accommodate the dictates of European television (where it aired during prime time in the evening hours) added to the difficulties of the coverage from the American perspective. This foreshadowed an anomaly in the tournament itself, as European demands to show the games in prime viewing time in Europe made for World Cup soccer games played in the noontime (or early afternoon) summer heat of such cities as Orlando, Dallas, Los Angeles, and Washington, D.C. In the months and weeks prior to the World Cup, most newspapers in host cities occasionally ran non–sports section feature stories about the local preparations and political maneuvers associated with staging the matches and hosting "soccer tourists," often under a subheading typically entitled "Countdown to World Cup '94," or something similar. Most occasionally ran short feature columns with a similar heading in their sports sections, usually including in the same column general soccer news in brief from wire services, items that otherwise would often have been omitted. Coverage of soccer and the World Cup was not extensive on television in this period, particularly on the sports segments of local and network news shows. Most World Cup television features, such as those on cable networks CNN and CNBC, tended to focus on whether the World Cup would succeed and were accompanied by what seemed like obligatory footage of youth soccer with voice-overs noting that at least 12 million American kids were devoted to playing the game. There were several segments on news and business shows that explored the prospects for product marketing success tied into the World Cup, as well as speculation on the cash that "soccer tourists" would leave behind in host cities and points between. Most local television coverage echoed these themes while reporting on local preparations for the tournament, often with an ethnic touch. In Boston, for example, the North End (the city's Italian section) received special emphasis, as did the overwhelmingly Irish South Boston, the Portuguese sections of East Cambridge, and the Brazilian neighborhoods of Brighton.

Several newspaper sports sections devoted prominent editorial space to preview the U.S.-Mexico exhibition match at Pasadena on June 4, notably the *San Jose Mercury News*, and the *Los Angeles Times* (a local story, of course, but also a reflection of that paper's established soccer credentials and large Hispanic readership). Overall, "pro-soccer" sports sections gave the 1–0 upset victory by the United States prominent display and coverage, while less "soccer-friendly" newspapers submerged the story. What was billed as a "dry run" for the tournament was likely treated the same by some sports editors, as many writers who would cover the World Cup were on hand to file stories. Obviously, the prominence in headline treatment for this match was engendered by the surprising result. That an estimated 98 percent of the over ninety thousand spectators were rooting for Mexico (making the U.S. win all the more extraordinary) was a consistent theme in all reports. Many commentators addressed the telling predicament of American soccer: When a home game becomes akin to a difficult away match in a hostile environment, there is clearly a problem in popular support and public affection for the game and its players. Most newspapers that had yet to devote relatively heavy editorial space to soccer, or those that were not decidedly "pro-soccer," ran wire service copy on the match. That the game was a mere "exhibition" also contributed to its insignificant coverage in some papers, particularly those on the East Coast. Additionally, the result did not make deadline for some papers (such as both Chicago dailies, each of which ran short wire copy on the game two days after the match, in their respective June 6 editions). Despite the prominent display of headlines in some newspapers (including main news, page one teasers) for the U.S.-Mexico "shocker," coverage was still quite secondary in relation to coverage of basketball (NBA play-offs), hockey (Stanley Cup play-offs), baseball, and golf (U.S. Open). The U.S. upset of Mexico generally warranted a brief mention in the sports segments of that evening's local news programs. CNN's *Sports Late Night* gave it short shrift, though ESPN's SportsCenter included some brief interview footage and follow-up reporting. (ESPN, as the secondary carrier for World Cup matches in the United States, had an obvious interest in covering soccer during this period.)

Coverage of soccer was not extensive in most newspapers or on television two days after the U.S. upset of Mexico. However, on June 7, ABC's *Nightline* aired a feature entitled "The Quest," which explored the plight of the players on Team USA by highlighting the U.S.-Mexico exhibition. Host Ted Koppel began his monologue by proclaiming himself a soccer fan, someone who had played as a youth and "would choose to watch a good soccer match over the All-Star baseball game any day of the week." This confession coincided perfectly with the high-brow aura of the Stanford-educated Koppel, thereby underlining, once again, the fact that soccer in the United States remains a game of the educated middle classes rather than of the masses and "the people," as has been the case in every place in which it enjoys a hegemonic status in that country's sports culture. Koppel's voice-overs and interviews of Alan Rothenberg during the match, and later with American players Alexi Lalas (the dawning of newfound celebrity status for the gregarious and telegenic defender), Eric Wynalda, and others, highlighted the theme that both soccer and Team USA faced an uphill battle to win the collective hearts and minds of the American public, as did the World Cup and soccer itself. This *Nightline* feature was essentially the first national exposure for Team USA and the first national broadcast of an in-depth World Cup–related story on a major American television network. Koppel was repeating a theme being played out in the sports and feature sections of America's newspapers. That most Americans were still unaware that the World Cup was about to take place in their midst was a worry for soccer enthusiasts, and ammunition for soccer detractors and those of the international "soccer community" and media who had decried FIFA awarding World Cup '94 to the United States. While the American public maintained its apathy toward "the world's game," the sports sections of most newspapers and the sports segments on local television news programs were still relegating soccer coverage to marginal status less than ten days prior to the opening ceremonies of World Cup '94. Meantime, as another reflection of the presumed "upper-class" and well-educated nature of America's "soccer constituency," decidedly set apart from the mainstream of American sports culture, National Pubic Radio began to run features on soccer and the World Cup during this period, and continued to do so throughout the tournament. This also confirms the high-brow (or iconoclastic) appeal of the game in the United States, since it was well-nigh never that National Public Radio covered events pertaining to the American Big Three and ice hockey. (This changed during the late 1990s, as NPR occasionally presented feature stories on major developments in all sports, including the Big Three and One-Half.) Additionally, Charlie Rose devoted a few segments of his television show (syndicated on the Public Broadcasting System) to a discussion of soccer and the World Cup.

Yet, it would be remiss not to mention that David Letterman and Jay Leno—in many ways the most accurate voices of America's middle-class males and in no way high-brow or elitist by any stretch of the imagination—repeatedly mentioned the World Cup in their monologues and skits, though (tellingly) always in a negative way and with much derision for the sport of soccer. Letterman's and Leno's jokes about soccer's alleged deficiencies—too aimless, too low scoring, played with feet, no interruptions, too effete—best encapsulate the average American male sports fan's objections to this game and thus the World Cup. Still, it was David Letterman who invited Andres Cantor, the Univision announcer best known for his exuberant "*Gooooaaaallll*" shout (that equally celebrates every goal regardless of its importance) onto his show, thus making Cantor a nationally recognized celebrity, so much so that by 2000 NBC hired the famed announcer to call the play-by-play of its televised soccer games from the Olympics in Sidney, Australia.

World Cup coverage, as well as soccer coverage in general, picked up considerably during the week immediately prior to the tournament. Still, it was not until the matches were about to begin that most newspapers began to display articles on soccer prominently in relation to the traditional coverage of the Big Three and One-Half. Most papers, including all dailies with Sunday editions located in host cities, initiated their full World Cup coverage by running "World Cup Special" insert sections either on Sunday, June 12, four days prior to the opening ceremonies and first match; on "opening day" Thursday, June 16 (the *Detroit Free Press* and the *Detroit News*); or on Sunday, June 19, during the first weekend of the tournament. The *Chicago Tribune*, "paper of record" for the tournament's opening site, ran pieces of a World Cup special preview as full-page color daily features in its sports section over the course of the week prior to the opener.

All of these special sections included previews of first-round matches; sites, dates, times, and television schedules for the entire tournament; profiles of teams (usually devoting more space to the teams most likely to advance, as well as expanded profiles of teams playing and/or training locally); profiles of the players on Team USA; profiles, including schematic diagrams, capacity figures, and match schedules for the nine venues; listings of World Cup–related events such as cultural festivals, parades, and entertainments; tips to those planning to attend matches and to those planning to watch on television; and guides for "soccer tourists" concerning travel to matches and local points and events of interest. In recognition of the lack of an American soccer culture, nearly all of these special sections sought to alleviate the typical reader's presumed ignorance of the sport by including primers on how the game is played, with its rules, complete with diagrams. Some included soccer and World Cup lexica, as well as descriptions of the organization of international soccer with a "who's who" list. Most also published a section on soccer history, with an attendant time line. Many presented a lead article by a soccer enthusiast explaining that soccer was the number-one sport and passion for most of the world and that Americans were fortunate to have the opportunity to experience the foremost event of the world's foremost sport here at home. The general theme usually implied something along the lines of "Try it, you'll like it." Some such articles, or accompanying pieces, speculated on whether or not World Cup soccer would make any inroads into the sports consciousness of the American public.

During the "buildup" to the tournament, many newspapers inaugurated World Cup–related feature columns that would run throughout the tournament. Many such features, such as "World Cup Flashback," which chronicled past World Cup highlights, were apparently directed at typical American sports-page readers who lacked a "soccer culture" and "soccer memory." Additionally, some papers ran informational pieces on the geography, culture, history, and economics of specific nations sending teams to the tournament.

On the eve of the tournament, World Cup coverage finally broke into network news reports. On June 15, a ten-second clip of that day's World Cup Parade in Chicago was shown, with a voice-over by anchor Tom Brokaw, on the NBC *Nightly News*. The next day, CBS *Morning News* featured a longer report on "one of the best parades Chicago's ever seen," emphasizing the international flavor of the event. Correspondent John Davis ended his report by noting, over footage of two people speaking Spanish, that "in the crowd hardly a word of English was heard. Just about every other language was." That day, Thursday, June 16—the day before the tournament's first match—saw a variety of World Cup feature pieces on national news programs. Alan Rothenberg, striving to paint a rosy picture in the face of questioning that emphasized the American public's lack of awareness and interest in the World Cup, was interviewed on CNN's *Daybreak*. (One day earlier, Rothenberg and associates unveiled start-up plans for the MLS to begin the following spring. As location and ownership for only seven of the twelve franchises had been determined, and spectator commitments were far short of the pre-announced requisites, much of the coverage of MLS in the press throughout the World Cup tended toward skepticism.) CNN included World Cup feature interviews and reports on *International Hour* (wherein two foreign sports reporters were asked to expound on soccer's chances of finding the American public, among other things) and the *World Today*. Filling in on the *Osgood File*, CBS radio's Dave Ross noted the American public's apathy toward soccer and the slow pace of World Cup souvenir sales and used metaphoric humor seemingly to dismiss any relevance the World Cup—and its attendant hype—might have for the American public.

The "Competition"

"Outside of the Simpson murder mystery, the Stanley Cup and the NBA, all the World Cup had to compete with over the weekend [June 17 through 20] was a three-way tie in US Open golf, Darryl Strawberry's progress from drug treatment to the outfield of the San Francisco Giants, Lee Trevino's victory in a senior golf tournament, Mary Pierce's last-minute withdrawal from Wimbledon with rumors of interference from her father and a team record of 18 straight home

victories by the Cleveland Indians. Any sport that
has trouble outshining the Cleveland Indians
may find it difficult to create mass excitement
among U.S. fans."
—Al Dunning, *Washington Times*, 23 June 1994

By necessity, the World Cup had to compete with other sports and sports-
related news for media coverage and prominence; the buildup to the tournament and the first round often played second, third, or fourth fiddle to
other competing sports events. This included the final round of the NBA
play-offs, which pitted the New York Knickerbockers against the Houston Rockets, and the NHL Stanley Cup finals between the Vancouver
Cannucks and the New York Rangers in which the Rangers won the Cup
to end a 54-year-long angst-filled drought. The Rangers victory lead to a
celebration in New York City that prompted an estimated one million
New Yorkers to fill the city's streets barely a few days before the beginning
of the World Cup tournament. While the magnitude of such celebration
has become commonplace in the setting of the champions in The Big
Three and hockey, it continues to remain unthinkable for soccer in North
America.

With both the Knicks and Rangers playing in the championship rounds
of their respective sports, the sports media in America's number-one
media market were particularly focused on basketball and hockey in the
days leading up to the World Cup tournament and during the first
matches. Additionally, the running of the Belmont Stakes (the New York
leg of thoroughbred horse racing's "Triple Crown") took place during
the first weekend of World Cup action. During the first two weeks of
World Cup play (which included the celebrated Ireland-Italy match at the
Meadowlands), a surprisingly large amount of New York media space—
though only a minuscule fraction of the sports pages—was devoted to the
Gay Olympics.

The New York sports media were also augmenting their extensive coverage of local baseball, as the Yankees were in first place atop the American League East division. The new realignment of Major League Baseball
had created competitive pennant races, engendering greater interest in
baseball than in recent years while, perhaps coincidentally, baseball experienced an upturn in offensive production. With the San Diego Padres'
future Hall of Famer Tony Gwynn flirting with a .400 batting average,
and Matt Williams of the San Francisco Giants and Ken Griffey Jr. of the
Seattle Mariners on track to reach 60-plus home runs, June and July were
very exciting months for baseball that year. Columnists for newspapers
covering hometown baseball clubs doing well and/or making significant
player acquisitions, such as those in San Francisco, clearly focused on

baseball. The newspapers in the traditional "baseball town" of Boston continued to give baseball headline prominence, even as the Red Sox stumbled in the standings. Only World Cup news of a sensational nature or of singular importance (such as the U.S. upset of Colombia, the murder of Andres Escobar [the Colombian player whose own goal made that upset possible], the barring of Diego Maradona for drug use, and the tournament's semifinal and final matches), or of specific American, ethnic, or local interest (the fortunes of Team USA against Romania and Brazil, the Ireland-Italy face-off at the Meadowlands, or specific matches as covered by the newspapers in cities where they occurred) managed to dislodge first hockey and basketball, and later baseball, from lead headline dominance on America's sports pages. The U.S. Open Golf tournament and the All-England Lawn Tennis Championships at Wimbledon—both featured ingredients of their respective sports' "Majors" or "Grand Slams"—coincided with the World Cup. Although they did not directly affect the quantity or placement of World Cup news, these events most definitely provided subjects other than soccer and American team sports as material for many sports columnists.

The buildup to the World Cup coincided with sensationalist coverage of the investigation into the brutal murder of Nicole Brown Simpson, ex-wife of former football star O. J. Simpson. As every American who watches television, listens to radio, or reads newspapers could not avoid hearing and observing that week, police and media alike had focused on O. J. Simpson as the prime suspect for the crime. Though seemingly a story for the main news and feature sections of newspapers, Simpson's status as perhaps the greatest running back in collegiate football history and one of the finest in NFL history, in addition to his high profile as a sports announcer, movie actor, and commercial pitchman, made this a story for the sports pages as well. Simpson's flight from police custody in the instantaneously famous "low-speed chase" through the Los Angeles freeway system interrupted national telecasts of both the fifth game of the NBA finals from New York on NBC and the World Cup Spain–South Korea match from Dallas on ESPN, as well as all American national network programming. On the following day, all sports sections included pieces by columnists reflecting on the Simpson story, as well as ancillary stories related to the case. In the very important and relevant context of media coverage, the American sport space had temporarily expanded as World Cup '94 began, but it was for a sensational crime story with over-hyped drama and pathos, not soccer.

Tellingly, this spectacular incident featured an American sports star, bespeaking the powerful hegemony that such sports assume in a country's culture. Had Simpson been a star in a nonhegemonic sport or had he been merely a regular football player instead of a marquee Hall of Famer, the incident would have never attained the attention it garnered from the very beginning. Indeed, it is interesting to note that European commentators could simply not understand what the fuss was all about, since to them O. J. Simpson was—if known at all—only a fourth-rate actor in lousy action movies. To the European journalists in the United States en masse to report on a World Cup tournament already suspect (to them) for being held in America, it seemed, once again, that Americans had found yet something new—such as a ridiculous "soap opera"—to block out soccer. Only when bicultural commentators (in some cases, Andrei Markovits) explained to reporters (in this case, German and Austrian journalists) that Simpson's stature in the United States was every bit the equivalent to that of Franz Beckenbauer in Germany, did those Europeans with some readiness to learn desist from using this incident as yet another example of alleged "American crassness" and "cultural inferiority," and further confirmation of their negative views of America.

The Simpson case would soon move out of the sports sections of American newspapers and the sports segments of local news shows (though not from ESPN's SportsCenter), but not out of the general attention of the American (and international) media. It would continue to divert coverage, in varying degrees, from many news items and sports events, including the 1994 World Cup. The saga of O. J. Simpson would continue to garner the intense scrutiny and editorial space of the American media at the expense of other news, even well after Simpson's acquittal in September 1995.

The Openers

With the Simpson saga dominating the headlines and columns of both news and sports sections, and the NBA finals in full swing, the World Cup opening ceremonies on June 17 in Chicago received quite secondary placement and attention. Reports on the nonsoccer parts of the festivities ranged from upbeat and positive to mildly derisive. On the positive side were the speeches and attendance of President Clinton, German Chancellor Helmut Kohl, and other dignitaries and the "festive" atmosphere of the over sixty-seven thousand in attendance. On the negative side were the intense heat and humidity, the inane lip-synching performance of the rock band B-52's, an injurious fall (resulting in a severely sprained right knee) by Master of Ceremonies Oprah Winfrey, and the unintentionally comic attempt of singer Diana Ross to kick a ball through a makeshift goal (she missed, and the "goal" fell apart).

The opening match, a German victory over Bolivia, was also generally submerged in Simpson and NBA stories, though it received extensive coverage in "soccer friendly" sports sections and the Chicago dailies. The South Korea–Spain tie taking place that evening in Dallas garnered far less attention than the Chicago match and ceremonies, though several newspapers ran sidebars and/or accompanying pieces that examined the "atmosphere" at the Cotton Bowl. Most tended toward ambivalence, noting that the match was not sold out. But the clichéd note of "and a good time was had by all" crept into many such reports.

Both matches were also criticized by reporters, a journalistic practice more prevalent with soccer than with other sports. The Chicago match was overwhelmingly graded as "boring," "dull," "sloppily played," "a highlight film of officiating," and "only marginally entertaining." The Dallas contest was overwhelmingly trumpeted as "exciting and action-packed," "well-played," and "tension-filled." The practice of "reviewing" the action in lieu of quotes from the participants is a feature of soccer reporting somewhat at odds with American sportswriting traditions and practices. With its lack of statistics and meaningful quantified events (save goals, of course), soccer reporting often requires the subjective angle for an accurate report. Non-American sportswriters traditionally write this way, as access to participants is restricted, thus limiting quotes. However, in terms of American reporting of matches, there was an underlying theme that soccer was, to some extent, on trial as far as the American public and sporting media were concerned. The lack of a "soccer culture" put some American sportswriters in the unfamiliar position of writing about a sport with which they were not completely comfortable and of which they were not sufficiently knowledgeable. As the tournament proceeded, reports on the matches became slightly less reviewlike and more practical, though soccer continues to elude accurate reporting by tried-and-true American sportswriting techniques. Similarly, television highlights of World Cup play on news broadcasts usually consisted solely of goals, or near goals in tense moments. For a sports viewership and media weaned on scores, statistics, and ultimate outcomes, quality of play not related to the final score is usually regarded as superfluous, even if it qualifies as "spectacular."

The First Round Games, 18–30 June 1994

The first round games consisted of a round-robin contest among the four teams comprising each of the six groups. In order to qualify for the next round to be played by sixteen teams in a simple head-to-head, winner-take-all knockout fashion, a team had to place first or second in its group. This twelve-team cluster was further augmented by the four third-placed teams with the best record, thus yielding the necessary sixteen for the second round. While each of the six groups was headquartered in one of the nine venues, all teams traveled away from their "home" to play at least one game in another city.

Saturday, June 18, featured the United States in its debut as host against a mediocre Swiss team that, however, sported some first-rate players who had attained starlike profiles in Europe's most demanding professional leagues, such as the German Bundesliga. Notably, this game was the first match in World Cup history—indeed at any international FIFA-sanctioned tournament—played in an indoor arena. The Silverdome in Pontiac, Michigan, was the site of this unusual event, which ended in a well-deserved 1–1 tie. While a number of articles pointed to flaws in the American team—particularly pertaining to its inability to control mid-field play—most comments were cautiously positive regarding the U.S. team's auspicious start. Later that day, the tournament witnessed its first major upsets when in Pasadena, California, a much-respected but relatively unheralded Romanian squad soundly defeated Colombia, a team that had been touted by many—Pelé among them[11]—as one of the tournament's favorites, handicapped in third place together with three-time champion Italy, just behind the coleaders Germany and Brazil (the other three-time World Cup winners). The other upset occurred across the continent at Giants Stadium in East Rutherford, New Jersey, where underdog Ireland defeated mighty Italy, 1–0, in a battle that received substantial media coverage not for its athletic content, but rather because of its hint of ethno-cultural implications for American cities with large populations of Italian and Irish ancestry, such as New York, Chicago, and Boston. By Tuesday, June 21, all teams had played the first of their three round-robin games that comprised the World Cup's first round, and a few early trends had emerged that seemed to bode well for the tournament as a whole:

- There were more goals scored than in the previous World Cup in Italy, which had witnessed the absolute nadir in this crucial aspect of the game.

- Upsets had provided several weaker teams a real chance to advance to the second round.

- Crowd favorites such as Brazil and Argentina played attractive soccer, scoring many goals (against Russia and Greece, respectively).

- All venues were virtually sold out at 95 percent of capacity, thus fully on target toward making this the World Cup with the highest attendance in the tournament's history.

- The crowds were colorful, festive, cheerful, and passionately partisan for their teams without even a hint of the much-dreaded soccer violence that had been yet another much-cited stigma attached to the sport in the eyes of the American public.

- Perhaps most important of all, the weekend's television ratings were much higher than those originally expected by all media experts. Indeed, the USA-Switzerland match attained a 5.8 overnight rating on ABC, thereby surpassing the 5.0 for golf's prestigious U.S. Open later that day.[12]

The American victory against Colombia in Pasadena on 22 June was perhaps the first match ever in the history of the U.S. national team to garner any kind of attention in the American public beyond the small circle of American soccer aficionados. Had this event not completely coincided with the seventh game of the NBA championship, there is little doubt that this surprising American win would have been accorded even more prominent coverage than what it received the following day. Obviously, the comments were exuberant, as this win all but guaranteed the American team's advance to the next round, thus saving it from the potential ignominy of becoming the tournament's first and only host not to reach the second round of play. Moreover, the win was the first for the U.S. national team at a World Cup since its "miracle" 1950 victory over England. The game's 4.3 rating on ESPN, seen in 2.7 million homes, outdrew ESPN's highest-rated baseball game that season, 4.1 for the St. Louis–Cincinnati 1994 opener. While these numbers were immensely impressive and completely unexpected, they need to be placed in their proper comparative perspective alongside the results for the seventh game of the NBA championship on NBC: a 17.9 rating with 50 million Americans watching, making it the ninth-highest-rated game in NBA history.[13]

In the wake of the U.S. victory, there ensued a level of interest in the American team and—by extension in the tournament and soccer—that we have come to call the "four-day soccer boom." National Public Radio's *Morning Edition* ran a feature on June 23 with brief interviews with Paul Caligiuri, Roy Wegerle, and the ubiquitous Alexi Lalas. The *CBS Evening News* mentioned the victory, and ABC ran a story on Kearny, New Jersey, home to three of the American team's players—Tony Meola, John Harkes, and Tab Ramos. That the American team's prospects were discussed, however briefly, on "sports talk" radio—as was the case in Boston, Chicago, and Washington, D.C.—lends credence to the notion that for a brief moment, at least, soccer registered on the radar screen of the average American sports fan. The American soccer win was characterized as "incredible, historical, very cool." Assistant coach Steve Sampson commented: "We were on the cover of every newspaper [the day after the victory]. Color pictures. Stories. I even heard taped highlights of our game on the radio going to practice. That's never happened to us before. Never."[14] None more prominent than Pelé himself accorded the U.S. team high grades for its performance against one of the tournament's favorites. To be sure, there remained the skeptics, such as Steve Stark, the commentator on popular culture for CNN's *Showbiz Today* who argued—as we have, similarly—that once soccer missed entry into America's sport space in the late nineteenth century, the game simply had no chance to make its mark in a culture that has been saturated by more sports than any other. By pointing to soccer as a "terrible television game, and TV tends to make sports what they are today," Stark argued that television accentuated, rather than attenuated, historically anchored tastes in sports as culture and entertainment, thereby giving soccer no chance to make significant and lasting inroads into America's sport space regardless of the genuine, but momentary, joy generated by the U.S. team's victory against powerhouse Colombia.[15]

In addition to the sports pages and the local sections in newspapers where the World Cup had been receiving ample coverage from the beginning of the tournament, articles began to appear in the business sections of the nation's newspapers delineating the economic implications of the competition. "You may not give a hoot about World Cup soccer, but the rest of the world does. And the Gillette Corporation knows it," wrote the *Boston Globe*. The article described how major U.S. corporations with a decided global presence were eager to have their names associated with the world's foremost sporting event. Led by such giants as Coca-Cola, ITT Sheraton, MasterCard, McDonald's, and Gillette, among others, American companies paid $20 million each to be official sponsors of the World Cup. To a company such as Gillette, which rings in 70 percent of its sales in foreign markets, the fact that Americans "are greeting the World Cup with a yawn" remained secondary to the global exposure that sponsorship of such an event guaranteed.[16] Bespeaking the sudden surge of interest in the U.S. team, some of the better-known players were hired to endorse products: Goalie Tony Meola snagged an adidas ad and was hawking Reusch gloves; Paul Caligiuri washed his hair with Pert on television; and Lalas endorsed many products, from soft drinks to cereal. "Victory creates appeal," correctly noted Brian Murphy, the publisher of *Sports Marketing Newsletter*. "You have to move quickly," added David Burns, founder of Burns Sports Celebrity Service. "A month from now a lot of the opportunities will have come and gone." Bob Dorfman, of the well-known advertising agency Foote, Cone & Belding, emphasized the seasonality and ephemeral spontaneity of the marketability of soccer and its American stars by saying that once autumn begins "then the money goes back to basketball." By drawing a parallel between the short-lived fame of an American gold medalist in the Olympic downhill race and the

U.S. soccer team's Warholian fifteen minutes of fame, Dorfman asked, "I mean, can you tell me, where Tommy Moe is now?"[17]

Sure enough, the third series of the first-round matches did not end auspiciously for the American team. Before 93,869 enthusiastic fans and a national television audience, the United States lost on the beautiful Sunday afternoon of June 26 in Pasadena to the Romanians, 1–0. Even though the goal itself resulted from a grave error by goalie Meola, and despite the fact that the U.S. team had a few fine chances, it was clear to any knowledgeable observer of the match that the Romanians were superior to the Americans in every phase of the game. The Americans managed to finish third in their group, which meant they had to await the outcome of other games to know for certain whether they would be among the four best third-place finishers. By Tuesday night, it had become official that the United States would advance to the second round only to face Brazil on—of all days—4 July.

Driven by the American team's acceptable, though far from spectacular, showing (one win, one tie, one loss); an early proliferation of goals; the surprisingly entertaining play by teams such as Saudi Arabia, Romania, Sweden, and Nigeria; and the festive nature of the entire event, which conveyed to the casual observer that the whole thing appeared to be good fun, the television numbers for the first-round games were nothing short of astounding: ABC's overnight rating of 7.8 for the American loss to Romania (6.8 in its final rating with an 18 percent share) compared favorably to college basketball (6.6 for CBS's afternoon NCAA tournament games) and the early-round NBA play-offs (8.4 on NBC). Moreover, the rating for the U.S.-Romania game was almost double CBS's 4.0 regular-season baseball average for the previous four years. Just as important, other World Cup games not involving the United States attained ratings in the middle to high 4s, thereby surpassing all other summer sports competition. NBC's first weekend of Wimbledon had slipped 25 percent to an all-time low overnight average of 2.3. "I'd like to see the World Cup take soccer to a new level in the USA," opined John McEnroe, once a high school soccer player and now a tennis announcer for NBC in Wimbledon.[18] During those heady days of late June and early July 1994, when American soccer fans saw their dream come true in that their underdog team was to meet mighty Brazil in a winner-take-all showdown on the Fourth of July, McEnroe's wish seemed not all that unrealistic.

The opening round also saw a bevy of articles on individual stars, such as the telegenic and fluent English-speaking Jürgen Klinsmann of the German team; the equally handsome Dennis Bergkamp of the Netherlands; Romario, the cocky little striker of the Brazilians; the pony-tailed Buddhist Roberto Baggio from Italy; the ageless Roger Milla of Cameroon (well into his forties, though nobody seemed to know his exact age, thereby adding further to his mystique); the gruff Hristo Stoichkov of Bulgaria (whose wonderfully skilled play on the field was matched only by his ugly racism and excessive arrogance); the Russian Oleg Salenko, who scored six goals for Russia in its hapless effort to qualify for the second round; and, of course, Diego Maradona, who made headlines for both his former prowess as a soccer star and his many escapades and brushes with the law. Maradona's prominent, though largely negative, presence in the media was augmented by his expulsion from the tournament for testing positive for a forbidden performance-enhancing substance, a rarity in soccer. Maradona's ignominious departure was rendered grotesque by his accusations against FIFA, the American organizers, and various unnamed—though implied—conspirators (such as the Brazilians), all of whom allegedly wanted to see the Argentinean team fail at the World Cup. Even though soccer is a team sport, like all team sports it has fostered individual stars; this has always been the case and will remain so. Still, in an environment such as the American one, where the game has never been part of the country's hegemonic sports culture, featuring individual players in lieu of the team as a whole helped familiarize and personalize an otherwise abstract and distant game to a largely uninitiated audience.

The Round of the Sweet Sixteen, 2–5 July 1994

The greatest amount of attention from the American media was accorded to the U.S.-Brazil game played on the Fourth of July at Stanford Stadium in Palo Alto, California. While few sports writers and analysts gave the Americans a realistic chance of upsetting the Brazilians, the mere fact that the United States had an opportunity to play the most glamorous soccer team in the world in such an important game on such a unique stage in the global sports scene made this a special event in American sports, well beyond the small world of American soccer. The pregame buildup was substantial in all the media and with the match falling on the American national holiday (which happened to be a Monday that year), it was clear that for the first time, a soccer game would take unchallenged center stage in the American sports world. Pete Sampras had won his Wimbledon trophy on Sunday, Martina Navratilova had lost to Conchita Martinez in her valiant effort to win her tenth Wimbledon singles title on Saturday; so this event only had to contend with the regular baseball season on a Monday of a long holiday weekend. No hockey play-offs, no NBA finals, no Gay Olympics, no U.S. Open—the field was wide open for the American team.

On a beautiful sunny California afternoon, Brazil defeated the United States, 1–0, before a crowd of 84,147 spectators at Stanford Stadium and a national television audience of hitherto unparalleled numbers for any soccer game in American history: a final 9.3 rating and a 26 percent share.[19] This was an immense success by any measure other than, of course, the only one that ultimately counts—the result on the field and its consequences, which were dire for Team USA since the loss eliminated the American team from the tournament. While U.S. World Cup chief Rothenberg might have been a bit self-serving in his comment that the American team and the game had "been a part of (U.S.) sports history," there is little doubt regarding the overall veracity of his remarks when one considers this match within the context of American soccer history.[20]

Indeed, the event and the very fact of its occurrence were much more significant than the game itself, which, by all "measures," was a major disappointment. Though Brazil won by a lone goal, the vast difference in the quality of the two teams was evident for anyone even vaguely conversant with soccer. The Brazilians dominated throughout, and even with one man down for over forty-five minutes, their attacks threatened the American goal repeatedly. Conversely, the U.S. team managed only four shots on the Brazilian goal throughout the entire match, and just one seemed seriously threatening. It was clear that the Americans did not belong on the same field with the Brazilians, whose subpar performance was still plenty to outplay the American team in every phase of the game and win, thus ensuring Brazil's advancement into the quarterfinals. The comments in the media reflected this sober assessment of the game and the American team's performance. Still, while their attitude regarding the match remained low-key, many remarked on the sheer importance of the event, which could not help but be advantageous to American soccer— as well as soccer in America—in the near and far future. Optimism and approval far outweighed pessimism and criticism, best summarized here: "Brazil's absolute dominance in the second half of its 1–0 win, despite being a player down, showed the gap in ability [between the two teams] is still huge. But the effort from a U.S. team so heavily discounted at the start of the tournament should be applauded and remembered as a starting point."[21]

Among the eight other games of this round, the greatest coverage was accorded to the surprising Romanian upset of favored Argentina in Pasadena in front of 90,469 spectators. In what was arguably the most exciting and well-played game of the entire tournament, the Romanians defeated the Argentineans, 3–2, with the help of yet another beautiful goal by Gheorghe Hagi, who thereby followed up on his amazing free-kick goal against Colombia that was without any doubt the tournament's most celebrated and that was to convert many a casual observer into a soccer fan. This was the case for Mike Penner of the *Los Angeles Times* who—as noted in the next chapter—cites this Hagi goal against Columbia as his personal epiphany on the road to becoming a rabid soccer fan. Hagi's overall brilliance in that superb game, as well as the one against Argentina, proved him one of the World Cup's undisputed superstars. The German victory over Belgium also received solid coverage, though not for the brilliance of play but rather for the incompetence of the Swiss referee Kurt Roethlisberger, whose failure to call an obvious penalty for Belgium in the seventieth minute had a major influence on the match's outcome. Though the referee telephoned FIFA after the game and admitted his error in judgment, he was suspended from calling any further games in the tournament. Roberto Baggio's last-minute heroics saved the Italian team from a potentially embarrassing loss to upstart Nigeria that would have meant the end for the "Azzurri's" World Cup presence, while Sweden finally put a stop to Saudi Arabia's Cinderella run by eliminating the Saudis from the tournament.

After the completion of this round, the total tally by July 6 was nothing short of stellar for the reception of the competition by the American public. With eight games still left on the schedule—the four quarterfinal games; the two semifinals; the final; and the consolation game—the tournament's forty-four matches attracted 2,955,108 spectators, far exceeding the 2,517,348 who attended all fifty-two games in Italy in 1990. Ticket sales represented 97.7 percent of listed stadium capacity, a record in World Cup history.[22] The television ratings were much beyond the most optimistic projections, bordering (for some) on the unbelievable. "A year ago only a crazy man would have expected a soccer telecast to outdraw all other sports programs for a weekend. But after two weeks of World Cup play, it was predictable that Monday's U.S.-Brazil game on ABC would top the charts. It compiled a 10.6 overnight rating [in the Boston area] in line with a 10.4 achieved in the nation's thirty-one top markets, which ABC translated into an audience of 32 million, only a small percentage of the international audience, of course." Putting this success into perspective, the Boston Red Sox-California Angels baseball game attained a 4.1 rating in a city legendary for its loyalty to its beloved baseball team.[23] But the assessment by Jack Craig, television reporter for the *Boston Globe*, also placed these impressive numbers in their proper international context, where they remained insubstantial. Rudy Martzke, television writer for *USA Today*, characterized these developments in the following optimistic manner: "The size of interest in USA cities Monday for an event two-thirds of the country didn't know was coming a few weeks ago was enough to toss yellow cards at soccer skeptics." The overnight rating for the USA-Brazil game in a few major American television markets was truly spectacular: 16.6 in San Francisco, 13.9 in Los Angeles and Orlando, 11.7 in Washington, D.C., 10.6 in Boston, 10.5 in Philadelphia, 9.9 in New York, and 8.0 in Chicago.[24]

Once again conveying the unparalleled potency of national allegiance, identity, and interest as a binding force between spectators and fans on the one hand, and players and the actual activities on the other, was that the other seven games in the round of the "sweet sixteen" garnered a far smaller television audience than the U.S.-Brazil game. A 31-market average for the other seven games attained a 4.0 rating, a very respectable number and well beyond even the most optimistic predictions before the World Cup, but nowhere near the quantity generated by the interest in and identification with the home team. There simply is no substitute for the ingredient of nationalism and localism in the world of hegemonic sports cultures anywhere, including the United States. There is uniformity on this count, with no American exceptionalism at all, as it was not appreciation for world-class soccer, but patriotic rooting for an underdog with a reasonable chance for some success that attracted the American audience. Until the World Cup final on July 17, the U.S.-Brazil weekend attracted the largest soccer audience ever in America, easily surpassing the previous record set barely a week before by the match between the United States and Romania.

That the World Cup had managed to catapult soccer onto a qualitatively new stage in America's sport space was best exemplified by its emergence beyond its usual esoteric and marginal existence in the world of gambling and betting. One of the telltale signs of a hegemonic sports culture is its centrality to the wagering of its gamblers, both casual and serious. Indeed, soccer has generated a multi-billion-dollar—usually state-sanctioned and often state-monopolized—betting industry in the countries where it constitutes a hegemonic sport, just as the major American team sports have done in the less official but equally lucrative American betting world (legal only in the state of Nevada, but in existence in many other locales). Via the World Cup, soccer emerged as a real factor in the American world of sports gambling, as evidenced by expert opinion from casinos in Las Vegas and Reno. On the night of the U.S.-Colombia game, a couple hundred sports fans and gamblers were on hand at Harrah's in Reno, presumably killing time until the beginning of the seventh game of the NBA final between the New York Knicks and the Houston Rockets. With tip-off a minute away, the staff at Harrah's switched most of the lounge's video screens from the soccer telecast to the impending basketball game. Nobody was ready for the reaction of the sports-book patrons.

"It was as if a riot had broken out," said Terry Cox, Race and Sports Service Manager for Harrah's Reno. "People were screaming at us, standing on chairs, cussing, yelling 'Put the soccer back on for God's sake.' The US was winning and pulling off a huge upset and the folks wanted to see this. It really took us by surprise. We just assumed everyone was just waiting around for the NBA game and just watching the soccer because it happened to be on."[25]

Indeed, most of the crowd at Harrah's had turned out for basketball, as the comparatively few bets placed on the USA-Colombia match partly affirmed. But as the soccer game progressed, the surprisingly fine play and unexpected success of Team USA began to captivate the crowd, most of whom had not cared a bit about soccer one hour earlier. Calm was restored, relatively, when the screens were switched back to the soccer telecast. Proving once again that interest in and identification with a sporting event expand exponentially when there exists a basis for partisan rooting with the realistic chance to win, a few hundred basketball fans—most with money on either the Knicks or the Rockets—gladly delayed watching the climax to the premier event of the NBA season for, of all things, soccer. This was surely a first in the storied history of sports gambling in the United States.

The "handles" for the Brazil-USA game far exceeded those of the American upset of Colombia. The number of bets and the amount of cash on the table were both huge because of such favorable odds on the United States; after the arrival of all that money for the Americans, professional gamblers went massively for Brazil when the odds became irresistible. The final between Brazil and Italy also attracted an unusual amount of betting in Reno, though it is clear that some of that attraction stemmed from the World Cup's unexpected popularity in gambling circles garnered by the relatively good showing of the American team. Nothing comes even close to the enthusiasm and involvement generated by a little success for the home team.

Quarterfinals and Semifinals, 9–13 July

The following matches comprised the quarterfinals: Germany-Bulgaria in the Meadowlands, Italy-Spain at Foxboro, Brazil-Holland in Dallas, and Sweden-Romania at Stanford Stadium. This round also witnessed a major upset when the still underestimated Bulgarian team defeated the defending world champion Germans, 2–1, before the usual sell out crowd in the Meadowlands. "Bulgaria's win was not quite Angola beating the Dream Team, but it was something like that," opined Steve Fainaru of the *Boston Globe*.[26] Italy defeated yet another underachieving and disappointing Spanish national team, 2–1, with Roberto Baggio scoring the winning goal, a veritable routine and apparent requirement for all the "Squadra Azzurra's" games at this tournament. In a thriller and one of the best matches of the World Cup, Brazil defeated Holland, 3–2, after blowing a 2–0 lead only to get bailed out by a phenomenal shot by the midfielder Branco. Lastly, Sweden edged Romania in a penalty shoot-out to break a 2–2 tie after the ninety-minute regulation time plus the extra thirty minutes now added at the end of tied games.

Surprisingly, this was the very first time at this World Cup tournament that a penalty shoot-out became necessary to determine a game's winner. Sure enough, criticism of this tiebreaking mechanism arose in the American media immediately after the Sweden-Romania match. A number of commentators found this system appalling, in good part because they viewed the penalty shoot-out as only tangentially related to the game. Many used the analogy of having a major basketball game decided by a free-throw shooting contest or a game of "horse," an important football game by a field-goal contest, and/or a crucial baseball game via a home-run contest. Some commentators realized that any solution to breaking a tie in soccer was flawed, yet there was a general sense that the current system was deeply problematic and in need of replacement by a better and fairer solution at future tournaments. While the huge coverage accorded the previous round (when the Americans were still in contention) visibly diminished, there can be no doubt that the matches were given much prominence in the sports sections of all the newspapers that we surveyed. Indeed, in such soccer-friendly papers as the *Los Angeles Times*, the *Boston Globe*, the *Miami Herald*, *USA Today*, and the *New York Times*, continued coverage of the World Cup remained on the same level as it had been before the elimination of the American team. Moreover, papers featuring these matches gave these events plenty of attention well beyond the confines of the sports sections. The *Boston Globe* and the *Boston Herald* ran a number of articles on the North End, just as the *Dallas Morning News* featured stories on the Brazilians—fans of the world's most popular soccer team arriving at the home of the other football's self-anointed "America's team."[27]

Television ratings for the quarterfinal matches were obviously well below those attained by the U.S. team, but still quite respectable and well beyond what had been expected for such games before the tournament began. For the doubleheader on Saturday, July 9, 4 million of the country's 92 million homes were tuned to Spain-Italy, and 4.4 million watched the Netherlands-Brazil game that followed. Romania-Sweden was watched by 4.9 million homes, and Germany-Bulgaria by 4 million. All experts agreed that these were very impressive ratings for any sporting event in the middle of July. Still, these numbers trailed the previous weekend's U.S.-Brazil game (seen by more than 10 million homes) by a wide margin. The U.S. team's three appearances produced the largest audiences, by a significant margin, for all the World Cup telecasts on ABC (save the tournament final).[28]

It would be the first time in World Cup history that the two semifinal games were to be played on the very same day. On 13 July Italy was to meet Bulgaria at Giants Stadium, and later that day Brazil was to confront Sweden at the Rose Bowl in Pasadena, two matches auspiciously timed so that they would be played with virtually no competition on the American sports scene at all: 13 July was the Wednesday after baseball's traditional annual All-Star game (always held on a Tuesday followed by a game-free Wednesday). The British Open in golf would not begin until Thursday, 14 July, thus making 13 July perhaps the quietest day on that year's American sports calendar. The two games were to be telecast by ESPN which—in 1994—reached only two-thirds of American homes. In the first match, Italy defeated Bulgaria, 2–1, in what was arguably the most convincing performance of the "Squadra Azzurra" throughout the tournament. In a relatively relaxed manner, the Italians clearly outplayed the Bulgarians and won—as had become completely routine by this time in the World Cup—on the strength of Roberto Baggio's two goals. Alas, there was one negative and potentially decisive angle to Baggio's continued heroics: He departed the game with a strained hamstring and a chipped tooth, making his appearance in the final doubtful. More than any other player, Baggio had become a real star in the course of this World Cup, becoming one of the very few World Cup players who had transcended soccer and attained some recognition by American sports fans and the general public. "Roberto Baggio was mentioned more often during yesterday's Italy-Bulgaria World Cup telecast on ESPN than were Ken Griffey and Frank Thomas combined during Tuesday night's All-Star Game on NBC," wrote Jack Craig in the *Boston Globe*.[29]

After a 24-year absence from a World Cup final—a painful hiatus for all Brazilians and the team's millions of fans all over the world—Romario's goal against Sweden sufficed to advance the *seleçao* to yet another showdown against Italy, the same opponent that Brazil had last met in a World Cup final (in 1970, when a Pelé-led squad demolished a superb Italian side in Mexico City). Brazil had played well enough to win without displaying its usual magic—the famed *jogo bonito*—in vanquishing the surprisingly resilient Swedes. Both semifinal matches played to soldout stadiums in their respective venues, and both yielded the winner that virtually everybody in the world—excepting Swedes and Bulgarians—hoped to see in the final: Two three-time champions would decide who would become the sole "tetra" champion, thus the undisputedly best national soccer team of all times. It would have been hard for anybody to script a more desirable final in terms of glamour, pedigree, history, and the skills of the two contestants. Television ratings for the two semifinals were respectable, though far from the impressive numbers compiled by the three games featuring the U.S. team: With a 3.9, Brazil-Sweden drew ESPN's second largest audience of the twenty-eight World Cup games it televised; Italy-Bulgaria attracted a somewhat smaller viewership at 2.9.[30]

The Brazil-Italy final on Sunday, 17 July would be what in the Latin countries (e.g., both Brazil and Italy) is called a *clasico*, a classic matchup, a "real marquee final" as Seamus Malin called it; a rematch of arguably the greatest World Cup final ever, one for the ages, the dream finale to an amazingly successful tournament.[31] Could the event live up to all these expectations?

The World Cup Final on 17 July and Its Aftermath

The simple answer has to be that it most certainly did not. For the first time in World Cup history, a final yielded no goals through regular playing time, and the extra thirty minutes that followed—also a World Cup first— failed to break the goalless deadlock. Adding insult to injury, the game itself offered few beautiful moments and was indeed precisely one of those rare 0–0 contests that lack any drama, not only for the paucity in scoring but also by the absence of any compelling play on the part of either of the two teams. While the Brazilians most definitely had the upper hand throughout the game, they failed to crack the famed Italian *catenaccio*-like defense. The Italians—who always play a defensive style of game featuring few, but often deadly, counterattacks—seemed altogether lacking in this match. In short, the final between Brazil and Italy yielded exactly the kind of match that American soccer critics always bring up when denouncing the sport as boring, slow, lacking in direction, and—ultimately—lacking in scoring. For the first time, a World Cup final had to be decided by penalty kicks; as fate would have it, it was Baggio's missed kick in the penalty shoot-out—with the ball sailing way over the crossbar—that sealed Italy's fate and gave Brazil its much-desired "tetra" championship. The headline for Dan Shaughnessy's column in the *Boston Globe* asked the question on the mind of virtually every American who had watched this game: "Why not just flip a coin to find winner?"[32] Informal and impromptu surveys of American soccer fans and casual viewers of the World Cup final revealed massive disappointment with the shootout as the ultimate tiebreaker of such a crucial game as the World Cup final. The negative reaction by the fans appeared totally congruent with that of the vast majority of media commentaries across the nation. Many believed that the very integrity of the game of soccer was somehow compromised by such a frivolous way of crowning a world champion, no matter how deserving the eventual winner might be.[33] Indeed, in our survey of newspapers covering the World Cup we could not find one commentary that defended the existing shoot-out as a legitimate tiebreaker of any soccer game, let alone a World Cup final. Some went to the trouble of explaining FIFA's rationale for this method, but none approved of it.

Most commentators and media reports concurred that the World Cup final was a disappointing end to an otherwise fine and often glorious tournament. However, a vast majority of analysts also declared Brazil a worthy winner, not only by virtue of its storied pedigree but also by dint of the team's performance throughout the tournament. Most also agreed that even in this lackluster final game, Brazil was the better team as it played with more grace, energy, and perhaps even skill than the Italian team. As expected, the final in Pasadena was played in front of a usual sellout crowd of 95,000 people. The global audience was estimated at 1.8 billion for the match. Also as expected, this game's viewership in the United States surpassed the previous record for a soccer game, set by U.S.-Brazil on July 4. The overnight rating of 12.4 for the thirty-one largest American cities eventually dropped to a final nationwide 9.5 rating with a twenty-four share, still immensely impressive numbers. The World Cup final swept past all other weekend network sports, almost doubling the audience for ABC's baseball extravaganza on the day before the soccer match. This feat was all the more impressive as the baseball game was shown in prime time and featured the sport's hottest teams and most exciting player of that season (the Eastern Division–leading New York Yankees, always a major television draw, confronting the Western Division–leading Seattle Mariners featuring Ken Griffey Jr., one of the best players in baseball and a very popular marquee star). The World Cup telecast crushed the British Open coverage on Sunday by tripling the numbers of this major golf tournament, one of the four majors of the sport.[34]

Despite the disappointing final, the overall numbers for the tournament were nothing short of astounding: The 52-match World Cup tournament, played in the United States for the first time, drew a record 3,578,598 fans, produced $210 million in gate receipts, filled all nine venues to virtual capacity, offered more goals than the previous World Cup in Italy, and provided a multicultural atmosphere that was clearly second to none. "The speculation about spectator violence, violence in the streets, never happened. The number of arrests were less than for a high school football game and less than that of an NFL game. We had a month-long love-in," declared Rothenberg, rightly proud of the achievements by his organization in producing such a resoundingly successful tournament.[35] To be sure, there were a few negatives that marred the overall quality of the tournament, first and foremost the murder of Colombian defender Andres Escobar by his countrymen for kicking a goal into his own net against the much-hated "Yanquis."[36] Additionally, there was Maradona's banishment for taking prohibited drugs; Tab Ramos's fractured skull thanks to Leonardo's elbow; Luis Enrique's broken nose from other elbows; a few serious misjudgments by referees that altered the outcomes of certain games; and the scheduling of games according to the dictates of Europe's prime time, which meant that quite a few contests suffered in quality of play because of the excessive heat quite commonplace at midday in late June and early to mid-July in most of the United States. Yet, even the most cynical of European reporters and the most skeptical of commentators had to admit—however grudgingly—that the World Cup in the United States was a resounding success.

Regarding the future of soccer in the United States, the question on everybody's mind was: What next? What might be the legacy of such a superb tournament for soccer's fate in America? Would it have any, or would it prove ephemeral, thus making the World Cup a fine temporary event whose organizers wisely rented a country that offered not only un-tapped market opportunities, but also an unparalleled infrastructure to make possible such a huge undertaking? What would be the World Cup's long-term impact on soccer in America and—more broadly—American sports culture? In the concluding section of this chapter, we attempt to shed some light on the debate of these issues as it occurred among the country's sports columnists during the course of the tournament. We deem these voices an appropriate gauge of the complex and conflicting sentiments of America's sports fans and the public at large regarding the 1994 World Cup and soccer in general.

The Columnists

During the buildup to the World Cup and as the tournament opened, sports sections, as well as feature sections utilizing columns and articles by nonsportswriters and columnists, began to include "pro and con" essays, often in tandem, debating the merits of soccer and its chances to break into mainstream American sports culture. This dialogue would continue in sports and feature pages throughout the tournament, though such col-umns appeared most often during the buildup, the first round, or within two days after the final match. Most newspapers, at some point, ran col-umns of this nature, though not always in the sports section. All newspa-pers ran pieces by both sports and feature columnists either before, dur-ing, or after the tournament (or all three) that examined the merits of soccer and the World Cup, the potential for soccer to succeed as a "big-time" professional sport in the United States, and what effect the World Cup might have in the promotion of American soccer.

There were several writers who displayed an undisguised hostility to-ward both soccer and the World Cup, though not all newspapers pub-lished pieces of this sort. There were many more writers who generally had positive things to say about the World Cup, and some who took up the cause of defending soccer for its own sake in response to negative or ambivalent attitudes toward the sport. Most pieces that examined the "American soccer attitude" and whether or not the sport could succeed in the United States were not necessarily an expression of a writer's personal views toward the sport itself. Hence, many writers who were soccer friendly were not sanguine regarding the potential successful establishment of MLS as a result of World Cup USA '94. Most recognized the difference between a successful World Cup and the success of soccer in capturing the permanent allegiance of the American public. There were some soccer-friendly writers who unabashedly wrote of their passion for the game and often exhorted their readers to take up the "soccer cause," though these sentiments were usually expressed by "guest" feature writers, not sportswriters. Most "pro-soccer" columnists made a point of not preaching for "the cause" and simply asked their readers to give the game, as it would be played in the World Cup tournament, a chance to entertain. There were some columnists not overtly friendly to the sport but who expressed a willingness to keep an open mind. Though tending to proclaim a loyalty and preference for the Big Three and One-Half, they generally wrote with a positive interest about the World Cup, viewing it as a temporary diversion that made for some good times, interesting experiences, and a firsthand opportunity to see what the rest of the world found so enthralling. The World Cup also gave many American sports columnists who make a point of writing with sarcasm and humor an opportunity to apply their craft to a newfound topic. (See appendix B for a sample of the opinions from sports columnists and journalists regarding the 1994 World Cup.)

Perhaps there is no better characterization of the essence of World Cup '94 in the United States than the words of Bob Ryan of the *Boston Globe*. We therefore deem them an appropriate way to conclude our chapter on this important episode in American soccer as well as sports history. Ryan described the change of mind he experienced over the course of the tournament, from an initial skeptic toward soccer and the World Cup to a respectful admirer (if not quite a fan) of the game and this unique event:

> OK, are you ready? I was wrong. I thought it would be sacrilegious to bring the World Cup to the United States, but I was in error. Do I think I could improve soccer? Sure. Do any of the two or three billion people on the planet who happen to like the game just the way it is care about what one (representative) mainstream American sportswriter thinks? No. Nor should they. The point is that they have loaned us their treasure and we have enhanced it. We turned out not to be heathens at all, but respectful curators instead. We have set an organizational and enthusiasm standard for *them* to match in the future. . . . It

turns out we were the perfect country to host the World Cup. Name the ethnic group, and it's here on our shores, somewhere. No team went unsupported or unloved. . . . What they've [the foreign journalists, visiting teams, and fans in general] found is that we have the best *stadia*, the best communications, the best overall transportation and the greatest fan mix in the world. Many a foreign journalist has noted that 1990 World Cup matches not featuring Italy itself often played to half houses, whereas in 1994 an empty seat for any Cup game in a US stadium might be the lead story on the 11 o'clock news. . . . It is always instructive for fat-headed Americans to learn that there is an entire world out there that ridicules our cavalier use of the word 'world' as in 'World Series,' and that views us as haughty and out of step with everyone else. We may not need their game as part of our daily mix, but we should understand its importance in the rest of the world. There is good and bad soccer passion, and we have been exposed to only the good. . . . The day may never come when we Americans will acquire a comparable passion for the game, but that doesn't mean we can't, or shouldn't, once again offer our halls for hire. No one else will do a better job."[37]

Seven ....

The Coverage of World Cup '98 by the American Media and the Tournament's Reception by the American Public

THERE SIMPLY can be no doubt that in the course of the last two decades of the twentieth century, coverage and awareness of the quadrennially held world championship of soccer, otherwise known as the World Cup, has grown tremendously in the United States. The data are clear: While barely present in the sports pages—let alone the general news sections—of American "papers of record" such as the *New York Times*, the *Washington Post*, and the *Los Angeles Times*, as well as America's leading sports weekly *Sports Illustrated*, until the mid 1980s, all of these publications covered the subsequent tournaments with increasing intensity and expertise to the point where—by the 1990s—the World Cup formed a featured part of their sport section during the tournament's actual duration.[1] This was already true for the World Cup of 1990 held in Italy in which—tellingly—the United States was present for the first time after a forty-year hiatus.

Of course, the coverage intensified mightily four years later when the championship was hosted by the United States. Interestingly, the quantity and prominence of World Cup coverage in 1998 did not substantially decrease from what it had been in 1994 (save, of course, from "local angle" news features in the nine host cities of that year). All major American newspapers devoted large parts of their sport sections to the World Cup; most had their own reporters in France who wrote daily stories. In addition, these newspapers utilized articles from wire services such as Reuters and the Associated Press. A number of times, World Cup stories and/or photos appeared on the very first pages of prominent American papers, including those mentioned above, plus the *Boston Globe*, the *Philadelphia Inquirer*, the *Miami Herald*, and the *San Jose Mercury News*. Just as in 1994, *USA Today* offered some of the most extensive and best-informed reporting on the World Cup in France. All sixty-two games were televised live on either ESPN, ESPN 2, or ABC, as well as by Univision, the Spanish-language network. While no local sport station sent any of its reporters to France, and few, if any, led their nightly sports news with World Cup–related matters, they all reported the daily scores of the matches and regularly featured highlights of the goals. Anybody in the

United States who wanted to be informed of virtually every aspect of the World Cup and/or follow every game could easily do so. About 670,000 non-Hispanic American soccer fans and approximately 850,000 Hispanic soccer aficionados clearly did so on a regular basis. The World Cup in France was eminently accessible to any American even vaguely interested in sports and/or international news, but whether this accessibility trans- lated into real interest and knowledge—let alone passion—is rather doubtful. The only poll (taken during the second week of the tounament) explicitly focused on Americans' awareness of the World Cup offered rather discouraging numbers. Only 74 percent had heard or read about the World Cup; a mere 52 percent knew that it was a soccer competition; only 25 percent were aware that the tournament was being played in France; and a mere 19 percent had watched part or all of a game, of which 24 percent enjoyed watching a "great deal" and 31 percent "quite a lot," while 45 percent liked it "not much."[2]

Despite these rather discouraging numbers, there can be no doubt that the sport of soccer and its premier event, the World Cup, have become better known in the United States in the past twenty years than ever be- fore. The most notable reasons for this include the NASL, the tremendous growth of soccer as a recreational activity for millions of Americans (espe- cially for youngsters and young women), World Cup 1994 held in the United States, MLS, the presence of the American national team at the last three World Cups, the global dominance and success of the American women's national team, the changed ethnic and cultural composition of immigrants to the United States in the wake of the 1966 Immigration Act, and the globalization of sports through television. All of these represent ephemeral steps on their own and under no circumstances would individ- ually help soccer's cause in terms of its gaining a meaningful presence in America's sport space. But taken together, these forces offer a window of opportunity that just might alter soccer's sorry marginalization in Ameri- can sports culture throughout the twentieth century, perhaps leading it to a brighter future in the twenty-first.

This chapter will first look at the "buildup" in the American media toward the 1998 World Cup, observing how this stage almost exclusively focused on the qualifying and preparatory games played by the U.S. na- tional team. The subsequent section of this chapter will analyze the tour- nament's presence in the United States between June 10 and July 12, 1998. In particular, we consider the following issues: other major sports events occurring concurrently with the World Cup—such as the NBA Fi- nals, the Stanley Cup Finals, the U.S. Opens (both men and women) in golf, the All-England tennis championships in Wimbledon, the All-Star game in baseball, the fate of the American team at the World Cup in France—and the reporting of key developments from the tournament, such as major matches as well as events outside the stadiums proper. By looking at this particular angle, we hope to gain some insight regarding the World Cup's attempt to establish a presence in the crowded American sport space. Our sources are television data from the three English-speaking and the Spanish-speaking television channels; analysis of newspapers hailing from every single one of the twelve U.S. cities that have an MLS team as well as from cities that were hosts to World Cup games during the 1994 tournament but do not have an MLS franchise (such as Orlando); important newspapers (such as the *Philadelphia Inquirer*) published neither in MLS cities nor in those that hosted games during the 1994 World Cup; sports weeklies; sports radio; and a month-long immersion into the world of sixty-two soccer games broadcast live from France and subsequently reported on by the media.[3]

The "Buildup"

The U.S. national team's road to the 1998 World Cup received an unprecedented degree of attention. (The United States—as the host nation—had automatically qualified for the tournament in 1994, so it did not have to undergo the grueling series of qualifying games within the so-called CONCACAF group, a FIFA designation comprising Central American and Caribbean countries, as well as the United States, Canada and Mexico.) To be sure, Paul Caligiuri's goal in the cauldron of Port Au Prince against Trinidad and Tobago that qualified the United States for the tournament in Italy in 1990 did get some attention in 1989, but on the whole, the American team's qualifiers had remained completely unknown other than to a very select group of soccer fans. Newspapers reported only the final scores, if that, and the games were never telecast; in short, these games were played in virtual obscurity. As a consequence of soccer's higher profile in the United States resulting from World Cup 1994 and the (belated) presence of Major League Soccer beginning in 1996, however, the U.S. team's qualifying games for the World Cup in France were all televised nationally and reported on with regularity.

    The U.S. team's tie with Mexico on 2 November 1997, was perhaps the first salient event. Never having won against Mexico in Mexico City and having been outscored by Mexico in that stadium, 69–13, since 1937, the Americans were confronted with a gargantuan task made all the more acute since a loss to Mexico would have placed the U.S. team in a precarious position for qualification. Even though one of the American players— Jeff Agoos—was sent off the field, and the team had to play much of the game one man short, the Americans attained a 0–0 draw, a tremendous success given the importance of the game, its location, and its history laden with failure and humiliation.[4] Above all, this tie placed the Americans in an excellent position to qualify for France. While getting some ink on the sports pages of the nation's newspapers, the game was not even televised beyond a complicated closed-circuit arrangement that excluded virtually everybody. One week later, the United States defeated Canada, 3–0, in Burnaby, British Columbia, to qualify for the World Cup for the third straight time. Comments after this victory repeatedly mentioned what America's qualifying for the Big Show would possibly mean for soccer's enhanced visibility in the United States.[5] There seemed to be no clear consensus as to how this positive development would prove beneficial to soccer's presence in the United States; but at the same time, there was near unanimity that a failure on the part of the American team to qualify for France would have meant a major setback for the future of soccer in the United States.[6]

The first event in which the World Cup entered the consciousness of most Americans well beyond hard-core soccer fans and even the larger sports world was on 4 December 1997, when FIFA held its World Cup draw in Marseilles, France, and America's opponents in Group F were determined to be Germany, Yugoslavia, and Iran. With the possible exceptions of Iraq and Cuba, the United States could not have drawn two more politically controversial opponents than Iran and Yugoslavia. Bitter enmity had informed America's relationship with Iran since the fall of the Shah's government in 1979 and the taking of hostages at the American embassy in Teheran by Iranian radicals. As to Yugoslavia, relations between the two countries had reached a nadir ever since the United States led a NATO intervention to curb a predatory Yugoslavia in its brutal war against Bosnia-Herzegovina in which Yugoslavia-supported Bosnian Serbs committed genocidal atrocities against Muslim Bosnians, particularly in the village of Srebrenica. It was after Serbian-led massacres there that the United States intervened, forcing Yugoslavian "strongman" Slobodan Milosevic to desist from further military campaigns in Bosnia. Poor relations between the United States and Serbia had already been further aggravated by Serbia's repeated military intervention in its autonomous region of Kosovo, inhabited almost exclusively by Muslim Albanians. Even though the American team's head coach, Steve Sampson, and many of the players insisted that these were only two soccer teams whom the Americans were to confront in France, it was clear that much more was involved. Concepts such as "soccer diplomacy," especially in relation to the game against Iran, made the rounds as an obvious analogy to the "Ping-Pong diplomacy" of the early 1970s that opened the door to relations between China and the United States. Soccer diplomacy was accorded particular importance because Iran's moderate new president, Mohammed Khatami, had made a number of gestures that—given the context of Iran's unmitigated hostility toward and hatred for the United States ("the Great Satan") for nearly two decades—could have been interpreted as clear overtures toward better relations. That is exactly how President Clinton and Secretary of State Madeleine Albright viewed Khatami and his policies, particularly in contrast to those of Khatami's main rival in Iran, Ali Khameini, the hard-line anti-American leader of the mullahs' continued conservative rule. Indeed, the president and the secretary of state would use the soccer game between Iran and the United States during the World Cup to make important conciliatory gestures toward Iran and give major policy speeches that indicated a willingness on the part of the United States to reconsider the hostile relations between these two countries. The Iran-U.S. game scheduled for 21 June 1998 in Lyons instantly became the most talked-about matchup of the World Cup's first-round games six months before it was actually played. Soccer in America had attained something of an unexpected boost from the world of global politics.[7]

While garnering nowhere near the attention of the World Cup draw, the U.S. team's 1–0 victory against Brazil on the evening of 10 February 1998 at the Los Angeles Coliseum stunned the sparse crowd of 12,298 as much as it did the soccer world. Preki's picture-book shot yielded the first goal that the Americans had scored against the Brazilians in sixty-eight years.[8] It was also the very first time that the American national soccer team had ever defeated Brazil. An otherwise little-known American tournament, the Gold Cup, had made headlines in the international soccer world (though not so much at home). Maybe the Americans were much better than everybody believed. Perhaps things had improved phenomenally since the abysmal performance of the team at the World Cup in Italy in 1990 and the respectable, but still meager, showing at home during World Cup 1994. For the goal's aesthetic beauty and by virtue of its leading to a victory against the very best national team in the game, Preki's shot received some television exposure on sports shows well beyond the L.A. area, though it was still quite secondary to basketball and hockey news.

The victory against Brazil catapulted the United States into the Gold Cup final against Mexico. Played at the L.A. Coliseum on 15 February 1998, it highlighted one of the major predicaments of soccer's existence in the United States: Unlike the Brazil game (which drew an embarrassingly low turnout given the pedigree of the opponent), this time 91,255 official spectators filled the Coliseum with an additional 10,000 admitted without tickets. Another 6,941 fans watched Mexico earn a Gold Cup "three-peat" with a 1–0 win on closed-circuit television inside the adjacent Los Angeles Arena.[9] The problem with these impressive numbers was simple: The fans were all Mexicans, making the crowd Mexico's "twelfth man" instead of one for the American team. It is worth quoting at length from *Soccer America*, the leading soccer publication in the United States, to give a flavor of how sad it must have been to the American players that their home game in Los Angeles bore all the characteristics of a difficult and hostile away game.

> A lone American flag fluttered at half-mast on the perimeter, surrounded by a whole host of Mexican Tricolores. Any remaining doubts about the identity of the home team were dispelled when the two teams took the field. The fans came, saw, booed and threw things—at the United States. Whistles greeted the U.S. national team when it took the field and during its national anthem. Every lost possession was greeted with cheers. Every U.S. throw-in or corner was hailed by flying debris. Cups and bottles containing beer, soda, water and the end-product of consumption rained onto the field.[10]

Certainly not an inviting image to make soccer more popular to the average American sports fan.

Even though television ratings for the concurrent winter Olympics in Nagano were more than disappointing, they still were sufficient to block out the Gold Cup for the regular American sports viewer.[11] Games against Belgium (3–0 loss), Holland (2–0 loss), Paraguay (2–2 tie), Austria (3–0 win, with detrimental consequences at the World Cup, as elaborated subsequently), Scotland (0–0 tie), Macedonia (0–0 tie), and a few other so-called friendlies against weaker international teams served as preparation for the team's trip to France. These warm-up games received little, if any, attention outside the soccer community, but they were all dutifully covered in the sports sections of the country's leading newspapers. By May there were a number of feature stories on the U.S. team as well as on some of its individual players, such as Tom Dooley, David Regis, Preki Radosavljevic, and Claudio Reyna. The gist of all these articles emphasized the polyglot and multicultural nature of the U.S. team, which, while immensely impressive and inviting on one level, could yet again serve to reinforce soccer's image for average American sports fans as a sport for and by foreigners.[12] Lastly, Coach Sampson's surprising decision to cut John Harkes from the U.S. team's final 22-man squad for France made the sports pages on account of Harkes's status as arguably one of the three most successful American players in the course of the 1990s, a stalwart member of the national team throughout much of the same decade, and one of the most important contributors to DC United's first two MLS championships.

By early June, the World Cup began to make its presence felt in American newspapers beyond the sports sections. Travel sections ran specials on France and Paris with a particular World Cup angle, such as transportation to the stadiums, intercity travel and cultural events such as special exhibits, open air concerts, and other similar programs organized around the World Cup.[13] Articles appeared that analyzed the World Cup's commercial attraction and marketing potential, while many featured the World Cup's unique reach, emphasizing that the tournament's projected cumulative global audience (as in the number of viewers for all the games represented as one sum total) would be in the vicinity of 37–40 billion viewers. By comparison, the viewership for the Super Bowl is typically 133 million, 128 million for the NBA finals, and 185 million for the World Series, with the latter two numbers the total for a series of games rather than one single event like the Super Bowl. Even the Olympics—with 3.5 billion total cumulative viewers—remains far behind the World Cup. While the World Cup attracts a global audience wherein the American share is minuscule, all of these other events appealed almost exclusively to an American viewership. Even the Olympics—in stark contrast to the World Cup—included a large portion of American television viewers in its worldwide audience.[14] As at the World Cup in the United States, there were yet again a number of major American-based multinational corporations participating as major sponsors of the World Cup. At the very top were Coca-Cola, SNICKERS, McDonald's, Gillette, MasterCard, and Opel (the German division of General Motors), who, along with adidas, Fujifilm, JVC, and Philips, comprised the ten global sponsors of the event and formed the inner core of sponsors. In addition to the six American companies whose logos graced the barricades of every stadium and whose names were ubiquitous in every possible venue related to the World Cup, companies such as Nike, Reebok, Hewlett-Packard, Time Warner, Electronic Data Systems, and Walt Disney were prominently represented at this event.[15]

Nike sponsored and clothed a number of teams, including the Americans, Dutch, Italians, South Koreans, Nigerians, and, most prominently, the Brazilians. Nike paid the American team $120 million for the right to be its sole outfitter through 2006, while establishing a unique relationship with Brazil whereby it paid the Brazilian Soccer Federation (CBF) $200 million. In return, the Brazilian team committed itself to wear Nike products exclusively for ten years (not unusual) as well as staging a certain number of exhibition games each year for the company (highly unusual).[16] Reebok clothed a number of South American teams, including Chile and Paraguay. Hewlett-Packard was in charge of running the event's main networking and computing systems, while Walt Disney's affiliates ABC, ESPN, and ESPN2 telecast all sixty-two games to the United States. In contrast to American sports fans, some of the country's leading multinational corporations were deeply engaged in the World Cup for one simple reason: With the earnings and revenues from their international operations often far surpassing those from their domestic markets, these companies were utilizing the global appeal of soccer and its premier event, the World Cup, to solidify their presence as global players, something they have done since the 1994 Cup and that they will continue to do for many Cups to come. Soccer and the World Cup had become major venues for these American companies, as well as others, to reap financial success in an increasingly globalized economy.[17] Once again, as Marx correctly demonstrated, the most efficient productive forces are by their very nature eager to break conventional boundaries, as they are inherently cosmopolitan, as opposed to the less efficient forces of production, which tend toward protection and parochialism in one form or another. This is a fortiori true for culture—including sports culture—that remains "sticky" and local; but markets and production are not completely separate from culture; there exists a slow but definite interaction. That said, there can be no doubt that by dint of the deep involvement with soccer (and the World Cup) on the part of these major American corporations, the game's future in the United States is a lot rosier than at any previous time in its century-long history. The immense resources of Coca-Cola, McDonald's, and Nike may yet succeed where everything else has thus far failed: making soccer an integral part of America's sports culture and sport space.[18] Indeed, that was the very essence of "Project 2010"—also known as the "Rothenberg Initiative"—which was announced in New York a few weeks before the beginning of the World Cup. With the assistance of corporate sponsorship by Nike and the International Management Group to the tune of more than $50 million (above and beyond the $120 million paid to the U.S. team), the United States is to wean a cadre of 120 superb soccer talents of under seventeen years of age at the Bollettieri Academy in Bradenton, Florida, and mold them into a squad that by 2010 can have a realistic chance to win the World Cup (and thus make the United States world champion in the game it will always call soccer even as the rest of the world calls it football). A plausible plan or a chimera—who can tell? However, the very fact that such a plan existed and was hatched in the late 1990s said much about the changing nature of soccer in the United States at the end of the twentieth century.[19]

The days before the beginning of the tournament saw all major newspapers run extensive previews of the World Cup with a complete listing (sometimes even short profiles) of the thirty-two teams, the dates and matchups of the preliminary round-robin segment of the tournament, brief histories of the World Cup, the television schedules of all sixty-two games, and an almost ubiquitous portrait of Ronaldo, the Brazilian superstar whom some touted as the new Pelé. Some newspapers published entire World Cup supplements.[20] *Sports Illustrated*, though featuring yet another Michael Jordan cover with the title "MJ Rises Again," included Ronaldo's name on the cover page alongside those of Mark McGwire (home run leader), Juan Gonzalez (RBI leader), Monica Seles (surprise French Open finalist), and the Detroit Red Wings (on the verge of re-peating as Stanley Cup Champions). Inside, there was a fine preview of the tournament and the requisite article on Ronaldo, in addition to full-page photographs of other prospective stars such as France's Zinedine Zidane, Italy's Alessandro Del Piero, England's Alan Shearer, Holland's Clarence Seedorf, and Germany's Oliver Bierhoff. Though *Sports Illus-trated* was to run weekly articles on various aspects of the tournament in the course of its duration, it was the "preview" issue that offered the most extensive exposure to the World Cup in America's most popular sports magazine. *Sport* also published a "World Cup Soccer Preview" in its June 1998 issue, though it chose to put Kobe Bryant and Shaquille O'Neal of the Los Angeles Lakers on its cover. Of course, the magazine ran the al-most requisite feature on Ronaldo in its July issue. However, just like in 1994, the *Sporting News* published absolutely nothing on the World Cup. Still, any interested American newspaper and magazine reader had ample opportunity to become extremely well informed about the impending tournament.

The World Cup Itself

June 10 featured the opening match of the tournament, which—as re-quired by tradition—pitted the champion, in this case Brazil, against one of its opponents from its round-robin group, in this case Scotland. Ameri-can papers ran articles on the Brazilian team; the traditions of Brazilian soccer; Ronaldo's life story from the rags of Rio's favelas to the riches of the world's most recognized and revered soccer star; Scotland's complete futility at the World Cup (where it had yet to advance to the second round); human interest stories on fans from various parts of the world; the Parisians' blasé attitude toward the whole tournament; and many arti-cles on the American team, its prospects, its preparations, its chances against its first opponent Germany, and why winning the World Cup might be the only chance to have soccer become part of America's sports culture.[21]

Brazil's 2–1 victory over Scotland received prominent display in the American press. The *New York Times* of 11 June 1998 featured a two-column Agence France-Presse picture of a Ronaldo header on the top section of the newspaper's front page. While the main story on the first page of the sports section read "Bulls Drive the Next-to-Last Nail in the Coffin" above a towering photo of Scottie Pippen grabbing a rebound, the Brazil-Scotland game appeared on the bottom section of the page re-ceiving exactly the amount of display given to a win by the Yankees'

Cuban pitcher Orlando Hernandez ("El Duque") in an interleague game against the Montreal Expos. George Vecsey's page-long column on the left-hand side of the page was entitled "World's Team Kicks Off World Cup." *USA Today* also featured yet another Ronaldo header in the top left-hand corner of its front page on 11 June, though the Bulls' victory over the Jazz with a huge picture of Michael Jordan passing the ball received much more prominent placement on that page. On the front page of the sports section, too, the Bulls received the most visible and extensive coverage, though the Brazil victory also appeared on that page. While the *Boston Globe* and the *Boston Herald* did not announce the Brazilian victory on their respective front pages, both gave the game at least as much coverage as they did to the Bulls' victory over the Jazz, arguably slightly more considering that the *Globe*'s first sports page featured a huge picture of a somersaulting Cafu celebrating a Brazilian goal instead of Michael Jordan or Scottie Pippen. The prominence of the article on the Brazil-Scotland game was also far superior to the Bulls' victory against the Jazz and—surprise—the Red Sox's 10–6 win in a rare interleague game against the mighty Atlanta Braves in which the Red Sox's star pitcher, Pedro Martinez, suffered a rare subpar outing. The *Los Angeles Times* ran eleven items on the World Cup that day, from a detailed report of the Brazil-Scotland game to an analysis of three American players, from worries on the Italian team, to Coach Sampson's difficult choice between two American attackers. A number of newspapers printed human-interest stories on Brazilians and Scotsmen watching the game in the United States; on how ethnic neighborhoods were gearing up for four weeks of nonstop soccer; on American soccer enthusiasts in France, of whom the most dedicated had come to be known as "Sam's Army"; but also on American sports fans in the United States who most certainly were not infected by soccer fever and seemed oblivious to the World Cup.

Friday, Saturday, and Sunday saw the papers report in respectable detail about the games played in the tournament, giving the France–South Africa game (3–0, for the French) particular attention on account of its pitting the tournament's host against a team that had never appeared in the World Cup. There were articles on the pressures confronting the French, who had "underachieved" throughout their often talented soccer history—most recently in the years between 1986 and 1998, when, most glaringly, they failed to qualify for both the 1990 and 1994 World Cup tournaments—and who were expected to perform very well on account of enjoying home-field advantage throughout the World Cup. As in all countries, team sports in South Africa also acquired certain meanings and content. With rugby associated with the former white apartheid regime, soccer had become—faute de mieux—the sport identified with blacks and the new integrated regime of Nelson Mandela. American newspapers featured this theme, but other games also received ample coverage. For example, Italy's opener with Chile (a 2–2 tie) saw a number of articles discuss the controversial penalty near the end of the game that gave the heavily favored Italians a lucky draw. Harking back to the Cup in the United States, where Roberto Baggio became one of the most prominent players in the tournament, a number of articles underlined Baggio's superb play in the game, leading to one of the tournament's most beautiful goals (Baggio's assist to Christian Vieri).

Naturally, there was an array of articles on the American team: that the players were bored and antsy in the Chateau de Pizay, a gorgeous but solitary retreat in the countryside, and that they felt calm and confident before the big game against Germany. And there were features on Coach Sampson, on Thomas Dooley, on Joe-Max Moore, and on Kasey Keller, the goalie. One of the themes to emerge repeatedly was the ever present and powerful "Dangerfield complex" that occurs in every sport: lack of respect. Article upon article discussed how the Germans—and their coach Berti Vogts, in particular—did not respect the United States. Sampson felt that by walking out early on the February U.S.-Belgium match in Brussels, Vogts had shown that "in Europe, they have no respect for the United States." Sampson then wisely added: "Frankly, we haven't earned it."[22] There were also discussions about Sampson's plan to use a so-called 3-6-1 system (i.e., three defenders, six midfielders, and one lone attacker) against Germany, a configuration the United States had employed with great success against the Austrians in a surprise 3–0 win back in April.

But the coverage was by no means confined to the American team. Hence, for example, the *Boston Sunday Globe* of June 14 ran a header above the newspaper's logo on the front page in red: "World Cup '98," while the caption underneath said: "The Netherlands ties Belgium, 0–0, in an intense, defensive soccer struggle—D17." Saturday's papers gave the Utah Jazz's surprise victory in Chicago more prominent coverage than the World Cup, especially since most observers had been expecting a Bulls win to give them their sixth championship in front of the hometown crowd. On account of his disappointing play in the series up to that point, Karl Malone's sensational play in that game garnered much attention. On Sunday, the Red Wings' third victory against the Washington Capitals in the Stanley Cup final also received extensive coverage on a par with that given the World Cup. As can well be imagined, the coverage of the Bulls in the two Chicago papers and of the Red Wings in the *Detroit Free Press* were much more detailed and prominent than those given the World Cup, though it should be noted that the latter received as much space as the Tigers (in Detroit) and the White Sox (in Chicago), though somewhat less than the ever popular and surging Cubs with their slugger Sammy Sosa going on a home-run binge that would land him on the cover of *Sports Illustrated* one week later.[23]

The first all-important television ratings of the World Cup appeared as well over that weekend, confirming what many had expected: A precipitous decline in viewership compared to that during the World Cup in the United States. Brazil's 2–1 victory over Scotland netted a 0.8 cable rating, which translates to 592,000 of the 74.0 million homes that receive ESPN, a 56 percent decline from 1994's equivalent event when then title-holder Germany opened the tournament at Chicago's Soldier's Field against Bolivia (winning the match, 1–0) and attained a rating of 2.2, or 1.39 million homes, on ESPN. Corroborating the experts' expectation that the games would be watched by a hard-core soccer crowd, the numbers for the World Cup's second game between Morocco and Norway (hardly marquee clubs) achieved numbers similar to those of the opener featuring world champion Brazil, about 0.8. Numbers for matches on ESPN2 were lower still, only garnering 0.6 rating points, a 25 percent decline from 1994.[24]

The most significant reason for the lower numbers in 1998 compared to 1994 was, of course, the inauspicious time of day that the games were televised in the United States: The early games aired at 11:30 A.M. eastern daylight savings time, with the later games televised at 3:00 P.M., hardly ideal for working people on regular nine-to-five schedules, though perfect for academics and night watchmen. And yet, there was a silver lining even in these early rather disappointing television numbers: Despite the low viewership, it still doubled ESPN's normal ratings. In the second quarter of 1998, ESPN averaged a 0.4 during the 11:00 A.M. eastern time slot and a 0.2 during the 3:00 P.M. Eastern slot.[25] Moreover, the World Cup was on its way to becoming a huge success with America's Hispanic viewers. During the first week of competition, Univision's numbers were already record breaking, exceeding those of ESPN in absolute numbers by about 100,000 homes, a figure that was to increase steadily with the tournament's progress. Still, to put these numbers in perspective: During the very same week, the NHL's leadership was busy trying to put a positive spin on the league's "ice cold ratings," which had just been published and were attracting a lot of media attention. ESPN and Fox had taken substantial hits in their NHL play-off coverage, as ESPN aired thirty-two games and averaged a rating of 1.2, down 29 percent from the 1.7 rating it attained in 1997. ESPN's tally for the Stanley Cup finals suffered even more, with the 1998 ratings at 2.6, a 37 percent decline to the comparable events one year earlier. Fox did a bit better by garnering a 3.3 rating for the opening game of the final series between the Detroit Red Wings and the Washington Capitals, though this, too, was 17 percent under the 1997 opener of the Stanley Cup finals.[26] These numbers were considered so bad that Gary

Bettman, the NHL commissioner, had to hold a press conference to explain them away with a positive spin. In a major article centered on these poor television numbers *Sports Illustrated* simply asked, "Is Anyone Watching?"[27]

What were considered catastrophic numbers for hockey would have been stellar for soccer. But truly stellar numbers were the 22.3 rating and 38 share for Game 6 of the NBA Finals, making it the highest-rated game in NBA history. This number surpassed Game 6 between the Bulls and the Phoenix Suns in 1993 and Game 7 between the Detroit Pistons and the Los Angeles Lakers in 1988, both of which drew a 21.2 rating and 37 share (the former on NBC, the latter on CBS). NBC estimated that 72 million viewers watched all or part of the Bulls' victory over the Jazz in Game 6 of the championship series, which averaged a national rating of 18.7 for its duration, also a record. Among the top ten most-watched television shows in America (all on NBC) during the week of June 8, the first week of the World Cup competition, a record six featured the NBA Finals: (1) NBA Finals, Game 6 (22.3 rating and 38 share); (2) NBA Finals, Game 5 (19.8 rating and 37 share); (3) NBA Finals, Game 4 (19.1 rating and 33 share); (4) NBA Finals, Postgame 6 (16.7 rating and 29 share);(7) NBA Finals Tip-Off, Game 5 (12.8 rating and 25 share); and (8) NBA Finals Tip-Off, Game 4 (11.8 rating and 21 share).

The NBA and Michael Jordan continued to dominate the sports pages on Monday, 15 June, the day of the American team's much-anticipated game against three-time world champion Germany in Paris. The World Cup all but disappeared from the front pages of America's newspapers that day and took a backseat in the sports sections of most major newspapers: It was "Michael's miracle finish" on the front page of *USA Today* and "Bulls Deep-six Jazz" on the paper's first sports page; the *New York Times* ran a two-column front-page article entitled "At the End, Jordan Yet Again Takes Bulls to Another Title," with a prominent photo of Jordan gracing the page's center. This event dominated the *Times* sports section with a huge title covering the entire width of the section's first page reading "Jordan Steals the Show As Bulls Win Sixth Title." While Jordan dominated the front page of the sports section for the *Boston Globe*, the paper did run two articles on the bottom of that page written by John Powers (one of two *Globe* journalists covering the World Cup): "Winning Is Their Business" featured an analysis of the German team with an accompanying picture of two of its stars, Lothar Matthäus and Andreas Möller; "Tough Opening Act for United States" was an ominously prescient statement of what was about to occur on the field.

ABC televised the Germany-U.S. game, preempting the regular airing of *General Hospital*, surely the first time in American television history that an episode of a popular soap opera was delayed in favor of a soccer game. Seamus Malin, color commentator for ABC and ESPN, noted the kickoff with the following words: "Here we are finally where we always dreamed to be; where the American soccer community yearned to be for ages: Paris; packed Parc des Princes stadium; Germany as the opponent; the World Cup as our stage. This is it. It does not get any better than this, nor more important. This is a major moment in American soccer history." Malin had barely finished these words when the United States found itself one goal down, as Andreas Möller scored a completely avoidable goal in the ninth minute of the game, making the United States play what still must be among the most embarrassing and hapless first halves in recent national team history. Even though the play of the Americans slightly improved in the second half, yet another mistake by the otherwise reliable team captain, Thomas Dooley, led to Germany's second goal and to the American team's first defeat. It was not so much the U.S. loss to power-house Germany that was worrisome and humiliating, rather it was its manner that proved so embarrassing.

"Ouch!" said the *Boston Herald*'s two-inch headline over nearly a full-page picture of an exasperated Thomas Dooley on the back cover of its June 16 edition. The *Boston Globe* featured a picture of a dejected Kasey Keller on its front page, and highlighted the U.S. loss with two further pictures—a beaten Keller entangled in the net of the goal and a shell-shocked Claudio Reyna holding his head (*Soccer America* featured the same picture on its cover with the caption "Nightmare in the Parc")—on the first page of its sports section accompanied by two articles entitled "Americans Get Off on Wrong Foot" and "At Least They Went Down Kicking." The *New York Times* chose to feature a fight between English and Tunisian fans in Marseilles over the caption "Soccer Fans Turn Violent at World Cup Site" on its front page, but also gave the Germany-U.S. game unchallenged prominence on the first page of its sports section, featuring Möller's goal under the headline "U.S. Starts Out Awed and Finishes Dominated." *USA Today* ran a short teaser in the upper left-hand corner of its front page ("U.S. Falls Flat in World Cup Opener: Offense Is a No-Show in 2–0 Loss to Germany"), while a main article dominated the first page of its sports section under the caption "Germany Stymies USA, 2–0." The *Los Angeles Times* published a major story written by Grahame Jones under the headline "Beginning of the End?". *Sports Illustrated*, in an issue featuring a cover of Michael Jordan taking the legendary jump shot that beat the Jazz (appropriately captioned "The Man" to Jordan's right and "The Shot" to his left), buried the U.S. loss in its wrap-up of the World Cup's first week under the title "Wake-up Call."[28] Television ratings bespoke the dilemmas confronting the World Cup in the United States. While the Americans' first game at the tournament drew far and away the biggest rating since the beginning of the World Cup, even these numbers were considerably lower than they were for the U.S. games during World Cup 1994. The U.S.-Germany match garnered a 4.4 rating on ABC, which was substantially inferior to the 7.0 average rating that ABC had attained televising three U.S. games during the 1994 tournament.[29] Then again, who had time to watch a soccer game telecast at 3:00 P.M. on a Monday afternoon?

Wednesday's sports sections featured the repeat Stanley Cup champion Detroit Red Wings, who had swept the Washington Capitals in four games. There were also a number of articles on the NBA's impending lockout and the NBA players' decision to forego the basketball world championship to be played in Greece in late July and early August. Moreover, the speculation began regarding Michael Jordan's future as a basketball player and a Chicago Bull. Still, all newspapers continued their coverage of the World Cup with reports on games from the previous day, and the first articles analyzing the U.S. loss and possible remedies emerged. All commentators agreed that the Americans played poorly, were in awe of the mighty Germans, and failed to get their playmaker, Claudio Reyna, into the game. Much criticism centered on the lifelessness of the American offense, due in part to Eric Wynalda's subpar performance (Was he still nursing an old injury? Was he thrust into such an important game prematurely and without having played very well before the tournament?) but also to Sampson's deficient 3-6-1 concept that might have worked wonders against a weak Austrian squad in a meaningless "friendly" in April, but was simply anemic against a powerful German team with the experience and reputation as one of the very best big tournament clubs ever to play the game of soccer. Additionally, a new American star had emerged in the midst of this gloom and doom: Frankie Hejduk, the California "surfer dude," played the second half of the game during which he almost scored a goal and repeatedly penetrated the German defense.

For the first time, a phenomenon appeared in the sports sections of some papers, regular fare in all hegemonic team sports be they the Big Three and One-Half in the United States or soccer in the rest of world: specifically, a discussion about past mistakes, lots of second guessing, Monday morning quarterbacking, criticisms directed against the coach, suggestions as to how to make things better for the next game, who to play and who to bench. All of these topics are the daily bread and butter of hundreds of sports radio shows all across the United States, but they focus on baseball, basketball, football, and hockey, rarely, if ever, on soccer; this was true during the World Cup as well. With very few exceptions, American sports radio completely ignored the World Cup other than to offer the occasional derogatory remark directed at the tournament and its sport, meaning that the vast number of America's regular sports fans simply did not pay much attention to the events in France, even when the U.S. team was playing. This was considerably different for sports journalists, who did in fact engage in "sports talk" about the World Cup, particularly regarding the fate of the American team. By Thursday, Friday, and Saturday of that week, all eyes were directed at the game against Iran.

As can be imagined, the Iran match received much coverage in the United States. A number of themes emerged that are best characterized in the following two categories:

First, it was only a game devoid of any politics. Many articles and interviews with American players highlighted this aspect of the forthcoming contest. Some American players were aware of Madeleine Albright's major policy-setting speech regarding America's potential reevaluation of its hostile position toward Iran and of President Clinton's address to the world and the Iranian people scheduled for the day of the game. But they downplayed this angle completely, repeatedly arguing that they regarded the contest as yet another soccer game. Some Iranians were also extensively quoted expressing a similar attitude. The Iranian coach, Jalal Talebi, was particularly prominent, receiving much attention for being a resident of the San Francisco Bay Area with a wife and family still residing there. Talebi had coached soccer at De Anza Community College, just up the road from Santa Clara University where Steve Sampson had begun his coaching career. And just like Sampson, Talebi was just a soccer man, not an ideologue.

Second, though only a soccer game, politics could not help but be part of it. Here, one needs to mention the various statements—again mainly by Talebi and a few Iranian players—that the Iranian team would make extra efforts during the introductory ceremonies to go beyond the conventional forms of courtesy displayed at such occasions and offer special gestures and gifts to the American players, precisely to demonstrate that even though the relationship between the two countries had been hostile for the past two decades, soccer players had their own community, identity, and communication, which did not necessarily conform to that dictated by "big politics." This was the positive, conciliatory response to the portrayal of the game as a political event in addition to a soccer match. However, there were other voices from the Iranian side that bespoke a much more negative attitude toward the Americans. The Iranian team's official leadership felt it a particular provocation that just a few days before the big game against the United States, one of the French television stations chose to air a 1991 movie starring Sally Field, called *Not Without My Daughter*, based on the true story of an American woman who escaped Iran with her daughter against the wishes of her Iranian husband. Talebi also found it disturbing that this movie was aired at this particular time and "insulting to people who come here to be friends."[30] Khodadad

Azizi, Iran's star player, openly called the game "the most important match in my life," clearly referring to it not as an opportunity to maintain the only possibility of qualifying for the next round but as an opportunity to beat the United States. (Still, he joined MLS in subsequent years.) Other players were dedicating this game to the "martyrs" who had fallen in the brutal eight-year war between Iran and Iraq during the 1980s (a conflict that many Iranians blame on the United States for allegedly instigating Iraq to attack Iran, and then providing assistance to Saddam Hussein throughout the intense hostilities). While it was clear that to all American players the game was all about soccer, this was much less the case for many Iranians. The *Boston Globe* put it best: The contest was a "one-sided grudge match"; soccer for the Americans, a cause for the Iranians.[31]

It was only a soccer game, but a crucial one for both sides, as the predicament for both Iran and the United States was simple: Lose and you are out of the tournament, win and you still might have a chance—slight though it was—to advance to the next round. Pressure mounted on Sampson to field a team that would play much better than the one against Germany. The manner in which the United States lost to Germany was awful but—when all was said and done—losing to the world's second most successful national team in soccer history was not a tragedy for the Americans. Indeed, it showed considerable hubris to have believed even for one second that the U.S. national team had any real chance to upset Germany. Reality had merely set in, that was all. However, the situation was completely different against Iran. Right after the World Cup groups were announced in early December 1997, Sampson had made it quite clear that defeating Iran was simply a must if the Americans were to have any chance of advancing in the tournament. Moreover, it was evident that throughout all the long months of preparation, most soccer experts in the United States, as well as the players and coaches, fully believed that the United States could and would beat Iran. After all, in its unimpressive soccer history, Iran had only qualified for one World Cup (in 1978) where it lost all its three games and was thereby eliminated early from the tournament. To be sure, the current Iranian team had a few excellent players who earned their living as professionals in some of Europe's top leagues, such as the German Bundesliga. But so did the United States. In short, the anticipation in the American media that Sunday was quite clear: A win over Iran was not only a must, it was also a distinct possibility. The result was a real shock to the American players, to American soccer, and to the soccer fans in the United States (who were the only ones back home to whom this contest mattered). Even a game against a nation led by a regime as hated as Iran's theocracy failed to put soccer on the radar screen of most American sports fans, let alone the public at large.

The 2–1 loss to Iran on Sunday, 21 June in Lyons was such big news that all American papers that we surveyed featured it on their front pages in some manner. On its front page, the *Boston Herald* ran a page-length photo of an exasperated Claudio Reyna, yet again holding his head, under the caption "What Happened?"[32] Its cross-town rival, the *Boston Globe*, featured a picture of a dejected Ernie Stewart standing all alone in the midst of jubilantly embracing Iranian players. The title of the piece underneath the photograph read "U.S. Soccer Quest Comes to Abrupt End."[33] On its front page, the *New York Times* featured the same Associated Press photo of Stewart and the Iranian players, with the accompanying article entitled "Enmity Past, U.S. Meets Iran and Suffers Bitter 2–1 Defeat."[34]

USA Today featured two pictures on its front page, one showing an Iranian and an American player contesting a high ball with their heads, the other an American and an Iranian fan, painted faces and all, sharing a good laugh. The headline on the main story read "Iran Kicks U.S. from Cup, 2–1." The smaller header underneath the photo of the cheerful fans read "On the Field, in the Stands, Politics Just Didn't Matter."[35] *Sports Illustrated* headlined its account of the game with "Go-o-o Home!" and *Soccer America* with "Lights Out." Calls arose in the media, as well as among the American players in France, that part of the blame lay with Sampson for starting a number of players who were relatively new to the team, instead of the tried-and-true veterans who had played for the American side for years to form a cohesive unit. The obligatory finger-pointing had inevitably begun.

However some of the best analysis of the American loss to Iran—and the U.S. team's inferiority even vis-à-vis the mediocre squads in the World Cup tournament, let alone the powerhouses—was offered by Ian Thomsen in *Sports Illustrated*: "The Iranian players . . . grew up playing in the streets or on dirt fields with cheap plastic soccer balls. They had no coaching to speak of until their mid-teens and no realistic hope of their national team's advancing to the world's greatest stage, yet they persisted. In defeating the Americans for Iran's first World Cup victory, they exhibited an ear for the game, whereas the U.S. players seemed to be reading from sheet music."[36]

Michael Gee from the *Boston Herald* also provided fine insight regarding the American loss: "To the normal American non-soccer fan, the message of World Cup 1998 is obvious: We stink. . . . Player after player said something [along] the lines of, 'They won but we were the better team.' Payne Stewart lost the U.S. Open the same day on some of the most monstrous strokes of luck imaginable, then said, 'I didn't play well enough to win.' . . . If the United States can do better in the next World Cup, the sport's popularity will advance accordingly. If it can't, all the youth leagues and family-friendly Revolution [the Boston-area Major League

Soccer team] promotions and Nike money in the world won't make any difference. My son and daughter have played soccer for years. They were sad to hear the United States lost to Iran. But they weren't really upset. If U.S. soccer can't make losing hurt worse for its faithful, it's going to end up as missionary stew."[37] Did Michael Gee's kids only "hear" about the American loss to Iran? Were they not watching the game? Might they have been watching the Red Sox playing the Tampa Bay Devil Rays, or the U.S. Open? Most likely they were doing neither, but were indulging in their soccer activities, instead of sitting in front of the television imbibing it as culture. The revealing comments by Thomsen and Gee are perhaps the best possible illustration of the difference between sport as activity and sport as culture. The former is mechanically playing music from a sheet, the latter is playing it with history as an integral part of its production; the former is being sad about a loss, the latter is being damn upset about it.

In terms of newspaper coverage and television time, the World Cup met with stiff competition from golf's U.S. Open, played at the Olympic Club in San Francisco on the weekend of the U.S.-Iran game. With Payne Stewart playing brilliantly until the last day, and with Lee Janzen's nail-biting, come-from-behind, one-stroke victory over Stewart, the Open once again delivered on its promise as one of golf's most exciting and popular tournaments. Just as with the Bulls in the two Chicago papers and the Red Wings in the *Detroit Free Press*, the three Bay Area newspapers—*San Francisco Chronicle, San Francisco Examiner* and, perhaps to a lesser extent, the *San Jose Mercury News*—gave the U.S. Open much greater coverage than they accorded the World Cup. But other than that, the pull and unusual circumstance of the U.S.-Iran game rendered this event sufficiently important and exotic to place soccer coverage on a par with that of a major golf event. Indeed, the U.S. loss to Iran received greater attention in some papers than the Janzen victory over Stewart at the Open. In terms of television viewership, both events fared respectably well, though their ratings dropped from years past. The U.S. loss to Iran, on ABC, drew a 4.8 overnight rating, representing a 38 percent drop from the U.S. team's second game in the 1994 Cup (also played on a Sunday). The U.S. Open, televised by NBC, attained a 6.7 overnight rating, which was down by 14 percent from the event's viewership in 1997, and the Open's weekend average was even 18 percent lower than the previous year's.[38]

Soccer's television numbers were a typical case of glass half full or half empty, depending on who was doing the measuring and the spinning. On the half-full side, Mark Mandel from ABC noted the network's long-term deal with Major League Soccer: "All the real experts understood the US and Iran were evenly matched, that a US win wasn't a foregone conclusion. We're still committed to soccer, including the 2002 Cup." For a middle-of-the road voice, ex-CBS Sports president Neal Pilson ruminated on what the 1998 World Cup might mean to U.S. soccer's television future: "Soccer has a secure niche. It's just not the niche soccer would like to be in. The public has voted with their TV clickers; soccer has to work harder to make people familiar with its stars." On the half-empty side of things, Jon Mandel of Grey Advertising said, "I didn't know soccer even had a future on American TV. And the Cup games without the U.S. don't draw anything." This Mandel certainly had a point, if one considers that ABC's Holland–South Korea game on Saturday afternoon attained an overnight rating of 1.9, just slightly better than the abysmal 1.6 that CBS received for its John McEnroe–Jimmy Connors ("old-timer") tennis exhibition on Sunday.[39] Still, Germany-Yugoslavia reached a 2.4 rating in the greater Boston area, a respectable number if one considers that two New York Yankees–Cleveland Indians games, featuring two of the American League's best clubs and the Boston Red Sox's most immediate rivals in the pennant race, received a 2.6 rating on Saturday and a 1.9 rating on Sunday.

The United States had one more game to play in which there was nothing at stake other than preserving a modicum of the American team's pride and the possibility of playing the spoiler for Yugoslavia. In the days preceding the 25 June match, the newspapers were full of reports about dissent among the American players and an open revolt against Sampson on the part of some frustrated veterans who felt slighted by the coach for not getting what they considered sufficient (or, in some cases, any) playing time. Other topics receiving regular coverage in the American press were the riots caused by English and German hooligans; the ticket scams and scandals, which left thousands of soccer fans without access to the stadiums to see their teams (though many had paid good money); the problems with the inconsistent officiating in the tournament; along with a steady dose of often detailed reporting on other games of the World Cup.

On the day of the Yugoslavia game, the sports sections of U.S. newspapers provided significant coverage of the NBA draft and increased attention on Wimbledon, where Marcelo Rios, (the number two seed) and Greg Rusedski (number four) were both eliminated in early rounds. Then came the 1–0 loss to Yugoslavia that ended the American team's miserable run at the World Cup, placing the team dead last among the thirty-two contestants, since the only other team to lose all three of its games, Japan, had managed to score two goals to the meager one of the Americans. "USA Falls to Yugoslavia: Bitter End for Winless Cup Stint," proclaimed *USA Today* at the center of its first sports page. "The United States Concludes a Miserable World Cup Campaign," wrote the *New York Times* as a header for the paper's C section, announcing its feature on the first sports page inside. "Shame and Blame: Ousted U.S. Players Eye Scapegoats," wrote the *Boston Herald*; and "Yankees Go Home," wrote the *Los Angeles Times*, concluding the piece with the tally of America's sorry performances in World Cup history for good measure: World Cup appearances: 6; World Cup record: 4-12-1; World Cup goals for/against: 18-38. In the three World Cups in which the United States contested in the 1990s (Italy in 1990, the United States in 1994, and France in 1998)—it had not qualified for any of the tournaments since the one in Brazil in 1950—the record reads 1-8-1, with goals for/against at 6–17. (The American attack actually only produced five goals in ten games since one goal—against Colombia—was an "own goal" by the Colombian defender Andres Escobar, for which he was assassinated upon his arrival in his homeland.)

Once the mudslinging by Tab Ramos and Alexi Lalas against their coach subsided, and once Sampson had resigned as coach of the team, a brief period of postmortem emerged in the newspapers (and even on sports radio for a few minutes) concerning reasons for the debacle and possible ways to avoid it in the future. The many topics discussed in the numerous articles of the papers that we surveyed included names of candidates for the next coach of the national team, the pros and cons of an American or foreign coach, the role of MLS in helping—or possibly hindering—the U.S. national team, Alan Rothenberg's most likely successor (since he was to depart from his presidency of the USSF by August 1998), the problems posed by the college system for the development of first-rate players, the viability of Project 2010 ("Can one buy experience and history?" "Can one buy the World Cup?" with the overwhelming answer being negative), the importance of developing homegrown stars who could really garner much-needed popularity for the game and for the U.S. team. In short, there was no angle of the game in the United States and regarding the American team that was not discussed at some length. To be sure: This was short-lived and never attained the dimensions that develop with regularity and predictability in similar situations with the Big Three and hockey. There are still far too few people interested in and passionate about soccer as culture—not as activity—in the United States for that to occur. But for a few days after the American team's ignominious elimination from the World Cup, sports fans well beyond the narrow circle of soccer aficionados asked themselves: What went wrong and what can we do about it? That, perhaps, constituted a minor atmospheric shift in soccer's favor within the American sport space.

There was, of course, passion in the United States for the World Cup among the various ethnic communities whose teams played in the tournament and, especially, for those whose "home countries" advanced to the second round and who followed the games avidly and passionately. Indeed, for the first time in American history, passion engendered by soccer reached European and Latin American proportions in the form of riots and violence. Mexicans and Mexican Americans in Huntington Beach, California, battled the police on two occasions, both involving "their" team: The first confrontation occurred when Mexico tied Belgium, 2–2, in an exciting come-from-behind game to qualify for the next round. The second occurred just a few days later when, in the first game of that next round, Mexico lost to Germany, 2–1 (after blowing a 1–0 lead), and was thus relegated from the tournament. We note this particular aspect of the World Cup to highlight two reasons we believe central in maintaining soccer's negative and "foreign" image in the United States for most American sports fans: First, it lends firsthand evidence to the widely held image among Americans that soccer's milieu and culture—as opposed to the game—are violent. And second, it clearly reinforces the notion that people who have lived in the United States for a long time, and are its citizens in many cases, continue to root for "their" country instead of showing any kind of similar passion and commitment to the American team. And we sincerely doubt that this would have been any different had the American team been more successful at the tournament. To be sure, a better result by the national team would have created much more interest in—if not yet any passion for—the American team and soccer in the larger world of American sports. But as to the real allegiance and genuine pathos of most Mexicans in the Los Angeles area, there can be no question that it would have remained first and foremost with the Mexican team, even if the American team had performed brilliantly instead of abysmally. One need only look at the ethnic composition of the most loyal and devoted fans of the American team—"Sam's Army"—to discover how thoroughly white, suburban, and middle class America's coterie of soccer fans continues to be.

The World Cup without a U.S. Team

With the American team's departure, World Cup coverage did not decrease in the newspapers that we surveyed. Instead, the emphasis shifted to more substantial reporting on games, which were becoming more important and played by better teams by the day. Many newspapers wrote long and detailed articles on such exciting games as Argentina-England, rhapsodizing about English phenom Michael Owen's goal, arguably the most aesthetically pleasing of the tournament; or about Nigeria's surprising and disappointing loss to an exuberantly attacking Danish team; or Argentina's loss to the Dutch by way of Dennis Bergkamp's masterful goal as regulation time was about to expire. Brazil, as the world's most popular team and defending champion, received especially detailed and lively coverage of its matches against the Danes and its subsequent semifinal win against Holland following a penalty kick shoot-out. For example, on Wednesday, July 8, the *Boston Globe* featured a huge photo on its front page depicting an ecstatic Claudio Taffarel celebrating after blocking two shots to help Brazil defeat the Netherlands to advance to the World Cup final.

It is important to note that there were two events during the first week of July that traditionally receive great attention in the American sports world and could clearly have displaced the World Cup from the pages of America's newspapers: the Wimbledon finals (July 4 and 5) and the baseball All-Star game (7 July). The former featured Jana Novotna's triumphant victory, her very first Grand Slam event after many close calls and a disappointing second place to Steffi Graf in an earlier Wimbledon final when Novotna inexplicably let her all but assured title victory slip away into a bitter defeat. On the men's side, Pete Sampras was going for his fifth Wimbledon title, which would equal Bjorn Borg's modern-day record while also representing an eleventh Grand Slam for Sampras, one short of Roy Emerson's record. Additional interest in the tournament came from Sampras's opponent, Goran Ivanisevic (a former loser in a Wimbledon final to André Agassi), now in quest of his first Grand Slam title. Ivanisevic, a Croatian, played Sampras exactly one day after the Croatian soccer team had defeated Germany, 3–0, in what must be seen as that young country's largest victory in its most beloved sport. Ivanisevic nearly pulled off what would have been a memorable weekend for Croatian sports, but in the end he succumbed to Sampras's experience and savvy.

Baseball's midseason classic was particularly attractive in 1998 in that it featured the game's most exciting home run hitters at Coors Field in Denver, Colorado, arguably the most auspicious park for home runs in the majors. On 7 July, newspapers ran stories about the players' gathering in Denver, as well as accounts of the home run contest that has become one of the All-Star game's major attractions. This was especially the case for this game, since the entire 1998 season featured the chase of Roger Maris's record of 61 home runs by three sluggers—Mark McGwire, Sammy Sosa, and Ken Griffey Jr.—all present at the All-Star game (Griffey won the home run contest). The starting pitcher for the American League was David Wells, who had pitched a perfect game earlier in the season for the New York Yankees. The Yankees themselves were on a record-setting pace for the best regular season in major league history. In short, baseball provided a number of great attractions to fans in the summer of 1998. On 8 July, the newspapers presented their annual heavy coverage of the game, conveying perhaps even more excitement than usual on account of it having been a slugfest with 31 hits (the American League finally won, 13–8).

In terms of television viewing, here is how the World Cup measured up to its competition: The men's final between Sampras and Ivanisevic, and other tennis on Sunday, attained a 5.5 rating; the women's final between Novotna and the Frenchwoman Nathalie Tauziat, as well as other matches on Saturday, received a 3.1 rating. Interestingly, the U.S. Women's Open in golf, played at the same time as the Wimbledon finals, outranked women's tennis by reaching a 3.7. Brazil-Denmark was the most watched World Cup game that week with a 3.7, Netherlands-Argentina scored a nearly identical 3.6, and Germany-Croatia attained a 2.8 rating. ABC averaged a 3.4 rating for its four quarterfinal games, in contrast to the 4.0 rating the network had averaged for the quarterfinals played in the United States in 1994.[40] The 1998 All-Star game was watched by an estimated 38 million viewers and was the highest rated since 1994, the year baseball went into a tailspin as a result of the strike that canceled the rest of that season. But baseball had not fully restored its pre-strike appeal, as the 1998 contest garnered the fourth lowest ratings in the history of televised All-Star games.[41]

The last week of the World Cup featured many articles on the four semifinalists: Brazil, Holland, Croatia, and France. In Brazil's case, most contributions described the singular passion that the game of soccer has consistently engendered in that country. Once again, there were a number of articles on Ronaldo, as well as on Brazil's coach Mario Zagalo who, in one form or another, had been directly involved with all of Brazil's four championships: as a player in 1958 and 1962, as the coach in 1970, and as an assistant coach in 1994. There were the requisite pieces on Brazil's famed style of play, the so-called *jogo bonito*, and how that was—or was not—compromised by a modern ethic that valued results much more than style. Brazil, analysts pointed out, faced not only the burden to win, but also the pressure of having do so in an aesthetically pleasing manner so as to satisfy its demanding fans. In Holland's case, commentators remarked that—along with Hungary's legendary "golden team" of 1954—the Dutch were arguably the best club never to have won the World Cup, having twice been the bridesmaids (in 1974 and 1978). A number of stories focused on the tensions between the black players mostly of Surinamian origin and the team's white players, an issue that was very divisive at the European Championships in England in 1996 and led to one player being sent home in the middle of the tournament. Elements of racial tension were once again present at the World Cup, but they seemed to have abated with the team's victorious advancement to the semifinals.

Regarding Croatia, there was obvious focus on the fact that this country had existed in a different guise at previous World Cups where it had played as part of Yugoslavia, now its bitter enemy. Features focused on the team's controversial coach, Miroslav Blazevic, who, among other things, had been a close confidant of the country's president, Franjo Tudjman, and viewed the Croats' mission in France as a statement of Croatian nationalism as well as an assertive manifestation of Croatia's superiority over its archenemy, the Serbia-dominated Yugoslavia. Other pieces discussed Croatia's midfielder Zvonimir Boban, whose kicking of a Serbian policeman during a Dynamo Zagreb–Red Star Belgrade match had become an important spark to initiate the cauldron of Croat-Serb enmity that led to the tragedy of the Yugoslav succession wars of the early to mid-1990s. A few articles focused on Davor Suker, Croatia's most prolific scorer and the eventual winner of the tournament's goal-scoring title. However, in notable contrast to a number of European newspapers and other media outlets, American reporting remained silent on the hostile and dismissive remarks Blazevic publicly directed at Serbs. Moreover, while the European press discussed the problematic issue of the Croatian team's jerseys (which prominently featured the country's red-checkered flag known as *sahovnica*), none of the American papers we surveyed or telecasts we watched ever raised such thorny political issues.[42] Instead, the tenor of American reporting on the Croatian team featured the small territory of this participant and how much its immense success at this most important of sports tournaments must have meant to the pride and passion of its people.

Lastly, host France was the subject of a bevy of articles in the week preceding the final. Regarding the team, there were features on its better-known players, especially Zinedine "Zizou" Zidane, the playmaker, wearer of the number 10 shirt (still the most distinguished in soccer), successor to the great Michel Platini (without any doubt France's best soccer player of all times and president of the World Cup Organizing Committee for this World Cup). France's quiet and methodical coach, Aimé Jacquet, had for years run the crucible of ill will and irony from the French press and was now poised to prove wrong all his adversaries and detractors. There were stories on the multiethnic and multicultural composition of the team, whose players—by birthplace and/or parentage—hailed from a diversity of locations, including Senegal, Ghana, Algeria, the Caribbean, Polynesia, Armenia, and Argentina, and whose success was the most powerful way to silence, at least for the time being, France's often vocal (and sometimes violent) xenophobic rightwing.[43] The sudden growth of enthusiasm for the tournament and for soccer among the French public attained a fair amount of attention, as many Frenchmen and Frenchwomen—especially in Paris—had initially greeted the tournament with aloofness and a certain distance. This changed when French defender Laurent "Lolo" Blanc scored the World Cup's only "golden goal" (i.e., one occurring in "sudden death" overtime) against Paraguay on 28 June, saving France from the real possibility of an embarrassingly early elimination, instead sending it to bigger and better things.

By the weekend of the World Cup final between France and Brazil on 12 July, the American media—print as well as electronic—had covered virtually every angle of this most prominent global event in sports. Just like in the days before the tournament had begun in early June, articles appeared outside the sports sections of major newspapers. A number of pieces, mostly in business sections, mentioned once again that a total of 4 billion people would be watching the final game and that the tournament as a whole might approach a cumulative audience of nearly 40 billion people. Surveys were published that women—perhaps for the first time—were watching these games in large numbers in many European countries, most notably Italy, Holland, and France. Tellingly, a few key articles appeared in important segments of the weekend papers that—though not hostile to soccer—explained, perhaps even welcomed, the fact that Americans would once again be apart from the rest of the world. Thus, on the first page of the Week in Review section of the *New York Times*, Kirk Johnson argued that soccer was trying to sell Americans "a bill of goods."[44] In the *Boston Sunday Globe*'s Focus section, Matthew Brelis made a powerful argument that soccer—regardless of all the efforts over the years—would continue to remain marginal to the sports interests and passion of Americans.[45] And in *USA Today*'s The Forum section, Sandy Grady confessed that his optimism regarding the rosy promise he foresaw for soccer in the 1970s had been rather misplaced.[46]

To virtually everyone's surprise, Brazil lost the final to France, 3–0. Every newspaper in our survey reported this score in some fashion on the front page of its Monday edition, and each ran at least one photograph on its front page as well. Moreover, in every case, the World Cup final received the most prominent display in the sports sections. There was a bevy of articles on the final match, and the tournament and its aftermath, on both the Monday and Tuesday after the game. Everything was discussed, from the French team's brilliant defense to the mystery surrounding Ronaldo's poor performance and his illness before the game; from the sadness in Brazil to the ecstasy in France; from the next tournament (jointly hosted by Japan and South Korea in 2002) to the problems of penalty kicks deciding key games and the fate of teams and players in such an important event as the World Cup. And, of course, soccer's presence in the United States was revisited in discussions of the American failure in the tournament and the future of the American national team, its prospective coach, and the prospective next president of the USSF.

A World Cup Wrap-up

In concluding this chapter, let us offer the television statistics, since these are—perhaps more than any other—the decisive data in evaluating the presence of any phenomenon in contemporary advanced industrial societies. On this count, the United States is most certainly not an exception: The final game between France and Brazil produced a 6.9 rating/17 share, 46 percent lower than the 12.8 rating for the Brazil-Italy final in 1994. For the twelve games televised by ABC, it averaged a 2.3 rating/7 share, a 51 percent drop from the network's results in the 1994 tournament. Compared to their 1994 numbers, the ratings for ESPN declined by 50 percent (from 1.7 to 0.8) and 38 percent (from 0.8 to 0.5) for ESPN2. The results for Spanish-language Univision: 22.2 rating/46 share for the final game; the 1.715 million households that tuned into the game were a Univision World Cup record. The tournament as a whole brought Univision an average of 850,000 households for the fifty-six live games, easily eclipsing ESPN (670,000 households) and ESPN2 (114,000 households).[47] For fifty games in which Univision went head-to-head against ESPN or ESPN2, Univision scored higher in TV households on forty-three occasions; ESPN came out ahead seven times. However, each of ABC's twelve broadcasts outdrew Univision. In addition to the final, some of Univision's numbers were truly impressive: 1.5 million households for Germany-Mexico, 1.4 million for Belgium-Mexico, 1.3 million for South Korea–Mexico. Games that did not involve Mexico also tallied impressive numbers on Univision: Argentina-England drew 1.1 million households, France-Paraguay 1.0 million; and Nigeria-Denmark—a match not featuring any Latin American team—still attracted 979,000 households to Univision.[48]

Once again, the interpretation of these data rests completely in the eye of the beholder. On the negative side, there is simply no argument against the fact that the numbers for the three English-speaking and Disney-owned channels were low. To be sure, there are many reasons for this, most important of all, the time difference between France and the United States, which—as we noted—made viewing these games other than on weekends virtually impossible for a working population. However, that the numbers were not significantly better precisely on those weekends conveys—at least to some extent—that the issue of scheduling was not the whole story. The predominant reason, we would argue, is that World Cup '94 in the United States was an event, a unique occurrence that attracted a following interested first and foremost in the games because they were held in the United States. Once the same tournament switched to another country, the interest waned.

On the positive side, a number of items require mention: ABC's 2.3 World Cup rating, though low, was not very far from Fox's baseball rating of 2.7. It most certainly exceeded the 1.8 that NBC attained for its Women's National Basketball Association games, and could compete honorably with hockey's television numbers, including the NHL's Stanley Cup play-offs. Moreover, the World Cup netted higher ratings among men ages 18-49 than baseball, golf, and tennis. Its final received higher ratings than telecasts of the Kentucky Derby (6.7) and the Belmont Stakes (6.6) on ABC, and the final round of the men's U.S. Open in golf (6.7) on NBC.[49]

Because the tournament was held in France instead of the United States, opinions about the World Cup and the game of soccer were far less polarized and vocal than in 1994. To be sure, there were many American sportswriters and sports fans who simply could not warm to the game and its culture in any way. They found the game too slow, too boring, too low scoring, too disjointed, its fans too violent and obnoxious, the penalty kicks a ridiculous way to decide major games; they found it uninteresting because it was played with feet instead of hands—in short, they voiced all the objections to the game that have become commonplace in Americans' dislike or ambivalence regarding soccer. Jay Leno and David Letterman, the nation's (mostly) uncensored voices who often well reflect the attitudes, worries, and beliefs of the American "everyman" (but much less "everywoman"), made constant jokes about soccer being boring. Among other put-downs of soccer, Letterman featured a top ten list called "Top Ten Ways to Make Soccer More Exciting," and Leno peppered his nightly monologues with soccer's alleged somnambulant ambience as such a low-scoring game.[50] Rick Reilly wrote a scathing critique of soccer, the World Cup, and its milieu in his column "The Life of Reilly" in *Sports Illustrated*, where he took soccer to task on issues ranging from the sight of coaches and even players smoking on the field to the riots caused by its fans; from the travesty of penalty kicks deciding games to the players feigning injuries to a degree not witnessed in other World Cups.[51] Just as in 1994, most critics of soccer and the World Cup found it somewhat annoying, and most certainly beside the point, that soccer's advocates always presented this tournament and its game as the world's most popular, which implicitly meant (or sometimes explicitly included statements) that there was something amiss about Americans for not joining this global enthusiasm.[52]

On the other side, there were the usual put-downs of American sports and especially their fans by writers such as George Vecsey, who once again berated Americans for being parochial isolationists by not appreciating soccer and according the World Cup its proper due.[53] Soccer advocates again appeared to feel the need to blame American sports fans for their alleged provincialism and to denounce American sports for their supposed inferiority in order to build their case for soccer's qualities as a sport and those of the World Cup as a tournament. But on the whole, the wide-ranging mutual animosities so commonplace in 1994 appeared muted during the World Cup of 1998. Dispassionate but well-informed analysis characterized the American media's presentation of the tournament and its culture. At least at that level, soccer as played quadrennially in the World Cup appears to have made it in the American sports world.

Conclusion ....

THE UNITED STATES has played a preeminent role in the twentieth century and it has done so in most facets of human endeavor, be it in science and politics, the arts and economics, social organization and culture. What rendered the United States such an original, dynamic, valuable—but also controversial—contributor to all these aspects of the human condition in the twentieth century was the fact that its very own history and existence were part of a larger whole, yet separate from it. In particular, America's intimate, yet also conflicting, relations with its European progenitors has been the source of wonderful creativity and attraction, as well as of much misunderstanding and angst on both sides of the Atlantic. From the days of Alexis de Tocqueville and Harriet Martineau to our jet age, when millions of European tourists flock to all parts of the United States on a yearly basis, America has been a complex and puzzling entity to most Europeans precisely for being so similar to Europe, yet at the same time so different from it.

These commonalities and differences have been the source of many a fruitful comparison of the United States with Europe as a whole (or with a few select countries as its representatives) in virtually every field of the social sciences as well as in many of the humanities, cultural studies perhaps the most prominent among them. We see the essence of our book precisely in this vein, as yet another attempt to look at a particular aspect of American culture in light of its exception vis-à-vis a European—and in our case, even global—commonality. In our study, too, the mixture of similarities and differences renders the comparison fruitful but also complex. On the one hand, the United States is no exception at all in our story. Like all industrial countries, it developed what we have termed "hegemonic sports culture," that is, a structure wherein team sports played with some kind of a ball or puck attained such societal importance that they became part of popular culture in every industrial nation throughout most of the twentieth century. This hegemonic sports culture began in the latter quarter of the nineteenth century and had solidified by the 1930s. Its adherents and protagonists were almost exclusively male, among whom the working classes and the commercial middle classes played a leading and decisive, if not necessarily exclusive, role. This culture proliferated in a commodified manner and became an intrinsic feature of modern industrial and urban life. As such, it shared a deep affinity with nationalism, one of the most ubiquitous expressions of modern industrial culture. Similarities—better still, commonalities—defined this part of our story.

However, when we look at the actual form and content of this hegemonic sports culture as it manifests itself in the United States and its family of industrial democracies, our story shifts away from the similarities and focuses on the differences. Here we realize that the very similar male industrial and white-collar workers (in terms of class position, age, social milieu, cultural consumption, to mention but a few key sociological markers) in Europe and the United States spend their days (and nights) thinking, talking, dreaming, hoping, worrying, and perhaps even playing different sports, the former most likely soccer and the latter most likely baseball, football, basketball, hockey—or perhaps all four—of the sports that we identified as comprising the American sport space.

The central task of our book has been to explain this difference. We believe that this difference and its explanation matter for one simple reason: a better understanding of American culture in the comparative context of industrial modernity. And no matter how globalized this culture became in the course of the twentieth century, key aspects of it remain local and apart from that of the norm elsewhere. They remain exceptional, not in a normative sense but in an empirical one.

Studies of this kind are by necessity historical. They have little, if any, predictive power and value. Hence, we have no idea whether the story we have presented in this book will continue, and if it does, for how long. We have no way of knowing whether America's hegemonic sports culture will remain the same during the twenty-first century as it is at its outset. Soccer seems to be in a much better position at the beginning of the twenty-first century than it was at the beginning of the twentieth in terms of entering America's sport space. Then again, this space itself has drastically changed. Just because America's soccer exceptionalism remained a staple of American culture for more than one hundred years is no reason to assume that this will continue into the indefinite future. Indeed, changes may be afoot that could possibly herald a new development in terms of soccer's entry into America's hegemonic sports culture. To be sure, this will take generations. But the beginning may be more auspicious this time than at any previous point in the history of soccer in America.

To wit, pronouncements such as the following would have been unthinkable one hundred years ago: "U.S. Soccer's mission statement is very simple and clear: to make soccer, in all its forms, a preeminent sport in the United States and to win the FIFA World Cup (men's) by the year 2010."[1] Is this a realistic project or a chimera? Might the indestructible optimism so characteristic of American pragmatism prevail in reaching such a seemingly hopeless goal? Will American "can-doism" succeed yet again, as it did with the Apollo project (a task that—to be sure—was a good deal more important than winning a soccer world championship, but also much more calculable)? In short, will soccer finally become ingrained in America's main culture and not remain the subculture it continues to be despite the major advances the sport experienced in the 1980s and 1990s? Will soccer become a major topic on sports-talk radio, or will it remain for most Americans a pleasant recreational activity for families, young people, and children?

We believe that our study offers powerful arguments for both scenarios: For soccer's continued marginalization in American sports culture and American life, and for its becoming a solid fifth team sport in America's sport space on the level of ice hockey, perhaps even a tad closer to the Big Three. We would like to conclude this book by delineating the trajectories and possibilities that might create either of the two scenarios, thereby reprising some of the key themes developed in our study.

The pessimistic scenario of soccer's continued marginalization in America's sport space relies on the observation that all team sports that attained cultural power in America, as elsewhere, succeeded in gaining a decisive foothold in the respective country's sport space between 1870 and 1930, a crucial era in the political, economic, and cultural modernization of industrial societies. By having the advantage of first-comers, these sports then reproduced themselves by establishing histories and affective ties with a large number of the population that then developed into an integral part of the respective country's mass culture, meaning baseball, football, and basketball in the United States, with hockey assuming enough of a hybrid status to qualify in our definition of culture. Soccer—so our argument—fulfilled a commensurate function in virtually all European and Latin American countries. These sports cultures—rendered popular by the commercial middle and working classes—became mass sports or "the people's games" in their respective countries and have remained so to this day. Despite the immense political, economic, and cultural changes that affected modern industrial societies in the course of the twentieth century, their sports cultures, in notable contrast to their sport activities, remained surprisingly resilient. The countries in Europe and Latin America, where soccer became king by the 1920s, still revere it as their premier sport despite the advent of various other sport activities since the late 1960s, including American sports such as baseball, basketball, and football.[2] To be sure, basketball and (to a lesser extent) American football have eked out a nice little niche in Germany's sport space, just like baseball has established a cultlike following with its own leagues and complete infrastructure in Holland and Italy. Basketball has indeed developed into a rather well-received popular game in countries such as Spain, Italy, Greece, Croatia, Yugoslavia, and Israel; yet it still does not come close to soccer's popularity by any measure. Using the immense power of television and other forms of modern communication, these hegemonic sports succeed in augmenting their already dominant position in a country's sport space by constantly reproducing their hegemony to the direct detriment of newcomers. Add in the power of habit, familiarity, knowledge, emotional attachment—to name but a few key ingredients in identity formation—and the task for any newcomer becomes perhaps more than formidable.

As a necessary but certainly not a sufficient condition, all sports cultures emerge through a complex interaction of grassroots activity "from below" and the setting of institutional parameters "from above." While these two dimensions are absolutely indispensable for the creation of any sports culture, they far from guaranteed its successful and continued existence throughout such a turbulent century as the twentieth. Once a symbiotic relationship between these two mechanisms has evolved, it then assumes a life of its own and becomes a successful new entity, in our case a hegemonic sports culture. As we have discussed throughout this book, soccer in America (until the 1980s) lacked both necessary prerequisites— grassroots activity from below and appropriate institution building from above—to warrant consideration as a viable candidate in a country in which it could never become part of the sports culture. During the course of the last two decades of the twentieth century, American soccer made tremendous strides on both dimensions: From below, it has become one of the nation's main recreational and physical activities since the early 1980s; with the formation of MLS and the concomitant streamlining of soccer's organizational framework, more important strides to establish soccer's institutional setting from above were achieved in the late 1990s than in the preceding one hundred years. But will this be enough? Can one establish culture by fiat, by following a blueprint? Here are some voices from unnamed American soccer experts, the gist of which would lead one to a pessimistic view of soccer becoming part of American sports culture in the foreseeable future.

> Nigerians play in the street. Latin Americans play in the street. Also, those who have had fathers who played will play. In the United States of America, we have no street soccer and fathers who did not play soccer.

> Soccer is not ingrained in the main culture. It is still a sub culture sport in the USA.

> The reason we can't compete and win at the international level, is we do not have a soccer culture on a daily basis.

> USA soccer is, in fact, still a feel good arena. Look at the folks who swarm around the game, and too many of them are simply participating in a fad. I often wonder how many U.S. youth, high school or college coaches could name a real world eleven and the clubs they play for.[3]

The pessimistic scenario is that sports cultures cannot be established in an "in vitro" fashion. And, after all, Project 2010 will be a kind of in vitro soccer creation from above designed to forge a World Cup winning team out of two- to three-dozen exceptionally talented athletes chosen from the millions of soccer-playing children and youth across the United States. This French-style planning approach—perhaps even more appropriately labeled East German–style strategy—to winning a major international tournament might work well in individual disciplines like track and field or lugeing, for example. But this is very hard to accomplish in team sports that are deeply anchored in complex cultural webs reinforced by structural networks of organizations and leagues on all levels of the game. Further complicating matters is that among team sports, soccer in particular—in notable contrast to American football and baseball, and to a lesser degree even basketball and ice hockey—relies much more on improvisation and an ephemeral, but all the more decisive, "feel" for the game that emanates from the sport's culture, rather than from learned strategies and set plays that can be conveyed at the level of activity but leave the game's overall quality far below the threshold of excellence required to be considered world class. Indeed, such top-down, blueprint style approaches to forging a winning soccer team at the highest level of global competition are exceedingly hard—perhaps impossible—to implement, as best demonstrated by East Germany's conscious decision not to pursue such a plan for its soccer teams (national or club) even though soccer assumed a much more prominent place in East Germany's sports culture than it ever has in the United States, including the game's boom period beginning in the early 1980s.[4] Put differently, a Project 2010–style approach to creating world-class excellence is much more controllable, confined, and thus realistic in sports such as gymnastics and bicycling than it is in a very fluid and culture-bound team sport such as soccer.

To be sure, even though a successfully accomplished Project 2010—unlikely as it may seem at this juncture—would be a necessary condition to catapult soccer onto the level of hegemonic sports culture in America, it would most definitely not be a sufficient one. A winning national team will still be no guarantee for the sustained articulation of a quotidian culture, which is ultimately the only way to make any sport part of the social fabric and create the "organic" basis for continued excellence in quality of play and competitive success. As long as little boys—and it is doubtful that little girls could carry this burden all by themselves, barring a fundamental change in the ways in which the vast majority of women and girls approach sport as culture—do not start playing one-on-one or two-on-two soccer with anything resembling a ball on any surface that masquerades as a playing field, as long as they rely on their soccer moms to drive them to organized soccer practice on well-appointed grassy grounds supervised by coaches (who have learned much of their trade by reading the myriad publications on the techniques of coaching soccer),

soccer will not be "the people's game" in the United States, and thus will never escape the levels of mediocrity on the global scene. Lastly, soccer continues to bear one further burden that impedes its development as culture in America's sport space: its virtual absence in the African American community with few, if any, signs of this lacuna abating in the foreseeable future.[5] The essence of the pessimistic scenario is simply that the shadows of American soccer's sad history have been far too dark and gloomy to have a ray of sunlight alter the fundamental presence of darkness. The continuity of soccer's marginalization in American culture will prevail despite a few sporadic successes.

But let us close this book by delineating the optimistic scenario for soccer's development in the United States during the first two decades of the third millennium. With MLS establishing a steady presence, soccer will gradually become a regular fixture in America's crowded sport space, not at its center, to be sure, but also far from the exotic fringes where it had barely subsisted for one century. The quality of its product—its games, its coaching, its players—will significantly improve, raising the level of competition on the field, establishing team rivalries, and developing into a solid summer sport that will become a respectable second to baseball. This will in turn improve the quality of the American national soccer team, thus making impressive victories such as the two consecutive ones against Germany and the one against Argentina in 1999 much more common and meaningful than in these largely inconsequential games. If such victories against comparable soccer powers increase in their frequency, if, in short, the American national team develops a consistency in its quality of play on an international level that will garner the soccer world's steady respect and lead to further wins in significant tournaments, then these victories will ignite a national pride, which—as we have argued—serves like virtually no other catalyst to ignite a sport's popularity and to catapult it from the realm of activity to that of culture. Consider how the success of the U.S. women during the World Cup tournament in 1999 developed into a national celebration. To be sure, women's soccer has been more popular in the United States than anywhere else in the world, constituting yet another of the many American exceptionalisms discussed in the course of this book. But the power of national allegiance, if not necessarily nationalist fervor, proved far more important in the vast popular accolades that the women's team received than the love for the game in which it attained its success. For let us be clear: Had the final been contested between, say, Brazil and China, or Norway and Germany—teams with virtually equal playing skills to those of the Americans—very few people outside the narrow confines of the American soccer community proper would have noticed, let alone cared. As we argued in chapter 1: The power of nationalism in popularizing a sport cannot be overstated. Here, the United States constitutes absolutely no exception and conforms to the norm that so forcefully governed the sports world throughout the twentieth century. One can discern no signs that this trend might abate, let alone disappear, during the first decades of the twenty-first. If anything, quite the opposite seems to be the case.

As a consequence of soccer's growing visibility and respectability in America's sports culture, triggered by the success of its national teams in international competitions, the game will gain a greater presence than ever before in America's inner cities and among its economically less advantaged social groups. With soccer thus becoming a viable means of earning good money, thereby offering a genuine venue for escaping the blight of poverty for a talented athlete and his family, the sport will for the first time become a serious option for athletes who previously would have had to act against their best interest had they chosen a career in professional soccer instead of one of America's Big Three and One-Half. Sooner or later this confluence of positive forces will give rise to a genuine American soccer star—if not quite at the superstar level of Michael Jordan, Joe Montana, Ken Griffey Jr., and Wayne Gretzky, to pick appropriate representatives of the four team sports currently comprising America's sports culture—who will create the necessary buzz in his wake that every successful professional sport in America has always exacted and received.

There is a possible variation to this scenario, a "positive offshoot," as it were: The success of a women's league might fully utilize the institutions of primary competition and global excellence coupled to a concurrent change in the ways in which girls and women relate to sports and sports culture. As discussed in chapter 5, the creation and proliferation of following and affect on the part of women for women's sports, specifically soccer—the one sport not a part of American hegemonic sports culture and not claimed by American men—is necessary for a women's league in the United States to elevate soccer to a position approaching at least that of ice hockey. In such a hypothetical case, interest in MLS and the U.S. men's national team might piggyback on the popularity of the women's game and engender a wide proliferation of interest in soccer for many American sports fans, male and female alike. This would be sacrilege and/ or farce to most of the millions of (male) soccer aficionados in Europe, Latin America, and elsewhere, but well in tune with the American exceptionalism in sport. However, we once again reiterate that fundamental changes in the relationship of women to sports must occur for this "offshoot" of the positive scenario to become a reality. Put starkly, as long as women continue to confine their involvement with sports to the realm of activity (doing) and do not let it expand to that of culture (following), as long as "talking sports" remains strictly a "guy thing" and does not become part of "girl talk," the transformative power of women's activities in sports will remain culturally limited.

America, like the rest of the advanced industrial world, has become much more varied in the taste of its consumers. Concomitant with an obvious trend toward uniformity in culture in the wake of what is now called globalization, we also observe the exact obverse: a definite process of segmentation and fragmentation. These two opposing, yet also mutually reinforcing, social and cultural trends inform contemporary life in the United States. Certain aspects of American culture have become uniform across this vast continent as never before. Yet, an equally impressive array of identity-forming experiences have undergone processes of fragmentation and segmentation that are new. Indeed, America's new uniformity lies precisely in the motley variety that is widely enjoyed by millions of citizens coast to coast. The proliferation of Starbucks and of local microbreweries represent but two examples of the nationalization of diversity, multiplicity, and variety that for decades remained confined to the ethnic enclaves of big cities and the country's cosmopolitan centers mainly, though certainly not exclusively, arrayed on its two coasts. To be sure, this new culture of diversity has not displaced the more conventional culture of standardized American conformity; rather, the two exist side by side with their own publics, which, however, are increasingly overlapping in all areas of consumption. Bagels, café latte and microbrewed beers have not replaced doughnuts, Maxwell House instant coffee, and Budweiser beer in contemporary America; rather, these products and their cultures have found a relatively comfortable way of coexisting in America's consumption space. However, this space either got larger or much more diverse—or most likely both—in the course of the last two decades of the twentieth century. The world of sports mirrors both of these processes. On the one hand, advances in technology and developments in media ownership have rendered local clubs such as the Chicago Cubs, Chicago Bulls, and Atlanta Braves nationally observable phenomena. Yet, on the other hand, the very same technological and media-related forces are in the process of creating a world where fans of a particular local team will be able to watch their team from anywhere in the country—indeed the world. American sports, just like American society, exist in toto; but they also exist in discrete and separate niches. Until the late 1970s and early 1980s, there existed very few outlets apart from the three national networks and their local affiliates to impart sports culture to the vast American public. This handful of channels has now been supplemented by well over fifty in most areas of the United States. This has led to a niched sports world in which hitherto obscure and marginalized sports have been able to develop and retain their specialized audiences apart from, as well as in addition to, the national audiences of the Big Three and One-Half, which succeeded in developing their audiences in an earlier age with far fewer options. Hence, soccer in America—like wrestling, bowling, car racing, curling, skateboarding, and any number of sports and activities—has its very own well-defined world of experts, activists, participants, and followers with its newspapers, magazines, web sites, mailing lists, and all other accoutrements that render it a legitimate culture. However, we feel that only through a major triggering event associated with a surge in popularity—caused by national pride and affect—can we expect this culture to depart from its enclave and emerge as a force on the national scale.

This is the optimistic scenario that we feel is not unreasonable to envision for soccer's future in the United States. Given the demographic changes that will occur in the United States in the course of the next twenty years and given the country's astounding economic and cultural dynamism, which has always characterized it and shows no signs of abating, it seems plausible to argue that America's sport space—just like its consumer space—will increase. In so doing, it will allow a certain growth in diversity, since we believe that the already entrenched actors will not be replaced or even substantially weakened; the immense staying power that they have attained over more than a century's worth of tradition and institutional presence will continue. Try as the involved actors might, through lengthy strikes, lockouts, or other actions that most certainly do not serve the image and cause of their sports, the Big Three and hockey will remain indestructible staples of America's sports culture. But there may well be possibilities for new members by virtue of the increasing diversification of this culture and the growth of America's sport space. If this scenario occurs in the next decade or two, we believe that soccer in America is in a fine position to join the club. The necessary groundwork was successfully laid in the last two decades of the twentieth century. It would be a terrible shame for soccer in the world, and for sports culture in the United States, were this—like in other instances with soccer in America—to have yet again been for naught.

Appendixes..

Appendix A ....

A Statistical Abstract on Recreational, Scholastic, and Collegiate Soccer in the United States

A MORE detailed breakdown of the social composition of the 18,226,000 so-called total participants impressively highlights soccer's growth between 1987 and 1997, while also providing insight into the demographic character of those who participate.

Participation in soccer by income breaks down (for 1997) in the following manner: 4,639,000 (25.5 percent) came from families that earned less than $25,000; 5,791,000 (31.8 percent) were in the $25,000–$49,000 range; 3,926,000 (21.5 percent) had family income between $50,000 and $74,999; and 3,870,000 or 21.2 percent comprised those who earned $75,000 or more per year. That soccer had become a geographically evenly distributed activity in the United States is confirmed by the following data in terms of regional participation: 4,256,000 (23.4 percent) in the Northeast; 4,632,000 (25.4 percent) in what the survey terms North Central (presumably similar to, if not identical with, what is usually called the Midwest in the American vernacular); the South tallied 4,466,000 (24.5 percent) and the West 4,872,000 (26.7 percent).

The top ten soccer states in 1997 were California with 2,154,000 registered participants, followed by New York (1,354,000), Texas (1,277,000), Ohio (1,116,000), Pennsylvania (1,070,000), Michigan (781,000), New Jersey (643,000), Florida (613,000), Minnesota (561,000), and North Carolina (467,000). It is interesting, however, to see which states emerged on top when the number of soccer players was computed as a percentage of that state's overall population, thus offering perhaps a more accurate measure of soccer's presence than provided by absolute numbers. Utah led the nation with the highest rate of soccer participation, as 17.3 percent of the state's residents age six and over played the game at least once that year. In order, it was followed by Kansas (14.1 percent), Iowa (12.6 percent), Missouri (11.8 percent), and Minnesota (10.8 percent). The Midwest also featured the cities in which soccer was played at the greatest rate in 1997: Kansas City (20.3 percent), Cincinnati (14.6 percent), Minneapolis/St. Paul (12.5 percent), and St. Louis (10.1 percent)—the only major American city to have had any kind of soccer tradition prior to the soccer boom of the 1980s and 1990s.

As expected, figures reflecting participation by ethnicity emphasize the game's particularly strong appeal to Whites (13,987,000 or 76.7 percent) and Hispanics (2,793,000 or 15.3 percent) and the concomitantly low involvement by African Americans (860,000 or 4.7 percent); 586,000 participants—or 3.3 percent—belonged to ethnic groups simply classified in composite as "other."

To substantiate the picture, here are a few additional categories that demonstrate soccer's impressive growth between 1987 and 1997: Total adult participants (eighteen years of age and older) increased from 2,849,000 in 1987 to 4,599,000 in 1997, a whopping growth of 61.4 percent. Similarly, the so-called frequent participants (those who have played soccer on twenty-five days or more per year) increased from 5,929,000 in 1987 to 8,502,000 in 1997, a growth of 43.4 percent. The so-called core participants (those indicating that they played fifty-two or more days per year) grew by 47 percent during the same decade. The "aficionados"—those who listed soccer as their favorite sport—increased by 34.4 percent in one decade, from 3,002,000 in 1987 to 4,036,000 in 1997. The average number of days per year that these respondents said they played a game of soccer went from thirty in 1987 to thirty-six in 1997, an increase of 20 percent. The number of soccer players per one hundred people increased by 5.6 percent during this decade, from 7.2 in 1987 to 7.6 in 1997. Total participant days in millions grew by 42.1 percent, from 461.6 in 1987 to 656.1 in 1997. Participants under the age of eighteen, numbering 12,593,000 in 1987 increased by 8.7 percent to 13,627,000 in 1997. Even more impressive was the 34.3 percent increase in the under-age-twelve category, which grew from 6,439,000 in 1987 to 8,646,000 in 1997, another indicator of soccer's immense attraction as an activity for children and young adolescents. The only category to experience negative growth—even though a relatively small one at 1.5 percent—was the number of new participants, which went from 3,920,000 in 1987 to 3,860,000 in 1997.[1]

Data from the United States Amateur Soccer Association for the annual growth of registered soccer-playing adults over nineteen years of age conveys an impressive picture: Whereas 103,737 adults registered with the association as amateur soccer players in the 1985–86 season, that number more than doubled to 221,408 by 1996–97. Perhaps most significant of all the data for the game's immense growth, solid presence, and, perhaps, even rosy future in the United States pertains to the number of registered soccer coaches in the country: In 1941 there were the 10 who founded the National Soccer Coaches Association of America. By 1960 their number had increased to 400; in 1980 it was 2,300, and by 1997 it had ballooned to 14,650.[2]

Immensely impressive in terms of soccer's meteoric rise in the United States as a major youth activity in the course of the 1980s and 1990s are the following data regarding youth soccer registration by the three largest institutions in the country comprising soccer played by young people under nineteen years of age: The American Youth Soccer Organization (AYSO), Soccer Organization for Youth (SAY), and United States Youth Soccer Association (USYS). In 1980 there were 199,055 young people registered in AYSO, 40,628 in SAY, and 649,022 in USYS, yielding a combined total of 888,705. In 1997 the respective figures were 591,934 in AYSO, 78,430 in SAY, and 2,722,898 in USYS for a grand total of 3,391,842 registered young soccer players in these three organizations. Assigning the 1980 level an index of 100 as a baseline, the tally reached 382 by 1997, an impressive growth by any measure.[3]

Organized youth team sports rankings for participants ages twelve to seventeen yielded the following results in 1997: (1) basketball (12,409,000); (2) volleyball (7,493,000); (3) soccer (4,981,000); (4) tackle football (4,879,000); (5) softball (4,509,000); (6) baseball (4,321,000); and (7) ice hockey (622,000). In the six- to eleven-year-old group, soccer's position was even more auspicious: It ranked number two with 8,646,000 participants, behind basketball (11,014,000 participants) but ahead of baseball (4,400,000), softball (4,243,000), volleyball (3,767,000), tackle football (2,740,000), and ice hockey (508,000).[4] None of these numbers are mutually exclusive, meaning that there can indeed be overlap in participation in these sports.

Soccer's growth in American high schools also confirms the sport's march from the fringes in the 1970s to a major activity twenty years later. In 1976–77, there were 115,811 boys registered as participating in soccer in American high schools. The corresponding figure for girls was 11,534, yielding a total of 127,345. By 1980–81, the base year to which the index of 100 has been assigned to all three measures—boys, girls, and combined—the boys' tally had increased to 149,376, the girls' to 41,119, and the combined total to 190,495. In 1996–97, the last year for which these figures were available, boys' registration had attained 296,587, girls' 226,636, and the total stood at 523,223. Beyond the absolute numbers, the immense change in the index is perhaps even more dramatically reflective of the growth in the sport at the high school level, particularly on the girls' side: The boys' index went from a 78 in 1976–77 to a 199 in 1996–97; the girls' from a meager 28 in 1976–77 to a whopping 551 in 1996–97, with the combined tally catapulting from 67 in the first period to 275 twenty years later.[5] Simply put, by the end of the twentieth century, soccer had become an integral part of the athletic scene of American high school life, transforming itself from an exotic and marginal activity to a normal option on an increasingly diversified menu.

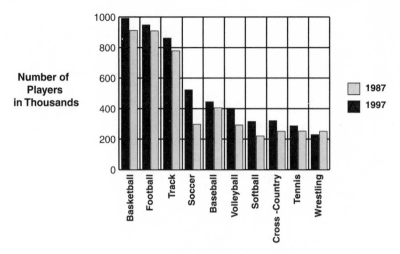

Figure A.1. Top ten sports listed by participation in high school programs

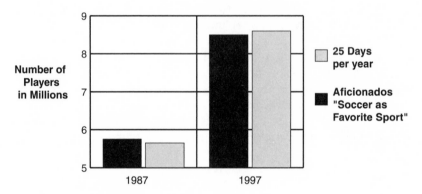

Figure A.2. Frequency of soccer play

Again, though not mutually exclusive (some sports that usually take place during the same season can be viewed in relation to each other), here is how soccer fared in 1996–97 compared to other sports at American high schools: On the girls' side, basketball remained the most popular sport with 447,687 participants, followed by outdoor track and field (385,605), volleyball (370,957), slow pitch softball (313,607), soccer (226,636), tennis (150,346), cross country (145,624), swimming and diving (123,886), field hockey (56,502), and indoor track and field (49,365). For the boys, football remained the most popular sport with 957,507 participants, followed by basketball (544,025), outdoor track and field (457,937), baseball (444,248), soccer (296,587), wrestling (227,596), cross country (174,599), golf (150,578), tennis (136,451), and swimming

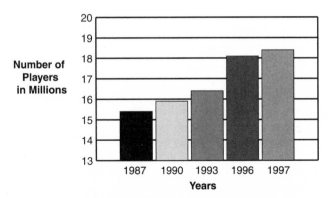

Figure A.3. Total participation in soccer, ages six and older

and diving (93,523). Participation in all high school athletics during 1996–97 stood at 6,195,247, an increase of 175,358 from the previous year and the second-highest mark in the twenty-seven years that the survey had been conducted, topped only by the "baby boom" figure of 6,450,482 in 1977–78. Data from the 1996–97 survey indicated another record participation for girls at 2,472,043, an increase of 104,107 from 1995–96. Boys' participation also grew by 72,173, to 3,706,225, the highest such figure since 1978–79. In addition to the 2,472,043 female and 3,706,225 male participants, the 6,195,247 total included 16,979 participants in coeducational sports.[6]

With an additional 17,349 newcomers since 1995–96, soccer registered the largest gain among all girls' athletic programs, ahead of the 13,481 opting for volleyball, 12,526 choosing swimming and diving, and 11,980 for indoor track and field. Soccer also led the way in registering the top increase in school sponsorship for girls' programs with an additional 445 schools, followed by indoor track and field (increase of 444), softball (443), golf (351), swimming and diving (332), and volleyball (317).

On the boys' side, too, soccer registered the biggest gain among all sports in 1996–97 with 12,859 new participants, followed by indoor track and field (increase of 12,725), swimming and diving (12,523), golf (10,567), wrestling (6,434), and cross country (6,396). In terms of school sponsorship among boys' sports, indoor track and field led the way with an additional 419 schools, followed by soccer with an increase of 250, golf (179), swimming and diving (176), basketball (130), and cross country (125).

The ten-year trend analysis (1987–97) (see figures A.1–A.3) of sports participation at American high schools yielded the following rank order of the top ten categories: (1) basketball (1987: 912,997; 1997: 991,712, an 8.6 percent gain); (2) football (11 player) (1987: 909,344; 1997:

958,247, a 5.4 percent gain); (3) track (outdoor) (1987: 778,126; 1997: 862,007, a 10.8 percent gain); (4) soccer (1987: 297,018—then in fifth place; 1997: 523,223, an amazing 76.2 percent gain, far and away the largest increase attained by any sport during this decade and nearly double the growth reached by the runner-up, fast pitch softball); (5) baseball (1987: 406,381—then in fourth place; 1997: 445,374, a 9.6 percent gain, not enough to prevent soccer from surpassing it and relegating baseball from fourth place in 1987 to fifth in 1997); (6) volleyball (1987: 292,043; 1997: 403,332, a handsome gain of 38.1 percent); (7) softball (fast-pitch) (1987: 220,322 then in tenth place; 1997: 315,571, an impressive 43.2 percent gain); (8) cross country (1987: 251,442; 1997: 320,223, a 27.4 percent gain);(9) tennis (1987: 252,277; 1997: 286,797, a 13.7 percent gain that was not enough to maintain tennis's seventh overall position in the 1987 rankings, slipping the sport to ninth place a decade later); (10) wrestling; the only loser in absolute numbers was wrestling, which held tenth place in 1997 with 229,225 participants, having slipped from ninth place in 1987 by incurring an 8.8 percent decline from the 251,299 participating in the sport a decade before.

Lastly, data on high school soccer sponsorship by state and gender offer ample evidence that the sport had become a central activity in the physical education and interscholastic competition of America's teenagers at the end of the twentieth century. To be sure, there are states such as Arkansas and South Dakota that sponsored zero high school soccer programs in the 1996–97 school year. But these were the only two states in the union to be so soccer free—or averse, as the case may be. In California, Connecticut, Florida, Massachusetts, New Hampshire, New York, and Washington, boys' soccer ranked an impressive second after basketball (which is the leading team sport in all fifty states). Here are the tallies: California—1,035 basketball; 879 soccer. Connecticut—170 basketball; 167 soccer. Florida—496 basketball; 332 soccer. Massachusetts—332 basketball; 313 soccer. New Hampshire—85 basketball; 82 soccer. New York—718 basketball; 633 soccer. Washington—375 basketball; 248 soccer. Vermont was the only state in the union in which soccer surpassed basketball as the leading state-sponsored high school sport, by a tally of 54 to 51. The picture on the girls' side was similar, with two revealing differences: First, though basketball was far and away the leading state-sponsored high school sport in most states, there were a number of states where volleyball (Florida, Hawaii, Illinois, Indiana, Iowa, Nebraska, and Nevada, for example) and softball (Vermont and the District of Columbia) surpassed basketball. Second, the gap between the leading sport and soccer was much narrower on the girls' side than it had been on the boys'. However, as far as Vermont was concerned, soccer was the leader among the girls as it had been among the boys, ahead of softball 52 to 42.[7]

Soccer's presence at the college level has paralleled its successes in high schools. Let us present some impressive evidence for soccer's advancement as a major presence at American institutions of higher learning. The NCAA member institutions that sponsor men's and women's soccer teams on the varsity level yield the following picture: Of the 752 institutional NCAA members in 1981–82, 521 (or 69 percent) sponsored men's soccer teams and 77 (10 percent) did so on the women's side. By 1997–98 the 985 institutional members sponsored 686 men's soccer teams and 721 women's, yet again underscoring soccer's immense growth as a major sport for women in the United States in the course of the 1980s and 1990s. In percentage terms, the men's side increased a mere point, from 69 to 70 percent, whereas on the women's side the number skyrocketed from 10 to 73 percent, in the process surpassing the men in absolute terms (721– 686) for the very first time in 1997–98. A more detailed breakdown of NCAA women's soccer sponsorship further highlights this amazing growth of soccer on the collegiate level. In 1981 there were a mere 17 Division I, 16 Division II, and 45 Division III schools that sponsored women's soccer. By 1997–98 the tally had changed in the following manner: 229 Division I, 153 Division II, and 339 Division III schools had college-sponsored varsity women's soccer teams in the United States. In relation to the two leading college team sports, notably men's basketball and football, here is soccer's position at American colleges and universities during the academic year 1997–98: For Division I there were 191 men's soccer teams, 231 football teams, 308 men's basketball teams, and 229 women's soccer teams. For Division II there were 160 men's soccer teams, 156 football teams, 279 men's basketball teams, and 153 women's soccer teams. For Division III there were 335 men's soccer programs, 217 football programs, 356 men's basketball programs, and 339 women's soccer programs. The total tally for all divisions was 686 for men's soccer, 600 for football, 943 for men's basketball, and 721 for women's soccer. By the end of the twentieth century, soccer had become a major sport for men and women in America's institutions of higher learning.

Appendix B ....

A Sample of Opinion from American Sports Columnists and Journalists regarding the 1994 World Cup

THE FOLLOWING is but a brief sample of some of the ruminations and statements by America's journalists regarding the World Cup.

Sampling the "Soccer-Friendlies"

The most pronounced of the soccer-friendly newspaper writers expressed their thrill in having the World Cup in the United States and their hopes (though usually qualified with a strong dose of reality) for a World Cup that would capture the hearts and minds of the American public while establishing soccer as a fifth major professional team sport in the United States. This included writers both in and out of the sports sections who likely qualify as part of America's "soccer constituency." Some of their pieces, particularly during the buildup and first round, dealt specifically with what made the sport so attractive and exciting on a personal level; narratives describing how the writer became "hooked on soccer" were almost always included. Though unabashedly hopeful, most were skeptical or noncommittal regarding the establishment of a pro soccer league in the United States. As these pieces were usually not written by sportswriters and as they tended to focus on personal soccer experiences, we have not included them in our survey of sports columnists and feature opinion editorials relating to the World Cup.

Most columnists recognized the significance and entertainment value of the tournament as separate from the issues regarding soccer's potential for success in the United States. Many of these writers stated, both implicitly and explicitly, that one need not be a lifelong soccer fan to enjoy the World Cup, and that soccer's marginal status in the United States was not an issue in doing so. Some criticized those so zealous and evangelical in their "pro soccer" rhetoric that they alienated many American sports fans. Some also bemoaned the tendency of the media and others who had a stake in promoting soccer in the United States to infer larger meanings to an event that could and should simply be enjoyed for itself. The general theme for many of these writers was: "We can enjoy the World Cup without having to express our undying devotion to soccer, and we shouldn't have to worry about the so-called grand implications. It should be fun and exciting, no big deal."

Nearly two weeks prior to the start of the tournament, an excellent representative of the "pro and con" soccer tandem ran in the *San Francisco Examiner* under the heading: "Should we care about the World Cup?" Ray Ratto's piece, the pro side of the argument, highlighted the entertainment value of the World Cup as opposed to embracing soccer per se: "Let's consider, though, the difference between what we are being asked to do by the soccer pressure groups, and what we need to do for our own enjoyment. And the World Cup is a pretty good way to spend a piece of summer." Ratto said that the quality of soccer played in the World Cup related as much to the soccer most Americans had seen as did an Ottawa-Edmonton hockey game to the Stanley Cup finals, or a Cincinnati Bengals football game to the Super Bowl. Ratto noted the spectacle and competitiveness of the tournament and the high-caliber skill of the teams and players. But for some, that is not enough and it creates problems for those who might simply want to watch a match or two:

"Some folks are even angry at what they know is going to happen next that as soon as the World Cup ends, soccer will return to its place as something our kids do between eating out of the dog's dish and discovering the opposite sex and taking the car without permission. Again, our choice. We don't work for the US Soccer Federation or any of its steel-plated minions, and we don't work for ESPN, or Nike, or Coca Cola, or any of the other official sponsors of the World Cup. . . .

"And if they care more than you, that's fine. You don't have to be that open-minded, or that pure of heart, or that globally conscious. You aren't taking a test to be the next national coach. You are sitting in your den with your feet up on the dog, watching a sport played at its highest level. Let's face it, you've watched much worse stuff than this and you know it."[1]

Ann Killion of the *San Jose Mercury News* voiced similar sentiments: "We won't be allowed to simply enjoy the event. Every TV rating, opinion poll and ticket sale will be sliced and diced and analyzed. . . . And unfair as it might be, pretty much everyone agrees that if the United States fails to advance to the second round, you can kiss your soccer dreams goodbye. . . . The World Cup should be exciting. Too bad it comes with so many strings attached."[2]

After experiencing the World Cup firsthand, some columnists made it a point to lobby their readers to do the same. After seeing the 1–1 tie between Mexico and Italy, Thomas Boswell of the *Washington Post* advised his readers to make every effort to be present for Saudi Arabia–

284 APPENDIX B

Belgium at RFK stadium, the one Washington match for which tickets might not be so hard to find.[3] There were columnists who, after attending some matches, either expressed a newfound interest in, or at least a newfound respect for, soccer. On the eve of the tournament, Boswell's colleague at the *Post*, Tony Kornheiser, expressed a vaguely positive view of the World Cup, though he too found fault with soccer and its fans: "Make fun of soccer and they'll write, 'Your criticisms are infantile. Obviously, the game eludes you; it has too many nuances for you to follow.' Well, it seems to me that trying to kick a round ball into a net ain't exactly quantum physics. Nuance, shmooance. . . . But it's only one month. Let's give it a try." Six days later, Kornheiser wrote: "Those of you who read this column regularly know it's fair to say . . . that I regarded soccer as somewhat less appealing than a case of hives. But I have been to two World Cup games now, and while I don't want to say I'm rolling over like a dog . . . scratch me behind the ear, and I'll fetch the paper for you."[4]

Some writers expressed a sort of "internationalist" and/or "multicultural" attitude as they exhorted their readers to avoid a display of an American sports chauvinism that could reflect a deeper provincialism, insularity, xenophobia, "cultural paranoia," irrational stubbornness, or self-imposed ignorance. Pieces of this nature were often in response to those that expressed overt "antisoccer" sentiments; some ran in tandem with a "soccer hostile" piece. Additionally, there was the explicit message asking Americans to give the sport a chance, if just to find out what the rest of the world found so captivating. The implication was that in doing so, Americans would thus become better world-citizens of the international community. Syndicated op-ed columnist Otis Pike sounded this theme on the eve of the World Cup opening ceremonies. "The rest of the world can't be all wrong," Pike wrote.[5]

Jay Mariotti of the *Chicago Sun-Times* bemoaned the "Ugly American" attitudes of xenophobia and chauvinism that were "spoiling [the] World Cup mood." But as citizens of a nation of immigrants, soccer is part of America too and "part of you will be represented on a field somewhere." Another problem was the alien nature of the game for most Americans. "Yeah, it's different," Mariotti wrote. "Yeah, it's strange. But give it a chance. The Cubs aren't worth your time, the Sox will be there later. You don't have to embrace the World Cup. But you might try to accept it for what it is, enjoy the unique spirit in the air and make these visitors feel good in a feel-good city. . . . I say Cup fever. You should say, why the hell not?"[6]

Lowell Cohen expressed similar sentiments in the *San Francisco Chronicle*. Noting that many Americans complain that soccer is "weird and foreign," Cohen pointed out that to most of the world, baseball and basketball were viewed this way. Additionally, American team sports, save baseball (which Cohen depicted not as a sport, but as "a pastime, guys standing around, deriving no health benefits from playing") are not egalitarian in their physical access, unlike soccer. Cohen viewed the reaction of most Americans to soccer as xenophobic, "the ugliest of American qualities . . . parochialism, isolationism, prejudice. It has everything to do with not liking what you don't understand, hating what's foreign to you. . . . Americans should stop being so condescending. It makes them seem ignorant, not to mention ungracious hosts."[7]

Writing a pro soccer piece, run in tandem with an extremely rude con piece by Gerry Callahan that bordered on explicit xenophobia, George Kimball of the *Boston Herald* responded: "That some people regard so religiously a game many Americans find almost incomprehensible is a concept at least a few people in my racket apparently view as threatening. . . . The oddest aspect of this reaction is that the very people who fear and loathe soccer the most are almost to a man ice hockey enthusiasts. Throw out the sticks and ice and have the participants play with their own teeth and what have you got but soccer? I'd be the first to admit that I'd rather spend a lazy summer afternoon watching a well-played baseball game, but that doesn't necessarily make the fellow who prefers soccer an idiot." Though skeptical about the potential for soccer to capture the hearts and minds of the American public, Kimball still believed that "the World Cup is a unique experience. We ought to be paying attention, if only to learn what all the fuss is about. . . . It is an opportunity to watch the very best players in the world perform on one stage, and to share in the emotional travails of their followers, who will bring a passion to these shores our own games could only hope to emulate. . . . Try it. You might like it."[8]

In response to a "con" soccer piece run in tandem on the eve of the tournament final, *Dallas Morning News* Metro reporter David Jackson echoed the call for tolerance: "None of this is better or worse, just different." Jackson found the World Cup "without a doubt one of the most exciting events in all of sports." Jackson noted that there are idiosyncrasies to all sports, and to dismiss soccer simply for being different from what one is used to was characteristic of provincialism and small-mindedness: "Many Americans would be upset, and rightly so, if baseball was bashed. Those foreign commentators would not understand how baseball has woven itself into the fabric of American life. Some Americans don't understand that soccer has done the same thing in other lands. If you find soccer boring, there is a simple solution: Don't watch. And don't worry: Millions of people are willing to take up the slack."[9]

A Sample of the "Soccer Hostiles"

Pieces hostile to soccer were not run in the quantity or frequency of pieces presenting positive views on the tournament, though they were often given prominent page placement, which provided a much higher profile than that provided by the former. The *Los Angeles Times*, the *New York Times*, the *New York Post*, the *New York Daily News*, and the *Miami Herald* did not run any pieces overtly hostile to soccer. The few negative viewpoints expressed by columnists in these papers concerned the poor chances that soccer and/or the World Cup had for making a positive and lasting impression on the American public and the problems with soccer as a televised event. Many of these remarks and observations were found in the Media Sports columns of these dailies. Toward the end of the tournament, *Newsday* and the *Chicago Tribune* published pieces by sports columnists who had covered the tournament and were now expressing a decided ambivalence to the game. The *Dallas Morning News* did not run a "soccer hostile" piece until a few days before the final, when it published a "pro and con" tandem in its Metro Section. The one "soccer hostile" piece to appear in the *San Jose Mercury News* did so during the first round in that paper's main news section.

The "soccer hostile" camp included those with a pronounced indifference, who, rather than expressing outright hostility, merely dismissed the sport and its relevance to the American public. It also was comprised of some with definite antipathies and hostilities toward soccer, the World Cup, and—often explicitly—foreigners in general. On the extreme were those who not only expressed a disdain for soccer, but also voiced a nativist and chauvinist attack on the sport and its fans. Prior to the opening of the tournament, several writers ascribed the rioting impulses prevalent at European and South American soccer matches to all foreigners traveling to the United States for the World Cup. This theme was used in several antisoccer pieces that appeared before the tournament. After the tournament began, and it became apparent that violence on the part of soccer fans would not be a feature of World Cup USA, this theme was for the most part dropped.

In the most extreme category of "soccer hostile," pieces by three Boston columnists at the beginning of the tournament stand apart with statements that were xenophobic and racist. After presenting a predictable sarcasm denoting an apathy and contempt for soccer, feature (Main News section) columnist Howie Carr of the *Boston Herald* wrote: "But, as if the INS hasn't got its hands full already, now we have a new wave of Eurotrash streaming onto our shores. Huddled masses, to coin a phrase, yearning not so much to be free as to party hearty."[10] A few days later, the *Herald* ran a pair of pro and con opinion pieces by two sportswriters in its op-ed pages. The headline over the antisoccer piece by Gerry Callahan read: "Beware the Bootheads Are Coming." Though more subtle and better written than Carr's diatribe, this essay also implied a nativistic contempt for soccer and foreign soccer fans. Callahan also had barbs for American "fans" of the sport: "Young suburban kids, who would rather be home killing frogs, will be forced into minivans and marched into Foxboro Stadium where they will fall asleep watching Bolivia tie South Korea, 1–1. The trendy yuppie types will go to games just so they can tell their trendy yuppie friends they went to games." After further disparagement of the sport, Callahan concluded with another shot at its spectators: "As the bootheads begin their assault on the area, we can only hope the town of Foxboro has plenty of available jail space and our state troopers don't forget the lessons they learned at the academy. Remember, boys. They give you nightsticks for a reason. Do not hesitate to use them." After the U.S. upset of Colombia, Callahan continued his belittlement of foreigners, soccer, soccer players, and "bootheads" in a prominently placed column entitled, "Keep the Cup." While citing the death threats by a drug cartel against a Colombian player as part of what it takes to pull off a major soccer upset, Callahan also presented his disdain for Spanish-language broadcaster Andres Cantor ("If I want to hear indecipherable howling I'll watch MTV"), compared Maradona to the midget of television's *Fantasy Island*, and inadvertently foreshadowed the tragic murder of Colombia's "own-goal" scorer Andres Escobar ("If he hadn't been gunned down by authorities last year, Uncle Pablo would not have been pleased.")[11] Writing in the presumably more genteel (i.e., nontabloid) *Boston Globe*, Mike Barnacle compared soccer to a Barbra Streisand concert: "It is a toss-up as to which event is more boring and both are totally irrelevant." On soccer being the game of the world's common people and a unifying force for nations: "That's because a lot of places like India, Egypt, Bolivia and South Korea have no country clubs . . . where men and women can relax and play a round of golf while telling anti-Semitic jokes. Most of these desperate nations don't even have bowling alleys. What do they know about fun?"[12]

No antisoccer columnists in the nineteen other newspapers surveyed matched this Boston trio for nativism, xenophobia, insularity, and rudeness. Most overtly antisoccer columns focused on why the game would fail in the United States and/or why Americans (including one particular newspaper writer) did not care for it. Local or American insularity as a virtue was a theme that occasionally appeared. In a piece that was not overtly "soccer hostile," Jake Vest of the *Orlando Sentinel* wrote: "The soccer crowd does have fun, no mistake about it. But I've yet to see anybody singly or in a group do anything you might not see at a Texas high school football game. For enthusiasm, I'd rate them just above league bowlers and way behind NASCAR. This may be the world's most-beloved sport, but the world always has been overrated. I'll take Lake County [Florida] anytime."[13]

Without the vitriol, rancor, or crudeness of a Callahan or Carr, perhaps most representative of "soccer hostile" pieces reflecting American nativism was a well-written column by Art Spander of the *San Francisco Examiner* that appeared in the sports section as the con side to Ray Ratto's aforementioned pro piece. "What we're going to find out," Spander wrote, "is whether a lot of anonymous players from countries not fortunate enough to have the legacy of Red Grange or Jackie Robinson can do anything about America's indifference toward the world's so-called most popular sport. Soccer isn't our game and never will be our game, but like a wreck on the Bayshore Freeway at rush hour, the World Cup can't be ignored." Spander predicted that the World Cup would succeed as an event because Americans like big events, but that the impact of soccer itself would be negligible. After pointing out several negative features relating to soccer (rioting fans and tragic deaths in the stands, bribes and game fixings), Spander noted that the mere mention of such things makes American soccer fans "apoplectic . . . whining that [American] sporting columnists have made it their devilish business to see the game never succeeds [in the United States]." But, noted Spander, baseball has its constant "knocks" with which the fans agree, yet baseball fans keep coming back. Regarding as propaganda the notion that interest in World Cup soccer makes for international citizenship, Spander wrote: "Don't fall for it. I promise, even if you never watch a moment, the merchants in Florence and Milan will still accept your lire when you're in Italy. . . ." Regarding the game itself, Spander wrote: "Soccer is boring, except for the chaos in the stands. Soccer doesn't have any statistics. Soccer doesn't have any recent American tradition in America. Soccer doesn't have any heroes." That the last two points could possibly be addressed with the establishment of a first-division American professional league; Spander commented as follows: "There's a better chance of a national health plan being passed by Congress than of a major pro league in America."[14]

Though expressing a sentiment of annoyance at soccer aficionados similar to those expressed by several prosoccer or pro–World Cup writers, Dan Shaughnessy of the *Boston Globe* had less sympathy. "They are the Soccer Krishnas," Shaughnessy wrote. "They are the Futbol Moonies. They are the Scientologists of Sport. They are the Maradona Witnesses. . . . It is not good enough when you tell them that baseball, basketball, football and hockey are your four basic spectator food groups. . . . No. You must love soccer. You simply must." Though the World Cup had great success "can't the Sports Scientologists just enjoy their event and leave us alone until July 17. Must they continue to insist that normal American sports fans convert to soccer? We are tired of having to explain ourselves. We just don't like watching the game. Never will. It is not going to happen for a lot of us. Hey, a lot of people like Garth Brooks. The French think Jerry Lewis is hysterical. Does that mean we all have to conform?" Tuna fish is great food, Shaughnessy wrote, "but I don't like it" so "does that mean I'm a bad guy or I have no taste?" Finally, Shaughnessy just desired "[n]o more tambourines, shaved heads, corner kicks or yellow cards. No more mailings from FIFA. Let me live in peace. Go watch another 0–0 game and tell each other how great it all is."[15]

Tom Knotts of the *Washington Times* expressed similar sentiments: "The game still looks foreign to me, and my passion meter is registering zero. One other thing: I'm getting tired of the soccer weenies lecturing me on what I'm missing. I have some news for them. Soccer is a game. That's all. You love the game. Fine. Great. Go for it. Work yourself into a frenzy over corner kicks. No problem. That's your business. But spare me your condescending rhetoric. I don't think we're talking a cure for cancer or anything." Knotts compared soccer and its aficionados to similarities with baseball: "I suspect if baseball dumped the World Series in Paris, the French would be saying, 'What the heck is this?' And I suspect George Will and his kind would go nuts trying to explain to the French the game's pastoral beauty and symmetry and other silliness. . . . Ultimately, I suspect, soccer will find its niche in the US on a level with track and field or one of the other every-four-years sports. Until then, the soccer weenies could use a chill pill."[16]

The lone "soccer hostile" piece to appear in the sports section of the *Washington Post* did so under the heading of "Other Voices: Another View of the World Cup in the United States." Norman Chad ("Special to the Post") found fault with the game's presentation on television, specifically for the lack of pauses for refreshments and/or a trip to the bathroom, and the game's paucity of scoring ("If I wanted 1–0 games at RFK, I'd ask Texas to give us back the Senators") and definitive moments. "Sure soccer aficionados talk about what a wonderful 'tactical game' soccer is, but then again so is chess and you don't see ABC rushing to televise 'Monday Night Checkmate.'" Admitting that he was not a big fan of the game, he at least had given it a chance on television. Chad believed his complaints were representative of most Americans and justified: "[F]rankly, I think this is one area in which the Stars and Stripes can flap in the wind proudly. Usually we're wrong in America when we think one way and the rest of the world thinks another, but I'm with Bubba and Verne and my good buddy Hank Williams Jr. on this one. I'm ready for some N-F-L *Football*!!!"[17]

The only negative piece on the World Cup to appear in the soccer-friendly *San Jose Mercury News* before or during the tournament ran in the Main News "South Bay Dispatches" column by Mike Cassidy, entitled "Who Cares about World Cup Soccer?" After dismissing the U.S. upset of Colombia as an event that few Americans actually witnessed or enjoyed, Cassidy included quotes from several San Francisco Bay Area residents to support his contention that most Americans find the sport not only foreign but boring, especially in comparison to traditional American sports. This included a visit to a San Jose sports bar where the patrons preferred to watch the U.S. Open golf tournament over the Saudi Arabia–Netherlands "soccer barn-burner." "Soccer simply isn't our game," Cassidy wrote. "We want high scores and instant results. We don't want a clock that adds minutes up instead of counting them down. And we don't want ties, for goodness sakes."[18]

The *Dallas Morning News* also ran just one overtly "soccer hostile" piece; on the eve of the final, a soccer pro and con tandem by guest columnists (both of whom were Metro staff writers) ran in that paper's features section. For the cons, Jeffrey Weiss's piece was entitled: "But for the Occasional *Goooaall*, It's *Boooorrring*." Weiss found the sport "interminable" and voiced the oft-heard complaint about soccer's lack of scoring and lack of defining action: "Call me a typical American, looking for instant gratification. But to me, soccer consists of lots of nothing. Or maybe that should be lots of the same thing leading to nothing." In American sports, noted Weiss, the potential for scoring is always there. "In baseball, every pitch has the potential of producing a score. . . . In American football, almost every play can end in a touchdown. (What's the biggest complaint about this game these days? Too many boring field goals. Booted by former soccer players. See?) . . . Basketball features the unremitting goad of a shot clock that pretty much guarantees a score a minute." The fourth favorite American team sport, hockey, somewhat resembles soccer: "And you know what? Most sports fans in the US find hockey an acquired taste. And some just go for the fights." Meanwhile, Weiss considered soccer a great game to play (and wonderfully inexpensive to equip and attire for), just boring to watch. "None of this, mind you, means I think America shouldn't be hosting the games," Weiss concluded. "Just include me out. I figure I did my bit as host, leaving one more spot for someone who cares."[19]

Another nonconvert to World Cup soccer was feature columnist Richard Roeper of the *Chicago Sun-Times* who found the Germany-Spain match at Soldier Field so boring that he asked: "Did not one hooligan make the trip overseas?"[20] The only "soccer hostile" piece to appear in the *Orlando Sentinel* (on July 4 in the last World Cup Today special section that paper would run) was more an expression of indifference to soccer as part of an indifference to all sports. Feature columnist Charley Reese echoed a metaphor used by several writers: "Soccer is un-American like the metric system, which Americans likewise won't voluntarily adopt." However, Reese put a different sort of nativist spin on the subject: "We did not draw a team whose fans are famous as hooligans, and I was rather disappointed that we didn't. I was looking forward to seeing what would happen when the British soccer hooligans discovered that America's generic hooligans carry guns and knives. Could have been another Battle of New Orleans with more or less the same results." But Reese made a point of not being chauvinistic regarding soccer and American sports: "So don't get the idea that I think soccer is an extra silly game. All games are silly, that's why we call them games. There is nothing essentially sillier about 22 men with fat calf muscles trying to kick a ball into a net than there is about 10 tall men trying to dunk or toss one through a hoop."[21]

Two pieces that if not overtly hostile to soccer expressed a definite ambivalence, stand out because of their authors and their timing. Sports columnists Steve Jacobson of *Newsday* and Bernie Lincicome of the *Chicago Tribune* covered the entire World Cup for their respective papers. Though Lincicome had written of his own indifference and skepticism regarding soccer and the World Cup two weeks prior to the tournament, after the admittedly dull Germany-Bolivia opener he had declared: "As official, and proud, host columnist for World Cup USA 1994, I refuse to be cynical."[22] Lincicome wrote pieces on various aspects of the tournament— both on and off the field—that were fairly insightful and accurate, though often in a facetious or sarcastic vein (which is, of course, a tradition of American sports journalism).

Throughout the tournament, Jacobson had written on numerous issues surrounding the World Cup, though most of his columns focused on the players and fans of various teams. Two days after the United States was eliminated by Brazil, Jacobson's column was entitled "Game's Appeal? Don't Ask Me." Comparing the appreciation of soccer to appreciation of certain modern art ("I didn't get it so it must have been me"), Jacobson wrote: "So I may not know art; I know what I like. . . . So I may not know soccer; I know what I like." Reciting many familiar American complaints about the game (such a paucity of scoring that a team can "dominate," 1–0, no use of hands, no breaks for players and spectators alike, nobody knows the real time left except the referee) and a complaint specific to sportswriters ("The rest of the world media does reviews, not interviews. So there are few interviews and few personalities emerging"). Jacobson expressed a nagging question looming beyond what on the surface is simply subjective preference: "But soccer is the king of sports in all its glory. Enjoy it. So it must be my failing. Unless the king has no clothes."[23] This column by Jacobson was the only truly negative piece on soccer to appear in any of the four New York dailies before, during, or after World Cup '94.

Four days later, Lincicome's "In the Wake of the News" column was titled: "Thanks, World, but It's OK: You Can Keep Your Game." With the United States now eliminated, many Americans were no longer interested nor was there really reason for American interest, save hosting the party. This was evidenced by the availability of tickets for second-round matches: "[I]t is fair to say that whatever seeds the World Cup has planted in American soil could still use some definite patriotic fertilizer. It is a mistake to believe that the World Cup has changed anyone's mind about soccer here. . . . We have only so much idiocy to go around, and we certainly don't need to be wasting it on soccer." Overall, Lincicome shared the belief that soccer simply isn't "our game," but that was fine: "No need to apologize about a lack of passion for soccer. Let's hope it never happens."[24]

As noted, some American sportswriters and columnists wrote negative pieces on soccer as a response to the real and perceived chauvinism of the foreign press and soccer community regarding soccer and American sports and the American public. Many American journalists found the methods and attitudes of those taking part and running the World Cup counterproductive, self-important, and arrogant; many found the foreign press unprofessional (particularly the absence of even a pretense of impartiality or objectivity by foreign journalists), condescending, and patronizing. The result was the occasional backlash from American writers, not all of it necessarily misplaced. Longtime sports columnist Joe Falls of the *Detroit News*: "I asked the Swiss coach, an English chap named Roy Hodgson, if he knew we were about to crown our hockey and basketball champions and if he cared about it. He said no, he didn't care at all. But we, I gather, are supposed to care about them."[25]

Perhaps the most biting piece by an American sports columnist in retaliation to "soccer chauvinists" was written by Scott Ostler of the *San Francisco Chronicle*, filed from London where he was covering the Wimbledon tennis tournament. After taking a few shots at soccer and the British, Ostler described a BBC-TV news segment from New York City wherein a reporter supposedly found no one who could identify particular soccer terms, but "I'm sure if anyone interviewed did know what a header or nutmeg is, their spoilsport butts wound up on the editing-room floor." The attitude of the British newsman's summation was basically "a smirk and a derisive snort." Ostler found that the British print media, particularly those actually covering the World Cup, displayed a similar attitude that implied: "Can you believe these unsophisticated rubes?" Ostler had some educational pointers for the English and the rest of the soccer world.

For one, American sports journalists consider it highly unprofessional to show any sort of partiality or enthusiasm when covering a contest, especially from the press box, "unless you are on fire. Such restraint is a useful skill. I once saw the statue of David, in person. While deeply moved, I did not lose control and leap on David's back in joy." Another point was that Americans were making a fine effort to stage, appreciate, and enjoy the tournament. Though it's unlikely that many will become soccer converts as a result of the World Cup, "we're willing to go along, to enjoy the spectacle, to help the world have a party. You don't have to be a pin-the-tail-on-the-donkey devotee to throw a hot birthday party for your 4-year-old." Finally, the American people did not decide to host the World Cup by plebiscite. "It came to America because some promoters thought they could make American money off it. You want the Cup back, blokes? Take it."[26]

The "Sport Pundits" on Soccer and Its Future in the United States

Many sports and feature writers examined the issue of whether or not soccer would continue to be marginalized as a professional U.S. sport. Most agreed that the World Cup itself would be successful as a big event, but were skeptical regarding what impact it would have on American soccer overall. Before the tournament began, almost all newspapers ran feature stories that explored the issue through interviews with interested (and some uninterested) parties. The overall consensus was that if the 1994 World Cup was a display comparable to that of 1990, "big-time" professional soccer in the United States was as good as dead. "Certainly, a slow, actionless tournament isn't going to turn on Americans," wrote Jake Curtis in the *San Francisco Chronicle*.[27]

In the days leading up to the tournament, often cited was the *USA Today*/CNN Gallup Poll that showed 66 percent of Americans unaware that the World Cup was taking place. A column syndicated to several American newspapers by the esteemed sports editor of the *Miami Herald*, Edwin Pope, addressed the finding from the same poll that showed only 9 percent of the American public interested in the World Cup. Pope cited three reasons for American apathy toward soccer, "as long as people understand that we are talking about US interest in the World Cup and not about the basic merits of soccer, which I, for one, consider by far the best sport for children." First, Americans could not identify (or identify with) soccer rivalries comparable to the ones, say, between the Boston Red Sox and New York Yankees in baseball or the Miami Hurricanes and Florida State Seminoles in college football; and they had no heroes like Ken

Griffey Jr. Second was soccer's aforementioned lack of definable plays that lead to resolution of the contest, including a paucity of scoring. Unlike sports where the potential for touchdowns, home runs, or slam dunks is always present, "soccer is a game of failure as far as US viewers are concerned. Players seem to run around forever without scoring." Third, soccer has nothing to match the pitcher versus batter of baseball, the driver/shooter versus defender of basketball, or the various individual matchups of football. "Mano a mano does the trick for Yankee Doodle Dandy," Pope wrote. "On top of everything else, the less soccer is on TV, the fewer people want to see it. . . . It's a vicious circle for the world's most popular game, which can't flip the electrifying switch in the United States even in the World Cup."[28]

Writing in the business section of the *Washington Post*, Jay Matthews pronounced the World Cup "a hit," but said that "hopes of affixing the world's most popular team sport to the American soul seem to be fading amid marketing miscues, a squabble among competing US soccer leagues and the stubborn belief of many sports fans that watching soccer is akin to being forced to sit through *Swan Lake*. 'I don't think soccer can be successfully marketed,' said Rick Jones, a former soccer coach who is now a vice president in the Atlanta office of sports promotion firm Advantage International. 'As Americans, we like instant gratification, lots of scoring, lots of action, and soccer is a lot like ballet in a lot of ways.' "[29]

Two days before the World Cup opening ceremonies, the *New York Post* ran a pair of pieces, each by a reporter experienced in covering "big-time" soccer, each of whom expressed complete skepticism regarding the future of professional American soccer beyond the World Cup. Writing as a "guest columnist" for the World Cup, the distinguished British journalist and internationally recognized soccer expert Brian Glanville predicted that "[t]he World Cup will be a colossal success in the USA. The subsequent professional soccer league won't. Not least because of the World Cup." After watching the greatest soccer players in the world, wrote Glanville, Americans won't "want to pay money to watch the equivalent of bush-league play. . . . Who'd pay money to watch Joe Soap, after they'd seen Roberto Baggio, Timmo Asprilla and Diego Maradona?" Recognizing that soccer has established itself as an American participatory sport, Glanville believes that in America soccer has run into a catch-22. Talented American players either go overseas (which, despite MLS, they will continue to do if they want top dollar) or must "waste four years playing junk soccer at college," after which "their hopes of earning a decent living as a pro in the US are minimal. . . . The Dallas tournament, in a Texas that once seemed an impregnable bastion of the gridiron game, will continue to be the largest, most ambitious youth tournament on earth. Flushing Park [in Queens, New York] on Sundays will go on being as full of football or soccer as the huge stretch of Hackney Marshes in East London. And pro soccer in the States will remain a mirage."[30]

On the opposite page, *Post* sportswriter Phil Mushnick told his readers "if you think the World Cup will leave in its wake the kind of fan devotion and enthusiasm to create and sustain a real-deal soccer league in this country, forget it. We've seen people bleed real money in that same pursuit. And if we need even one more reminder that sports is a business, soccer will provide ownership, not fans, with the downside reminder." Mushnick, who had covered the NASL, cited the precedent of that venture. "Same thing that killed hula hoops. Not that soccer is a fad, but buying tickets to regular-season pro league games in this country was a fad. And it came like a nova, and left like one." Mushnick wrote that soccer *is* dull compared to established American team sports, though he was quick to qualify that statement by noting that this observation is not derived from "bigotry-driven ignorance, nor as a matter of closed-minded protectionism. Don't forget, we covered soccer and immensely enjoyed the task. . . . Rather, we know of soccer's inherent dullness from internationals living in this country. They take to football and basketball as spectator sports quicker, and with a greater enthusiasm and lasting devotion, than Americans have taken to soccer as a spectator sport. In fact, Americans have not yet, on a continuum, taken to pro soccer as spectator sport. . . . The World Cup, should no one get killed, is a fabulous event. Enjoy it. And enjoy the next one. And if, in between, you patronize any and all pro soccer leagues that begin here, enjoy them too. They'll be gone faster than the girl over there with the hula hoop. See her? She's the one listening to the Monkees on the quadrophonic speakers."[31]

Mike Lopresti of *USA Today* listed thirteen reasons, most of which were facetious, why "nonbelievers" should watch the tournament. "But if anyone thinks revolution is at hand in this country with soccer," Lopresti concluded, "disappointment is ahead. It is not telegenic enough for US sports fans. It will not happen. Come July 17, one country will dance in the streets by the millions. Most US fans will return to the pennant races, glad to have seen this just once."[32] After viewing her first World Cup match, the Spain–South Korea opener at the Cotton Bowl, Cathy Harasta of the *Dallas Morning News* came away with overwhelmingly positive impressions. But she still was not sold on soccer's potential in the United States. "The planet's soccer officials constantly tout the glories of this game. The Cup's staging in America is intended to sell us on soccer. Friday night put soccer in a new light. But it will not become a national obsession overnight."[33]

Once the tournament had begun, and after the U.S. upset of Colombia, it became obvious that the World Cup had indeed captured a fair amount of attention from the American public. But that still did not necessarily translate into success in the United States for soccer itself. In the only piece he would write on the World Cup, longtime San Francisco sports columnist Glenn Dickey saw positive signs for the future of pro soccer in the United States and took a most interesting angle on what needed to be done. Dickey thought that MLS could succeed "if those in charge remember what it takes for a sport to work in this country. . . . They should work hard at the social aspects of the game, bringing in the bands, cheerleaders, and tailgate parties. They should have the large electronic boards to show replays and player interviews before the game and at halftime. Instead of thinking the rules are sacred, they should Americanize it whenever possible, remembering that the intent is to broaden interest, not to limit it to purists." Noting that the shoot-out was an American invention, Dickey thought that the offside rule should be changed to allow for the excitement of an offensive player taking a pass behind the last defender and, of course, to increase scoring. Lastly, Dickey counseled patience on the part of the new league, so as not to repeat the mistakes of the NASL. "Now, fans have been educated through the World Cup telecasts," Dickey concluded, "so the new league should be built on a basic support for the game. Maybe we'll discover why the rest of the world has been out of step all these years."[34]

Once the U.S. team had been eliminated by Brazil, World Cup coverage decreased markedly in most newspapers. During the period encompassing the rest of the second round, the quarterfinals and semifinals, there were significantly fewer sports and feature columnists writing about soccer. Those that did, often returned to an evaluation of the World Cup, the success of Team USA, and what it all meant for the future of soccer in the United States. Kevin B. Blackstone of the *Dallas Morning News* thought that the success of the American players might actually provide a major obstacle to the fledgling MLS, since these players would probably play in Europe. "The US team was too successful in World Cup '94 for the new league's good," Blackstone wrote. "This wasn't going to be an easy venture anyway. But without a galaxy of stars, the next launch of the US pro soccer league will be lost in orbit. And, the last thing US soccer needs is another failed opportunity."[35]

The tournament's singular success also led some nationally known sportswriters to change their minds from their initial skepticism and negative attitudes toward the game to a more measured outlook that most certainly extolled the success of the World Cup tournament, if not of soccer as a whole. In an editorial entitled "Goal!" published on its regular editorial page rather than in the paper's sports section, the *Boston Globe* wrote: "In New England, the defining and unexpected soccer moment came on June 23 when 54,000 fans filled Foxboro Stadium to watch not two of the top teams, but South Korea and Bolivia play to a 0–0 tie. The

crowd couldn't get enough. And this despite the pre-Cup analysis from
pundits, including the *Globe*'s Dan Shaughnessy, who posited, 'Soccer
won't sell in America because it lacks scoring and violence, and its running time won't allow for television commercials.' . . . Even Shaughnessy
came around after watching Argentina wump Greece. He wrote: 'I take
it all back. Futbol is my life.' "[36]

Notes ....

Preface

1. Indeed, this quarterfinal game between Brazil and France, played in Estadio Jalisco in Guadalajara, has attained a somewhat legendary status in the world of soccer. Many soccer experts and fans regard it as among the finest ever played in World Cup history, showcasing such talents as Michel Platini, Alain Giresse, Dominic Rocheteau, and Jean Tigana on the French side, and Socrates, Careca, Junior, Zico, and Josimar on the Brazilian team. The much-respected English football magazine *Goal* listed this game as number one on its list of the top fifty World Cup matches ever played (excluding the 1998 tournament in France). See Gus Martins, "History Repeats Itself" in the *Boston Herald*, 9 July 1998.

By using the term "American" throughout this book to denote citizens of the United States of America, I beg the indulgence of all readers who reside north or south of the border of the United States and are thus, of course, "American" though not citizens of the United States.

Introduction

1. On the concept of postmaterialist values, lifestyles, and milieus as essential categories of social stratification and cohesion, see Inglehart, *Culture Shift* and *The Silent Revolution*.

2. On the concepts of Pierre Bourdieu's "habitus" and "cultural capital," see Swartz, *Culture and Power*.

3. America's exceptional position is already evident in the difference between what this game is called in the United States and what it is called in much of the rest of the world. Whereas in the United States the game is known as "soccer" and the word "football" is reserved for a very different game that, however, shares its roots with soccer, most countries in the world refer to the game of soccer by its preferred name of "football" or its local linguistic variations, such as "futebol," "futbol," "fussball," "fotball," "fodbold," or "voetbal" to note but a few. Of course there is the Italian "calcio," the Finnish "sakkaa" (which derives from "soccer") and the Hungarian "labdarugas," but on the whole a version of "football" has come to denote this game virtually everywhere in the world but in the United States. In our book, we will refer to "soccer" when we mean the kicking game played all over the world and to "football" when we have the American running-and-passing game in mind.

4. See Matthew Brelis, "If an announcer today shouts Goooaaalll! Will anyone in this country hear it?" in the *Boston Globe*, 12 July 1998; Kirk Johnson, "Soccer Is Trying to Sell the United States a Bill of Goods" in the *New York Times*, 12 July 1998; and Bob Ryan, "Everyone in the World in on the Fun but US" in the *Boston Globe*, 10 July 1998.

5. See Rachel Shuster, "The American Century in Sports—The Birth of a Sports Nation" in *USA Today*, 31 December 1998.

6. Gardner, *The Simplest Game*, p. 210.

7. *Chronicle of the Olympics, 1896–1996*.

8. Geoffrey Wheatcroft, "Much More than a Game" the *New York Times*, 11 July 1998. Wheatcroft writes: "Soccer leaves most Americans cold, alas. And yet this indifference reflects the curious phenomenon of American exceptionalism."

Chapter One
The Argument

1. See Hobsbawm, *The Age of Extremes*, p. 198.

2. The literature dealing with American exceptionalism, or at least certain aspects of it, is extensive. Here we list only those works we have found particularly important in our teaching and research over the years: Hartz, *The Liberal Tradition in America*; Turner, *The Frontier in American History*; Lipset, *Political Man*; *The First New Nation*; *Revolution and Counterrevolution*; *Agrarian Socialism*; *Continental Divide*; *American Exceptionalism*; Lipset and Marks, *It Didn't Happen Here*; Laslett and Lipset (eds.) *Failure of a Dream?*; the exchange between Sean Wilentz and Michael Hanagan in *International Labor and Working Class History* Number 26, Fall 1984; and Karabel, "The Failure of American Socialism Reconsidered," pp. 204–27.

3. The original title of Sombart's work as published in Tübingen in 1906 by J. C. B. Mohr (Paul Siebeck) was *Warum gibt es in den Vereinigten Staaten keinen Sozialismus?* The English translation, *Why Is There No Socialism in the United States?* was first published by Macmillan, London, and by the International Arts and Sciences Press of White Plains, New York, in 1976. To be sure, socialism existed as little in Sombart's time in the Europe of the early twentieth century as at the century's conclusion, rendering the United States not particularly exceptional on that count. A far more appropriate, though infinitely less elegant, title for Sombart's book would have been "Why Is There No Large, Organized Working-Class Movement Led by a Social Democratic or Socialist Party in the United States?"

4. On the salience of ethnic cleavages over those of class as manifested in the greater importance of neighborhood as opposed to the workplace, see Katznelson, *City Trenches*.

5. Thus, for example, Antonin Dvořák in his famous Symphony in E minor, op. 95, known to music lovers as "From the New World," wanted to capture and convey something "typically American," not Canadian or Australian, to his European audiences. See Heller, "Antonin Dvořák: 9. Symphonie 'Aus der neuen Welt' ."

6. On this aspect of American exceptionalism, see Hartz, *The Liberal Tradition in America*.

7. Tocqueville, *Democracy in America*.

8. Williams, *Marxism and Literature*, p. 113.

9. While the *Boston Globe* is known for the quality of its sports journalism and the extensive coverage it gives to many sports, in addition to the hegemonic

team sports comprising much of the American sport space, the point can be generalized to other American newspapers covering any of these papers' home teams in the dominant American sports of football, baseball, basketball, and even hockey where pertinent.

10. Wise, *Sports Fiction for Adults*.

11. As quoted in Samuel G. Freedman, "Of Those Boys of Autumn, Neither Beloved Nor Lauded," the *New York Times*, 5 September 1998, p. 15. This is a wonderful piece analyzing why baseball and the "Boys of Summer" have held a decided preferential edge in American literature and culture over football and the "Boys of Autumn."

12. Thus, for example, in a virtual mirror image to the prominence of the Big Three in American literature, soccer's presence as a subject of study and literature in Britain is overwhelming. So, a compendium lists 5,629 sources on soccer. Seddon, *A Football Compendium*.

13. Durkheim, *The Division of Labor in Society*; *Sociology and Philosophy*; and Nisbet, *The Sociology of Emile Durkheim*.

14. For a detailed study of the World Cup in France and its singular effects on French public life, see Andrei S. Markovits, "Reflections on the World Cup '98" in *French Politics and Society*.

15. See Guttmann, *A Whole New Ball Game*, pp. 1–12, esp. p. 6; and *From Ritual to Record*, p. 16. We agree with Guttmann that all industrial societies—that is "modern" societies—created modern sports in a very similar way; in this the United States is not an exception at all, precisely the point of the first part of our analytical discussion presented here. However, we disagree with Guttmann that the United States was no exception at all. Guttmann angrily rejects the notion of American exceptionalism, attributing to it only the normative notion of "exceptional" in the sense of being "better," of Americans feeling superior to others, of an "Only in America" belief and faith. What makes Guttmann's argument particularly weak on this important point is that he not only fails to mention, let alone engage, the huge body of scholarly literature discussing American exceptionalism in a serious empirical manner, but that he subsequently devotes entire chapters discussing precisely the different—and very unique—nature of American sports, American sports organization, and American sports culture. Sentences such as "Here, the United States is once again exceptional in that we have no Minister of Sports, nor, it must be added, are our amateur athletes governed by a single voluntary association" bespeak this contradiction (ibid., p. 46) We mean the term "exceptionalism" in an analytic sense, *not* in a normative manner, as Guttmann seems to (mis)interpret it.

16. Karl Marx writes in his *Preface to the Critique of Political Economy* about the contradiction and antagonism between the forces of production (i.e., technology) inherently forward looking and modernizing, and the relations of production (i.e., culture and social mores) retarding and tradition bound. See Marx, "Preface to the Critique of Political Economy"; For the perceptive concept of the "culture lag," see Ogburn, *Social Change*.

17. The best book delineating the often violent clashes between the globalizing tendencies of the economy and the localizing pull of culture remains Barber's *Jihad versus McWorld*. For two fine studies showing how the globalizing tendencies

of contemporary modernization do not lead to the demise, or even significant attenuation, of local—in particular national—cultures, see Robertson, *Globalization*; and Featherstone, *Undoing Culture*.

18. Weber, "The Social Psychology of World Religions."

19. Schumpeter, *Capitalism, Socialism and Democracy*.

20. Pierre Bourdieu uses the term "space of sports" which he sees as the methodological and conceptual equivalent of the field of power. See Bourdieu, *In Other Words*, pp. 156–67. We use the term "sport space" in its Bourdieuian sense, but also borrow it conceptually from the literature on political parties where the notion of "party space" has been advanced.

21. On sequence theory in political development, see Rustow, *A World of Nations*. Even though critical of modernization theorists, Moore also rested his analysis of modern political rule on sequences. His classic *Social Origins of Dictatorship and Democracy* is a brilliant exposé of comparative sequence theory at its best.

22. For a superb presentation of this nuanced view of sports space, see the fine article by Tomlinson and Sugden, "What's Left When the Circus Leaves Town?, pp. 238–58. See also Sugden and Tomlinson, *FIFA and the Contest for World Football*.

23. The concept of "sports space," developed independently by Markovits and the eminent British football historian Tony Mason, came under criticism by Waddington and Broderick for representing in their view "an implicit—and therefore unexamined—assumption that in each society there is a limited amount of 'space' for sports, and that once this 'space' has been 'filled' by one sport, there is no room for other sports." For Markovits, see "The other 'American exceptionalism,' " pp. 230–64. For Mason, see his book *Passion of the People?*; and for Waddington and Roderick, see their article "American Exceptionalism."

24. On the concept of the "liability of newness," see Stinchcombe, *Constructing Social Theories*; pp. 108–18.

25. For a cogently written argument on the power of feedback in reinforcing already existing conditions, see Pierson, "When Effect Becomes Cause," pp. 595–628.

26. On the concepts of "exit" and "loyalty" as options for social action, see Hirschmann, *Exit, Voice and Loyalty*.

27. On the concept of the "mechanisms of reproduction," see Collier and Collier. *Shaping the Political Arena*.

28. We are grateful to Paul Pierson for referring us to the literature on "barriers to entry" as relevant to our project at hand. According to Joe Bain, who did pioneering work in this field, the three mentioned factors are the most salient in defining barriers to entry into a market by newcomers. See Bain, *Barriers to New Competition*.

29. George Stigler identifies "inadequate demand" rather than "economies of scale" as a barrier to entry by new firms into a market. See Stigler, *The Organization of Industry*. For a nice comparison to Bain's and Stigler's analysis, see Nahata and Olson, "On the Definition of Barriers to Entry," pp. 236–39.

30. See chapter 8, entitled "The Dynamics of Monopoly and Oligopoly Pricing" in Scherer, *Industrial Market Structure and Economic Performance*, pp. 229–66.

31. Rosenbaum and Lamort, "Entry Barriers, Exit, and Sunk Costs," pp. 297–304. See also Weizsäcker, *Barriers to Entry*.

32. On the concept of "critical junctures," see the superb article by Pierson, "Path Dependence, Increasing Returns, and the Study of Politics"; on the concept of realignments and de-alignments in electoral politics and the topography of a society's party system, particularly that of the United States, see Burnham *Critical Elections and the Mainsprings of American Politics*; "Party Systems and the Political Process."

33. See, for example, Goodwin *Wait until Next Year*, as an example of the devotion and loyalty that a team—in this case the Brooklyn Dodgers—developed with its fans.

34. Roman Horak, as quoted in Demmel, "Ballfieber," p. 22.

35. Seabrook, "Tackling the Competition," pp. 42–51.

36. Lipset and Rokkan, "Cleavage Structures, Party Systems and Voter Alignment," pp. 1–64.

37. Barra, "The Best Quarterback Ever. Joe Montana? Otto Graham? Nope. By any statistical measure, it's the 49ers' Steve Young." The *New York Times Magazine*, 11 January 1998, pp. 28, 29.

38. In his otherwise insightful interpretation of modern sports, Allen Guttmann argues that one of the most essential characteristics of modern sports—as opposed to old games and traditional contests—is their quantification, measurability, and statistical accountability. While this is certainly true for the North American sports of baseball, football, basketball, and hockey, it has decidedly not been the case for soccer and rugby, for example, both of which most definitely qualify as "modern." See Guttmann, *From Ritual to Record*.

39. Bloch, *The Historian's Craft*.

40. The "Ernie Banks phenomenon" exists in the world of soccer and outside the United States as well. Many soccer greats never attained the pinnacle of their sport, in terms of winning the World Cup, the European Championship, or the Copa Libertadores with their country's national team, or of winning the European Champion's Cup, its South American counterpart, or the Super Cup with their club teams.

41. Here we are altering Paul Hoch's useful term of "sexual apartheid" to "gender apartheid" so as to underline what we believe to be mainly a socially and culturally constructed, rather than a physically based, form of discrimination. See Hoch, *Rip off the Big Game*, pp. 147–66.

42. The following data from a CBS News Poll of 13 September 1997 bear this out: To the question, "How much do you regularly watch or follow men's sports—a lot, some, not much, or not at all?" 29% responded "a lot," 30% replied "some," 24% "not much," and 17% "not at all." To the parallel question pertaining to women's sports, the corresponding figures were 3% "a lot," 28% "some," 34% "not much," 34% "not at all" (1% did not know, or provided no answer). When those who regularly watch sports were asked, "Which sports do

you enjoy watching the most—men's sports or women's sports?" the tally was as
follows: men's 78%, women's 7%, both equally 12%, don't know/no answer
3%. (The survey was conducted by telephone between August 17 and 19, 1997,
with a representative national sample of 1,307 adults in the United States.) Had
the survey differentiated between team and individual sports, the results would
have undoubtedly reflected an even stronger bias favoring male over female
sports.

43. "In the News," in *Soccer America*, volume 53, number 29 (27 July 1998),
p. 38.

44. The following event confirms the strongly gendered and historicized nature
of hegemonic sports cultures:

In August 1995 Andrei Markovits taught a course on sports, society, and politics in Germany to thirty German students hailing from a diversity of disciplines.
The group, all the equivalent to National Merit Scholars in the United States, was
equally divided between young men and women, most between the ages of twenty
and twenty-three.

To demonstrate the gendered and historicized nature of hegemonic sports, Markovits asked each individual in the class to write down as many names of the 1954
German World Champion team as he/she could. While none of the young women
came up with any names, all the young men knew the names of at least three
players, some knew as many as eight. Two male students recited all eleven members of the team, just as if they had been the team's contemporaries rather than
nearly two generations removed from it.

45. Moore, *Social Origins of Dictatorship and Democracy*.

46. Frederic Chambon, "Les Bleus jouent pour ceux qui n'ont pas de billets,"
in the World Cup supplement of *Le Monde*, 11 July 1998; and " 'Wake up'
Deschamps tells French fans" *Yahoo! Inc and Agence-France-Press*, 11 July 1998.

47. Christopher Clarey, "French Players Ask Fans for Loud Support inside Stadium" in the *New York Times*, 10 July 1998.

48. As quoted in Duncan Irving, " 'Team 3B' captures hearts and minds," in
Soccer America, volume 53, number 29 (27 July 1998), p. 12.

49. This is an interesting case, in which we can clearly see that national allegiance is accorded more to a person than to a machine. Thus, the German fans
and the general public follow and root for Michael Schumacher even though he
drives for Ferarri, an Italian construction. And they decidedly root against Schumacher's main rival, Mikka Hakkinen, a Finn who drives for Mercedes, a German
company.

50. For the intolerance on the part of the French crowd at Roland Garros fu-
eled by nationalism, see Bertrand Poirot-Delpech, "Les Nouveaux Dieux du
stade," in *Le Monde*, 10 June 1998.

51. See Markovits, "Reflections on the World Cup '98."

52. Patricia Jolly, "Naissance d'une nation de football," in *Le Monde*, World
Cup supplement, 7 July 1998, p. 3.

53. Thus, for example, it is commonplace in Germany to contextualize the
national team's performance within the framework of German politics. A number
of commentators have referred to the great 1972 European championship team
as an expression of the open-mindedness and progressive politics of the Brandt-

Scheel government of the time. The more plodding teams of the 1980s were often associated with the retrenchment and drabness of the Kohl-Genscher governments. For an excellent analysis of the parallels between the Federal Republic of the 1950s and Germany's 1954 World championship team as well as this team's alleged embodiment of West Germany's essence, see Heinrich, *Tooor! Toor! Tor.*

54. Great Britain and the United States dominated the five Olympic Games held before World War I (1896, 1900, 1904, 1908, and 1912). Among the total of 211 gold medals awarded in this period, the United States won 82 and Britain 36, bringing their total to 118 or 55.7 percent of all the gold medals obtained by winners in these five Olympics. Add the twelve gold medals won by Australians, South Africans, and Canadians, the "Anglo-Saxon" total of 130 gold medals yields 61.3 percent of all the gold medals awarded (*Encyclopedia Americana* Number 20 (1982); pp. 723b–23r.) This is yet another clear manifestation of the fact that the invention, development, and practice of organized sports were very much the domain of the most decidedly bourgeois societies at the turn of the century: the United States and Great Britain.

55. Thus, for example, the British invented yet another staple of modern life, that of mass tourism. First developed by and for the British middle class, it, too, just like sports, would become a mainstay of all industrial societies during the course of the twentieth century.

56. Michael Oriard has superbly captured the essence of this "special relationship" between Great Britain and the United States, highlighting the American side of the dilemma: "As former colonials, Americans looked to the mother country for leadership in athletic matters as surely as they imitated British art, literature, and other cultural expressions in the nineteenth century. But it is equally important to note our distinctive adaptations of English sporting customs. The historical moment of America's colonizing, the rejection of monarchy and aristocracy for an egalitarian ideal, and the consequent differences in American social, political, and educational institutions had profound implications for the native sports culture." Michael Oriard, *Sporting with the Gods*, p. 87. This passage is from the book's chapter two, "In the Land of Merriwell: Fair Play and American Sports Culture."

57. Still the most comprehensive comparative study showing the university system in the United States as much more comprehensive and all-inclusive than in any other country in the world is Ben-David, "The Growth of the Professions and the Class System," pp. 459–72. By analyzing detailed historical data from countries such as Belgium, Denmark, Holland, France, Great Britain, Germany, Switzerland, Sweden, Italy, Austria, Japan, and Canada, Ben-David convincingly demonstrates that the system of higher education in the United States has been far and away the most egalitarian of all. In addition to this comparative finding representing an important ingredient for this particular aspect of our "American exceptionalism" argument, it is crucial to note that Ben-David dates this egalitarian development in American higher education with the end of the Civil War (ibid., p. 472). This expansion coincides almost perfectly with the growth of American sports and the institutionalization of the Big Three in American life. The role of higher education in the development and institutionalization of sports as a mass phenom-

enon in America has been part and parcel of the same basic tenet: that of the early and thorough bourgeoisification of American public life and culture.

58. See Hoehn and Szymanski, "The Americanization of European Football," pp. 205–40.

59. Rudolf Hilferding uses the term "organized capitalism" in his influential *Finance Capital.*

60. See Katzenstein, *Policy and Politics in West Germany.*

61. Hoehn and Szymanski, "The Americanization of European Football", p. 213.

62. Bob Ryan, "Game of Numbers Fascinates," in the *Boston Globe*, 29 August 1998, p. G1.

Chapter Two
The Formation of American Sport Space

1. As quoted in Rachel Shuster, "The American Century in Sports: The Birth of a Sports Nation." in *USA Today*, 31 December 1998.

2. The Doubleday myth was persuasively disproved by Henderson in his 1947 publication *Bat, Ball and Bishop*. Henderson also sought to establish that base-ball, along with all ball and bat games and all racquet games, is "merely" a descendent of an ancient Egyptian fertility rite. Eventually, such rituals were co-opted by later pagans, and finally by Christian clerics. By the middle ages, games such as stool ball were being played by young men and women in conjunction with religious and quasi-religious festivals, and by boys and girls in more secular settings. Though Henderson's theory requires an unswerving faith in total cultural continuity (including the belief that the Egyptians somehow journeyed to the Americas, since ball and racquet games are also found in ancient Aztec rituals), he clearly demonstrates that the act of whacking a thrown object with a piece of wood was not an unheard of amusement in premodern times.

3. Ibid., 132–36, 140–42.

4. Ibid., 132–36. Harold Seymour, *Baseball, Volume I: The Early Years*, pp. 5–6.

5. Voigt, *American Baseball*, pp. xxi–xxvi. Charles Alexander, *Our Game*, p. 3. Kirsch, *The Creation of American Team Sports*, pp. 11–17. Kirsch cites and describes "the appearance of an ideological justification of athletics that would supercede the traditional religious and social objections to sport in the United States." See also, Adelman, *A Sporting Time*, pp. 99–100, 277–84.

6. Seymour, I: pp. 7–8. Henderson, pp. 145–60. Spalding, *America's National Game*, pp. 41–42. Smith, *Baseball*, pp. 26–28.

7. Voigt, xxv–xxvi. Kirsch, p. 3. Seymour, I: pp. 7–8. Spalding, pp. 29–37.

8. Voigt, xxvi. Henderson, passim. For analysis of the early American sporting scene, the development of an American "sportsman's ethic," and accounts of the origins and early histories of horse racing, boxing, and parlor games in the United States, see Dizikis. *Sportsmen and Gamesmen*. See Adelman, pp. 27–54, for an account of horse racing in its initial stages of modernization, and pp. 55–74, for "harness racing as the first modern sport."

9. Adelman, pp. 101–102. Kirsch, pp. 21–22.

10. Kirsch, pp. 26, 161. Seymour, I: pp. 14–15. Adelman, pp. 269–77. Any study of American sports in the nineteenth century will inevitably cite clippings from William T. Porter's *Spirit of the Times*, which had achieved popularity by the late 1840s. *The Spirit* "itself became a kind of national sporting center, one of those informal, voluntary associations that, at this time, so impressed Alexis de Tocqueville." (Dizikis, p. 55). For an account of Porter and his creation, see Dizikis, pp. 47–65.

11. Seymour, I: p. 15. Smith, pp. 32–36. Henderson, p. 161. Kirsch, p. 57. Spalding, p. 49.

12. Seymour, I: pp. 19–20. Henderson, pp. 163–65, includes the actual rules as originally written. Spalding, pp. 50–52. Alexander, pp. 4–6. See Burk, *Never Just a Game*, p. 245, for a chart of National League rule changes and institution of the "lively ball" in 1920 as compared to batting averages. Overhand pitching was not allowed until 1884.

See also, Goldstein, *Playing For Keeps*, pp. 48–53. Goldstein's thesis rests upon an analysis of the way baseball evolved from recreation, which could be construed as "boyish," to competition, which was viewed as "mannish." Both terms were "loaded" in nineteenth-century America; when baseball players began to "play for keeps" the game became widely acceptable as "manly" behavior.

13. Adelman (p. 122) finds that "several references in the *New York Herald* in late 1845, unnoticed by other historians, provide early insights into the New York Club and the early history of organized baseball" that qualify the New York Club as truly organized, "although not, in all likelihood, to the same degree as the Knickerbockers." The Knickerbockers' position as baseball's first organized team and Cartwright's reputation as the progenitor of modern baseball's rules remain mostly undiminished.

14. According to Adelman (pp. 122–24), "the occupational structure of the Knickerbockers indicates that the members were drawn at least from the middle class, but there is no evidence to support the contention that on the whole they were from the city's upper class or were wealthy urban gentlemen."

15. Seymour, I: pp. 20–22. Voigt, p. 8. Adelman, p. 124.

16. Seymour, I: p. 14. Adelman, pp. 126–27.

17. Seymour, I: p. 52: "*Spirit of the Times* reported that the large crowds at the Elysian Fields in 1857 were attracted by the chance to bet as much as by the game itself and the fame of the players. In an 1857 match between the Gothams and Atlantics, it was said that seven out of ten of cognoscenti were ready to 'plant their tin' on the Gothams at two and three to one. Worse yet, Mr. Morrow, an umpire, allegedly had a bet on a game in which he was officiating." Betting on cricket matches was commonplace.

18. Seymour, I: p. 24. Kirsch, pp. 125, 130–36. Adelman, pp. 125–26, 138–42. Goldstein, pp. 28–31. The organization of early baseball clubs was patterned after volunteer fire companies, who held competitions among themselves in the firefighting arts of the era. Goldstein sees an important link between the adoption of baseball uniforms (which resembled those of firemen) and the evolution of the game as a serious on-field activity and spectator sport. On the Tweed-Mutual connection (begun in 1857), see Vincent, *Mudville's Revenge*, pp. 89, 101–104.

19. Goldstein, p. 21. Seymour, I: pp. 62–63. Adelman, p. 129.

20. Voigt, p. 10. Seymour, I: p. 25. Kirsch, p. 59–60. Spalding, pp. 70–74. Brooklyn was still a separate municipality from New York at this time. Seymour, I: p. 36. Seymour, I: p. 35. Adelman, pp.127–28. Seymour, I: pp. 36–37. Kirsch, p. 64. Goldstein, pp. 44–48. Goldstein interprets this exclusion of players under the age of twenty-one as yet another reflection of the dichotomy between "boy-ishness" and "manliness." Seymour, I: p. 46, chart illustrating clubs represented at NABBP conventions, 1857–68.

21. Seymour, I: pp. 28–29: "Displacement of the 'Massachusetts game' dates from 1857, when Edward G. Saltzman of the New York Gothams went to New England to work at his trade of watch case making. He soon was teaching his shopmates how to play ball in the New York manner."

22. Kirsch, pp. 169–70. That cricket as played by gentlemen was (and still is) less exciting to watch than baseball for most of those familiar with baseball is part of the equation regarding why cricket failed in America. Whether this is due to national indoctrination or the actual structure of each respective game is likely to remain an unresolved debate between the adherents of both.

23. Tyrell, "The Emergence of Modern American Baseball c. 1850–80," pp. 205–26.

24. Kirsch, pp. 97–99, pp. 103–108. Adelman, pp. 107–10. Kirsch, pp. 29–33, 121, 195–96. Professional cricketers generally resembled the golf or tennis pro one may find nowadays at a country club. Their job was mainly to instruct club members on the finer points of the game, though they quite often participated in matches.

25. Spalding, 180–86. Though certainly not an unbiased source, Spalding participated in this contest. The first match was a baseball game won by the Americans at a score closer than expected.

26. Kirsch, pp. 99–103. Adelman, pp. 98–101, 110–16, 118–19.

27. Quoted in Adelman, p. 107. Adelman, pp. 107–108. Kirsch, pp. 33–34.

28. Seymour, I: p. 32. Kirsch, I: p. 60–61. Goldstein, pp. 18–19. *Brooklyn Eagle*, 30 October 1860, and *New York Clipper* 8 (2 February 1861), p. 322. Quoted in Adelman, p. 132, n. 56.

29. Voigt, *American Baseball*, p. 11: "Perhaps the largest crowd of the nineteenth century was the throng of forty thousand Union soldiers who watched a Christmas Day game in 1862 between two picked nines of their comrades." Seymour, I: pp. 47–56. Kirsch, pp. 230–56. Goldstein, pp. 84–100.

30. Goldstein, pp. 112–19. Vincent, pp. 123–29. The Red Stockings' owner and founder, A. B. Champion, established the club to further his own business and political ambitions. The Red Stockings' model for fielding a team was quickly copied by the Chicago White Sox . Voigt, pp. 23–34. Goldstein, pp. 112–19. Adelman, pp. 170–72.

31. Spalding, p. 193. For a detailed biography of Spalding and his role in baseball, see Levine, *A. G. Spalding and the Rise of Baseball.*

32. Seymour, I: pp. 75–85. Voigt, pp. 60–79. Vincent, pp. 123–56. Burk, pp. 50–80. Seymour, I: pp. 135–47. Voigt, pp. 121–53. Alexander, pp. 121–53. Vincent, pp. 163–64, passim.

33. On the reserve clause, see Burk, Voigt, Seymour, passim. For two opposing views on the General Agreement, see Obojski. *Bush League*; and Neil J. Sullivan.

The Minors. The traditional interpretation concedes—in Obojski's words—that "there has to be a minors in order for there to be a majors." However, Sullivan demonstrates that over the course of barely a decade, the National League was able to manipulate the short-term interests of ownership in all other leagues to impose its dominance and create first the perception and *then* the reality of "majors and minors."

34. A *New York Times* editorial of 30 August 1881 stated that "[as] base ball is gradually dying out in this country probably the time is now ripe for a revival of cricket. [Baseball] was in the beginning a sport unworthy of men—it is now, in its fully developed state, unworthy of gentlemen" (cited in Vincent, pp. 120–21). Vincent cogently explicates the class differences, perceptions, and timing in the proliferation of baseball and how the perpetual antipathy of American "high society" was not an obstacle to baseball's hegemonic capture of the American sports space.

35. Seymour, I: pp. 148–61, 221–39. Voigt, pp. 121–69. Vincent, pp. 180–221. Alexander, pp. 35–58. Burk, pp. 81–115. Baseball historians generally refer to the Players League as the "revolt of the serfs."

36. Seymour, I: pp. 289–306. Voigt, pp. 225–40. Alexander, pp. 58–75. Burk, 116–41.

37. Seymour, I: pp. 307–24, 343–44. Voigt, pp. 303–12. Alexander, pp. 75–83. Murdock, *Ban Johnson*, pp. 30–66. The rise of a reform-oriented enterprise such as the American League can be viewed within the context of the Progressive Era and increasing urbanization. Demands for the reform of baseball were part of an overall discourse regarding reform of American politics, government, social institutions, and business. See Riess. *Touching Base.*

38. Seymour, *Baseball, Volume II: The Golden Age*, pp. 3–18. The World Series was not played in 1904 because of a feud between Johnson and New York Giants manager John McGraw.

39. On minor leagues and minor league teams, see Obojski, *Bush League*; and Sullivan, *The Minors.* For a view of what likely was the most successful minor league in the twentieth century, see O'Neal. *The Pacific Coast League.* On the Federal League and its challenge to Major League Baseball, see Seymour, II: pp. 196–213.

40. Seymour, II: pp. 93–95.

41. The definitive work and source on the entire Black Sox scandal is still (and will likely always remain) Asinof, *Eight Men Out.* Also, see Seymour, II: pp. 294–330; and Murdock, pp. 179–92. On Landis, see Seymour, II: pp. 367–59, 419–22. Additionally, though occasionally lapsing into hagiography and completely eliding the issue of race and the judge's role in the perpetuation of baseball's "color line," see Spink, *Judge Landis and 25 Years of Baseball.*

42. That Landis "saved baseball" and revived interest in it after the Black Sox scandal is in good part myth. See Seymour, II: pp. 420–21.

43. It is also at this juncture that "Americanism" and American culture in particular began a successful intrusion into the Old World in a massive way. American films, music, dance, fashion, celebrities, production systems (Fordism and Taylorism)—but, tellingly, *not* American sports—became part of Europe's quotidian cultural fare in the course of the 1920s. On the transfer of Americanism and Amer-

ican culture to Europe in the 1920s, see Nolan, *Visions of Modernity*; and *Imagining America*; and de Grazia, *The Culture of Consent.*

44. Seymour, II: pp. 423–33. Spink, p. 95.

45. Aside from Ruth (whose fame was unsurpassed), athletes from other sports became media celebrities on a par with the biggest movie stars of the time (who, in turn, were also experiencing an exponential rise in income and fame). Boxing provided Jack Dempsey and his foil Gene Tunney, golf had Bobby Jones, and tennis "Big" Bill Tilden. Red Grange became known as "the Babe Ruth of football." Bill Gonsalves would become known as "the Babe Ruth of American soccer." In the 1970s, the American media often referred to Pelé as "the Babe Ruth of soccer."

46. For organized baseball in the 1920s, see Seymour, II: pp. 343–66; and Alexander, pp. 130–35. On the industrial leagues and company teams, see Seymour, *Baseball, Volume III: The People's Game*, pp. 213–75.

47. Seymour, II: p. 346; and Radar, *American Sports*, p. 118. Many networks and local stations featured "sports story" shows, usually consisting of anecdotes told by a sportswriter or coach. As many stations could not afford the telephone transmission rates to cover baseball games live on-site, the art of "re-creating" games from telegraph copy was utilized. (Among those who made a living, for a while, at this form of broadcasting was an aspiring actor named Ronald Reagan.) The technology to facilitate affordable live broadcasts of most sports contests was in general use by the end of the 1930s.

48. Seymour, I: p. 334; II: pp. 81–85.

49. Seymour, I: pp. 331, 334; I: pp. 278–79, 334; III: pp. 552–55. For history, accounts, and anecdotes of blacks and baseball, see Seymour, III: pp. 531–609; Peterson, *Only the Ball Was White*; and Chadwick, *When the Game Was Black and White*. Competitive all-black teams had been in existence since the 1890s, and several black leagues had come and gone. The National Negro League, founded in the early 1920s mostly through the efforts of African American pitching great Rube Foster, would survive the longest. Teams in and out of this league provided a place for black ballplayers to earn a living on occasion (though at conditions usually far below those offered to white players in the lowest minor leagues) and exhibit their talents and abilities until baseball became fully integrated in the 1950s. In short, organized baseball thrived while continuing to exclude from its ranks some of the very best players in the world.

50. Chuck Cascio, *Soccer U.S.A.*, p. 7.

51. For the various manifestations of soccerlike games in China, Greece, Rome, and medieval Europe, see Hollander, ed., *The American Encyclopedia of Soccer*, pp. 13–17.

52. Thus, for example, even though Italians decided to call modern-day football (or soccer) "*calcio*," as a game played in Florence during the Renaissance was called, the contemporary game played in Italy has absolutely nothing to do with its Florentine predecessor. See Lanfranchi's chapter on soccer in France and Italy entitled "Frankreich und Italien" in Christiane Eisenberg's fine collection of essays on soccer, *Fussball, soccer calcio.*

53. Hollander, p. 19; and Gardner, *The Simplest Game*, p. 210.

54. Prince, "Football at Harvard, 1800–75." Blanchard, ed., *The H Book of Harvard Athletics*, pp. 311, 314, 322, 328, 334; Hollander, *The American Encyclopedia of Soccer*, p. 20. Also, see Weyand, *The Saga of American Football*, pp. 5–6.

55. Prince, "Football Hollander, at Harvard, 1800–75;" 348; *The American Encyclopedia of Soccer*, p. 21.

56. Hollander, *The American Encyclopedia of Soccer*; 21–22, 24.

57. Prince, "Football at Harvard, 1800–75,"pp. 350–53. It still remains somewhat unclear as to why Harvard students so steadfastly refused to play the kicking game. One hypothesis might be that the university's Anglophilia and strong preoccupation with imitating Oxford and Cambridge as closely as possible led it to identify with rugby as the "proper" sport for students. Prince (Harvard Class of 1875) writes that the Harvard students initially preferred to have a football "club" that would "encourage and provide for the sport within the college"; in other words, inclusive recreation for all rather than establishing and promoting "a team" of only the best players for intercollegiate competition. In this view, the dislike by Harvard students of the "kicking game" played by the other schools was simply a way to reject the exclusivity and competitive nature (i.e., "playing for keeps," as Warren Goldstein cogently framed it regarding baseball's development a few years earlier) of intercollegiate rivalry in favor of "the joy of playing and the history of the Boston Game." Still another hypothesis (likely favored by American football players and fans) is that the Harvard students decided to stick with the "Boston Game" simply because they considered it more fun to play.

58. Ibid., p. 358.

59. Hollander, *The American Encyclopedia of Soccer*, p. 25; Prince, "Football at Harvard, 1800–75," p. 363.

60. Prince, "Football at Harvard, 1800–75," pp. 364–68; also Bealle, *The History of Football at Harvard, 1874–1948*, pp. 22–23. As with matches between the Knickerbocker-type baseball clubs of a quarter century earlier, the game was almost incidental. But unlike the Knickerbockers and their fellow baseball enthusiasts, the Harvard students were mostly of genuine upper-class status. Hence, football and attendant festivities such as dinners and dances were initially a vehicle for socializing between the students of two elite universities, long after the baseball world had abandoned such rituals. (See Prince, pp. 368, 370.)

61. Prince, "Football at Harvard, 1800–75," pp. 370–71. Weyand, *The Saga of American Football*, p. 8.

62. Cate, "The First Harvard-Yale Game," Blanchard, ed. *The H Book of Harvard Athletics*, p. 372. As the game at the time was much different (and much closer to rugby) than the football of just a few years later (and exceedingly different from what is played today), so were the rules and methods regarding scoring: One goal (i.e., a ball kicked through the opponent's goal) was worth four touchdowns (i.e., a ball carried over the opponent's goal line) (Cate, p. 376). The definitive sublimation of the kicking aspect of the game (and the total break with what would become soccer) had yet to occur.

63. Hollander, *The American Encyclopedia of Soccer*, p. 26. Weyand, *The Saga of American Football*, p. 14.

64. Prince, "Football at Harvard, 1800–75," p. 370. Italics in original.

65. *The NFL's Official Encyclopedia History of Professional Football*. New York: Macmillan Publishing, 1977, p. 10. In this context, it is interesting to note a parallel between the leadership of Camp and Seymour Martin Lipset's analysis of George Washington's role as the first president of the Republic in the Weberian terms of "charismatic authority." See Lipset, *The First New Nation*, 21–26.

66. *The NFL's Official Encyclopedia History of Professional Football*, p. 10. For additional Camp hagiography, see Allison Danzig, *The History of American Football*, 124–28.

67. Riesman and Denney, "Football in America," pp. 318–19; and Oriard, *Sporting with the Gods*, p. 112.

68. Danzig, *The History of American Football*, pp.14–20. Oriard, *Sporting with the Gods*, p. 107.

69. Danzig, *The History of American Football*, pp. 21–29. Also, Fleisher, Goff, and Tollison, *The National Collegiate Athletic Association*, pp. 35–42. The NCCA would eventually become the sole arbiter of all college sports in the United States. Fleisher et al., clearly explicate how it operates as a cartel in a very true economic sense of the term.

70. On the evolution of rules regarding the forward pass, and the utilization of the passing game itself, see Danzig, *The History of American Football*, 30–47.

71. See Ross, "Football Red and Baseball Green," in Comley et al., eds., *Fields of Writing*, pp. 251–59.

72. Oriard, *Reading Football*.

73. Soccer's reappearance at several elite colleges and secondary schools in this period (c. early 1900s) was a direct reaction to the violence of football, banned at these particular schools. Hence, the perception of soccer as a genteel and effete game for those not up to the rigors of football was attached to the former, eventually to further the negative connotations soccer invoked to many Americans. (See chapter 5).

74. Danzig, *The History of American Football*, passim; Weyand, *The Saga of American Football*, pp. 55–60, 104–28.

75. Weyand, *The Saga of American Football*; pp. 25–26: "In 1883, the Harvard committee on athletics [ordered] the Harvard team . . . disbanded, but it so happened that the Harvard Athletic Association badly needed the money that would accrue from important games. Jarvis Field was in the process of being re-modeled at a cost of $13,000. Yale was in much the same plight."

76. Ibid., p. 35. Legend has it that the game of softball—the recreational variant of baseball that was initially played indoors—was invented in 1884 by young men passing time at a Chicago gymnasium while awaiting the final score for that year's "Game" to come over the telegraph. (See Bealle. *Softball Story*. The prominence of the annual Harvard-Yale contest greatly decreased over the years, and it now does not receive the national attention it received as recently as the 1950s.

77. See Robert W. Wheeler. *Jim Thorpe: World's Greatest Athlete*. Norman: University of Oklahoma Press, 1987; Jack Newcomb. *The Best of the Athletic Boys: The White Man's Impact on Jim Thorpe*. Garden City, N.Y.: Doubleday & Co., 1975; Gene Schoor with Henry Gilford. *The Jim Thorpe Story: America's Greatest Athlete*. New York: Julian Messner, 1962. When it was revealed by officials of the American Olympic Association that he had played minor league base-

ball prior to his Olympic appearance, Thorpe was stripped of his medals. After baseball and a few years in the early NFL, Thorpe spent most of the remainder of his life in obscurity. He was honored by the American sportswriting establishment as "The Greatest Athlete of the Century" in 1950. In 1983, the International Olympic Committee reinstated Thorpe's gold medals—thirty years after his death.

78. Danzig, *The History of American Football*, pp. 124, 176, 203–04; on "the Golden Age of the coaches" (c. 1912–20), pp. 203–31.

79. In the context of discussing professional football's precursors, *The NFL's Official Encyclopedia History of Professional Football* (p. 11) provides an account of the atmosphere underlying the formation of American sports (especially football), which—if not explicitly anti-British—was clearly conducive to separating the "new world's" sports from those of the "old."

80. Peterson, *Pigskin*, pp. 23–44. Such a geographic origin for professional football in the United States bears a striking similarity and parallel to soccer's professionalization in the midlands and the industrial north of England.

81. Ibid., pp. 13, 14–16. Peterson cites evidence that both Harvard and Princeton were paying some of their players in the late 1880s, actually making these the first professionals in football.

82. See *The NFL's Official Encyclopedia History of Professional Football*, p. 12.

83. See Vincent, *Mudville's Revenge*, pp. 8–10.

84. Riffenburgh and Clary. *NFL*, pp. 41–42, 51–52. As many players in baseball and hockey might not attend college, Major League Baseball and the National Hockey League each has its own "amateur draft." Major League Soccer also utilizes such a system.

85. Ibid., pp. 39–40, 41. The marginalization of the professional game is clearly evident in that two of the older sources for this chapter—Weyand's *Saga of American Football* (originally published in 1955) and Danzig's *History of American Football* (1956)—almost completely ignore the existence of the NFL or any other professional football entity, though the titles of both books implicitly denote the "complete history" of the sport.

86. Riffenburgh and Clary, *NFL*, pp. 55–56. For the old American Football Leagues and minor league football, see Peterson, *Pigskin*, pp. 98–100, 120, 123–24, 136, 142, 167, 180–81.

87. Riffenburgh and Clary, *NFL*, pp. 53–58, 63–65, 66. Also, Neft, Cohen, and Korch, *The Football Encyclopedia*, pp. 112–13.

88. Peterson, *From Cages to Jumpshots*, p. 3.

89. Ibid., pp. 15–21, 27. Gutman, *The History of NCAA Basketball*, pp. 8–11. Sachare, ed., *The Official NBA Basketball Encyclopedia*, p. 1. McCallum, *College Basketball*, pp. 30–35. Isaacs, *All the Moves*, pp. 19–20. Vincent, *Mudville's Revenge*, pp. 227–30.

90. Peterson, *Cages to Jumpshots*, pp. 4, 8, 9, 33–34. "The cage lived on in the nation's sports pages for two generations after its disappearance from the court because sports editors found 'cagers' and 'cage game' were fitted more easily into headlines than 'basketball players' and 'basketball' " (p. 34).

91. Peterson, *Cages to Jumpshots*, pp. 22, 24. Gutman, *The History of NCAA Basketball*, p. 11.

92. Peterson, pp. 4, 32–33, 47–48.

93. Ibid., pp. 34, 41, 42, 48.

94. Peterson, *Cages to Jumpshots*, pp. 85–86, 89, 120–26. Vincent, *Mudville's Revenge*, pp. 246–47, 248–49. Peterson, *Cages to Jumpshots*, pp. 56–61.

95. Vincent, *Mudville's Revenge*, pp. 250–51. Peterson, *Cages to Jumpshots*, pp. 54–55, 89. The fluid organizational boundaries of professional basketball throughout this early period of the game's existence is best demonstrated by the fact that in 1919, for example, Joe Lapchick played for four teams in four leagues at the same time.

96. Sachare, ed., *The Official NBA Basketball Encyclopedia*, pp. 9, 11. Peterson, *Cages to Jumpshots*, pp. 95–101.

97. Sachare, ed., *The Official NBA Basketball Encyclopedia*, pp. 11–13. Peterson, *Cages to Jumpshots*, pp. 105–107.

98. Sachare, ed., *The Official NBA Basketball Encyclopedia*, pp. 6–9. Peterson, *Cages to Jumpshots*, pp. 84–93.

99. Peterson, *Cages to Jumpshots*, pp. 99, 107. Vincent, *Mudville's Revenge*, pp. 291–92.

100. Peterson, *Cages to Jumpshots*, pp. 124–25, 148, 150, 166–67. Sachare, ed., *The Official NBA Basketball Encyclopedia*, pp. 15–20. Vincent, *Mudville's Revenge*, pp. 280, 289–305.

101. See Flath, *A History of Relations between the National Collegiate Athletic Association and the Amateur Athletic Union of the United States (1905–1963)*.

102. Gutman, *The History of NCAA Basketball*, pp. 12, 13.

103. See Vincent, *Mudville's Revenge*, pp. 238–42.

104. Isaacs, *All the Moves*, pp. 71–75. Gutman, *The History of NCAA Basketball*, p. 24. Peterson, *Cages to Jumpshots*, p. 108.

105. Isaacs, *All the Moves*, pp. 76–80. McCallum, *College Basketball, USA*, pp. 54–61, 62. Gutman, *The History of NCAA Basketball*, pp. 26–31.

106. The CCNY scandal was not the first such incident (one of the most well-known precursors occurred in 1945, involving Brooklyn College and Akron), just the most infamous, and the one with the greatest impact. See Vincent, *Mudville's Revenge*, pp. 267–78; McCallum, *College Basketball, USA*, pp. 93–96; Gutman, *The History of NCAA Basketball*, pp. 62–67.

107. See Isaacs, *All the Moves*, pp. 159–64; McCallum, *College Basketball, USA*, pp. 96–97.

108. See Arthur Fleisher III et al., *The National Collegiate Athletic Association*, pp. 46–51.

109. On the concept of dyads—in particular the relationship between the United States and Canada in a very telling comparative context—see von Riekhoff and Neuhold, eds., *Unequal Partners*.

110. As quoted in Gruneau and Whitson, *Hockey Night in Canada*, pp. 38, 39. McGill University played a pivotal role in the development of three of the four occupants of the American sports space: The two series of games between Harvard and McGill in 1874 set Harvard on the path away from a soccer-style kicking game and toward a rugby-style running game. Additionally, it was as a student at

McGill that James Naismith developed his fondness for team sports as a recreational activity.

111. Gruneau and Whitson (pp. 65–67) make the fascinating argument that it was mainly baseball that mobilized working-class Canadians into organized sports and "provided an early model for the possibility and legitimacy of professional team sport in Canada" (p. 67). The prevalence of baseball in Canada is another confirmation that the boundaries between the United States and Canada have been very porous in terms of sports culture.

112. Hollander, ed., *The Complete Encyclopedia of Hockey*, p. 1.

113. As quoted in Gruneau and Whitson, *Hockey Night in Canada*, p. 73. McFarlane, *One Hundred Years of Hockey*, pp. 4, 6.

114. On the difference between American and Canadian values and culture, especially in terms of the allegedly greater commodification and commercialization of the former when compared to the latter, see Lipset, *Continental Divide*.

115. Gruneau and Whitson, *Hockey Night in Canada*, p. 74.

116. From McFarlane, *One Hundred Years of Hockey*, p. 240. We could have presented many more incidents of violence from this book.

117. Gruneau and Whitson (pp. 175–96) devote an entire chapter of their fine book to the issue of violence in hockey. Such a major voice in Canadian hockey as Don Cherry's has repeatedly encouraged the continued use of violence as part of the game's very essence and has legitimated it by invoking Canadian chauvinism. To Cherry, it has been European "sissies" who have led the campaign against hockey's violence, which to people like Cherry forms very much the Canadian essence of the game.

118. Ibid., p. 13; and Hollander, ed., *The Complete Encyclopedia of Hockey*, p. 2.

119. McFarlane, *One Hundred Years of Hockey*, pp. 39, 43.

120. The term "hat trick" comes from criket in which it denotes getting three batsmen out on three consecutive balls.

Chapter Three
Soccer's Trials and Tribulations

Many thanks to Susanne Katzenstein for assistance with the research for this chapter.

1. Foulds and Harris, *America's Soccer Heritage*, p. 11.

2. Cascio, *Soccer U.S.A.*

3. Paul Gardner, *The Simplest Game*, p. 212. Foulds and Harris offer an important qualification of this point in this context: "Surprisingly, few of the clubs used ethnic names. In most cases the amateur clubs represented the employees of industrial corporations or took the names of community sponsors. In fact the 'ethnic' naming of teams was a product of the post World War Two era." Foulds and Harris, *America's Soccer Heritage*, p. 31. To be sure, Foulds and Harris begin this very paragraph in their book with the statement: "Many of the soccer clubs were ethnic in their origin." So, according to these two authors, the ethnic naming

of the clubs, rather than their ethnic base in terms of players and fans, was a post–World War II phenomenon.

4. Foulds and Harris, *America's Soccer Heritage*, p. 24.

5. Ibid., pp. 24–25.

6. Gardner, *The Simplest Game*, p. 213.

7. As quoted in ibid., p. 213. Dr. Manning also became a prime mover in the formation of the German Football Association—Deutscher Fussballbund (DFB)—which was founded in 1900. He helped it obtain FIFA recognition. See Foulds and Harris, *America's Soccer Heritage*, pp. 25, 227–28.

8. Foulds and Harris, *America's Soccer Heritage*, p. 32.

9. Ibid., p. 142; also Ciccarelli, "A Review," pp. 56–59; and Frommer, *The Great American Soccer Book*, pp. 69–70.

10. Helmut Kuhn, *Fussball in den USA*, p. 77.

11. Foulds and Harris, *America's Soccer Heritage*, p. 62.

12. To be sure: Soccer in other countries has also not always been organized along national lines. Indeed, in key soccer countries such as Brazil, regional state championships like those of Rio de Janeiro, São Paolo, or Minas Gerais (Bello Horizonte) are still much more important to soccer culture than the national play-off system that eventually determines the national champion on an annual basis. In Germany the national Bundesliga was not established until the 1960s, with soccer flourishing in regional leagues whose winners then determined the German champion in an annual play-off system. Still, in Brazil and in Germany—as well as in other countries where regional leagues assumed organizational primacy in soccer's indigenous history—all these formations had monopolistic standings in society, culture, and economy, with no rival leagues allowed, no challengers tolerated. Moreover, even in the countries with decentralized league structures, all soccer leagues—from the most minor to the major—have been under the uncontested jurisdiction of a national federation, which in turn has been sanctioned by soccer's world federation, FIFA.

13. Foulds and Harris, p. 12; and Ciccarelli, "A Review," p. 23.

14. As quoted in Foulds and Harris, *America's Soccer Heritage*, p. 14.

15. Ibid., pp. 14–15.

16. We encountered an interesting difference of interpretation concerning this matter in Foulds and Harris on the one hand and Ciccarelli on the other. Whereas the former argue that the owners did in fact hope to attract immigrants to these games, Ciccarelli hypothesizes that the owners purposely sought to exclude non-natives so as to attract "society" and its emulators to the games; hence no Saturday matches. However, key to our purpose here is their unequivocal congruence: that the owners, for whatever reason, failed to market their product in a fashion that would have had much of a chance of being accepted by the American sports-interested public.

17. Ciccarelli's research on the *New York Times* is particularly helpful in this context. See Ciccarelli, "A Review," pp. 24–27. Foulds and Harris, *America's Soccer Heritage*, pp. 13–14; and Ciccarelli, "A Review," p. 28.

18. For this point, see Rasmussen, "Historical Analysis."

19. Ciccarelli's repeated emphasis of this point, though often exaggerated and somewhat simplistic, has been helpful.

20. Foulds and Harris, *America's Soccer Heritage*, pp. 16, 38. '

21. Ibid., pp. 39–40.

22. Ciccarelli, "A Review," pp. 56–58.

23. Foulds and Harris, *America's Soccer Heritage*, p. 40; for the most comprehensive and meticulous study of the American Soccer League, see Jose's monumental *American Soccer League 1921–1931*.

24. Foulds and Harris, *America's Soccer Heritage*, p. 41.

25. Hakoah might arguably have been among the very best soccer clubs of the world at the time, since Austrian soccer—Viennese soccer to be precise—was among the finest in the world. No city in the world, not even London, could claim to have such a bevy of excellent teams at the time as Vienna. Indeed, virtually every one of the city's then twenty-one districts had its own soccer team with its own colors, icons, character, culture, and fans. It was not uncommon during the twenties to have ten of Vienna's clubs occupy all the available positions in Austria's top soccer league. Hakoah-Vienna was an all-Jewish soccer club that attracted soccer stars from many countries and gained a worldwide reputation through its many travels. It became the first non-British club to defeat an English team on English soil when it demolished London's venerable West Ham United, 5–0, on its home field in 1923. To be sure, it was a "friendly" and United did not field some of its best players, but this should in no way diminish Hakoah's impressive feat. For a fine history of Hakoah, see John Bunzl (ed.) *Hoppauf Hakoah: Jüdischer Sport in österreich. Von den Anfängen bis in die Gegenwart* (Vienna: Junius Verlag, 1987); for a superb history of Viennese soccer, especially of that era, see Roman Horak and Wolfgang Maderthaner, *Mehr als ein Spiel. Fussball und Populare Kulturen im Wien der Moderne* (Vienna: Loecker Verlag, 1997).

26. Jose, *American Soccer League*, p. 10.

27. Ibid., p. 7 and the book jacket: Thus, Jose speaks of the "American Menace," which drew the best players in the Scottish leagues to American clubs that offered better money. The resulting teams, many of them ethnic, beat the best teams in the world at that time. The decade from 1921 to 1931 became known as the "golden years" of American soccer. See also Foulds and Harris, *America's Soccer Heritage*, pp. 40–42; and Hollander, *The American Encyclopedia of Soccer*, p. 265.

28. Foulds and Harris, *America's Soccer Heritage*, p. 41.

29. Hollander, *The American Encyclopedia of Soccer*, p. 265; and Jose, *American Soccer League*, p. 11. Jose writes that Stark scored 67 goals in 44 games for Bethlehem Steel in the 1924–25 league season, and three more in Cup competition.

30. Foulds and Harris, *America's Soccer Heritage*, p. 42; and Jose, *American Soccer League*, pp. 124, 191.

31. Ibid. Here we follow Jose's superb account very closely.

32. Foulds and Harris, *America's Soccer Heritage*, p. 43. What Foulds and Harris, as well as other authors, call Eastern Professional League, Jose labels Eastern Soccer League.

33. Foulds and Harris, *America's Soccer Heritage*, p. 44. Jose, *American Soccer League*, p. 191.

34. Hollander, *The American Encyclopedia of Soccer*, p. 272.

35. Foulds and Harris, *America's Soccer Heritage*, p. 57.

36. Hollander, *The American Encyclopedia of Soccer*, p. 511.

37. Kuhn, *Fussball in den USA*, p. 34. The following accolade demonstrates the respect that Gonsalves commanded among his peers: " 'Pelé could hit a ball,' said Jack Hynes, who was one of the ASL's greatest scorers himself, 'but he was nothing compared to Billy Gonsalves. Billy could hit a ball and make it fly. He was the greatest.' " (Hollander, *The American Encyclopedia of Soccer*, p. 265.)

38. Jose, *The United States and World Cup Soccer Competition*, p. 101. Walter Bahr's sons Chris, Casey, and Matt also became soccer players who were good enough to play for the United States. Chris played on the American Olympic team at the Montreal games in 1976, Casey on the 1972 Olympic team in Munich, and Matt, the youngest of the boys, played for the Tulsa and Colorado franchises of the NASL. Chris became a rather successful place kicker for the Oakland Raiders of the National Football League and won a Super Bowl Championship with the Pittsburgh Steelers. His younger brother Matt followed in Chris's footsteps, so to speak, by winning a championship with the New York Giants. "My boys' hearts always beat for soccer, but their wallets longed for football," confessed Walter Bahr to a German journalist, aptly characterizing soccer's predicament in the American sports space. Matt's salary for the Philadelphia Eagles in 1993 was $400,000 a year; he had earned $8,000 playing soccer in the NASL exactly a decade earlier. See Kuhn, *Fussball in den USA*, pp. 55, 56.

39. Hollander, *The American Encyclopedia of Soccer*, p. 263; and Foulds and Harris, *America's Soccer Heritage*, p. 56.

40. Gardner, *The Simplest Game*, p. 215; and Foulds and Harris, *America's Soccer Heritage*, p. 56.

41. Kuhn, *Fussball in den USA*, pp. 54, 55. A picture of a smiling and kicking Marilyn Monroe in high heels graces the cover of Kuhn's book and is reproduced twice inside it.

42. Foulds and Harris, *America's Soccer Heritage*, p. 56.

43. In addition to having some of the world's best players at the time, Inter also had an innovative and world-famous coach in Helenio Hererra. An Argentine who had become prominent by coaching in Europe's top leagues, Hererra had invented a defensive strategy known as "catenaccio," which he successfully implemented with Inter. Copied by others, this system emphasized ironclad defense with the occasional surgical offensive strike that was to lead to victory. Many argued that, though effective, Hererra's "catenaccio" lowered goal scoring in top-level soccer and thus rendered the game much less exciting and fun to watch.

44. Gardner, *The Simplest Game*, p. 216. Concerning Cox, Gardner writes on the same page: "Caught betting on his own team, he [Cox] was banished from baseball by Commissioner Judge Landis."

45. The Polo Grounds, prior to its demolition in 1964, had been home to baseball's New York Giants before they departed to San Francisco in 1958. It remained home to New York's new National League franchise, the Mets, until completion of Shea Stadium, where the Mets continue to play to this day. The seating capacity

of the Polo Grounds was nearly seventy thousand, thus dwarfing the usual attendance at ISL matches.

46. Gardner, *The Simplest Game*, p. 216.

47. Jose, *The United States and World Cup Soccer Competition*, pp. 18, 19.

48. Foulds and Harris, *America's Soccer Heritage*, p. 32.

49. For the finest account of this fascinating event and its nonexistence in American sports lore and history, see Geoffrey Douglas, *The Game of Their Lives.*

50. See Arthur Heinrich, *Tooor! Toor! Tor!* Heinrich and other German students of the Bundesrepublik have argued very persuasively that the real founding of this republic was not in May 1949, as the official date would have it, but in July 1954 with Germany's winning the World Cup against a hugely favored Hungarian team on—of all dates—4 July 1954 in the Wankdorf Stadium in Bern, Switzerland. Film buffs will remember the last scene in Rainer Werner Fassbinder's "The Marriage of Maria Braun," which features precisely this moment as it is being broadcast on German radio with the announcer going crazy shouting "Tooor, Toor, Tor" for minutes as the German team's Helmut Rahn scored the third and decisive goal in the 83rd minute of the game to give the underdog Germans their first of three world championships.

51. The contemporary rules concerning permission to play for a country's national team are much stricter: A player has to be a country's full and complete citizen before he can represent it on its national team. Moreover, a player who has played even one competitive match for one country's national team can no longer represent another at any point in his career.

52. Foulds and Harris, *America's Soccer Heritage*, p. 109.

53. Hollander, *The American Encyclopedia of Soccer*, pp. 33–36.

54. Ibid., pp. 135–41. Foulds and Harris, *America's Soccer Heritage*, p. 110.

55. Indeed, the fall season's intensity in American college soccer is—in terms of the sheer quantity of scheduling and the physical demands placed on the players—higher than in the German Bundesliga. This is in the esteemed judgment of Manfred Schellscheidt, a German soccer expert who has been the longtime and successful coach of Seton Hall's soccer team, one of the Big East's most successful. See Kuhn, *Fussball in den USA*, pp. 61, 62.

56. A visit to the sports section of any respectable book store in the United States will reveal a bevy of "how to" books on soccer emphasizing the mechanics of playing, shooting, dribbling, passing, and, of course, coaching, while simultaneously saying little, if anything, about the game's culture and history. It is clear that absent soccer culture in the United States, most books about it must confine themselves to techniques, methods, and mechanics.

57. Currently, underclassmen are eligible for the NFL draft after their junior year, though the league will not grant eligibility to any player until he reaches his twentieth birthday. One or both of these barriers may soon face legal challenges. In direct opposition to soccer—and, in various degrees to baseball and basketball—a legitimate chance at an NFL career almost always requires the background of a college football program. The number of exceptions have been minuscule, most notably a few naturally gifted athletes or impressive physical specimens from other organized sports.

Similar to the NFL's policy prior to the late 1980s, the National Basketball Association had a ban on underclassmen until the early 1970s when, as a direct by-product of the NBA-ABA rivalry, it became possible for any player of any age to apply for the draft. Several have done so directly from high school, most famously Moses Malone (the pioneer of the practice, with the old ABA), Darryl Dawkins, Kobe Bryant, and, after a year out of high school, Shawn Kemp. Of course, there have also been direct-from-high-school players who flunked out of the NBA. The first round of the NBA draft is usually dominated by college underclassmen. It should be noted, however, that a fair number of basketball players who have "come out early" would likely have done much better in the NBA if they had decided to stay in college the full four years. Several ended their professional careers quite ignominiously and much earlier than if they had been the beneficiaries of serious seasoning at the college level. Unlike in soccer, the American college experience usually enhances one's basketball savvy and skills, as evidenced by the many foreign players who opt to come to the United States to learn the college game before returning home to their respective professional leagues, let alone the NBA.

Chapter Four
The Formation and Rearrangement of the American Sport Space

1. See Leifer, *Making the Majors*.
2. Indeed, Robinson had previously been best known for his football skills as a productive running back at UCLA before the war. On this and Jackie Robinson's crucible in general, see Tygiel, *Baseball's Great Experiment*.
3. Radar, *American Sports*, pp. 241–243; Patton, *Razzle-Dazzle*, p. 26.
4. See O'Neal, pp. 101–18; and Sullivan, pp. 209–25, 235–55.
5. *Baseball Encyclopedia*, p. 2083.
6. For an explanation of baseball's antitrust exemption and its long-term affect on the sport, see Seymour, p. 420; also Zimbalist, *Baseball and Billions*, pp. xiv, 8–19, 151–56, 178–82. In 1922 the Supreme Court declared that baseball was not involved in interstate commerce and therefore was not subject to the country's antitrust laws. The high court reaffirmed this decision in 1953, and again in 1972. Baseball stands alone among professional sports in its exemption. Baseball is a legal monopoly, euphemistically known in the field of law as the "baseball anomaly" (p. xiv).
7. The first emancipated baseball free agent was actually Jim "Catfish" Hunter, in 1975. However, this represented a special case regarding a violation of his contract with the Oakland Athletics not related to the challenge of the reserve clause.
8. Staudohar, *Playing for Dollars*, p. 32.
9. As exhibited in the cover story of *Time* Magazine, 27 July 1998, "The Power Boys of Summer," as well as the cover stories of virtually all magazines in early September when McGwire surpassed Maris's record on the Tuesday after Labor Day. See also the Special Section of the *New York Times*, 23 October 1998 appropriately labeled "A Season to Remember."
10. Riffenburgh and Clary, *NFL*, p. 67. Also, Riger and Maulle, *The Pros*, p. 22. "[I]t was to prove the most intelligent move in the long history of pro football.

[Rams owner Dan] Reeves did it in the face of strenuous opposition from the rest of the league; he had to walk out of the league meeting in New York and threaten to quit football before the other owners granted him permission to move." Ironically, Los Angeles—the second largest "media market" and population center in the United States—is currently bereft of an NFL franchise, as the Rams are now located in St. Louis, while the Raiders have returned to Oakland after a thirteen-year sojourn in Southern California.

11. Riffenburgh and Clary, *NFL*, pp. 67–69.

12. Ibid., pp. 69–71.

13. Peterson, *Pigskin*, pp. 169–80. Also, John M. Carroll, *Fritz Pollard*.

14. Peterson, *Pigskin*, pp. 147–67, 193–95. Neft et al., *The Football Encyclopedia*, p. 187. Riffenburgh and Clary, *NFL*, pp. 71–75, 80–82. Weyand, *The Saga of American Football*, pp. 180–90.

15. Phil Patton, *Razzle-Dazzle*, pp. 31–34, 37, 41–42. Peterson, *Pigskin*, pp. 195–201.

16. Patton, *Razzle-Dazzle*, pp. 37–40. As many now forget, this game was blacked out in the New York metropolitan area. Two years later, Huff and the NFL were lionized as part of the prime-time CBS series *The Twentieth Century* with a piece hosted by Walter Cronkite entitled "The Violent World of Sam Huff," considered a landmark of sports television (p. 44).

17. To this day, this has been the only NFL championship game (including the Super Bowl era beginning in 1967) that was decided in "sudden death" overtime. This modus for deciding the outcome of a tied game had only been used for play-off games, where it has occurred very rarely. In 1974, the NFL introduced an additional quarter of sudden-death overtime for its regular season games, which it maintains to this day. NCAA Division I football instituted one quarter of a modified sudden-death overtime in 1996. Deviating from the global norms of soccer and adapting to the alleged American malaise with ties, draws, and uncertainties of winner and loser, Major League Soccer (MLS) initially institutionalized the so-called Shoot-Out to follow—and decide—every league game that ended in a tie after regulation time. MLS was the only soccer league in the world to do so. However, as a consequence of major displeasure by America's soccer purists regarding this American exception—some called it abomination—this method to break a tie was abolished by MLS at the beginning of its fifth season in April 2000. In addition to this change, MLS instituted a few other reforms in 2000 that were to "de-Americanize" the game and render it much closer to the rules and habits pursued everywhere else in the soccer world. Thus, for example, whereas until then MLS had its game clocks count down—as is common in football, basketball, and hockey—as of April 2000, its game clocks counted up as has been common to soccer for over one century.

18. Patton, *Razzle-Dazzle*, p. 39. Guttman, *From Ritual to Record*, p. 141.

19. Patton, pp. 49–57. Rozelle's only significant misstep in this period was the decision to have the NFL play its full schedule of games two days after the assassination of President John F. Kennedy. The games were not televised (all regular television programming in the United States was preempted that weekend for news coverage), and Rozelle initially refused to credit CBS for the loss of revenue. Later, he quietly relented.

20. Ibid., pp. 79, 82, 83–84, 88–89. Riffenburgh and Clary, *NFL*, pp. 89–94.

21. Riffenburgh and Clary, *NFL*, p. 92. Patton, *Razzle-Dazzle*, p. 90.

22. In our opinion, the only pro football player to achieve a greater "cross-over" cultural impact and "celebration" than Namath did so for overwhelmingly negative reasons having nothing to do with football, and long after his playing days were over, was O. J. Simpson.

23. Riffenburgh and Clary, *NFL*, p. 95. Patton, *Razzle-Dazzle*, pp. 96–97. The game was not officially called the Super Bowl until 1970. Previously, its official title was the Professional World Championship Game, though the media (and subsequently the public) had begun calling it the Super Bowl before the first such game in January 1967. (Neft et al., *The Football Encyclopedia*, p. 418).

24. Patton, *Razzle-Dazzle*, pp. 90–91: "The next day, a tabloid headline ran: Raiders 43, Jets 32, HEIDI 14. The NBC switchboard seized up like the nervous system of a junkie undergoing withdrawal; the Circle-7 exchange in Manhattan, of which its phones were a part, was blown out of action. The switch was a result of mistakes within NBC . . . that indicated how little conscious NBC was of the fast pace of the league's play or of the devotion of its viewers."

25. Ibid., p. 92. The game itself was nothing spectacular, as the Jets defeated the Colts by playing tough defense and relying on a conservative, grind-it-out offensive game plan featuring the running of fullback Matt Snell, though Namath completed several key passes. The Jets of the wide-open, pass-oriented AFL had beaten the Colts by playing "NFL-style" football.

26. Thus, for example, millions of Americans learned of the murder of John Lennon from Monday Night Football's most widely known and inimitable commentator, Howard Cosell ("the man they love to hate") during the telecast on 10 December 1980.

27. Gregg Krupa, "Ted Turner Eyes a League of His Own," *Boston Globe*, 3 June 1998, C1, C5.

28. Leonard Shapiro, "NBC Gets In on WWF Football," *Washington Post*, 30 March 2000; p. D2. Ted Turner (who had broadcast NFL games under the old contract on his Turner network, now part of the Time Warner conglomerate) had also seriously considered taking part in the introduction of a new football league.

29. Staudohar, *Playing for Dollars*, p. 77.

30. Sachare, ed., *The Official NBA Basketball Encyclopedia*, pp. 21, 53–60.

31. Sachare, "The Shot Clock That Saved the NBA" in *The Official NBA Basketball Encyclopedia*, pp. 61–64. The NCAA eventually instituted its own shot clock in the 1970s, initially forty-five seconds, now thirty.

32. Peterson, *From Cages to Jumpshots*, p. 182.

33. Ibid., pp. 170–71.

34. McCallum, *College Basketball, USA*, pp. 190–98. Sachare, ed., *The Official NBA Basketball Encyclopedia*, pp. 68–76.

35. In what still remains the single most remarkable achievement for any individual player in basketball history, Chamberlain averaged 50.4 points per game in the 1961–62 season, becoming the only player to surpass 4,000 points in one season (4,029) while leading the league in rebounding (25.7 per game) and placing second in field-goal percentage at .506. Highlighting Chamberlain's year was his 100-point effort against the New York Knicks on March 2, a feat that continues

to boggle the mind. Sachare, ed., *The Official NBA Basketball Encyclopedia*, p. 74.

36. Ibid., p. 135.

37. Staudohar, *Playing for Dollars*, p. 108.

38. When Michael Jordan announced his retirement on Wednesday, 13 January 1999, the international reactions were truly remarkable: German television's most established and leading channel, ARD, made this its featured story on its evening news show *Tagesschau*. So did Israeli, Italian, Chinese, Australian, and Lithuanian television stations. "'From Warsaw to Rome, Sydney to Santiago, Jordan was given the kind of page 1 coverage Wednesday that American sports seldom receive outside North America. In a world in which soccer dwarfs the NBA, Jordan received the highest possible accolade: he was likened to the legendary soccer star Pelé. The London tabloid the *Sun* said: 'The shattering retirement announcement will even drive Bill Clinton's sex scandal off America's front pages. If you thought boxer Mike Tyson, football legend Pelé or racing driver Ayrton Senna were the most recognized names in the world—forget it.' Italy's *Il Gazzetta dello Sport* said: 'His popularity is unprecedented and without limit. He's way better known than basketball itself because he goes beyond its limits: Jordan is myth, poetry.' . . . A headline in the Polish paper *Gazeta Wyborcza*: 'NBA without Jordan?' " All quoted material hails from Stephen Wade of the Associated Press as reported in "Announcement Makes Waves around World," in *USA Today* (14 January 1999); and "Highest Accolades Worldwide" in *International Herald Tribune* (14 January 1999). Leave it to the deep anti-Americanism of the French to give even this unique event a negative spin: "But no American moment can pass unmolested by French cattiness. 'The status of American blacks doesn't bother him,' opined the daily *Le Monde*. 'Simply, MJ is a professional basketball player with an acute sense of business and an oversized ego.' " Peter Finn, "Worldwide, Praise Goes out to Jordan," in *International Herald Tribune*, 15 January 1999.

39. McCallum, *College Basketball USA*, pp. 208–11.

40. Vincent, *Mudville's Revenge*, pp. 314–15. Gutman, *The History of NCAA Basketball*, p. 99.

41. See Vincent, *Mudville's Revenge*, pp. 315–24.

42. Jere Longman, "An Exciting If Little Noticed A.B.L. Final," the *New York Times*, 16 March 1998, p. 59.

43. McFarlane, *One Hundred Years of Hockey*, p. 59.

44. See on this point, Gruneau and Whitson, *Hockey Night in Canada*, pp. 2, 280. Gruneau and Whitson repeatedly emphasize how these regular Saturday night broadcasts created a sense of "Canadianness," reaching its height during the 1950s and 1960s, and declining thereafter for a number of reasons that were to transform the game from its Canadian and North American confines to a global sport. Additionally, commodification of this Canadian icon renamed it "Molson Hockey Night in Canada," making it clear that even a former national treasure could not escape the exigencies of commercialization.

45. Hollander, ed., *The Complete Encyclopedia of Hockey*, p. 399.

46. Ibid., pp. 118, 377. Also Mc Farlane, *One Hundred Years of Hockey*, p. 112.

47. Hollander, ed., *The Complete Encyclopedia of Hockey*, p. 379.

48. Ibid., p. 377.
49. Staudohar, *Playing for Dollars*, p. 140.
50. Quoted in Grahame L. Jones, "When It Comes to a Stadium, Galaxy May Want to Downsize," *Los Angeles Times*, 6 March 1999, p. D10.

Chapter Five
From the NASL to the MLS

1. Myers, "The Formation of Organizations," pp. 29–34.
2. Gardner, *The Simplest Game*, p. 216. In addition to focusing on the four environmental factors that she sees as essential to the formation of a sports league, Myers also features a category that she labels "influential individuals," whom she characterizes as "sports entrepreneurs" with "the wealth, and therefore the risk-taking ability, of an entrepreneur plus a great love of sports." Myers, "The Formation of Organizations," p. 40.
3. Colin Jose, *NASL*, p. 12.
4. Ibid., p. 13; Gardner, *The Simplest Game*, pp. 216–18; Gardner offers an excellent account as to the amateurish nature and churlish attitude of the USSFA. See also Frommer, *The Great American Soccer Book*, pp. 76–78; and Hollander, ed., *The American Encyclopedia of Soccer*, pp. 281–82.
5. Kuhn, *Fussball in den USA*, p. 66. To wit: Boston (Shamrock Rovers from Ireland), Chicago (Cagliari from Italy), Washington (Aberdeen from Scotland), Houston (Bangu from Brazil), Toronto (Hibernians from Scotland), Dallas (Dundee United from Scotland), Cleveland (Stoke City from England), Vancouver (Sunderland from England), Detroit (Glentoran from Ireland), Los Angeles (Wolverhampton Wanderers from England), San Francisco (Ado Den Haag from Holland), and New York (Cerro from Uruguay).
6. Gardner, *The Simplest Game*, p. 218. Frommer, *The Great American Soccer Book*, pp. 76–78. Jose, *NASL*, p. 14.
7. Jose, *NASL*, p. 14.
8. Even a cursory perusal of Colin Jose's encyclopedic compilation of all NASL data and players reveals to any soccer fan the amazing array of top talent that played in this league at one time or another. Were one to judge a league by the famous players performing in it, the NASL could compete with the very best of them. While it is true that most of these renowned players joined the NASL in the twilight of their careers, it is still amazing to read the who's who of world soccer that graced the stadiums of this nation now completely forgotten by all but the most devoted of its soccer fans.
9. Gardner, *The Simplest Game*, p. 220.
10. Ibid., p. 221.
11. Among the 2,243 players (including goalkeepers) listed in the All-Time NASL Player Registry from 1967 until 1979—thereby including the United Soccer Association (USA) and the National Professional Soccer League (NPSL)—published by Zander Hollander in his *The American Encyclopedia of Soccer*, we counted 184 players who were born in the United States or Canada (thus in North America, excepting Mexico). This is less than 10 percent. Interestingly, St. Louis was mentioned by a plurality of U.S.-born players as their place of birth, Vancou-

ver in the case of the Canadians. (Not all birthplaces were listed, making the exact tally impossible.) Still, the order of magnitude is a revealing and accurate reflection as to just how foreign the NASL really was. Hollander's data stop in 1979, since his book was published in 1980. For the NASL's subsequent five years, we consulted Colin Jose's *NASL*. Whereas in the former category (U.S.-born players) the tally continues to hover around 10 percent, it increases to about 18 percent in the latter category (U.S. citizens) by dint of a number of foreign-born players assuming U.S. citizenship in the course of their soccer-playing careers in America.

12. Hollander, *The American Encyclopedia of Soccer*, p. 263.

13. As quoted in Gardner, *The Simplest Game*, p. 222.

14. Ibid.

15. *Dallas Morning News*, 19 June 1994. For a more detailed discussion, see Andrei S. Markovits and Steven L. Hellerman, "Soccer in America: A Story of Marginalization," in *Entertainment and Sports Law Review*, volume 13, number 1–2, 1995–96, pp. 247, 248.

16. We gratefully thank Nathaniel Pine for providing the graphs for this section and those in the chapter's appendix.

17. All these data emanate from *Soccer in the USA 1998: An Overview of the American Soccer Market* produced by *Soccer America* in conjunction with the Soccer Industry Council of America, 1998.

18. See Dermot Pugavie, "Women to Rescue of Uncle Sam," in the *Observer*, 19 July 1998, p. 7.

19. U.S. Soccer Federation, *U.S. Soccer Federation Media Guide*, 1998, p. 162.

20. Paul Kennedy, "1998: A Year When the Numbers Will Count," in *Soccer America*, volume 53, number 4 (9 February 1998), p. 25.

21. Harvey Araton, "A Pioneer in Her Sport and Beyond," in the *New York Times*, 28 July 1998; p. C23.

22. John Powers and Shira Springer, "Profits Starting to Add Up," *Boston Globe*, 10 July 1999, p. G12. "Soccermania Grips U.S.: It's a Sellout for Women's World Cup Final," *International Herald Tribune*, 10–11 July 1999, p. 19. *USA Today*, 25 June 1999, p. 26C.

23. Rudy Martzke, "ABC's Soccer Goal: Big Buzz about World Cup," *USA Today*, 9 July 1999, p. 2C.

24. Richard Sandomir, "Postive Ratings for Soccer Are Raising Some Eyebrows," the *New York Times*, 9 July 1999, p. D5.

25. Bob Herzog, "Lovefest Continues for U.S. Women's Team," *Newsday*, 14 July 1999, p. A65; and Steve Zipay, "Women's TV Numbers Join '99 NBA Finals, '98 Series," *Newsday*, 12 July 1999, p. A43.

26. Jere Longman, "Pride in Their Play, and in Their Bodies," the *New York Times*, 8 July 1999, pp. D1, D4. This was in particular contrast to many of the female soccer players from other nations, notably the Brazilians who seemed to emulate male players with their close-cropped hair styles and somewhat masculine and/or androgynous appearances.

27. See Richard Sandomir, "Was Sports Bra Celebration Spontaneous?" the *New York Times*, 18 July 1999, p. S6; and "Sports Bra's Flash Could Cash In," Melanie Wells and Ann Oldenburg, *USA Today*, 13 July 1999, p. 2A.

28. See Melanie Wells and Bruce Horowitz, "World Cup Loses Ad Game: Red-Hot U.S. Women's Team Fires Up Fans, but Endorsers Stay Lukewarm," *USA Today*, 9 July 1999, pp. 1B, 2B.

29. Carol Beggy and Beth Carney, "Names & Faces: Their Goal Is Now Complete," the *Boston Globe*, 12 August 1999, p. E2. Players from MLS can be found on boxes of Kellogs's Raisin Bran, though this does not carry anywhere near the prestige of a Wheaties "enshrinement."

30. Christine Brennan, "U.S. Team's Impact Will Reach Far, Wide," *USA Today*, 9 July 1999, p. 3C. Such a venture could not be launched before 2001 at the earliest, as the women's national team first embarked on a "barnstorming" tour in preparation for the 2000 Olympic Games.

31. Richard Sandomir, "Sale of Cup Merchandise Just Didn't Take Off," the *New York Times*, 13 July 1999, p. D4.

32. Nancy Lieberman-Cline, "A Women's Pro Soccer League Requires a Kick-Start," *New York Times*, 27 February 2000, p. 37.

33. Grahame L. Jones, "WUSA," *Los Angeles Times*, 23 April 2000, p. D3.

34. Grahame L. Jones, "MLS Embraces Women's League," *Los Angeles Times*, 25 May 2000, p. D3.

35. Joseph Blatter, "USA '94: One Tournament—Two Targets," in *FIFA News*, February 1993, p. 1.

36. For the finest critical book on FIFA in general and its role in World Cup '94 in the United States, see John Sugden and Alan Tomlinson *FIFA and the Contest for World Football*, especially chapter 9 entitled "FIFA's Final Frontier: USA '94."

37. MLS, *1997 Major League Soccer Official Media Guide*, p. 24.

38. According to MLS, twenty-two cities submitted formal applications to be awarded with an MLS franchise. Apart from disqualification for not possessing the proper venues in which this FIFA-sanctioned league was to play its games—the surface had to be lawn, not artificial turf as has been so common in many North American stadiums—most failed because they could not demonstrate a sufficient fan base, as measured by the minimum of ten thousand annual season ticket holders. See Ralf Goeken, "Soccer in den USA: Ein europäisches Spiel in der Neuen Welt" (unpublished Master's thesis, Department of Sport Studies, University of Muenster, 1998), p. 87.

39. MLS, *1998 Major League Soccer Official Media Guide*, p. 15.

40. Ibid., p. 13.

41. Ibid., p. 14.

42. Peter Brewington, "Intimate Facility 'Designated with the Fan in Mind,' " in *USA Today*, 13 June 1999, p. 10C.

43. Ibid., p. 15.

44. "The Official Site of Major League Soccer," www.mlsnet.com.

45. MLS, *1998 Major League Soccer Official Media Guide*, p. 58. Telemundo replaced Linovision in 1999 as the Spanish-language television channel for MLS.

46. Alex Yannis, "A Change of Command at the Struggling MLS," *New York Times*, 4 August 1999.

47. Alex Yannis, "League Turning to NFL, Hires New Commissioner," the *New York Times*, 5 August 1999. If Garber's record is gauged by American foot-

ball's fate in Europe, the future of MLS may face difficult times. Rather than attempting to convey the appeal of the game itself to Europeans, NFL Europe has instead opted to emphasize a circus-style entertainment package in which cheerleaders and other performers are often more important than the sport itself. While people in Barcelona, Amsterdam, Glasgow, and three German cities might go to their respective stadiums to partake in an afternoon of fake Americana and mindless fun, this league's lasting effect on European sport and culture is next to nil. NFL Europe is ultimately little more than a seasoning venue for American players trying to make it in the NFL back home. Some actually succeed, as did Kurt Warner who, after playing in Amsterdam, returned to the United States to lead the St. Louis Rams to Super Bowl victory in January 2000.

48. MLS, *1997 Major League Soccer Official Media Guide*, p. 61.

49. Paul Kennedy, "Francisco Marcos on the State of League," in *Soccer America*, volume 53, number 45 (16 November 1998), p. 16.

50. MLS, *1997 Major League Soccer Official Media Guide*, p. 61.

51. MLS, *1998 Major League Soccer Official Media Guide*, p. 358.

52. U.S. Soccer Federation, *U.S. Soccer Federation 1998 Media Guide*, p. 285.

53. MLS, *1998 Major League Soccer Official Media Guide*, p. 360.

54. Poul Swain, "Schools Come to Terms with the Project-40 Effect," in *Soccer America*, volume 54, number 2 (25 January 1999), p. 22.

55. MLS, *1997 Major League Soccer Official Media Guide*, pp. 45, 60.

56. MLS, *1998 Major League Soccer Official Media Guide*, p. 42.

57. "*Chicago gewinnt Titel, doch Probleme allerorten*," in *Frankfurter Rundschau*, 27 October 1998; and Duncan Irving, "A World Cup Summer Awaits," in *Soccer America*, volume 53, number 19 (25 May 1998), p. 8.

58. "The Official Site of Major League Soccer," www.mls.com.

59. Unpublished research by Christopher S. Allen and Morgan Holmquist, communicated to Andrei Markovits in an e-mail dated 10 October 1998.

60. MLS, *1998 Major League Soccer Official Media Guide*, p. 12.

61. All the data pertaining to the social composition of MLS spectators hail from MLS communications and were provided by Sunil Gulati to Andrei Markovits on 6 October 1997.

62. All television data come from ESPN Major League Soccer and National Hockey League ratings for 1996, 1997, and 1998 obtained by Andrei Markovits from ESPN in Bristol, Connecticut, through the good offices of Bob Ley and Seamus Malin.

63. *Soccer America*, "Soccer on the Air," 13 December 1999.

64. MLS, *1998 Major League Soccer Official Media Guide*, p. 12. For the World Cup averages, see chapters 7 and 8.

65. Jeff Rusnak, "United Too Tough for South America's Best," in *Soccer America*, volume 53, number 50 (21 December 1998), pp. 8, 9: "Vasco da Gama, which began playing soccer in 1915, played both games in the Interamerican Cup with very little rest after grueling transcontinental flights. The Rio de Janeiro–based club beat D.C. United, 1–0, November 14, just two days after closing out its Brasileiro season at league rival Goias. Game 2 came four days after the 1997 Brasileiro champions lost to Real Madrid, 2–1, in the International (Toyota) Cup in Tokyo. Vasco flew 20 hours to Fort Lauderdale and essentially had only two

full days to get ready for United" for the second game between the two which United won, 2–0, winning the Interamerican Cup contested annually between the club champions of South America and CONCACAF.

66. Ridge Mahoney, "Blossoming of Youngsters Bodes Well: More Americans Took Their Places Among League's Elite," in *Soccer America*, volume 53, number 45 (16 November 1998), p. 10.

67. Anne-Marie O'Conner, "Roar of Soccer at Coliseum: *Futbol* Is the Fastest-Growing Sport in California, and a Huge Immigrant Fan Base is Proving an Attractive Target for Marketers." *Los Angeles Times*, 29 April 1999, pp. A1, A24, A25.

68. Ibid.

69. Grahame L. Jones, "MLS Seeks International Flair, Even if It Won't Talk About It," *Los Angeles Times*, 7 April 2000, p. D3.

Chapter Six
The World Cup in the United States

Many thanks to Daniel Benjamin and Josh Gorfinkle for their assistance with the research for this chapter.

1. "Scoring in Someone Else's Game," *Dallas Morning News*, 14 June 1994, p. D1.

2. Barry Horn, "Networks Hope Americans Warm to Blanket Coverage," *Dallas Morning News*, 12 June 1994, p. P2.

3. Andrea Stone, "For USA, Once in a Lifetime," *USA Today*, 17 June 1994, p. A4. According to a Harris Poll conducted 23–26 May 1994, 71 percent of Americans were not aware that the 1994 World Cup was taking place in the United States.

4. Pelé, "Pelé Predicts Successful Soccer Story", *USA Today*, 17 June 1994, pp. C1–C2.

5. "Argentine Genius Prevails," *San Jose Mercury News*, 24 June 1994, p. C9

6. Rudy Martzke, "Malin: Brazil-USA No Rating Surprise," *USA Today*, 6 July 1994, p. C3; Richard Sandomir, "ABC Snores Its Way for 120 Minutes," *New York Times*, 19 July 1994, p. B11.

7. This chapter is based on a research survey of daily newspapers covering, but not limited to, the period of 1 June 1994 to 31 July 1994, including *USA Today*, the *New York Times*, *New York Newsday*, the *New York Post*, the *New York Daily News*, *Boston Globe*, *Boston Herald*, *Washington Post*, *Washington Times*, *Orlando Sentinel*, *Miami Herald*, *Chicago Tribune*, *Detroit Free Press*, *Detroit News*, *Los Angeles Times*, *San Francisco Chronicle*, *San Francisco Examiner*, *San Jose Mercury News*, *Santa Cruz Sentinel*, and the *Dallas Morning News*; various American sports magazines including *Soccer America*, *Sports Illustrated*, and the *Sporting News*; interviews with several American sportswriters and sports editors; transcripts from network television programs; and many hours of simply watching television. In terms of foreign publications, we followed the German, French, Austrian, and English press by reading publications such as, *Frankfurter Allgemeine Zeitung*, *Süddeutsche Zeitung*, and *Frankfurter Rundschau*; *Le Monde*, *Le*

Figaro, and *L'Equipe*; *Der Standard*, *Die Kronen-Zeitung*, and *Der Kurier*, and the *Times*, the *Independent*, and the *Guardian*.

8. It is also interesting to note how often European journalists decried the fact that the United States—a country without a viable soccer culture—was awarded the World Cup. This often bordered on the downright hostile. Some journalists argued that awarding the soccer World Cup to the United States was the equivalent of holding a major skiing competition in an African country. Most agreed that holding the tournament in the United States was FIFA's ploy to make lots of money and had little to do with the game itself. Indeed, many argued that the game would somehow be further demeaned by holding its most cherished tournament in a country that simply did not care about the sport and had no tradition in it. These critics saw the World Cup's presence in the United States as merely another manifestation of the continued commodification and commercialization of the game. As it is well known, many Europeans view the United States as the epitome of crass commercialism and tastelessness. This opinion was widely replicated in almost all European commentaries on the World Cup's presence in the United States. Virtually no European journalist welcomed this development. To many, Americans were simply too stupid to appreciate the world's foremost game and the usual sentiments associated with anti-Americanism reared their ugly head. Above all, the United States simply could not get it right whichever way it turned; it was damned both ways. On the one hand, European commentators decried it for not playing soccer and not having a soccer culture, and on the other hand, they denounced it for being arrogant and/or incompetent for even trying to attain one by hosting such a sacred and hallowed tournament. Even the fact that the World Cup in the United States was the most successful in the tournament's history in terms of attendance at games (nearly 3.5 million) was interpreted by some Europeans as prima facie evidence of America's crassness and materialist obsession. Interestingly, these negative attitudes and sentiments were much less prevalent among Latin American reporters. Could it be that due to proximity of cultures and also a much greater interdependence of soccer traditions and publics, the Latin Americans had developed a greater respect for U.S. soccer and America's potential for the game's cultural presence than had the Europeans? Seamus Malin, the first-rate television commentator, certainly thinks so (interview with Seamus Malin, 30 July 1994). For the various manifestations of anti-Americanism in Europe, see Andrei S. Markovits, "Anti-Americanism and the Struggle for a West German Identity," in Peter H. Merkl, ed., *The Federal Republic of Germany at Forty* (New York: New York University Press, 1989), pp. 35–54.

9. *Miami Herald*, 12 December and 16 December 1993; *New York Times*, 16 December 1993.

10. *Miami Herald*, 30 January 1994; 19 February and 21 February 1994.

11. Pelé, "Pelé Predicts Successful Soccer Story," in *USA Today*, 17 June 1994, pp. C1, C2.

12. Jerry Langdon, "Openers a Bit Short on Goals," in *USA Today*, 20 June 1994, p. C1.

13. Rudy Martzke, "U.S. Cup Win Gives ABC/ESPN a Hit," in *USA Today*, 24 June 1994, p. 3C.

14. As quoted in Paul Oberjuerge, "Soccer Now in the U.S. Public Interest," in *USA Today*, 24 June 1996, p. 6C.

15. "Americans Take Little Interest in World Cup," CNN *Showbiz Today*, 23 June 1994.

16. Alex Pham, "The Other World Cup Players," in the *Boston Globe*, 23 June 1994, p. 37.

17. All these quotations are from Ellen Neuborne, "U.S. Cup Players Kick into Endorsement Gear," in *USA Today*, 30 June 1994, p. B1.

18. As quoted in Rudy Martzke, "World Cup Ratings Exceed Expectations," in *USA Today*, 28 June 1994, p. 3C. All the television data mentioned hail from this article.

19. "The World Cup," in *Nielsen Media Research*, Facsimile Communication, 24 August 1998.

20. As quoted in Dick Patrick, "USA Out Amid Tears, Cheers," in *USA Today*, 5 July 1994, p. 1A.

21. Rachel Shuster, "Give U.S. Team Credit: Sport Is Here to Stay" in *USA Today*, 5 July 1994, p. 9C.

22. Jerry Langdon, "Attendance Already at an All-Time High," in *USA Today*, 7 July 1994, p. 9C.

23. Jack Craig, "Telecast a Winner in Ratings," in the *Boston Globe*, 6 July 1994, p. 49.

24. Rudy Martzke, "Malin: Brazil-USA No Rating Surprise," in *USA Today*, 6 July 1994, pp. 3C.

25. Interview with Terry Cox, Reno, Nevada, 27 July 1995.

26. Steve Fainaru, "Bulgaria Heads Off Defending Champs: Germany Stopped in Shocker" in the *Boston Globe*, 11 July 1994, p. 37.

27. See for example, Usha Lee McFarling, "North End Cafés Just the Ticket for Cup," in the *Boston Globe*, 10 July 1994, p. 25.

28. Jack Craig, "Without United States, Soccer on TV May Be Losing Its Stock," in the *Boston Globe*, 12 July 1994, p. 30.

29. Jack Craig, "Baggio Is Talk of Tube," in the *Boston Globe*, 14 July 1994, p. 46.

30. Steve Woodward, "World Cup Exceeds Ratings Predictions," in *USA Today*, 15 July 1994, p. 3C.

31. As quoted in ibid.

32. Dan Shaughnessy, "Why Not Just Flip a Coin to Find Winner?" in the *Boston Globe*, 18 July 1994, p. 38.

33. For a representative piece of this view, see Paul Oberjuerge, "Soccer the Real Loser with Shootout Policy," in *USA Today*, 18 July 1994, p. 7C.

34. Jack Craig, "Americans Tuned In; Were They Turned On?" in the *Boston Globe*, 19 July 1994, p. 66.

35. Frank Dell'Apa, "For United States, a Cupful of Memories," in the *Boston Globe*, 19 July 1994, p. 66.

36. Sunstantial and credible evidence has emerged since that Escobar's assasination was only tangentially related to his scoring an own goal against the United States.

37. Bob Ryan, "Cup Is on Good Footing in United States," in the *Boston Globe*, pp. 47, 62.

Chapter Seven
Coverage of the World Cup '98

Many thanks to Kate Fichter for her assistance with the research for this chapter.

1. The data tell an important story as the trajectory becomes crystal clear: the *New York Times* basically did not cover any World Cup with its own reporter until the event in England in 1966. During the first tournament in Uruguay, there were six short Associated Press reports, mainly of various game results and—curiously—a brief cable on July 21, reporting that the United States (of all countries) was favored to win the first World Cup of soccer. For the subsequent tournaments in Italy (1934), France (1938), Brazil (1950), Switzerland (1954), Sweden (1958), and Chile (1962) there were never any pictures from the tournaments, nor articles by *Times* reporters—nothing but very short wire-service notes reporting the results. For the Cup in England, the *New York Times* dispatched its first reporter, Granger Blair, who wrote two short reports on game results and four features on teams and individual players. Four years later, there were three reporters covering the matches for the *Times*, including the noted soccer expert Brian Glanville. Even though only Alex Yannis, still one of the *Times*'s soccer journalists twenty-five years later, covered the World Cup in Germany in 1974, he wrote regularly on the event, filing eleven short game reports as well as eleven longer feature stories. Beginning with the World Cup in Argentina in 1978, the *New York Times* regularly sent two seasoned sports reporters to the tournaments in Spain (1982) and Mexico (1986), with the stories and coverage increasing consistently from twenty-two pieces in 1978 to thirty-eight pieces by 1986. By the 1990 World Cup in Italy, the *New York Times* had a number of sportswriters as well as general reporters (such as Ferdinand Protzman and Clyde Haberman) cover the event that yielded nearly eighty items in the course of the tournament, ranging from small reportlike pieces to lengthy and detailed features. Lastly, the frequency by which articles about the World Cup appeared on the front page of the sports section increased steadily from tournament to tournament, peaking at twenty-two in 1990, which meant—in essence—that the World Cup received prominent coverage on a daily basis throughout its three-week duration. By the time the World Cup was to reach the United States four years later, it had become an integral and featured part of the *New York Times*'s sports reporting and commentary.

A parallel pattern can be observed in the case of the *Washington Post*. Not until the tournament in England in 1966 can one speak of any kind of coverage for this event. It was at this World Cup that the paper published its first photo from this event and also listed the teams' standings. From tournament to tournament, the quantity and quality of the reporting increased steadily. At the World Cup in 1970, the *Post* ran ten short reports of games and their results plus eleven articles of analysis, substance, and detailed features. These numbers increased to thirty and forty-three, respectively, by the 1990 Cup in Italy. Just like the *New York Times*, the *Post* also began to feature World Cup coverage on the front page of its sports section in consistently larger numbers: from eleven times in 1970 to thirty-four in 1990. Lastly, the *Los Angeles Times* confirms this trend. Perhaps as a harbinger for its current preeminence as America's daily newspaper with the finest soccer coverage at all levels of the game (rivaled only, perhaps, by soccer reporting in *USA Today*, the *Boston Globe*, and the *Boston Herald*), the *Los Angeles Times* had slightly more coverage of the early World Cups than its two rival papers of record. But until the Cup in England, these items were minor to the point of being negligible. This begins to change with consistency by the early 1970s to the point that by the World Cup in Italy in 1990, the *Los Angeles Times* ran fifty short, result-reporting pieces of the games accompanied by eighty-seven substantial features on every conceivable aspect of the tournament. Among the latter, forty-nine appeared on the front page of the newspaper's sports section. The number of articles *Sports Illustrated* published for World Cups (the magazine did not exist until 1953): 1954: 0; 1958: 1; 1962: 1; 1966: 1; 1970: 2; 1974: 4; 1978: 3 (with the last one the issue's cover story of Argentina's winning the championship at home); 1982: 4; 1986: 5; 1990: 6; 1994: 14 (when the tournament was held in the United States); and 1998: 6.

2. Louis Harris and Associates' telephone poll of one thousand adults on a nationwide basis between 17 June and 22 June, 1998. See also "The Harris Poll" in *USA Today*, 7 July 1998, p. C1.

3. This chapter is based on a research survey of daily newspapers covering, but not limited to, the period 7 June 1998 to 15 July 1998. It includes *USA Today*, the *New York Times*, *Newsday*, the *New York Post*, the *New York Daily News*, the *Boston Globe*, the *Boston Herald*, the *Washington Post*, the *Washington Times*, the *Orlando Sentinel*, the *Miami Herald*, the *Tampa Bay Tribune*, the *Chicago Tribune*, the *Chicago Sun-Times*, the *Columbus Dispatch*, the *Dallas Morning News*, the *Detroit Free Press*, the *Kansas City Star*, the *Rocky Mountain News*, the *San Francisco Chronicle*, the *San Francisco Examiner*, the *San Jose Mercury News*, the *Los Angeles Times*, the *Philadelphia Inquirer*, and the *International Herald Tribune*, which, though published in Paris, we classify as an American newspaper. In addition, our survey also covers weekly magazines such as the *New Yorker*, *Sports Illustrated*, *Sport*, the *Sporting News*, and *Soccer America*. In terms of foreign publications, we analyzed the following on a regular basis immediately preceding, during, and after the World Cup tournament: *L'Equipe*, *Le Monde*, *Le Figaro*, *Liberation* from France. *Süddeutsche Zeitung*, *Bild*, *Frankfurter Rundschau*, *Frankfurter Allgemeine Zeitung*, *die tageszeitung* from Germany. *Der Standard* from Austria. *Neue Züricher Zeitung* from Switzerland; the *Independent*, the *Observer*, the *Daily Telegraph*, the *Times*, the *Financial Times* from England; *La Stampa*, *Corriere della Sera*, *La Gazzetta dello Sport* from Italy. We also obtained transcripts from television programs, listened to sports radio in New York and Boston, and watched many hours of television on all three English language channels—ESPN, ESPN2, and ABC—as well as the Spanish language channel Univision.

4. Sam Dillon, "Americans Are Waiting to Exhale," in the *New York Times*, 2 November 1997; "Americans Get a Golden Point," in the *New York Times*, 3 November 1997; see also Steve Fainaru, "US Leaves the Mexicans Fit to Be Tied,"

in the *Boston Globe*, 3 November 1997; and Frank Dell'Apa, "Tie Supplies United States with a Cup Boost," in the *Boston Globe*, 4 November 1998.

5. See, for example, Jere Longman, "Victorious Americans Qualify for France," in the *New York Times*, 10 November 1997.

6. See, for example, Frank Dell'Apa, "US Makes Strides but Has Ground to Cover," in the *Boston Globe*, 11 November 1997.

7. John Powers, "It's Political Football for US in Cup," in the *Boston Globe*, 5 December 1997; Frank Dell'Apa, "United States Faces Iran Game," in the *Boston Globe*, 9 December 1997; and Jere Longman, "It's a Draw: Politics Aside, the Pieces Fall in Place; Group Hug? Doubtful When It's United States-Iran," in the *New York Times*, 5 December 1997.

8. Grahame L. Jones, "A Shocker: U.S. Beats Brazil for the First Time," in the *Los Angeles Times*, 11 February 1998, p. C1.

9. Duncan Irving, "Coliseum Rocks As Tricolores Three-Peat," in *Soccer America*, volume 53, number 7 (2 March 1998), p. 8.

10. Ibid. See also Frank Dell'Apa's description of this disgraceful event on the bottom of the first page of the *Boston Globe's* Monday sports section: "United States Lacks Kick in Final Against Mexico," in the *Boston Globe*, 16 February 1998, pp. E1, E11. Also Frank Dell'Apa, "Losing Their Footing at End: U.S. Soccer Made Strides in Cup, but Last Slip Shows Work Remains," in the *Boston Globe*, 17 February 1998, p. D11.

11. The average ratings for the Nagano Olympics were a disappointing 16.8 on CBS, down from a 25.4 in Lillehamer in 1994 and a 20.0 in Albertville in 1992. See Christopher Clarey, "Lugers Tell of Drug Temptations," in the *New York Times*, 14 February 1998, p. B18.

12. Indeed, David Regis, a superb defender and essentially a Frenchman born in Martinique, was made an American citizen on May 20, barely three weeks before the World Cup through a little-known provision in U.S. immigration law that permits the spouse of an American citizen to attain citizenship immediately if the American citizen is employed by an entity furthering the economic and/or cultural interests of the United States abroad. Thomas Dooley, the captain of the American team, was German born and became an American by virtue of having had an American GI as a father. Preki Radosavljevic—simply known as Preki to the world's soccer fans—hailed from Belgrade, where he was one of the rising stars of that city's premier soccer club, Red Star, before leaving for America. Roy Wegerle was originally South African; Ernie Stewart was essentially Dutch. Claudio Reyna, Tab Ramos, Marcello Balboa, although either American born or long-time residents of the United States, learned their soccer from their Latin fathers and their South American environment.

13. See, for example, Corinne LaBalme, "What's Doing in Paris," in the *New York Times*, Sunday Travel Section, 7 June 1998, p. 10.

14. Gregg Krupa, "Cup Runneth Over," in the *Boston Globe*, Sunday Business Section, 7 June 1998, p. F1.

15. Stuart Elliott, "A Big World Wide Web Site by Time Inc. New Media Is Devoted to the 1998 Soccer World Cup," in the *New York Times*, 1 June 1998, p. D12.

16. Richard Sandomir, "Nike Swoops In and Pays United States $120 Million," in the *New York Times*, 23 October 1997, p. D30.

17. To be sure, not all American experts and advertising specialists viewed the World Cup as such a boon to business. " 'The World Cup, a magnificent international event, is a joke for most American companies' according to David D'Alessandro, president of John Hancock Mutual Life Insurance Company, which is heavily involved in the Olympics and a myriad of local and international sports events. 'People are looking at the millions of kids who play soccer in this country and they think it's going to become the American pastime. They were wrong in '94, when the Cup was here, and they're wrong now.' " As quoted in Gregg Kupa, "Cup Runneth Over," *Boston Globe*, Sunday Business Section, 7 June 1998, p. F7.

In a provocative counterintuitive piece, Simon Kuper of the *Financial Times* argued that the whole ballyhoo about the World Cup becoming a commercial event on an unprecedented scale was little more than hype. "Not compared to the Citicorp-Travelers merger, it hasn't. The television rights for this World Cup were sold for L73 million [approximately 100 million U.S. $]—a figure of barely credible tininess—and the tournament's sponsors are forecast to spend about L750 million [approximately 1 billion U.S. $] on rights plus advertising. All that money together would not buy 1 percent of Citigroup." Simon Kuper, "Fictions Worthy of a Red Card," in the *Financial Times*, 5 June 1998, p. 11.

18. Mike Jensen, "With Big Business' Bucks, Soccer's Future Has Arrived," in the *Philadelphia Inquirer*, 7 June 1998, p. A1.

19. "A 12-Year Plan for Developing the Best" in the *New York Times*, 2 June 1998, p. D22.

20. Among the best was the *Philadelphia Inquirer*'s entire Section H from 10 June 1998, the opening day of competition in France. Few European newspapers produced World Cup previews of comparable detail and quality of presentation. Also excellent were the *Boston Globe*'s "World Cup '98 Preview" of 9 June 1998; *USA Today*'s "World Cup Preview" of 8 June 1998, which was announced in big letters accompanied by pictures of Brazilian superstar Ronaldo and U.S. goalie Kasey Keller on the very first page of the newspaper right below the paper's logo and above a picture showing Scottie Pippen of the Chicago Bulls making a move against a Utah defender topped by the caption "Bulls Bash Jazz 96–54"; and the *New York Sunday Times* of 7 June 1998.

21. Mike Penner, "Soccer Can Make It in the United States As Soon As United States Can Make It in the World Cup," in the *Los Angeles Times*, 10 June 1998. Penner offers a fine analysis as to why such a win might be a necessary, but certainly not a sufficient, reason to render soccer truly popular as a cultural phenomenon in the United States. While Penner has acquired a decent, though far from nuanced, understanding of soccer, his analyses of the game and its position in American culture are marred by the fanaticism common to any convert's belief in his new cause—in Penner's case, to soccer. Penner—converted to soccer by Gheorghe Hagi's brilliant and beautiful free-kick goal in Romania's match against Colombia at the Rose Bowl during World Cup '94—has to express his appreciation for his newfound love by putting down American sports. See his "Confession of an Obsession: It Only Took One Shot in '94 to Convert This Sportswriter into a

Genuine Socceraholic," in the *Los Angeles Times*, 9 June 1998. In this article, Penner alludes to a commentary that he wrote in the wake of his transformation by the Hagi kick in which he outlines "Thirty reasons why soccer is better than baseball. (There are more than thirty reasons, I know; space was limited that day.)" As we stated in the introduction, we find such put-downs misplaced, misguided, and (specific to the "soccer cause") counterproductive.

22. Ronald Blum, "Sampson: Europe Must Be Won," in the *Boston Herald*, 12 June 1998, p. 98.

23. See "Watch Out Mark McGwire! Here Comes Slammin' Sammy—Sammy Sosa Is on a Record Home Run Binge," *Sports Illustrated*, 29 June 1998 (cover story).

24. Jim Baker, "Cup Spills," in the *Boston Herald*, 19 June 1998, p. 94.

25. "U.S. Viewing Falls," in the *New York Times*, 13 June 1998, p. B18.

26. Howard Manly, "Ice Cold Ratings," in the *Boston Globe*, 19 June 1998, p. E13.

27. Michael Farber, "Is Anyone Watching?" in *Sports Illustrated*, 15 June 1998, pp. 46–55.

28. The *Boston Herald*, the *Boston Globe*, the *New York Times*, *USA-Today*, the *Los Angeles Times*, all of Tuesday, June 16. *Sports Illustrated*, 22 June 1998.

29. "World Cup Daily Report: World Cup Ratings Down Significantly," in the *Los Angeles Times*, 17 June 1998.

30. John Powers, "Iranians Are No Fans of U.S. Film in France," in the *Boston Globe*, 18 June 1998, p. F6.

31. John Powers, "World Cup Match: One-Sided Grudge—It's Soccer for United States, Cause for Iran" in the *Boston Sunday Globe*, 21 June 1998. That this game was much more than a soccer to the Iranians can best be attested by the following little-known but very telling incident. For the World Cup in France, FIFA institutionalized a pre-game handshake in which—following the playing of the two national anthems—one country's players would proceed in single file to shake the hands of the other country's eleven players who would "receive" them. FIFA decreed that global rankings of the teams would decide which of the two country's players would stay put (be the "recipient" of the handshakes, so to speak), and which team would "offer" the handshakes by walking over to the other team. Following this scheme, it should have been the Iranian players who walked over to the American side to "offer" their handshakes to the American players because the United States enjoyed a higher global ranking by FIFA that Iran at that time. But the Iranian players categorically refused to do this since they considered it a servile and subservient gesture. Thus, lest the game be canceled and an incident of international proportions damage an already tense political situation, it was the higher ranked American team—contrary to FIFA protocol— that went over single file to the Iranian side to save the day and spare everybody of a terrible scandal.

32. "What Happened?" *Boston Herald*, 22 June 1998.

33. John Powers, "U.S. Soccer Quest Comes to Abrupt End," in the *Boston Globe*, 22 June 1998, p. A1.

34. Jere Longman, "Enmity Past, U.S. Meets Iran and Suffers Bitter 2–1 Defeat," in the *New York Times*, 22 June 1998, p. A1.

35. Marco R. Della Cava, "On the field, in the Stands, Politics Just Didn't Matter," in *USA Today*, 22 June 1998, p. A1.

36. Ian Thomsen, "Go-o-o Home!" in *Sports Illustrated*, 29 June 1998, p. 34.

37. Michael Gee, "Apathy Fatal for U.S. Soccer," in the *Boston Herald*, 26 June 1998, p. 90.

38. Michael Hiestand, "Cup, U.S. Open Ratings Drop from Years Past," in *USA Today*, 23 June 1998, p. 3C.

39. Ibid.

40. Howard Manly, "Nothing to Kick About," in the *Boston Globe*, 8 July 1998, p. D7.

41. Rudy Martzke, "All-Star TV Ratings Rise 13% from '97," in *USA Today*, 9 July 1998, p. 7C.

42. An op-ed piece by Geoffrey Wheatcroft in the *New York Times* did address this issue, albeit only in brief. Wheatcroft writes: "It's true that the red-and-white-checker 'sahovnica' adorning the Croatian soccer players' shirts is part of the heraldry that President Franjo Tudjman borrowed from the pro-Nazi wartime regime of Ante Pavelic. And some Bosnian Croats celebrated the victory over Germany by beating up Muslims." Geoffrey Wheatcroft, "Much More than a Game," in the *New York Times*, 11 July 1998, p. A23.

43. For a fine article on this topic, see Anne Swardson, "The French Tricolor: White, Black and Brown" in the *Washington Post*, 8 July 1998, p. C3.

44. Kirk Johnson, "Soccer Is Trying to Sell the U.S. a Bill of Goods," in the *New York Times*, Week in Review, section 4 (12 July 1998), p. 1.

45. Matthew Brelis, "If an Announcer Today Shouts Goooaaalll! Will Anyone in This Country Hear It?" in the *Boston Sunday Globe*, Focus, section D (12 July 1998), p. 1.

46. Sandy Grady, "World Cup Frenzy Has No Kick for Yanks," in *USA Today*, 9 July 1998, p. 13A.

47. Josh Dubow, "World Cup TV Ratings Low," in the *Los Angeles Times*, 13 July 1998.

48. Richard Sandomir, "Gooooaaaallll! Univision's Audience Takes Off," in the *New York Times*, 3 July 1998, p. C18.

49. Rudy Martzke, "In the Eye of the Beholder," in *USA Today*, 10 July 1998, p. 2C; "TV Ratings Fare Well," in *USA Today*, 14 July 1998, p. 8 C.

50. David Letterman, "Top Ten Ways to Make Soccer More Exciting":

10. Foreign countries play for the right to nuke each other.

9. Every five seconds, goal or no goal, have that nutty Spanish guy scream "Gooooooaaaaalllll!"

8. Use clever ad slogans like, "Soccer—You'll Get a Kick out of It!"

7. Stop bein' a bunch of old ladies and let 'em use their hands, for God's sake.

6. Add four bases, a ball, and a bat like a real damn sport!

5. Get all them damn foreigners off the field.

4. How about some cars gettin' smashed up real good?

3. Lewinsky!

2. Replace ref with Jerry Springer and let the fun begin.
1. Less corner kicking, more coach-kicking.

Here are two examples of the many Leno jokes: "Medical science has come up with some new—and definitive—research on the various stages of sleep. First, there is REM sleep—rapid-eye-movement sleep—which is deep. But deeper still is the second stage known as Alpha sleep. Lastly, the deepest stage of sleep is provided by soccer, known as the World Cup stage of sleep."

"One of the Spice Girls—Posh Spice—just got pregnant. We assume that her boyfriend, the English soccer player, is somehow involved in this, though I am a bit doubtful since we know how rarely, if ever, soccer players really score."

51. Rick Reilly, "World Cup Lessons We Have Learned," in *Sports Illustrated*, 13 July 1998, p. 96.

52. For a cogent piece defending Detroit and Washington, D.C., for preoccupation with the Stanley Cup and ice hockey instead of following the dictates of the world's fascination with the World Cup and soccer, see Thomas Boswell, "Soccer Can't Match Hockey's Kick," in the *Washington Post*, 13 June 1998, p. C4.

53. George Vecsey, "The Roundness of the Ball, the Madness of the Feet," in the *New York Times*, 7 June 1998, pp. 7, 8 of the Sunday Sports Section.

Conclusion

1. United States Soccer Federation, *U.S. Soccer Yearbook 1998*, p. 6.

2. According to Christiane Eisenberg, one of Germany's foremost sports scholars and soccer historians, the German Sports Federation listed 189 sport categories in which Germans engaged in 1998.

3. All of these voices hail from the third part of the so-called Queiroz Report, called "We can fly 2010." Carlos Queiroz, a Portuguese soccer coach with extensive American experience, was asked by the United States Soccer Federation to write a detailed report on the state of American soccer following the national team's awful showing in the World Cup of 1998. In this report, Queiroz delineates steps that, in his view, need to be taken in order to improve the quality of soccer in America and—ultimately—make the game part of America's sports space. In the course of his research Queiroz interviewed many American soccer experts from the most diverse parts of the American soccer constituency. Queiroz's report was posted on the Internet on the U.S. Soccer web page.

4. As is well known, East Germany's strategy to excel in international sports targeted the "amateur" Olympics and consciously excluded the "professional" soccer World Cup. It designated individual sports as targets of opportunity precisely because they were much more easily implemented in a top-down manner than team sports (which required a much greater network of grassroots activity and a larger pool of potential candidates for excellence). With the state's prime aim to gain as many Olympic medals as possible, simple calculation showed it much cheaper and easier to attain medals in single sport disciplines than in team competition. After all, a country was awarded one medal for individual swimmers and track-and-field athletes and one medal for a successful soccer team with a 22-

member roster. Team sports, in short, were a good deal less efficient and much too costly in terms of human resources when compared to individual sports. Hence, soccer in the East Germans' grand sports plan was surrendered to the capitalist West. Basketball was briefly considered as a possible target by the state authorities, only to be abandoned when it became obvious that the brotherly Soviet Union already had a top-notch team that was always in contention for an Olympic medal. As a result, there was exactly one basketball court in all of East Germany.

5. When a reporter for the *New York Times* asked black teenagers at Polo Grounds Towers in New York City to rank their favorite sports, he received the following unanimous reply: "Basketball, football, baseball, and hockey." "And Soccer?" queried the reporter. To which the telling answer: "You've got to interview some Australians about that." Jesse McKinley, "On Baseball's Hallowed Grounds Young Worship Basketball," the *New York Times*, 10 October 1999.

Appendix A

We extend our thanks to Nathaniel Pine for providing the graphs for this appendix.

1. All these data emanate from *Soccer in the USA 1998: An Overview of the American Soccer Market,* produced by *Soccer America* in conjunction with the Soccer Industry Council of America, 1998.

2. *Soccer in the USA: A Statistical Abstract on Soccer Participation Tracing the Historical Development of Organized Soccer in America,* Summer 1998 Edition, produced by the Soccer Industry Council of America.

3. Ibid.

4. Ibid.

5. Ibid.

6. Ibid. "The National Federation of State High School Associations (NFHS) had compiled the survey since 1971, based on figures from its 51-member state associations [includes Washington, D.C.]. With the exception of a slight decrease from 1987–88 to 1988–89, participation had risen each year since 1983–84. The 1984–85 total stopped a six-year downward spiral in which participation dropped for five years."

7. Ibid.

Appendix B

1. Ray Ratto, "Should We Care about World Cup?" *San Francisco Examiner,* 5 June 1994, pp. D1, D7.

2. Ann Killion, "Yanks Have Their Work Cut Out: Win—*and* Make United States Love Soccer," *San Jose Mercury News,* 17 June 1994, pp. A1, A28. Most of this piece dealt with the way those organizing the World Cup had failed to take advantage of the event to establish and market professional soccer in the United States.

3. Thomas Boswell, "Pay Your Respects to Passing Cup," *Washington Post,* 29 June 1994, pp. C1, C7.

4. Tony Kornheiser, "Soccer in a Sauna: Drip Till You Drop," *Washington Post*, 16 June 1994, pp. B1, B6; "Suddenly, Filled with Cup Fever," *Washington Post*, 22 June 1994, pp. C1, C7.

5. Otis Pike, "Culture Shock of Watching Soccer Is Worth It," *Chicago Sun-Times*, 15 June 1994, p. 45.

6. Jay Mariotti, "Too Many Ugly Americans Spoiling World Cup Mood," *Chicago Sun-Times*, 16 June 1994, p. 111.

7. Lowell Cohen, "Ugly American Should Be Quiet," *San Francisco Chronicle*, 17 June 1994, p. D2.

8. George Kimball, "The Game Could Just Catch on Here," *Boston Herald*, 20 June 1994, p. 21.

9. David Jackson, "Soccer: Beloved or Bemoaned: Let's Show More Tolerance for a Hugely Popular Sport," *Dallas Morning News*, 16 July 1994, pp. C1, C3.

10. Howie Carr, "Warning to Visiting World Cup Wackos: Get Your Kicks from Soccer," *Boston Herald*, 17 June 1994, p. 4.

11. Gerry Callahan, "Beware the Bootheads Are Coming!" *Boston Herald*, 20 June 1994, p. 21; "Keep the Cup," *Boston Herald*, 24 June 1994, pp. 110, 120.

12. Mike Barnacle, "Seeing the Cup As Totally Empty," *Boston Globe*, 23 June 1994, p. 25.

13. Jake Vest, "World Tour Includes a Touch of Country," the *Orlando Sentinel*, 22 June 1994, p. C1.

14. Art Spander, "Should We Care about World Cup?" *San Francisco Examiner*, 5 June 1994, pp. D1, D7.

15. Dan Shaughnessy, "Sorry, Soccer Pitch Is Wasted on Some," *Boston Globe*, 26 June 1994, p. 59.

16. Tom Knotts, "Hey, Soccer Nuts—It's Only a Game," *Washington Times*, 6 July 1994, pp. B1–B2.

17. Norman Chad, "Give Me a (Commercial) Break, Please," *Washington Post*, 21 June 1994, p. C7.

18. Mike Cassidy, "Who Cares about World Cup Soccer?" *San Jose Mercury News*, 26 June 1994, p. A1, A26.

19. Jeffrey Weiss, "Soccer: Beloved or Bemoaned: But for the Occasional Goooaall, It's Boooorrring," *Dallas Morning News*, p. C1, C3.

20. Richard Roeper, "Slight World Cup Fever Cools Down in a Hurry," *Chicago Sun-Times*, 22 June 1994, p. 11

21. Charley Reese, "Soccer? (Yawn) It's Not an American Game, So Why Should I Care about It?" *Orlando Sentinel*, 4 July 1994, p. C7. The *Sentinel* provided a tremendous amount of World Cup coverage until that point. On July 4 Orlando hosted its last game of the tournament, and the *Sentinel*'s coverage of the World Cup dropped precipitously.

22. Bernie Lincicome, "United States Won't Catch World Cup Fever, but That's Normal," *Chicago Tribune*, 5 June 1994, section 3, p. 1; "About All Those World Cup Thrills, When Do They Start?" *Chicago Tribune*, 18 June 1994, section 2, p. 1.

23. Steve Jacobson, "Game's Appeal? Don't Ask Me," *New York Newsday*, 6 July 1994, p. A65.

24. Bernie Lincicome, "Thanks, World, but It's OK: You Can Keep Your Game," *Chicago Tribune*, 10 July 1994, section 3, p. 1.

25. Joe Falls, "Cultures Clash Aplenty As Swiss Squad Scrimmages," *Detroit News*, 15 June 1994, p. F6.

26. Scott Ostler, "Soccer: We Yanks Just Don't Get It," *San Francisco Chronicle*, 22 June 1994, p. B8.

27. Jake Curtis, "Battle for the Heart of America," *San Francisco Chronicle*, 13 June 1994, pp. D1, D7.

28. Edwin Pope, "In U.S., Soccer Induces Sleep," *Miami Herald*, 13 June 1994, p. D1, D9.

29. Jay Matthews, "Soccer's Tough Sell: The World Cup's a Hit, but Don't Look for a Homegrown Major League," *Washington Post*, 23 June 1994, pp. H1, H14.

30. Brian Glanville, "World Cup a Catch-22 for Soccer in America," *New York Post*, 15 June 1994, p. W20.

31. Phil Mushnik, "Cup Won't Runneth Over: Professional Soccer Still Lacks Staying Power to Succeed in America," *New York Post*, 15 June 1994, p. W21.

32. Mike Lopresti, "Thirteen Reasons for Nonbelievers to See Tournament," *USA Today*, 17 June 1994, p. C14.

33. Cathy Harasta, *Dallas Morning News*, 18 June 1994, pp. 1B, 5B.

34. Glenn Dickey, "World Cup Enthusiasm Fuels Hope for Soccer in U.S.," *San Francisco Chronicle*, 27 June 1994, p. B2.

35. Kevin B. Blackstone, "U.S. Success May Be New League's Failure," *Dallas Morning News*, 7 July 1994, pp. B1, B4.

36. "Goal!" in the *Boston Globe*, 15 July 1994, p. 16.

Bibliography ....

Secondary Sources

Adelman, Melvin. *A Sporting Time: New York City and the Rise of Modern Athletics, 1820–70.* Chicago: University of Illinois Press, 1986.

Alexander, Charles C. *Our Game: An American Baseball History.* New York: Henry Holt and Co., 1991.

Andre, Judith, and David N. James, eds. *Rethinking College Athletics.* Philadelphia: Temple University Press, 1991.

Ashe, Arthur R. *A Hard Road to Glory: The African American Athlete in Football.* New York: Amistad Press, 1988.

Asinof, Eliot. *Eight Men Out: The Black Sox and the 1919 World Series.* Evanston, Ill.: Holtzman Press, 1963.

Bain, Joe. *Barriers to New Competition.* Cambridge, Mass.: Harvard University Press, 1956.

Baker, William J., and John M. Carroll, eds. *Sports in Modern America.* St. Louis: River City Publishers, 1981.

Barber, Benjamin. *Jihad versus McWorld.* New York: Times Books, 1995.

Baseball Encyclopedia: The Complete and Official Record of Major League Baseball. New York: Macmillan, 1976.

Bealle, Morris A. *The History of Football at Harvard: 1874–1948.* Washington, D.C.: Columbia Publishing Company, 1948.

———. *Softball Story: The Complete Story of Softball and All Ball-and-Bat Games, B.C. 1250 to A.D. 1962.* Washington, D.C.: Columbia Publishing Co., 1962.

Ben-David, Joseph. "The Growth of the Professions and the Class System," in Reinhard Bendix and Seymour Martin Lipset, eds., *Class, Status, and Power: Social Stratification in Comparative Perspective.* New York: The Free Press, 1966.

Blanchard, John A., ed. *The H. Book of Harvard Athletics: 1852–1922.* Cambridge: Harvard Varsity Club, 1923.

Bloch, Marc. *The Historian's Craft.* New York: Vintage Books, 1953.

Bourdieu, Pierre. *In Other Words: Essays toward a Reflexive Sociology.* Stanford: Stanford University Press, 1990.

Bunzl, John. Hoppauf Hakoah: *Jüdischer Sport in Österreich. Von den Anfängen bis in die Gegenwart.* Vienna: Junius Verlag, 1987.

Burk, Robert F. *Never Just a Game: Players, Owners, and American Baseball to 1920.* Chapel Hill: University of North Carolina Press, 1994.

Burnham, Walter Dean. *Critical Elections and the Mainsprings of American Politics.* New York: W.W. Norton, 1970.

Burnham, Walter Dean. "The 1980 Earthquake: Realignment, Reaction, or What?" in Thomas Ferguson and Joel Rogers, eds., *The Hidden Election: Politics and Economics in the 1980 Presidential Campaign.* New York: Pantheon, 1981.

———. "Party Systems and the Political Process," in Walter Dean Burnham and William Nisbet Chambers, eds., *The American Party System: Stages of Political Development.* New York: Oxford University Press, 1967.

Byers, Walter, with Charles Hammer. *Unsportsmanlike Conduct: Exploiting College Athletes.* Ann Arbor: University of Michigan Press, 1995.

Candelaria, Cordelia. *Seeking the Perfect Game: Baseball in American Literature.* Westport, Conn.: Greenwood Press, 1989.

Carroll, John M. *Fritz Pollard: Pioneer in Racial Advancement.* Chicago: University of Illinois Press, 1992.

Cascio, Chuck. *Soccer U.S.A.* Washington, D.C.: Robert B. Luce, 1975.

Cate, Martin L. "The First Harvard-Yale Game," in John A. Blanchard, ed., *The H. Book of Harvard Athletics: 1852–1922.* Cambridge, Mass.: Harvard Varsity Club, 1923.

Chadwick, Bruce. *When the Game Was Black and White: The Illustrated History of the Negro Leagues.* New York: Abbeville Press, 1992.

Chronicle of the Olympics, 1896–1996. New York: DK Publishing, 1996.

Chyzowych, Walter. *The Official Book of the United States Soccer Federation.* New York: Rand McNally, 1978.

Ciccarelli, Daniel J. "A Review of the Historical and Sociological Perspectives Involved in the Acceptance of Soccer As Professional Sport in the United States." Ph.D. diss., Temple University, 1983.

Collier, Ruth Berins, and David Collier. *Shaping the Political Arena: Critical Junctures, the Labor Movement, and Regime Dynamics in Latin America.* Princeton, N.J.: Princeton University Press, 1991.

Danzig, Allison. *The History of American Football: Its Great Teams, Players, and Coaches.* Englewood Cliffs, N.J.: Prentice Hall, 1956.

Demmel, Gerald. "Ballfieber." *Werkstattblätter* 9(4) (September 1997).

Dickson, Paul. *The Worth Book of Softball.* New York: Facts on File, 1994.

Dizikis, John. *Sportsmen and Gamesmen.* Boston, Mass.: Houghton Mifflin, 1981.

Douglas, Geoffrey. *The Game of Their Lives.* New York: Henry Holt and Company, 1996.

Dryden, Ken, and Roy McGregor. *Home Game: Hockey and Life in Canada.* Toronto: McClelland and Stewart, 1989.

Durkheim, Emile. *The Division of Labor in Society.* New York: The Free Press, 1950.

———. *Sociology and Philosophy.* New York: The Free Press, 1974.

Durocher, Leo, and Ed Linn. *Nice Guys Finish Last.* New York: Simon and Schuster, Pocket Books, 1976.

Eisenberg, Christiane, ed. *Fussball, soccer calcio: Ein englischer Sport auf seinem Weg um die Welt.* Munich: Deutscher Taschenbuch Verlag, 1997.

Encyclopedia Americana Number 20. Danbury, Conn.: Grolier, 1982.

Erickson, Hal. *Baseball in the Movies: A Comprehensive Reference, 1915–91.* Jefferson, N.C.: McFarland & Co., 1992.

Farrell, James T. *My Baseball Diary.* New York: A. S. Barnes and Company, 1957.

Featherstone, Mike. *Undoing Culture: Globalization, Postmodernism, and Identity.* London: Sage, 1995.

Fischler, Stan. *Fischler's Illustrated History of Hockey.* Toronto: Warwick Publishers, 1993.

Flath, Arnold William. *A History of the Relations between National Collegiate Athletic Association and the Amateur Athletic Union of the United States, 1905–63.* Champaign, Ill.: Stipes Publishing, 1964.

Fleisher, Arthur A., Brian L. Goff, and Robert D. Tollison. *The National Collegiate Association: A Study in Cartel Behavior.* Chicago: University of Chicago Press, 1992.

Fleming, G. H. *The Unforgettable Season (1908).* New York: Penguin Books, 1981.

Foulds, Sam, and Paul Harris. *America's Soccer Heritage.* Manhattan Beach, Calif.: Soccer for Americans, 1979.

Frommer, Harvey. *The Great American Soccer Book.* New York: Atheneum, 1980.

Gardner, Paul. *The Simplest Game: The Intelligent Fan's Guide to the World of Soccer.* New York: Collier Books, 1994.

Gelber, Steven M. "Working at Playing: The Culture of the Workplace and the Rise of Baseball." *Journal of Social History* (Summer 1983).

Glanville, Brian. *The Story of the World Cup.* London: Faber and Faber, Ltd., 1993.

Goeken, Ralf. "Soccer in den USA: Ein europäisches Spiel in der Neuen Welt." Master's thesis, Department of Sport Studies, University of Münster, 1998.

Goldstein, Warren. *Playing for Keeps: A History of Early Baseball.* Ithaca, N.Y.: Cornell University Press, 1989.

Goodwin, Doris Kearns. *Wait until Next Year: A Memoir.* New York: Simon and Schuster, 1997.

Grazia, Victoria de. *The Culture of Consent: Mass Organization of Leisure in Fascist Italy.* New York: Cambridge University Press, 1981.

Gruneau, Richard, and David Whitson. *Hockey Night in Canada: Sport, Identities, and Cultural Politics.* Toronto: Garamond Press, 1993.

Gutman, Bill. *The History of NCAA Basketball.* New York: Crescent Books, 1993.

Guttmann, Allen. *From Ritual to Record: The Nature of Modern Sports.* New York: Columbia University Press, 1978.

———. *Sports Spectators.* New York: Columbia University Press, 1986.

———. *A Whole New Ball Game: An Interpretation of American Sports.* Chapel Hill: University of North Carolina Press, 1988.

Hartz, Louis. *The Liberal Tradition in America: An Interpretation of American Political Thought Since the Revolution.* New York: Harcourt, Brace, 1995.

Heinrich, Arthur. *Tooor! Toor! Tor!.* Hamburg: Rotbuch Verlag, 1994.

Heller, Friedrich C. "Antonin Dvorak: 9. Symphonie 'Aus der neuen Welt'" in Playbill of the Salzburger Festspiele 1985, 29 July 1985.

Henderson, Robert W. *Ball, Bat and Bishop: The Origin of Ball Games.* New York: Rockport Press. 1947.

Hilferding, Rudolf. *Finance Capital: A Study of the Latest Phase of Capitalist Development.* London: Routledge and Kegan Paul, 1981.

Hirschmann, Albert O. *Exit, Voice, and Loyalty: Responses to Decline in Firms, Organizations, and States.* Cambridge, Mass.: Harvard University Press, 1970.

Hobsbawm, Eric. *The Age of Extremes: A History of the World, 1914–91.* New York: Pantheon Books, 1994.

Hoch, Paul. *Rip Off the Big Game: The Exploitation of Sports by the Power Elite.* Garden City N.Y.: Anchor Books, 1972.

Hoehn, Thomas, and Stefan Szymanski. "The Americanization of European football." *Economic Policy* 28 (April 1999).

Hollander, Zander. *The American Encyclopedia of Soccer.* New York: Everest House Publishers, 1980.

Hollander, Zander ed., *The Complete Encyclopedia of Hockey,* 4th ed. Detroit: Visible Ink Press, 1993.

Horak, Roman and Wolfgang Maderthaner. *Mehr als ein Spiel. Fussball und Populare Kulturen im Wien der Moderne.* Vienna: Löcker Verlag, 1997.

Ikenberry, G. John. "History's Heavy Hand: Institutions and the Politics of the State" (paper prepared for the conference, "The New Institutionalism," University of Maryland, 14–15 October, 1994).

Inglehart, Ronald. *Culture Shift in Advanced Industrial Society.* Princeton, N.J.: Princeton University Press, 1990.

———. *The Silent Revolution: Changing Values and Political Styles among Western Publics.* Princeton, N.J.: Princeton University Press, 1977.

Isaacs, Neil D. *All the Moves: A History of College Basketball.* New York: Harper Colophon Books, 1984.

Johnson, Arthur T. *Minor League Baseball and Local Economic Development.* Chicago: University of Illinois, 1993.

Jose, Colin. *The American Soccer League 1921–1931: The Golden Years of American Soccer.* Lanham, Md.: Scarecrow Press, 1998.

———. *NASL: A Complete Record of the North American Soccer League.* Derby: Breedon Brooks, 1989.

———. *The United States and World Cup Soccer Competition: An Encyclopedic History of the United States in International Competition.* Metuchen, N.J.: Scarecrow Press, 1994.

Karabel, Jerome. "The Failure of American Socialism Reconsidered." *The Socialist Register* (1979).

Katzenstein, Peter. *Policy and Politics in West Germany: The Growth of the Semi-Sovereign State.* Philadelphia, Pa.: Temple University Press, 1987.

Katznelson, Ira. *City Trenches: Urban Politics and the Patterning of Class in the United States.* Chicago: University of Chicago Press, 1982.

Kirsch, George. *The Creation of American Team Sports: Baseball and Cricket, 1838–72.* Chicago: University of Illinois Press, 1989.

Klinkowitz, Jerry, ed. *Writing Baseball*. Chicago: University of Illinois Press, 1991.

Kuhn, Helmut. *Fussball in den USA*. Bremen, Germany: Edition Temmen, 1994.

Lanfranchi, Pierre. "Frankreich und Italien" in Eisenberg (ed.), *Fussball, soccer calcio*.

Laslett, John M., and Seymour Martin Lipset, eds. *Failure of a Dream? Essays in the History of American Socialism*. Garden City, N.Y.: Anchor Press, 1974.

Leifer, Eric. *Making the Majors: The Transformation of Team Sports in America*. Cambridge, Mass.: Harvard University Press, 1995.

Levine, Peter. *Ellis Island to Ebbetts Field*. New York: Oxford University Press, 1992.

———. *A.G. Spalding and the Rise of Baseball*. New York: 1985.

Lieb, Fred. *Baseball As I have Known It*. New York: Gosset & Dunlap, 1977.

Lipset, Seymour Martin. *Agrarian Socialism: The Cooperative Commonwealth Federation in Saskatchewan*. Garden City, N.Y.: Doubleday, 1968.

———. *American Exceptionalism: A Double-Edged Sword*. New York: W. W. Norton, 1996.

———. *Continental Divide: The Values and Institutions of the United States and Canada*. New York: Canadian-American Committee, 1989.

———. *The First New Nation*. Garden City, N.Y.: Doubleday Anchor Books, 1967.

———. *Political Man: The Social Bases of Politics*. Baltimore, Md.: Johns Hopkins University Press, 1981.

———. *Revolution and Counterrevolution: Change and Persistence in Social Structures*. Garden City, N.Y.: Doubleday, 1979.

Lipset, Seymour Martin, and Gary Marks. *It Didn't happen here: Why Socialism Failed in the United States*. New York: W. W. Norton, 2000.

Lipset, Seymour Martin, and Stein Rokkan. "Cleavage Structures, Party Systems, and Voter Alignment: An Introduction," in Seymour Martin Lipset and Stein Rokkan, eds., *Party Systems and Voter Alignments: Cross-National Perspectives*. New York: The Free Press, 1967.

Major League Soccer: *1997 Major League Soccer Official Media Guide*. n.p.

Major League Soccer: *1998 Major League Soccer Official Media Guide*. n.p.

Markovits, Andrei S. "Anti-Americanism and the Struggle for a West-German Identity, " in Peter H. Merkl, ed. *The Federal Republic of Germany at Forty*. New York: New York University Press, 1989, pp. 35–54.

———. "The Other 'American Exceptionalism': Why Is There No Soccer in the United States?" *International Journal of the History of Sport* 7(2), 1990.

———. "Reflections on the World Cup '98" in *French Politics and Society*, Volume 16, number 3, summer 1998.

Markovits, Andrei S., and Steven L. Hellermann. "Soccer in America: A Story of Marginalization," *Entertainment and Sports Law Review*, volume 13, number 1–2, 1995–96.

Marx, Karl. "Preface to the Critique of Political Economy," in Robert C. Tucker, ed., *The Marx-Engels Reader*. New York: W.W. Norton, 1972.

Mason, Tony. *Passion of the People? Football in South America*. London: Verso, 1995.

McCallum, John D. *College Basketball, U.S.A. since 1892*. New York: Stein and Day, 1978.

McFarlane, Brian. *One Hundred Years of Hockey*. Toronto: Summerhill Press, 1990.

Mead, William B. *The 10 Worst Years of Baseball*. New York: Van Nostrand Reinhold, 1982.

Mink, Gwendolyn. *Old Labor and New Immigrants in American Political Development: Union, Party, and State, 1875–1920*. Ithaca, N.Y.: Cornell University Press, 1986.

Moore Jr., Barrington. *Social Origins of Dictatorship and Democracy: Lord and Peasant in the Making of the Modern World*. Boston, Mass.: Beacon Press, 1966.

Mote, James. *Everything Baseball*. New York: Prentice Hall Press, 1989.

Murdock, Eugene C. *Ban Johnson: Czar of Baseball*. Westport, Conn.: Greenwood Press, 1982.

Myers, Phyllis Marie Goudy. "The Formation of Organizations: A Case Study of the North American Soccer League." Ph.D. diss., Purdue University, 1984.

Nahata, Babu, and Dennis O. Olson. "On the Definition of Barriers to Entry." *Southern Economic Journal*, 56(1) (July 1989).

Neft, David S., Richard M. Cohen, and Rick Korch. *The Football Encyclopedia: The Complete, Year-By-Year History of Professional Football from 1892 to the Present*. New York: St. Martin's Press, 1994.

Newcomb, Jack. *The Best of the Athletic Boys: The White Man's Impact on Jim Thorpe*. Garden City, N.Y.: Doubleday and Co., 1975.

The NFL's Official Encyclopedia History of Professional Football. New York: Macmillan Publishing, 1977.

Nisbet, Robert A. *The Sociology of Emile Durkheim*. New York: Oxford University Press, 1974.

Nolan, Mary. *Imagining America, Modernizing Germany: Fordism and Economic Reform in the Weimar Republic*. New York: Oxford University Press, 1994.

———. *Visions of Modernity: American Business in the Modernization of Germany*. New York: Oxford University Press, 1994.

Obojski, Robert. *Bush League: A History of Minor League Baseball*. New York: Macmillan Publishing, 1975.

Ogburn, William Fielding. *Social Change*. New York: Viking Press, 1992.

O'Neal, Bill. *The Pacific Coast League, 1903–88*. Austin, Tex.: Eakin Press, 1990.

Oriard, Michael. *Dreaming of Heroes: American Sports Fiction, 1868–80*. Chicago, Ill.: Nelson-Hall, 1982.

———. *Reading Football: How the Popular Press Created an American Spectacle*. Chapel Hill: University of North Carolina Press, 1993.

———. *Sporting with the Gods: The Rhetoric of Play and Game in American Culture*. New York: Cambridge University Press, 1991.

Patton, Phil. *Razzle-Dazzle: The Curious Marriage of Television and Professional Football*. Garden City, N.Y.: Dial Press, Doubleday, 1984.

Peterson, Robert W. *From Cages to Jump Shots: Pro Basketball's Early Years.* New York: Oxford University Press, 1990.

———. *Only the Ball Was White.* New York: Oxford University Press, 1970.

———. *Pigskin: The Early Years of Pro Football.* New York: Oxford University Press, 1997.

Pierson, Paul. "Path Dependence, Increasing Returns, and the Study of Politics." (paper, Harvard University, Center for European Studies, 1997).

———. "When Effect Becomes Cause: Policy Feedback and Political Change." *World Politics* (July 1993).

Prince, Morton H. "Football at Harvard, 1800–75," in John A. Blanchard, ed., *The H. Book of Harvard Athletics: 1852–22.* Cambridge, Mass.: Harvard Varsity Club, 1923.

Radar Benjamin. *American Sports: From the Age of Folk Games to the Age of Televised Sports.* Englewood Cliffs, N.J.: Prentice-Hall, 1994.

Rasmussen, Wayne Douglas. "Historical Analysis of Four Major Attempts to Establish Professional Soccer in the United States of America between 1894 and 1994. " Ph.D. diss., Temple University, 1995.

Riekhoff, Harald von, and Hanspeter Neuhold., eds. *Unequal Partners: A Comparative Analysis of Relations between Austria and the Federal Republic of Germany and between Canada and the United States.* Boulder, Colo.: Westview Press, 1993.

Riesman, David, and Reuel Denney. "Football in America: A Study in Culture Diffusion." *American Quarterly* 3(4) (Winter 1951).

Riess, Steven A. *Touching Base: Professional Baseball and American Culture in the Progressive Era.* Westport, Conn.: Greenwood Press, 1980.

Riffenburgh, Beau, and Jack Clary. *NFL: The Official History of Pro Football.* New York: Crescent Books, 1990.

Riger, Robert, and Tex Maule. *The Pros: A Documentary of Professional Football in America.* New York: Simon and Schuster, 1960.

Roberts, Howard. *The Story of Pro Football.* New York: Rand McNally, 1953.

Roberts, Randy, and James S. Olson. *Winning Is the Only Thing: Sports in America since 1945.* Baltimore, Md.: Johns Hopkins University Press, 1989.

Robertson, Roland. *Globalization: Social Theory and Global Culture.* London: Sage, 1992.

Rosenbaum, David, and Fabian Lamort. "Entry Barriers, Existence, and Sunk Costs: An Analysis." *Applied Economics* 24(3) (March 1992).

Ross, Murray. "Football Red and Baseball Green." In Nancy R. Comley, et. al., eds. *Fields of Writing: Readings Across the Disciplines.* New York: St. Martins Press, 1984.

Rote Jr., Kyle, and Basil Kane. *Kyle Rote Jr.'s Complete Book of Soccer.* New York: Simon and Schuster, 1978.

Rustow, Dankwart. *A World of Nations: Problems of Political Modernization.* Washington, D.C.: The Brookings Institution, 1967.

Ruth, Babe, and Bob Considine. *The Babe Ruth Story.* New York: E. P. Dutton, 1948.

Sachare, Alex, ed. *The Official NBA Basketball Encyclopedia*. 2d ed. New York: Villard Books, 1994.

Samson, Leon. *Toward a United Front*. New York: Farrar and Rinehart, 1933.

Scherer, F. M. *Industrial Market Structure and Economic Performance*, 2d ed. Chicago, Ill.: Rand McNally, 1980.

Schoor, Gene with Henry Gilford. *The Jim Thorpe Story: America's Greatest Athlete*. New York: Julian Messner, 1962.

Schumpeter, Joseph A. *Capitalism, Socialism and Democracy*, 3d ed. New York: Harper and Row, 1950.

Seabrook, John. "Tackling the Competition. *The New Yorker* (8 August 1997).

Seddon, Peter J. *A Football Compendium: A Comprehensive Guide to the Literature of Association Football*. Boston: The British Library, 1995.

Seymour, Harold. *Baseball, Volume I: The Early Years*. New York: Oxford University Press, 1960.

———. *Baseball, Volume II: The Golden Age*. New York: Oxford University Press, 1971.

———. *Baseball, Volume III: The People's Game*. New York: Oxford University Press, 1990.

Shannon, Mike. *Diamond Classics: Essays on 100 of the Best Baseball Books Ever Published*. Jefferson, N.C.: McFarland & Co., 1989.

Sifakis, Stewart. *Who Was Who in the Civil War*. New York: Facts on File, 1988.

Smith, Robert. *Baseball: A Historical Narrative of the Game, the Men Who Have Played It, and Its Place in American Life*. New York: Simon and Schuster, 1947.

———. *Illustrated History of Baseball*. New York: Basic Books, 1973.

Soccer Industry Council of America (SICA), and *Soccer America*. "Soccer in the USA: Statistical Abstract on Soccer Participation,"1998

———. "Soccer in the USA: An Overview of the American Soccer Marketplace," 1998.

Sombart, Werner. *Warum gibt es in den Vereinigten Staaten keinen Sozialismus?* Tübingen: JCB Mohr (Paul Siebeck), 1906.

Spalding, Albert G. *America's National Game*. New York: American Sports Publishing Co., 1911.

Spink, J. G. Taylor. *Judge Landis and 25 Years of Baseball*. St. Louis, Mo.: The Sporting News Press, 1974.

Staudohar, Paul D. *Playing for Dollars: Labor Relations and the Sports Business*. Ithaca, N.Y.: Cornell University Press, 1996.

Stigler, George. *The Organization of Industry*. Chicago: University of Chicago Press, 1968.

Stinchcombe, Arthur L. *Constructing Social Theories*. New York: Harcourt, Brace, and World, 1968.

Sugden, John, and Alan Tomlinson. *FIFA and the Contest for World Football: Who Rules the Peoples' Game?* Cambridge, U.K.: Polity Press, 1998.

Sullivan, George. *The Complete Guide to Softball*. New York: Fleet Publishing Company, 1965.

Sullivan, Neil J. *The Minors: The Struggle and the Triumphs of Baseball's Poor Relations from 1876 to the Present*. New York: St. Martin's Press, 1990.

Swartz, David. *Culture and Power: The Sociology of Pierre Bourdieu*. Chicago, Ill.: University of Chicago Press, 1997.

Tocqueville, Alexis de. *Democracy in America*. New York: Harper Perennial, 1988.

Tomlinson, Alan, and John Sugden. "What's Left When the Circus Leaves Town? An Evaluation of the World Cup USA 1994." *Sociology of Sport Journal* (13)3 (1996).

Turner, Frederick Jackson. *The Frontier in American History*. New York: Holt, 1947.

Tygiel, Jules. *Baseball's Great Experiment: Jackie Robinson and His Legacy*. New York: Oxford University Press, 1983.

Tyrell, Ian. "The Emergence of Modern American Baseball c. 1850–80," in Richard Cashman and Michael Mckernan, eds., *Sport in History: The Making of Modern Sporting History*. Queensland: University of Queensland Press, 1979.

U.S. Soccer Federation. *U.S. Soccer Federation Media Guide, 1998*. n.p., 1998.

Vincent, Ted. *Mudville's Revenge: The Rise and Fall of American Sport*. Lincoln: University of Nebraska Press, 1994.

Voigt, David Quentin. *American Baseball: From Gentleman's Sport to the Commissioner System*. Norman: University of Oklahoma Press, 1966.

———. "Reflections on Diamonds: American Baseball and American Culture." in *Journal of Sport History* 1(1) (Spring 1974).

Waddington, Ivan, and Martin Roderick. "American Exceptionalism: Soccer and American Football," in *The Sports Historian*, British Society of Sports History, volume 16 (May 1996), 1996, pp. 42–63.

Wagg, Steven, ed. *Giving the Game Away: Football, Politics, and Culture on Five Continents*. London: Leicester University Press, 1995.

Weber, Max. "The Social Psychology of World Religions," in Hans Gerth and C. Wright Mill, eds., *From Max Weber: Essays in Sociology*. New York: Oxford University Press, 1946.

Weizsäcker, C. C. *Barriers to Entry: A Theoretical Treatment*. Berlin: Springer Verlag, 1980.

Wenner, Lawrence A., ed. *Media, Sports, and Society*. Newbury Park, Calif.: Sage Publications, 1989.

Weyand, Alexander M. *The Saga of American Football*. New York: Macmillan, 1961.

Wheeler, Robert W. *Jim Thorpe: World's Greatest Athlete*. Norman: University of Oklahoma Press, 1987.

Williams, Raymond. *Marxism and Literature*. New York: Oxford University Press, 1977.

Wise, Suzanne. *Sports Fiction for Adults: An Annotated Bibliography of Novels, Plays, Short Stories and Poetry with Sporting Settings*. New York: Garland Publishers, 1986.

Zimbalist, Andrew. *Baseball and Billions: A Probing Look Inside the Big Business of Our National Game*. New York: Basic Books, 1992.

Zipter, Yvonn., *Diamonds Are a Dyke's Best Friend*. Ithaca, N.Y.: Firebrand Books, 1988.

Newspapers and Magazines

Bild
Boston Globe
Boston Herald
Chicago Sun-Times
Chicago Tribune
Columbus Dispatch
Corriere della Sera
Daily Telegraph
Dallas Morning News
Detroit Free Press
L'Equipe
Le Figaro
Financial Times
Die Frankfurter Allgemeine Zeitung
Frankfurter Rundschau
Gazeta Wyborcza
Independent
International Herald Tribune
Kansas City Star
La Gazzetta dello Sport
Liberation
Los Angeles Times
Miami Herald
Le Monde
Neue Züricher Zeitung
New York Newsday

New York Post
New York Times
New Yorker
Observer
Orlando Sentinel
Philadelphia Enquirer
Rocky Mountain News
San Francisco Chronicle
San Francisco Examiner
San Jose Mercury News
Soccer America
Sport
Sporting News
Sports Illustrated
La Stampa
Der Standard
Die Süddeutsche Zeitung
die tageszeitung
Tampa Bay Tribune
Time
Times
USA Today
Washington Post
Washington Times
Yahoo! Inc and Agence-France-Press

Interviews

Terry Cox, Race and Sports Service Manager, Harrah's Casino in Reno, Nevada; 27 July 1995.

John Paul Delacamera, sports announcer, specializing in hockey and soccer at ESPN, ABC, and other television stations; 21 August 1997.

Frank Dell'Apa, sportswriter and journalist for the Boston Globe; 29 August 1994, and 1 July 1997.

Dan Giesan, sportswriter and journalist for the San Francisco Chronicle; 18 April 1995.

Sunil Gulati, Deputy Commissioner of Major League Soccer (MLS); 29 September 1997.

Andreas Herren, Press Secretary and Spokesman of FIFA; 18 August 1995.

Ted Howard, former deputy commissioner of the North American Soccer League (NASL) and market analyst at the National Basketball Association (NBA); 11 July 1997.

Colin Jose, North America's most eminent soccer historian; 20 August 1997, 30 September 1997, and 23 June 1998.

Ann Killion, sports columnist and journalist for the *San Jose Mercury News*; 9 May 1995.

Richard Lapchik, Director of the Center for the Study of Sports and Society at Northeastern University; 20 September 1994.

Nye Lavelle, President of Sports Marketing, Inc.; 23 January 1995.

Bob Ley, sports announcer and journalist, specializing in soccer at ESPN and ABC; August 21 1997.

Seamus Malin, soccer announcer for ESPN, ABC, and other television stations; 10, 30 August 1994,10 July 1997, 4 August 1998; 6 September 1998, and 6 September 1999.

Gus Martins, sportswriter and journalist for the *Boston Herald*; 29 August 1994.

Alice McGillan, Deputy Director of the Women's Basketball Association (WNBA); 29 September 1997.

Rafael Morfi, press secretary and media spokesperson for Major League Soccer (MLS); 11 July 1997.

Ron Newman, head coach of the Kansas City Wizzards and the coach with the most wins in U.S. soccer on all levels of the game; 12 July 1997.

Derek Rae, soccer announcer for ESPN, ABC, and other television stations; 25 July 1997.

Adekunle Raji, researcher and soccer specialist at the Center for the Study of Sports and Society at Northeastern University; 11 August 1994.

John Seabrook, writer for the *New Yorker*, specializing in sports features; 29 September 1997.

Tommy Smyth, soccer announcer for ESPN, ABC, and other television stations; 21 August 1997.

Mike Soltys, Marketing Department at ESPN; 21 August 1997.

Guido Tognoni, press secretary and media spokesman at FIFA; thereafter European organizer and representative of NHL Europe; 29 November 1993, and 16 July 1996.

Mike Woitalla, senior editor of *Soccer America*; 17 April 1995.

Index...

AAFA (American Amateur Football Association), 100
AAFC (All-America Football Conference), 136–37
Aaron, Henry, 21
ABA (American Basketball Association), 148–49
ABC televised coverage, 143, 147
ABL (American Basketball League), 87, 154
Abner Doubleday myth, 54, 306n.2
AC Milan, 22, 31, 118, 119
Adelman, Melvin, 58
AFA (American Football Association), 100
AFL (American Football League), 140–41
African Americans: baseball anecdotes on, 310n.49; baseball segregation of, 69; Big Three desegregation and, 128–29; entrance into basketball by, 87, 146–47, 149; failure of hockey to appeal to, 158–59; post-W.W. II baseball and, 131–32; pro-football desegregation and, 137. See also ethnic groups
Agoos, Jeff, 237
AIAW (Association for Intercollegiate Athletics for Women), 153
Ajax Amsterdam teams, 22
Akers, Michelle, 178, 209
Alberto, Carlos, 167
Albright, Madeleine, 239, 250
All-America Football Conference, 136
Allegheny Athletic Association, 80
"All England Eleven," 60
All-England Lawn Tennis Championships (Wimbledon), 216, 222, 223, 236, 254, 257
All-Time NASL Player Registry (1967–1979), 324n.11
ALPFC (American League of Professional Football Clubs), 105–8
Altig, Rudi, 35
Amateur Athletic Union, 87, 88
Amateur Hockey Association of Canada, 94
Ameche, Alan, 139

America Hockey League, 88
American Association, 62, 63, 64
American baseball vernacular language, 65–66
American Civil War, 59–61
American Cricket clubs, 55–56
American culture: commonalties/differences between European, 264–65; hegemonic sports culture of, 9–13; intrusion into Old World by, 309n.43. See also United States
American Cup Competition (soccer), 108
American exceptionalism: commonalties/differences of, 264–65; debate over socialism and, 7–9, 300n.3; evidence of, 299n.3, 300n.8; literature dealing with, 300n.2; to soccer, 39–51; to university soccer teams, 121–27. See also hegemonic sports culture; United States
American Football League, 128
American League, 133, 134
American professional soccer: ALPFC experiment in, 105–8; ASL-USFA conflict, 112–14; beginnings of, 104–5; missed opportunity of first ASL, 109–14; Queiroz Report on, 337n.3; second ASL of, 114–19; World Cup competition through 1950 by, 119–21. See also MLS (Major League Soccer)
American soccer: age participation in, 173f, 279f; "Dangerfield complex" and, 245; development of professional, 104–19; exceptionalism of university, 121–27; future possible scenarios of, 265–72; gender participation in high school, 172f; high school participation in, 277–80; "how to" books on, 319n.56; identification/affect paradox of, 197–200; immigrant players of early, 102; impact of women's leagues on future of, 160–61, 269, 270–71; indoor soccer and, 170–71; media coverage on future of, 293–97; metamorphosis during 30 years of, 162–63, 171–74; organization of, 99–

School for Christian Workers, 83–84
Schumacher, Michael, 35
Schumpeter, Joseph, 14, 23
Scurry, Briana, 178
Seattle Metropolitans, 96
Seedorf, Clarence, 243
Seitz, Peter, 135
Seles, Monica, 243
Seoul Olympics (1988), 34
Shaughnessy, Dan, 230, 288–89, 297
Shearer, Alan, 243
Simpson, Nicole Brown, 216
Simpson, O. J., 21, 216–17
Slater, Duke, 137
Smyth, Tommy, 186
Sobotnick, Stuart, 185
soccer: American marginalization of, 52–54; baseball crowding out of, 54–57; diffuse institutionalization of, 159–60; nationalism feature of, 37–38; nationalism/national pride associated with, 34–39, 269–70, 316n.12; obstacles to television coverage of, 129–30, 131; played in U.S. by foreign teams, 118–19; possible impact of women on future of, 160–61; proletarian culture of, 28; as universalizing agent for sport, 7. *See also* American exceptionalism; American soccer
Soccer America, 240, 252
"Soccer Celebration" theme park, 193
soccer clubs: ethnic origins of, 315n.3; "organized capitalism" of European, 44–45
soccer diplomacy (World Cup 1998), 238–39, 249–52, 259, 335n.31
Soccer Industry Council of America, 172
"soccer mom," 162
"soccer war" (El Salvador–Honduras), 37
social class: American exceptionalism rooting in bourgeois, 39–40; American participation in soccer and, 171–72, 204–5, 211; hegemonic sports culture and, 25–26, 27–28; path dependence and, 28–33; statistical abstract on soccer U.S. by, 275
socialism exceptionalism (U.S.), 7–9, 300n.3
softball, 312n.76
Solid Six, 155
Sombart, Werner, 8
Sosa, Sammy, 136, 245–46, 257
Southern New York State Association, 113
Souza, Edward, 117, 120
Souza, John, 117, 120

Spalding, Albert, 62
Spander, Art, 288
Spanish-American War (1898), 108
Sport, 243
Sporting News, 134, 206, 243
sports: bourgeois codification of, 39–40; charisma and bureaucracy interaction in, 24–25; critical junctures of, 23–24; increasing women's participation in, 25, 26–27; managerial and bureaucratic attributes of, 24. *See also* hegemonic sports culture
Sports Broadcasting Act (1961), 132
SportsCenter (ESPN), 211
sports culture. *See* hegemonic sports culture
Sports Illustrated, 139–40, 178, 235, 242, 243, 246, 247, 248, 252, 262
Sports Late Night (CNN), 211
Sports Marketing Newsletter, 221
sport space: criticism of concept of, 302n.23; defining term use of, 302n.20; development in industrial societies of, 14–17, 301n.15; "freezing," 19–23. *See also* American sport space
"Squadra Azzurra" games (World Cup 1994), 227, 229
stalling, 146
Stallone, Sylvester, 11
Stanley Cup, 46, 94, 95, 96, 154, 155, 159
Stanley Cup ESPN ratings, 246
Stanley of Preston, Lord, 94
Stark, Archie, 111–12
Stark, Steve, 221
Starr, Bart, 22
Stern, David, 150
Stewart, Ernie, 252
Stewart, Payne, 252, 253
Stich, Michael, 35
Stoichkov, Hristo, 223
Stoneham, Horace, 110
Strawberry, Darryl, 18, 214
Strode, Woody, 137
Suker, Davor, 259
Super Bowl, 142

Talebi, Jalal, 250
Tampa Bay Mutiny, 184
Tauziat, Nathalie, 258
Team Canada, 48, 155, 156